CICERO
THE SENIOR STATESMAN

CICERO

THE SENIOR STATESMAN

THOMAS N. MITCHELL

Yale University Press
New Haven and London

Set in Times Roman type by
The Composing Room of Michigan, Inc.
Printed in the United States of America by
BookCrafters, Inc., Chelsea, Michigan.

Library of Congress Cataloging-in-Publication Data

Mitchell, Thomas N., 1939–
   Cicero, the senior statesman / Thomas N. Mitchell.
      p.   cm.
   Includes bibliographical references and index.
   ISBN 0-300-04779-7 (alk. paper)
   1. Cicero, Marcus Tullius.   2. Rome—Politics and
government—265-30 B.C.   3. Statesmen—Rome—Biography.   4. Orators—
Rome—Biography.   I. Title.
DG260.C53M58   1991
937'.05'092—dc20
[B]   90-38157
                                                               CIP

The paper in this book meets the guidelines for
permanence and durability of the Committee on
Production Guidelines for Book Longevity of the
Council on Library Resources.

10   9   8   7   6   5   4   3   2   1

CONTENTS

PREFACE

The present volume brings to a conclusion the study of Cicero's political life and thought begun in *Cicero, the Ascending Years*. It spans the last twenty years of his life, from the end of his consulship in December 63 to his death in December 43.[1] Its purpose is the same as that of my earlier volume: to provide a detailed and fully documented account of Cicero's political life that combines the story of his career with a comprehensive discussion of the political ideas and events that helped shape it. Its justification is also the same. Standard biographies tend to concentrate on biographical detail and have too little space to deal fully with Cicero's ideas or with the complexities of the political world in which he worked. His abiding interest and importance as a man, statesman, writer, thinker, and as a uniquely valuable source for a crucial era of Roman history justify a more complete study of a type long absent in the English language. It is hoped that these two volumes will help to bridge that significant gap.

My thanks are due to Trinity College, Dublin, for two terms of leave, during which the bulk of this volume was written. I am also grateful to three able secretaries, Rosemary Doran, Madeleine O'Siochain, and Vivienne O'Rafferty, for their enormous help in preparing the manu-

---

1. All dates are B.C. unless otherwise indicated.

script. I owe a special debt, as always, to my wife, Lynn, for unceasing support and valuable criticism.

Finally, I wish to thank the reader for Yale University Press for many helpful comments and the Press itself for its great efficiency and for patiently awaiting completion of the book, which was long delayed by a move to Dublin and by new administrative responsibilities.

ABBREVIATIONS

ABG	*Archiv für Begriffsgeschichte*
AC	*L'Antiquité classique*
AJAH	*American Journal of Ancient History*
AJP	*American Journal of Philology*
ANRW	*Aufstieg und Niedergang der römischen Welt*
B Stud Lat	*Bollettino di studi latini*
CJ	*Classical Journal*
CM	*Classica et Mediaevalia*
CP	*Classical Philology*
CQ	*Classical Quarterly*
CR	*Classical Review*
CW	*Classical World*
GLO	*Graecolatina et Orientalia*
HSCP	*Harvard Studies in Classical Philology*
JP	*Journal of Philology*
JRS	*Journal of Roman Studies*
LCM	*Liverpool Classical Monthly*
LEC	*Les Etudes classiques*

MAAR	*Memoirs of the American Academy at Rome*
MEFR	*Mélanges d'archéologie et d'histoire de l'Ecole Française de Rome*
Mn	*Mnemosyne*
Mus Helv	*Museum Helveticum*
PBSR	*Papers of the British School at Rome*
PCPS	*Proceedings of the Cambridge Philological Society*
PP	*La parola del passato*
QJS	*Quarterly Journal of Speech*
RAL	*Rendiconti della classe di scienze morali, storiche e filologiche dell'Accademia dei Lincei*
RCCM	*Rivista di cultura classica e medioevale*
RE	*Real-Encyclopädie der classischen Altertumswissenschaft*
REL	*Revue des études latines*
RhM	*Rheinisches Museum für Philologie*
TAPA	*Transactions and Proceedings of the American Philological Association*
ZRG	*Zeitschrift der Savigny-Stiftung für Rechtsgeschichte*

INTRODUCTION

Marcus Tullius Cicero was born on January 3, 106 B.C., in the town of
Arpinum, which lay in the Volscian highlands about seventy miles southeast of Rome. His family was old and distinguished, and had not only
achieved local prominence but had managed to build connections with
several of the most prestigious noble houses of the early first century.
Cicero's father had a close relationship with M. Cato, great-grandson of
Cato the Censor, and was also on intimate terms with L. Licinius
Crassus, the consul of 95, an association that was perhaps initiated by the
marriage of Cicero's maternal aunt to C. Aculeo, a noted jurist and a
bosom friend of Crassus. The friendship with Crassus brought contact
with the family of Crassus's wife, the Mucii Scaevolae, and a further
noble connection was added through a friendship that developed between
Cicero's uncle Lucius and M. Antonius, the consul of 99.

Cicero's family also had links to C. Marius, a fellow townsman and a
relative by marriage, his sister having married M. Gratidius, the brother-
in-law of Cicero's grandfather. The connection does not appear, however, to have had much effect on Cicero's early life. The link was indirect
and relatively remote, and was made more tenuous still by persistent
coolness between the Gratidii and the Tullii Cicerones. It warrants no
assumption of friendship between Marius and Cicero's family, and
Cicero nowhere claims a personal relationship with Marius or implies his
career was in any way helped or molded by the general's patronage or
influence.

It was the family's other noble associates that most closely touched

1

Cicero's early life and shaped his social and political outlook. He received the first stages of his education at the house of Crassus along with his brother Quintus and the sons of Aculeo. After assuming the *toga virilis* toward the end of 91, he became a pupil of Scaevola the Augur, consul of 117 and Rome's most distinguished expert on civil law. After the latter's death in the early eighties, he studied with Scaevola Pontifex, cousin of the augur, consul of 95, and a close friend and political ally of Crassus. He also had frequent contact with M. Antonius, who instructed him in a variety of subjects.

These noble mentors of Cicero formed the nucleus of an active and prestigious coterie of consulars in the nineties that heavily influenced political decision making throughout most of the decade. They were men of talent and industry who had come to prominence by traditional political means and who were committed by ideology and self-interest to the preservation of the traditional political and social structures of the Republic. They showed little concern for the problems that had emerged in the decades since the Gracchi and little inclination to work toward their solution. Their overriding objective was the stabilizing of aristocratic control through a dominant Senate, and they were inalterably opposed to any form of social, economic, or political change that threatened the underpinnings of oligarchic rule.

Their impact on Cicero was profound, as his own writings amply attest. He approved their basic political and social ideas and saw in them the main attributes of the good statesman—high ability, initiative, moral integrity, and dedication to the welfare of the Republic. Crassus in particular won his admiration and remained a potent source of inspiration for him throughout his political life. A similarity in their skills and careers helped strengthen Cicero's sense of identification with his patron. Crassus was, like Cicero, a gifted orator, broadly educated under the supervision of his father, his eloquence enriched by learning. He had used his oratorical abilities to good effect in the courts and his political success was due in large measure to his oratorical prowess as an advocate. Cicero also admired him for his general uprightness and for his political wisdom and good judgment. He closely represented Cicero's concept of the ideal civilian statesman, and was the perfect model of the authoritative *princeps* of the Senate, using his influence, eloquence, experience, and wisdom to mold and direct the course of public policy.

Cicero's upbringing and early political associations bound him closely therefore to the conservative tradition in late republican politics and left a lasting imprint on his own political ideas and aspirations. The effects of his conservative heritage were well illustrated in the eighties, a decade racked by political turmoil and civil war, in which the political choices were hard and fraught with danger. In normal circumstances Cicero would have launched his public career early in the decade by entering military service or commencing activity in the courts. Instead he refrained from any public involvements other than a brief term of military service in 89, and greatly extended the period of his education. He continued his legal studies with the Scaevolae, studied philosophy with Philo the Academician, who was in Rome in 88, attended lectures of the rhetorician Molo of Rhodes in 87, wrote, read, and practiced declamation on a daily basis, and was a frequent visitor to the Forum to observe politicians at trials and public meetings.

Cicero's long seclusion in study and his passive apprenticeship throughout the eighties reflected a deep antipathy to the regime of Cinna and a determination to eschew any association with it. His sympathies in the political struggles of the eighties were unequivocal. The Cinnan years he regarded as a period when the institutions of the Republic were disfigured, when the *improbi* and *indigni* held sway, and when one man was more powerful than the laws, subjecting the state to a *regnum*. He was later to characterize the regime of Caesar in 46 and 45 in strikingly similar terms.

Sulla's cause, seeking to rid the state of a hateful tyranny, was therefore just, the cause of the *respublica* and of the *nobilitas*. Cicero felt similarly about Sulla's forceful suppression of Sulpicius in 88; he considered Sulla's use of his legions on both occasions a legitimate response, on the principle that the safety of the state was the highest law and justified unauthorized or violent expedients when no other recourse was available. He did not approve Sulla's vengeful use of victory, which he regarded as a ruinous precedent and certain to sow the seeds of future civil wars, but he never wavered in his conviction that the cause was righteous.

Cicero did not, however, take any part in the overthrow of the Cinnan faction, a decision resulting from a deep abhorrence of civil war and from the influence of Scaevola Pontifex, with whom he remained closely associated throughout the eighties. Scaevola had remained in Rome under Cinna so as to avoid committing himself to bearing arms in a civil war, but he did not disguise his aversion to Cinna and refused any association with his regime. As the civil war drew closer, he attempted to find a peaceful solution. When he failed, he persisted in his determination not to bear arms and remained in Rome, where he was killed in 81 as an enemy of the Cinnan cause. Cicero was still too obscure a figure to share his fate, but there can be little doubt that he shared Scaevola's political views and had been guided in his responses throughout the eighties by the hardline conservative or optimate ideology epitomized by his patrons.

Cicero quickly became active in the courts after Sulla's victory and entered the political limelight in 80 when he successfully defended Sextus Roscius of Ameria on a charge of murder instigated by Sulla's powerful freedman Chrysogonus. Roscius had friends in several of Rome's leading families, including the Metelli, the Servilii, and the Scipiones. They rallied to his defense, also anxious, no doubt, to curb the power of Chrysogonus. Cicero became their agent and ably accomplished his task. He was continuing to cement his ties to the Roman nobility.

In the early seventies he took an extended break and traveled in Greece and Asia Minor, seeking to strengthen his voice and lungs and to refine his style of oratory. He returned to Rome about the middle of 77 and immediately began the task of building the reputation and the network of friends and influential connections essential for success in the Roman electoral system. Despite his family's many links to noble houses, he was still a new man lacking the inherited clients, connections, and prestige of his noble competitors, and certain to face a measure of hostility in a class-conscious society resentful or suspicious of those seeking to rise above their station. The higher offices of praetorship and consulship, jealously guarded by an exclusive aristocracy, would be especially difficult to attain.

Cicero's strategy was to build patiently through his work in the courts a network of friends throughout all sections of the electorate. He also strengthened his political base by marrying soon after his return in 77 the wealthy and well-born Terentia, who belonged to the distinguished Terentian *gens* and was half-sister of a Vestal Virgin who belonged to the patrician house of the Fabii. His first electoral success came in 76, when he was a candidate for the quaestorship and was among the first to be elected. He served in Sicily where he made many friends, but he found provincial service tedious and politically unrewarding, and he was glad to return to Rome. The remaining years of the seventies he devoted to ceaseless activity in the courts, building a following among the nobility, among the powerful business group, the *publicani,* and among the *collegia* of artisans and shopkeepers. He also worked hard to gain the friendship of leading figures in the country towns of Italy, a strategy that enabled him to gain a secure foothold in a significant number of the thirty-one rural tribes.

Cicero's forensic efforts took a new direction in 70 when he undertook the prosecution of C. Verres, a former governor of Sicily, on a charge of extortion. He was obliging his Sicilian clients and also availing of a particularly good opportunity to display his talent and industry. The trial was certain to become a cause célèbre. Verres' corruption was notorious, and he was coming to trial at a time when a major controversy surrounding the composition of juries was focusing particular attention on the criminal courts. Further interest was added by the distinction of some of Verres' defenders, among them Q. Hortensius, Rome's most outstanding orator in the seventies and consul-elect for 69. Cicero was confronting a prestigious and celebrated opponent in a well-publicized trial, circumstances ideally suited to advance the career of a new man seeking to advertise his abilities. Cicero made the most of the opportunity and assembled a mass of evidence that persuaded Verres to abandon his defense after the first stage of the trial.

The prosecution of Verres is sometimes linked to the political events of the late seventies and is variously seen as a boon to reformist elements eager to highlight any evidence of senatorial misgovernment, or as serving the interests of Pompey, who was anxious to protect his Sicilian clients and hand a defeat to the powerful noble clique supporting Verres. Cicero, on such interpretations, emerges as an ally of the reformers or a Pompeian partisan.

There is little direct evidence to support such theories. The trial, which began in early August, came too late to affect seriously the controversy over juries, which was already nearing resolution. Verres was, besides, a new man and a Cinnan renegade and, though he did have friends among the nobility, he was a poor instrument with which to seek to tarnish Rome's ruling elite, much of which, in any case, turned out to testify against him. Factional motivations for the prosecution are equally difficult to substantiate. The supporters and opponents of Verres did not represent rival factions, nor did they represent friends and foes of Pompey, who in any event appears to have had only the most peripheral involvement in the trial. There is no evidence that he gave active support to the Sicilians, and Cicero never claims him as an ally in the case. In the final analysis, the trial emerges as simply another in a long series of extortion cases that marked the late Republic, the participants on both sides motivated primarily by personal demands derived from various ties of *amicitia*. Cicero took the case because of his friendship with the Sicilians and because of the opportunity it offered to boost his reputation. The prosecution made no statement about his political views or sympathies, nor did it identify him with any particular political cause or coterie.

Cicero, in fact, carefully kept his distance from all the political controversies of the seventies and early sixties and conspicuously avoided association with reformist elements. He did not seek the tribunate, the office that most of all gave scope to younger politicians to keep their name before the public and court popular favor. He also avoided another important means of self-advertisement on a grand scale, the *contio,* maintaining a prudent silence on a succession of important political disputes. Especially notable was his failure to support the Gabinian law in 67, the measure that gave Pompey his extraordinary command against the pirates and that had wide support among the general public and the equestrian order. Cicero was keeping faith with his conservative heritage, patiently building his political base by time-honored means and avoiding the alternative route to electoral success through exploitation of popular grievances and attacks on senatorial power. And it was a strategy that served him well. He was elected to the plebeian aedileship in 70 and to the praetorship in 67, and he headed the poll on both occasions.

He did at last participate publicly in a political debate when, during his praetorship in 66, he delivered his first speech at a *contio* in support of a bill introduced by a tribune, C. Manilius, proposing that Pompey, who had lately successfully concluded the pirate war, should have his *imperium* extended to all of Asia Minor and assume command of the Mithridatic War. The bill was opposed by the leading conservative consulars, Q. Hortensius and Q. Catulus, but it also had many noble supporters. It was a sensible measure that promised an end to a protracted and costly war, and it raised none of the constitutional difficulties posed by the earlier Gabinian law, which had entailed the granting of *imperium* to a private citizen. Cicero was therefore able to make a bid for the political benefits of supporting a popular cause and a popular hero without abandoning the precepts or proponents of traditional republicanism.

He came closer to a collision with elements of the conservative nobility in 65, when he undertook the defense of Pompey's ally C. Manilius, and of a friend of his own C. Cornelius, both of whom had incurred the enmity of the Senate's leaders by their radical behavior as tribunes. Criminal prosecutions in retribution had quickly followed their departure from office. The trial of Manilius was disrupted by violence and had to be adjourned. When the court reconvened, Manilius failed to appear and was condemned. The trial of Cornelius was orderly and extended over four days, arousing great interest. Cicero delivered a spirited defense, and in the course of it expounded on the merits of the tribunate and of tribunician activism. Cornelius was acquitted by a large majority.

Cicero's defense of these radical politicians and his praise of the tribunate during the trial of Cornelius should not be taken to represent any change in the conservative political posture he had maintained since entering public life. The cases were part of his longtime strategy to build his electoral strength through the courts, a traditional and fully acceptable practice of republican politics. The ethics of the Roman bar did not restrict his right to defend anyone who sought his help, and certainly entitled him to come to the aid of a longterm friend such as Cornelius. He was further entitled to use his orator's craft to devise whatever arguments were likely to sway the jury. His contemporaries would have attached little significance to sentiments in a forensic speech that were clearly designed to vindicate a client, and the absence of any oligarchic resentment of his actions is well attested by the fact that, soon after Cornelius's trial, he had the offer of a *legatio* from Cornelius's foremost antagonist, C. Calpurnius Piso, consul of 67.

In 64 Cicero entered the toughest political contest of his career when he became a candidate for the consulship, the office most highly prized and jealously guarded by the nobility. His competitors—C. Antonius, son of the consul of 99, and L. Catiline, a patrician—both had murky reputations but came from famous families and were pushing their claims with bribery and extravagant promises. But Cicero was nonetheless able to defeat them with ease, and he won a famous victory, gaining election to the state's highest office as a new man, and doing so on his first attempt and in the first year in which he was eligible, and with an overwhelming majority. His tireless labors and brilliance in the courts had earned him the necessary connections among vital segments of the electorate—the equestrian order, the aristocracies of the country towns, the younger aristocrats, the clubs and associations. A long line of noble supporters can also be documented, and his shrewd and moderate political posture throughout his years as a candidate, linking him to popular figures such as Pompey but leaving no doubt about his commitment to traditional republicanism, made him broadly acceptable to voters of all classes. He had proven that merit still counted for something in the Roman electoral system, and that the barriers of aristocratic exclusiveness could be surmounted without espousal of revolutionary platforms or resort to corruption or demagoguery.

1: THE POLITICAL IDEAS BEHIND THE POLICIES OF 63

Cicero crowned his remarkable ascent to the consulship of 63 with an energetic and effective tenure of the office that won him at the end of his term high acclaim from his peers and demonstrations of approval from the general public. He had entered on his consulship at a particularly difficult time in Roman politics. The restoration of the powers of the tribunate in 70 had brought a quick return of disruptive activism by those who were willing to promote popular interests over the wishes of the Senate. The enrollment in the same year of large numbers of Italians in tribes and classes had greatly complicated electoral politics and sharpened rivalries. Pompey's impending return following his spectacular victories over the pirates and Mithridates was heightening political tensions and prompting moves to court his friendship or minimize his power. The divisive effects of the civil wars of the eighties and the many injustices of the Sullan years were continuing to foster unrest and alienation and to encourage political agitation and opportunism. Worsening economic conditions resulting from the long chain of domestic and foreign wars since 90 were producing similar effects.

These various sources of discontent and political disunity combined to provoke a fresh upsurge of political dissension and domestic turmoil in 63. In the early months a powerfully backed and politically volatile program of reform was introduced by the College of Tribunes, containing proposals for large-scale agrarian resettlement, the alleviation of debt, and the restoration of their rights to the sons of those proscribed by Sulla. A dramatic attempt was also made to highlight and limit the power of the Sullan oligarchy by means of a sensational trial centering on the controversial legal ramifications of the Senate's so-called ultimate decree. Later in the year came a determined bid by Catiline to win the consulship as a champion of the *miseri,* and soon afterwards his more desperate attempt to unite the politically disaffected in armed revolt.[1]

Cicero responded to the tribunician initiatives with repeated denunciations of the aims and methods of all so-called popular leaders, warning of specious promises from these falsely styled friends of the people whose only goal was self-aggrandizement and whose chief hope of success lay in dissension and civil disorder. He paraded a lengthy catalogue of damaging effects from the machinations of such self-seeking seditionists—disruptions of the peace, fear and uncertainty, a weakened structure of government and law enforcement, threats to private property, the abolition of credit and of all confidence in the state's financial stability, and ultimately the risk of anarchy and despotism. *Populares* were, he claimed, the one serious remaining threat to the security of the Republic, and he declared their defeat a primary goal of his consulship.[2]

He joined his attacks on popular reformers with efforts to restore confidence in the institutions and practices of the existing order and to reawaken support for the cornerstone of the system, senatorial supremacy in political decision making. He extolled the achievements of the ancestral constitution and the aspirations for which it stood and to which he pledged his own complete dedication, namely, liberty and dignity, law and order, peace at home and abroad, and the secure, untroubled enjoyment of their property by all citizens. These, he argued, were the only truly popular and important possessions of any people, and he appealed for the unity of honest and right-minded citizens from all orders in active defense of these precious benefits of their republican heritage. In his opposition to the proposals for agrarian reform and for the cancellation or reduction of debts, he stood forth as a particular defender of property owners and of the interests of the entire business class, and it was this numerous and powerful body of the prosperous, which he some-

---

1. The events of Cicero's consulship have been dealt with in greater detail in my *Cicero, the Ascending Years* (New Haven, 1979), 177–242.

2. *Leg. agr.* 1.22–27; 2.8, 10, 102. *Rab.* 33. *Cat.* 1.31; 2.11.

times described as the *lauti* and the *locupletes,* that he especially sought to convince of the advantages of the status quo and of the need for their firm and united support of the Senate to insure its preservation.[3]

Cicero's skill and forcefulness in opposing the advocates of change and in articulating and promoting traditional republican beliefs and practices had a telling effect. Only one relatively minor popular reform, relating to the election of priests, is known to have been carried into law during the whole of 63.[4]

The designs of Catiline he resisted with equal success. He helped bring about his defeat at the consular elections for 62 and his subsequent conspiracy he contained and eventually suppressed, skillfully exploiting it to rally support for his own brand of government and to vindicate his warnings of danger from all opponents of the status quo. His exposure of the plot brought a temporary fulfillment of his dearest objective, the unification of all orders in defense of the Republic under the resolute leadership of the Senate.[5]

Cicero's aggressive and outspoken stand in 63 in defense of the ancestral constitution and in opposition to any form of political action or movement for change that might endanger senatorial control or threaten private property or the financial interest of the well-to-do clearly revealed the abiding influence of his conservative heritage and early mentors and the depth of his commitment to the social and political structure of traditional republicanism. He was by no means unaware of the problems of corruption and disunity that were threatening the foundations of senatorial rule, or of the economic hardships that were alienating the lower classes and promoting demagoguery and violence. But his instinctive attachment to the established order and intellectual faith in its merits prevented him from seeking or accepting radical solutions. He had no vision of a better state than the *vetus respublica,* and could conceive of no remedy for the evils of his time that departed from the basic political and economic tenets of republicanism. Accordingly, he gave all his energies as consul to opposing change and to the revitalization of the Republic's

3. *Leg. agr.* 1.23, 26–27; 2.9, 102. *Rab.* 33–34. *Cat.* 4.15, 22. *Pis.* 7. *Att.* 1.16.6; 1.18.3; 1.19.4. *Fam.* 1.9.12. *Off.* 3.88. *Rep.* 2.40.

4. Dio 37.37.1–2. See L. R. Taylor, "The Election of the Pontifex Maximus in the Late Republic," *CP* 37 (1942), 421ff.

5. *Mur.* 52. *Sulla* 51. *Cat.* 1.11; 4.14, 17–22. *Pis.* 7. *Att.* 1.18.3. *Fam.* 1.9.12, 17. Dio 37.29. Plutarch, *Cic.* 14.3–6. Sallust, *Cat.* 26.

traditional political structures, and he measured the achievements of 63, not in terms of new directions or positive reforms, but of his success in thwarting the designs and weakening the support of those who would radically alter the status quo.[6]

Cicero never wavered in his belief in the superiority of the republican constitution and of the social and political ideals that he saw embodied in it. Even when the system had come close to collapse a decade later and, disheartened by the failure of his hopes and deprived of any meaningful role in public affairs, he turned to study and to theoretical consideration of the ideal state, the products of his reflections, the *De republica* and *De legibus,* did little more than reaffirm within a philosophical framework the enduring merits of the *vetus respublica.* In general, his philosophical and rhetorical writings, whenever they touch on social and political themes, attempt to bolster the political and moral traditions of the *respublica* by philosophic rationales. There is consequently a remarkable consistency of political and moral thought throughout Cicero's varied and voluminous writings. There are occasional shifts of emphasis and some concessions to political realism or opportunism, but the basic vision of the state and statesmanship is never discarded or seriously diluted. The present chapter will attempt to assemble the evidence for Cicero's political thought from all his writings and to show the intensity and persistence of his ideological attachment to the fundamental tenets of Roman republicanism.

Cicero's political ideas proceeded from an aristocratic view of the state and its management that presupposed a hierarchical social structure and a system of government dominated by the upper classes, and it closely reflected the thinking underlying the basic structures of the Roman state and its elaborate differentiation of citizens on the basis of wealth and *dignitas.*[7] Cicero did acknowledge and emphasize that a true *respublica,* founded on the idea that the state belongs to the people and exists for the good of the people, must recognize a high degree of equality among all

6. *Rep.* 1.70; 5.1–2. *Tusc.* 4.1. *Leg.* 3.37. *Fam.* 1.9.12. *Pis.* 6–7. *Phil.* 2.11–20. *Sulla* 28–29. *Off.* 2.84. *Att.* 1.16.7; 4.18.2. Cicero did attempt to implement two reforms, introducing an *ambitus* bill, which was passed, and a proposal to abolish *liberae legationes,* which failed. *Mur.* 3, 5, 67, 89. *Planc.* 83. *Sest.* 133ff. *Vat.* 37. *Schol. Bob.* 79, Stangl. Dio 37.29. *Leg.* 3.18. He was not opposed to reforms that curbed abuses and demanded higher standards of the ruling class.

7. Livy 1.42.4. Cato *apud* Festus 408, 33L.

citizens, but he viewed the form of equalitarianism inherent in the notion of *respublica* as relating primarily to law and the administration of justice. In these areas he is eloquently insistent that the principle of equality must be observed absolutely. He repeatedly stresses that a state is a partnership in justice, a community held together by a common agreement about the principles of right that should govern the conduct of citizens and their dealings with one another. These principles must be spelled out in the state's laws, whose purpose it is to insure that citizens may live honorably and happily in safety and peace in accordance with rules formulated in conformity with that shared sense of right that is the bond of society. It follows that the laws must be applied equally to all; there can be no legal privilege, for justice is one and necessarily the same for all.[8]

Further, law is the only master that a free people can endure, and no group or individual, whatever their position, can be allowed to become more powerful than the laws. Those who govern exercise authority, but do so by virtue of lawfully constituted offices. The authority of rulers comes from the law and they are creatures of the law.[9]

This equality before the law and the equal subordination of all to the law comprised for Cicero the essence of political freedom. Those were the conditions that made all citizens *pares libertate,* a form of equality demanded by justice and essential to the preservation of harmony and stability.[10]

8. *Rep.* 1.39, 42–43, 49, 53, 69; 2.31, 48, 50, 55, 69–70; 3.33, 45; 4.8. *Leg.* 1.18, 22–23, 35, 42; 2.8–13; 3.23–24, 34. *Planc.* 33. *Off.* 1.53, 124; 2.85. *De or.* 1.88. *Leg. agr.* 2.102. *Verr.* 2.5.169–70. See Ch. Wirszubski, *Libertas as a Political Idea at Rome* (Cambridge, 1960), 9–15. E. Fantham, "*Aequabilitas* in Cicero's Political Theory, and the Greek Tradition of Proportional Justice," *CQ* 23 (1973), 285–90. L. P. Kenter, *Cicero, De Legibus: A Commentary on Book I* (Amsterdam, 1972), 81, 157. G. H. Sabine and S. B. Smith, *Cicero, On the Commonwealth* (Columbus, Ohio, 1929), 45–56. E. Lepore, *Il principe ciceroniano e gli ideali politici della tarda reppublica* (Naples, 1954), 258–65. K. Büchner, *Cicero: Bestand und Wandel seiner gestigen Welt* (Heidelberg, 1964), 214–38. A. F. Cancelli, "Iuris consensu nella definizione ciceroniana di res publica," *RCCM* 14 (1972), 247–67. J. Hellegouarc'h, *Le vocabulaire latin des relations et des partis politiques sous la république* (Paris, 1963), 542–66. N. Wood, *Cicero's Social and Political Thought* (Berkeley, Calif. 1988), 70–89.

9. *Cluent.* 146. *Rep.* 2.43. *Leg.* 3.1–3. Toward the end of his life Cicero claimed that one of his foremost objectives had always been to insure that no individual became stronger than the laws. *Fam.* 5.21.2; 7.3.5. *Ad Brut.* 1.16.5. For Cicero's view of the law and use of it as an advocate, see C. J. Classen, "Cicero, the Laws and the Law-Courts," *Latomus* 37 (1978), 597–619.

10. *Phil.* 1.34. Cf. *Leg. agr.* 2.102.

Cicero did not, however, extend the notion of equality to the sphere of government. He conceded that the nature of a *respublica* and the nature of man as a political being and his perception of his rights and liberties required recognition of the principle that the people were the highest authority in the state and the ultimate source of all power wielded by those who governed. The same considerations led him to believe that some degree of participation in the conduct of public affairs must be given to all citizens.[11] But an equal share for all in the administration of the state was, he maintained, neither conducive to a free and stable political order nor in accordance with the principles of justice. The deliberations of mass gatherings were susceptible to manipulation by seditionists and characterized by an impulsiveness and impatience that left little room for the exercise of reason and judgment. Besides, the extreme conception of freedom and equality inherent in the idea that all citizens must have an equal part in political decision making had the inevitable effect of creating a society in which people thought only of their rights, not of their obligations, and became intolerant of all authority and restraint. Before long the excessive thirst for freedom brought the loss of all freedom, as the entire ordering of society and government became subject to the whims of a self-indulgent and undisciplined populace. There resulted a despotism of the multitude, a condition that fostered the rise of demagogues and the eventual emergence of one such leader with sufficient power to establish a tyranny and abolish every vestige of liberty.[12]

Cicero's Concept of Virtus

Cicero found one further critical flaw in the idea of government by the people. It failed to recognize the natural inequalities in the abilities of men and the justice and necessity of reserving the demanding and critically important task of ruling to those who showed superior gifts of leadership. These gifts he summarized in the term *virtus,* an elusive word variously used in the age of Cicero. Derived from *vis,* it basically meant

    11. *Rep.* 1.43, 53, 55, 69; 2.31, 39, 50, 55–57; 3.43. *Leg.* 3.23–26, 34, 38. *Sest.* 137.
    12. *Rep.* 1.65–68; 2.39; 3.45–47. Cf. *Flacc.* 16–17, 57. *Cluent.* 138. *Planc.* 9. *Dom.* 4. *Mur.* 35–36. *Phil.* 7.4. *Tusc.* 5.104.

manliness or courage, and often represented a general toughness of mind that produced resolute and courageous action.[13] It was also used to describe any commendable physical or mental quality and skill, or the sum of such attributes in the sense of all-round excellence or worth.[14]

In the strictly moral sphere it served to describe both the morally right and the qualities of character individually and collectively that enabled a person to recognize and follow the way of right conduct. Cicero variously defines the term in this latter sense as "all right conditions of mind," "nature developed and brought to the highest level of perfection," "a disposition of soul in harmony with the order of nature and with reason."[15]

Cicero was rarely concerned, however, with this philosophical and Greek conception of *virtus,* and he generally used the term in a thoroughly Roman way in relation to praiseworthy achievement, particularly in the area of government. He believed that *virtus,* to be meaningful, must be more than a mere state of mind or an internal possession. It had to find expression in action, and he considered that it found its worthiest expression in political activity, the area of human endeavor that he so fervently believed afforded the greatest opportunities for worthwhile accomplishment.[16] For him, therefore, *virtus* represented, above all else, excellence with respect to statesmanship, and in his writings it most often described either particular political merits or the entirety of the attributes that marked the good statesman and formed the basis of his right to a place of political leadership.[17]

Among these attributes Cicero included innate abilities and acquired

13. *Tusc.* 2.43. *Phil.* 3.34; 4.13; 5.2,4; 8.23; 13.5; 14.4, 35. *Quir.* 19. *Sest.* 86. Caesar, *BG* 1.1. See D. C. Earl, *Sallust* (Amsterdam, 1966), 5–40; *The Moral and Political Tradition of Rome* (London, 1967), 20–35. A. Ernout, "Les noms latins en -TUS," *Philologica Classica* (1946), 225ff. P. Kuklica, "Ciceros Begriff *virtus* und dessen Interpretation," *GLO* 7–8 (1975–76), 3–23. J. Ferguson, *Moral Values in the Ancient World* (London, 1958), 159–78. J. Sarsila, "Some Notes on *Virtus* in Sallust and Cicero," *Arctos* 12 (1978), 135–43. W. Eisenhut, *Virtus Romana. Ihre Stillung im römischen Wertsystem* (Munich, 1973).

14. *Arch.* 25. *Man.* 36. *Sest.* 136–38. *Cael.* 41. *Verr.* 2.5.181. *Balb.* 51. *Mur.* 17. *Mil.* 101.

15. *Tusc.* 2.43. *Leg.* 1.25. *Inv.* 2.159. Cf. *Deiot.* 26. *Mur.* 30, 65. *Phil.* 10.20. *Pis.* 69. *Cael.* 39–41.

16. *Rep.* 1.1–12, 33; 6.13. *Off.* 1.19, 28–29, 70–72, 92, 153–55. *Leg.* 3.3. *Mur.* 30. *Sest.* 86.

17. *Sest.* 136–37. *Verr.* 2.5.181. *Balb.* 51. *Mur.* 17.

skills as well as qualities of character. The former were chiefly represented for him in the terms *prudentia* or *sapientia, consilium,* and
eloquentia.

Prudentia in its widest sense he presents as the art that relates to the
conduct of life, providing those who possess it with the knowledge of
what is good and what is bad, or, put another way, knowledge of things to
be sought and things to be avoided. He derives it from *providere* and
gives *providentia,* the ability to foresee what will happen before it hap-
pens, as one of its main subdivisions. This ability to foresee was the chief
mark of the *sapiens,* and *prudentia,* therefore, came to be used as a
synonym for *sapientia.*[18] The latter, however, did retain a loftier significance. Cicero calls it the *gravissimum nomen* for wisdom and equates it
with the Greek σοφία, representing the higher knowledge attainable by
the perfect reason of the sage and encompassing an understanding of the
whole scheme of things human and divine. *Prudentia* had a more general
and less exalted meaning that corresponded to the sense of the Greek
φρόνησις, and it was the term that Cicero preferred in political
contexts.[19]

He does not, however, maintain a consistent distinction between the
two words. He often uses *sapientia* to describe general good sense and
perceptiveness and *prudentia* to indicate the deeper wisdom of the
learned and developed intellect. Both words served him as virtual synonyms to indicate either philosophical insight or more ordinary practical
farsightedness, or a combination of the two.[20]

Both words could also be used to mean wisdom or expertise in relation
to a particular profession or individual area of knowledge. For instance,
Cicero calls the special knowledge of physicians *prudentia physicorum*
and describes the legal expertise of the Scaevolae as *sapientia.* Similarly,
he speaks of *prudentia reipublicae gerendae* and *sapientia constituendae
civitatis.*[21]

---

18. *Fin.* 5.16, 18, 36. *ND* 2.58; 3.38. *Rep.* 6.1. *Leg.* 1.19, 60. *Div.* 1.111. *Inv.*
2.160. *Off.* 1.15, 153; 2.33; 3.71. *Sen.* 78. *Tusc.* 3.37. *Hort.*fr.33M. *Herr.* 3.3.
19. *Off.* 1.153; 2.5. *Leg.* 1.22, 58. *Tusc.* 4.57. *Part. or.* 76. *Fin.* 3.23–25. *Rep.*
2.45, 67. *De or.* 1.60; 2.4. *Div.* 1.24. *Att.* 12.4.2. See M. O. Liscu, *Etude sur la langue
de la philosophie morale chez Cicéron* (Paris, 1930), 235ff. G. Luck, "Etymologie et
usage du mot sapientia chez les Latins, notamment chez Cicéron," *ABG* 60 (1964), 203–
15.
20. *Deiot.* 4. *Marc.* 7. *Man.* 17. *Off.* 1.15. *Fin.* 5.36. *Part. or.* 76. *Tusc.* 3.37.
21. *Div.* 1.24; 2.11. *De or.* 1.214, 256; 2.59, 144, 154. *Fin.* 4.76. *Mur.* 28. *Herr.* 3.3.

Cicero's use of *prudentia* in relation to politics, or *prudentia civilis* as he terms it, incorporated all senses of the term, denoting both practical knowledge of public affairs and of the operations of government, and a broader political acumen aided by a theoretical understanding of the principles of ethics and political science and of all that pertained to the art of government.[22]

Such expertise and wisdom were obviously not easily acquired. Cicero considered them a possession of the very few, a product of unusual intelligence, informed and developed by the broadest possible training and education. In the *De inventione* he specifically lists *intelligentia* as one of the main components of *prudentia*. Elsewhere he constantly associates the word with sharpness of mind and the ability to reason, opposing it to *stultitia* and *stupiditas*.[23]

But native intelligence needed the addition of knowledge. *Prudentia* in all its senses was inseparable from *scientia;* Cicero asserts that it is in knowledge that *prudentia* manifests itself, and on knowledge rests its whole force and efficacy as a virtue. He is particularly insistent that political wisdom is based on *scientia*; the capacity to govern wisely is not an instinctive gift, not even for the intelligent or for the so-called *docti et sapientes* who lack specific knowledge of the governmental system and the science of politics. Statesmanship he considered not only an *ars* but the greatest and most important of all professional skills. In the manner of Socrates, he found the idea that it required no special training or expertise profoundly illogical.

Such ideas were also a serious threat to his concept of a select political leadership. They gave claims to political power to the *imperiti* and opened the way to the form of radical democracy that brought the downfall of Greece. On the other hand, they provided an excuse for political quietism for potentially able statesmen who claimed they need only enter politics in times of crisis.[24]

The practical expertise that Cicero demanded of the good statesman consisted first of all in a thorough understanding of the state's constitu-

---

22. *Rep.* 2.45. *Part. or.* 76. *Rep.* 1.11; 3.4–5. *De or.* 1.60, 85, 165, 193, 201.
23. *Inv.* 2.160. *ND* 2.18, 147. *Rep.* 3.28. *Off.* 1.81. *Lig.* 10. *Verr.* 2.1.115. *Man.* 68. *Phil.* 2.13.81; 5.50. *Mur.* 26. *De or.* 3.142.
24. *Part. or.* 76. *Rep.* 1.9–11, 33, 35; 3.4–5. *De or.* 1.165, 211; 3.142. *Tusc.* 1.94. *Off.* 1.122. *Flacc.* 16.

tion and organs of government. This required most obviously a knowledge of the functions and procedures of the political bodies and of all the mechanics of government. Actual experience, *usus,* was the best teacher in these matters. Cicero frequently exalts the value of *usus* in relation to the statesman's craft and sometimes explicitly links the word to *prudentia.*[25] But he also stresses the need for studies that would reinforce and complement experience, particularly the study of law and of the history of the state. Legal advocacy was, of course, a significant part of the activities of the majority of Roman politicians and an important means of winning friends and building influence, as is well illustrated by the career of Cicero himself. But, besides these practical benefits, Cicero saw in the study of law together with the study of the state's history the surest way to a necessary understanding of the character and spirit of the constitution and of the values and traditions that comprised the mind of the nation. Such studies also built pride in the Roman achievement and in the *prudentia* of past generations and thus promoted the political conservatism and dedication to the *mos maiorum* so fundamental to Cicero's political thought.[26]

Knowledge of all current affairs, national and international, is also given great emphasis by Cicero. The resources of the state, the condition of the empire, treaties, agreements, the rights of allies, friends, and tributaries—all these he lists as samples of the varied issues that have to be studied and grasped. He was seeking a government of experts, acting out of the fullest possible knowledge of the matters they confronted, and the degree of his concern with this high level of knowledgeability is evidenced in the *De legibus,* where he incorporates among the laws of his ideal state a specific injunction that senators must be well informed about all aspects of public affairs.[27]

There was a much more important side, however, to Cicero's concept of *prudentia civilis,* which required a wider and more profound form of knowledge. The true essence of political wisdom he regarded as an understanding of the forces and principles that govern the movement of political affairs and a resultant capacity to evaluate accurately the course of future events. It implied a superior knowledge and foresight that

25. *Rep.* 1.13, 36–37. *De or.* 1.211; 3.74. *Phil.* 10.6. *Cluent.* 84. *Fam.* 3.7.5.
26. *De or.* 1.159, 165–201; 2.337. *Orator* 120. *Rep.* 5.5. *Brut.* 161, 322.
27. *Leg.* 3.41. *De or.* 1.159, 201, 2.68, 337.

brought an awareness of all the implications and possible consequences of any situation and pointed the way to expedient action. It also implied a confident rationality that guarded against the rash response, tempering by informed and well-reasoned reflection the common tendency of talented and courageous men to resort to bold action.[28]

Such farsightedness and right judgments Cicero believed could only come from an intellect sharpened and enlightened by broad learning. *Doctrina* is a frequent companion of *prudentia* throughout his writings, the connection most closely made in the *De oratore,* where he states that part of his purpose in writing the dialogue was to show that men like the chief interlocutors, L. Crassus and M. Antonius, could never have achieved the *prudentia* and *eloquentia* they exhibited without *doctrina.*[29]

The learning Cicero had in mind included all the areas of knowledge that were considered in his day to comprise the *artes liberales.* This term sometimes referred to the curriculum of the lower levels of education, the *puerilis institutio* which corresponded to the Greek ἐγκύκλιος παιδεία, but in Cicero it generally has a broader application, denoting all the studies that befit the free.[30] At one time or another he includes under it geometry, astronomy, music, rhetoric, dialectics, literature, history, and philosophy.[31] All of these comprised a *doctrina* that was essentially one. All had a bearing on human life and contributed to man's understanding of himself and of the universe and man's place in it. Their systematic character and formative power also contributed to the student's intellectual growth, nurturing and expanding his mental capabilities.[32]

While Cicero insists on the oneness of the liberal arts and the need for the widest possible exposure to all the areas of knowledge they encompassed, he considered history and philosophy of particular importance in relation to *prudentia civilis.* He was himself an eager student of both. His interest in history verged on the antiquarian. His writings show a fascination not only with the great figures of Roman history and the institutions and traditions on which the Roman state and empire were built, but with

28. *Rep.* 2.45. *Off.* 1.81; 2.33. *Cat.* 2.25. *Div.* 1.111.
29. *De or.* 1.5; 2.1–7; 3.122, 142. *Off.* 1.156. *Leg.* 1.60. *Rep.* 3.4–6. *Lig.* 10. *Fam.* 3.7.5. *Q.F.* 1.1.29.
30. *De or.* 1.11, 72–73; 2.1; 3.21, 125, 127, 140. *Inv.* 1.35. *Arch.* 4. *Acad.* 2.1. Seneca, *Ep. mor.* 88.23.
31. *De or.* 1.187; 3.127. Cf. *Leg.* 1.60–62. *Orator* 113, 118–20.
32. *De or.* 3.20–21. *Arch.* 2, 15–16. *Rep.* 1.28, 30. *Leg.* 1.60. Cf. Quintilian, *Inst.* 1.8.8.

great men and great events everywhere. He recounts a visit to the tomb of Archimedes and to the haunts of the great men of Athens with the excitement of a man who was, to use his own language, *curiosus,* enchanted by the past and ardently anxious to know it.[33] He was widely read in the historical literature, Greek and Roman, of his time and had given much thought to the nature of historiography. Many of his theoretical writings, notably the *De republica,* involved him in extensive historical research, and the opening of the *De legibus* indicates that he seriously contemplated writing a history of Rome.[34]

In the end, however, it was philosophy that was to get precedence in his literary endeavors. It had always held a high place in his interests. He speaks many times of his devotion to it from his youth. He had become an eager student of Philo the Academician in the early eighties and about the same time began to work with Diodotus the Stoic, to whom he gave a home and with whom he developed the closest friendship. His enthusiasm for the discipline was renewed in the early seventies when, during lengthy travels abroad, he spent six months at Athens as a student of Antiochus of Ascalon, Philo's successor as head of the Academy, and also studied with Posidonius at Rhodes. He relates that after he entered public life he could devote only such time to philosophy as the claims of his friends and the state allowed, but he says he continued to read in the subject although there was no opportunity for writing. That opportunity did come when Caesar's victory in the civil war brought an enforced retirement. Cicero made full use of it and produced an impressive body of philosophical writings, seeking to provide consolation for himself and to give readier access to his countrymen to a discipline that he describes as too little known in Rome but most worthy to be known.[35]

Cicero comes back many times to the importance of history and philosophy in the education of political leaders. He urges the widest possible

33. *Fin.* 5.4–6. *Tusc.* 5.64–66.
34. *Leg.* 1. 5–10. *De or.* 2.51–64. See E. Rawson, "Cicero the Historian and Cicero the Antiquarian," *JRS* 62 (1972), 33–45. B. Shimron, "Ciceronian Historiography," *Latomus* 33 (1974), 232–44. P. A. Brunt, "Cicero and Historiography," *Miscellanea di studi classici in onore di E. Manni,* vol. 1 (Rome, 1980), 311–40. M. Rambaud, *Cicéron et l'histoire romaine* (Paris, 1953). C. W. R. Ardley, "Cicero on Philosophy and History," *Prudentia* 1, (1969), 28–41.
35. *Brut.* 306, 309, 315. *De or.* 1.1; 2.1. *Off.* 2.2–6. *ND* 1.6. *Tusc.* 1.1,5–6; 5.5. *Div.* 1.6–7. *Acad.* 2.6.

study of history, ranging over *omnis antiquitas*.[36] The benefits were of several kinds. In a very practical way a broad knowledge of history provided a treasury of *exempla,* which Cicero considered an important tool of persuasion.[37] National history provided the crucial information, alluded to earlier, about the traditions and social and political structures of one's own country. History also had an inspirational aspect that encouraged emulation of the actions and aspirations of heroic personalities. Associated with this was the practical guidance to be derived from the lives of the great, whose decisions and opinions constituted a rich legacy of accumulated wisdom.[38]

In a more general way history offered valuable lessons about human behavior and the ways of nations and governments. History was, in Cicero's phrases, "the witness of the ages," "the lifeblood of tradition," "the messenger of antiquity." It set forth the course and character of human affairs, the causes and consequences of events, and the nature and life of the principal figures. It was, therefore, "a teacher of life" and "a beacon of truth," and, severed from what it taught about what man had done, man lacked maturity and understanding of himself. Cicero made the point memorably in a well-known passage in the *Orator:* "To be ignorant of what happened before you were born is to remain forever a child. For what is the life of man if it is not interwoven with the life of earlier generations through the recollection of past events."[39] Like many before him and since, he saw a constancy and continuity in human experience that made man inseparable from his past and left all inquiry into human affairs in need of the illumination of history.

Philosophy he believed offered still greater rewards and was more necessary to the achievement of *prudentia civilis* in its fullest sense. He defines it in the standard way as *studium sapientiae,* its purpose to unearth by the power of the mind the probable truth about the significance, nature, and causes of all things divine and human and the proper system of life and conduct for man. It put an end to *inscientia* and was the source of true *doctrina,* its students the truly *docti*.[40]

36. *De or.* 1.18, 158, 165, 187, 256. *Orator* 120. *Brut.* 161, 322.
37. *De. or.* 1.18,201. *Orator* 120. *Brut.* 322. *Leg.* 3.41. *Part. or.* 96. See P. Defourny, "Histoire et eloquence," *LEC* 21 (1953), 156–66.
38. *Fin.* 5.6. *Arch.* 14.
39. *De or.* 2.36. *Orator* 120.
40. *Off.* 2.5. *De or.* 1.212; 3.56, 79, 142–43. *Rep.* 3.4–6. *Orator* 13.

Cicero did not demand, however, that the statesman should be schooled in all the varied concerns of philosophy. Two of the three ancient divisions of the discipline, logic and physics, he was prepared to dispense with altogether. He saw some value for the orator in the study of logic, and sometimes speaks in glowing terms about natural science and the pleasure and benefit of examining the nature and design of the universe and acquiring a cosmic view of human existence and human affairs, but neither study had a crucial bearing, to his mind, on the art of statesmanship.[41]

What chiefly concerned him was philosophy's third branch, ethics, and its subdivision political theory, the area that he described as dealing with the life and *mores* of man, with human relations and life in society, with the nature of states and government.[42] These were the *studia*, centered in Socratic fashion on man himself, that could both benefit people personally and make them useful to the state.[43] They were the means to self-knowledge and to the discovery of the morally right and of the moral duties associated with it. There was no other training that was more likely to lead to virtue and none that could contribute more to a good and happy life.[44]

The moral insight and probity that these studies could produce were obviously highly desirable traits in political leaders and, as we shall see later, Cicero attached the highest political importance to them. But he also saw other aids to wise and effective leadership in the study of moral and political philosophy. It gave an understanding of human nature and of the emotions and motivations underlying human responses that had obvious value for the statesman in his dealings with the public and in the promotion of his views.[45] But still more important, it confronted the fundamental questions relating to the establishment and governance of political communities—the social and political instincts that gathered men into states, the principles of justice on which human fellowship was founded, the rights and liberties that justice entailed, the forms of govern-

41. *De or.* 1.68. *Orator* 16, 113. *Leg.* 1.58–62. *Rep.* 1.26–29.
42. *De or.* 1.42, 48, 53, 85, 219; 2.68; 3.72, 122, 127. *Orator* 16. Cicero coined the adjective *moralis* to translate the Greek ἠθικός. *De fato* 1.
43. *Rep.* 1.15–16, 30, 32–33.
44. *Leg.* 1.58–61. *Off.* 1.4; 2.5–6; 3.5. *Rep.* 1.26–29; 3.4–6; 5.6. *Brut.* 322. *Tusc.* 3.6; 5.5. *Sen.* 2. *Div.* 2.1–3.
45. *De or.* 1.53, 60, 219.

ment compatible with it, the constitution and laws of the ideal state, the ideal statesman. Cicero subscribed to the sentiments he attributed to the Academician Charmadas in the *De oratore* that knowledge of these basic political issues had to be sought from philosophy, and it was a knowledge he believed no statesman could afford to neglect. In it was the key to the causes and remedies of political crises and the way to that superior perceptiveness and farsightedness in political affairs which constituted *caput prudentiae civilis*.[46]

Cicero's emphasis on *doctrina* did not mean that he was advocating long years of study or any ongoing immersion in book-learning for those who aspired to high political office. He was careful to avoid any impression that political leaders should be reclusive intellectuals and to discount any possibility of conflict between the pursuit of knowledge and the heavy demands of an active career in public life. He has Crassus directly confront this question in the third book of the *De oratore*. Crassus admits that acquiring knowledge is an endless and alluring occupation that often fills whole lives, but he insists that intelligent minds can quickly master any subject, if they are content to take from it what is of practical use to them and refrain from indulging in study for its own sake. He cites his own experience in illustration. He claims he can hold his own in any philosophical discussion though he has been able to devote little time to the study of philosophy since entering public life at a very early age. Cicero makes similar remarks about himself on various occasions, emphasizing that, despite his devotion to learning, his studies had become activities of leisure since the beginning of his political career and had never prevented him devoting his full energies to the service of the state.[47]

Cicero, in tune with the Roman spirit, held fast to the view that *virtus* must be expressed in action and that doing is more meritorious than mere thinking. He believed this applied especially in the sphere of politics. He therefore measured the intellectual activities of statesmen, once they extended beyond a recreational function, by strict standards of utility. Their purpose must be to aid political achievement, not to interfere with it. He was not seeking scholars or sages to lead the state, but men of

46. See n. 42 above; also *De or.* 1.60, 85–88. *Orator* 16–17. *Rep.* 1.35, 45; 2.45; 3.4–6; 5.5. *Leg.* 1.16, 19, 22. See G. Kennedy, *The Art of Rhetoric in the Roman World* (Princeton, 1972), 218–20.

47. *De or.* 1.1–2, 77–81; 3.74–77, 82–89. *Arch.* 12. *Rep.* 1.7–8. *Off.* 2.4.

action sufficiently acquainted with scholarly endeavors to extract from them and apply what was of value for the task of government.

The other attribute that Cicero associated with wise leadership, *consilium,* requires only brief discussion, as it was largely inseparable from *prudentia.* It signified good judgment, the ability to take the right decision. Cicero presents it as a product of high intelligence and unimpaired rationality, a deliberative faculty based solely on reason and independent of the influences of passion or emotion. It was properly a subdivision of *prudentia,* ancillary to the latter's powers of intellectual discernment and farsightedness, achieving the translation of the intellect's perceptions of political conditions and trends into a proper course of action.[48]

Prudentia and *consilium* were, in Cicero's view, the qualities which, when combined with justice, enabled a leader to win the full confidence of the public. People appreciated the utilitarian aspects of these abilities and willingly entrusted their lives, fortunes, and children to those who were seen to possess them, provided they were also seen to be *boni viri.* Such trust was, of course, indispensable to the smooth working of Cicero's conception of a governmental system dominated, with the consent of the masses, by the preeminent few.[49]

But despite the high place that he gives to *prudentia* and *consilium* among political virtues, Cicero saw them as incomplete and largely ineffective qualities without the addition of *eloquentia.* He speaks in exalted terms about the art in which he himself excelled and to which he had an intense devotion. It was in the ability to converse and express his thoughts in speech that man especially rose above the animals. Eloquence was the perfection of that ability and was the foremost hallmark of civilized man, an art of the greatest aesthetic and intellectual appeal, unsurpassed in the pleasure it afforded to ear and mind. It adorned the state and had done more to enhance its dignity than the bulk of military triumphs.[50]

Cicero speaks in a similar vein about the practical benefits of eloquence. There was no power greater or more admirable or more princely than the capacity it bestowed to sway the minds and feelings of any audience. This ability brought recognition and popular favor to the orator

48. *Rep.* 1.25, 55, 60; 2.30; 3.28. *Off.* 1.79, 81. *ND* 2.18, 79, 147; 3.75. *Fin.* 2.115. *Tusc.* 4.77. *Sen.* 67. *Div.* 2.85. *De or.* 1.8; 2.299.

49. *Off.* 2.33–34.

50. *De or.* 1.30–34; 2.33–35, 85; 3.55. *Inv.* 1.5. *Brut.* 255–57. *Orator* 142.

and also won him the close friendship and firm political support of the beneficiaries of his skills. It was the best means, aside from some outstanding achievement in war, of demonstrating one's fitness for political office and of building a political following.[51]

Cicero found the full measure of its appeal and benefits illustrated in the Roman experience. He relates that, after the acquisition of empire had brought a sense of lasting peace, there was scarcely a Roman youth with a sense of ambition who did not feel that he should devote all his energies to the pursuit of eloquence. Later, after contact with Greek orators and Greek literature and the arrival of Greek teachers, enthusiasm for the art grew to unbelievable proportions. It was given first place among civic accomplishments and provided rich rewards in prestige and influence for those who possessed it. It had continued to hold that primacy and to bring to distinction its ablest practitioners.[52]

But the value of eloquence was not confined to the pursuit of political success. Cicero considered it an equally important resource in the administration of political office. It was only with its aid that the benefits of *prudentia* and *consilium* could have real effect. He argued that all wisdom needed the resources of the art of speech if it was not to remain inchoate and introversive. Eloquence was the lamp of human intelligence that gave light to ideas. If the wise did not use it to communicate their knowledge to the world, they discarded the chief benefit of knowledge, which lay in its application to the service of humanity. He rehearses these themes at greatest length in the *De oratore,* where he dwells repeatedly on the inseparability of knowledge and eloquence and insists that the power to think and express thought must be considered one. Their separation he attributes to Socrates and calls an absurdity, a sundering, as it were, of tongue and brain.[53]

Political wisdom, therefore, like all wisdom, Cicero considered deficient without eloquence, but, viewed as an attribute of the statesman, he found it especially so, since it was the statesman's function not merely to discover and expound the expedient course but also to secure its acceptance and implementation. Political leaders, to win success in the Roman system, obviously had to be able to gain public approval for their mea-

51. *De or.* 1.15, 32–33; 2.33. *Mur.* 22–24. *Man.* 1–2. *Cael.* 46. *Off.* 2.48.
52. *De or.* 1.13–15. *Tusc.* 1.5. *Orator* 141.
53. *De or.* 1.54, 56, 61–63; 2.34–38; 3.19–24, 56–61, 69–73, 122–43. *Off.* 1.153–56. *Brut.* 59.

sures and public rejection of the arguments of their opponents. But beyond that, Cicero maintained, the true statesman needed the capacity to shape the direction of the nation in a more general way. He needed the skill and influence to mold the character and spirit of the people, to arouse and inspire them to honorable endeavors, and to deflect them from impetuous or evil courses and the influence of the pernicious. Above all, he needed to command full and continuous trust and respect from the public, for in no other way could the ascendancy of the aristocracy of merit that Cicero was seeking emerge and endure. Such an ascendancy he was convinced could not be established in law, since he believed the nature of the state and the political nature of man required that a balance of rights and functions be maintained between governors and governed and enough liberty and power given to the latter to allow them to feel secure and in ultimate control of their destinies. But he felt the assertion of its power by the people would be minimized and effective control relinquished to the aristocracy if its members were held in high esteem and had the moral authority to win voluntary acceptance of their views. He saw several examples of such a development in the history of the Republic and he describes the resulting situation, which recognized a certain equality among citizens and preserved the *potestas* of the people, but in circumstances of harmony and trust that made it subservient to an esteemed and eminent aristocracy, as the ideal form of government.[54]

The prestige and moral authority necessary to secure such control of a country's outlook and affairs could not be achieved, in Cicero's opinion, without the help of eloquence. He considered it a delicate and difficult task to win agreement about matters of high political importance, particularly from the general public, which was volatile and unpredictable in its reactions. It required mastery of the full panoply of deliberative oratory: an authoritative presentation; a style of a certain grandeur and distinction suited to the dignity and seriousness of affairs of state and capable of stirring the emotions in favor of or against a particular course; an awareness of the many ways in which the feelings of the crowd can be alienated; a sensitivity to popular concerns of the moment; and, finally, variety and wit to maintain interest and goodwill.[55]

Cicero recognized, of course, that these skills of oratory needed the

---

54. *Leg.* 1.62; 3.24–25, 28, 39. *Rep.* 2.55–57, 59, 61. *De or.* 1.202; 2.35.
55. *De or.* 1.33–34; 2.35, 333–37; 3.55, 76. *Inv.* 1.3, 5.

backing of other ingredients of *auctoritas* to be fully effective, but eloquence remained for him the most vital precondition for lasting political influence. He comes back time and again to its unequaled importance as a formative force in the affairs of nations. He repeats the Greek commonplace that it was the power of eloquence that first gathered the scattered race of man into states and turned them from a savage and lawless existence to a peaceful and civilized way of life in well-ordered societies. He maintains that eloquence had continued to exert a dominant influence in every political community that enjoyed peace and liberty. History abounded in examples. Pericles, the first near-perfect orator produced in Athens, had charmed and dominated the Athenians with his oratorical power for forty years and, even when he spoke against popular measures and popular men, he was able to keep his own popularity. In Rome, Cato the Censor, C. Laelius, and Scipio Aemilianus were leaders who had similarly crowned great ability and wide learning with eloquence and had achieved as a result unrivaled *auctoritas*.[56]

Cicero, therefore, classified eloquence alongside *prudentia* or *sapientia* as a central part of the *ratio civilis*. Wisdom unspoken or badly articulated was politically impotent. It was only in conjunction with artful and persuasive speech that it could move the minds and inclinations of the body politic and give its holders the recognition and influence to translate wise perception into action.[57]

As in the case of *prudentia*, Cicero considered *eloquentia* a most difficult skill to acquire, demanding great natural talent, arduous technical training and practice, and the broadest possible learning. The natural requirements were formidable and were both physical and mental—strength of body, a good voice, attractive appearance and bearing, a sharp, inventive mind, facility with language, a good memory. The training was also formidable and likely to deter all but the most dedicated.[58] It involved, first of all, a schooling in the precepts of the art of rhetoric. Cicero had some reservations about calling rhetoric an art, but he accepted that valid rules for good speaking could be formulated from observation and analysis of good speeches, and that the study of these rules was undeniably useful. But he was careful to point out that elo-

56. *De or.* 1.30, 33, 215–16; 2.33, 154; 3.138. *Brut.* 25, 44–45. *Orator* 141. *Inv.* 1.2–6. *Top.* 78.
57. *Inv.* 1.3, 6.
58. *De or.* 1.17–19, 113–15; 2.30, 85–88, 147; 3.125. *Cael.* 45–46.

quence did not derive from rules, and he was obviously impatient with what he saw as a pedantic obsession with technical details on the part of many rhetoricians that demeaned and distorted the nature of the art.[59] He placed a much higher value on the study and imitation of good models and on practice of a realistic nature.[60]

But the ingredient in the education of the orator with which Cicero was chiefly concerned was *doctrina*. He considered a general training in all the liberal arts an essential first step in laying the broad foundations of eloquence.[61] In addition, particular areas of learning helped develop particular oratorical skills and provided a variety of aids to effective speech. The study of literature, especially poetry, helped develop the memory along with skill in criticism and argumentation. It also provided material and examples for speeches. Knowledge of law was clearly necessary for the legal advocacy that was a primary function of oratory. History and public law provided a vast store of precedents and examples with which to add authority and credibility and charm to one's arguments. Logic gave insight into the art of disputation. Knowledge of natural science helped add loftiness and grandeur to an orator's style. Ethics provided an increased understanding of human psychology that was indispensable to the effective use of pathos—persuasion by appeal to the emotions. Knowledge of philosophy in general was useful in enabling a speaker to deal more fully and authoritatively with basic concepts and emotions that continually cropped up in speeches.[62]

But the prominence that Cicero gave *doctrina* in the training of the orator was not due primarily to this broad familiarity with the various divisions of learning that he considered essential to an orator's fluency and technical proficiency, but to the belief that true eloquence was impossible without complete comprehension of one's subject matter. This was the other side of the leitmotif of the *De oratore* that knowledge and eloquence should be regarded as inseparable. Just as knowledge needed eloquence to give it completeness and effect, so eloquence needed knowledge to give it weight and substance. If an orator did not speak with a full understanding of his subject, he became a mouther of glib inanities,

59. *De or.* 1.23, 52, 102, 107–10, 145–47; 2.30–33, 75–77, 133; 3.75.
60. *De or.* 1.147–57; 2.90–92. Cf. *Brut.* 309–10.
61. *De or.* 1.72–73, 158; 2.85; 3.125.
62. *De or.* 1.18, 53–54, 60, 157–58, 201; 2.72, 85. *Brut.* 161, 322. *Orator* 12–17, 113–20. *Arch.* 2, 12. *Tusc.* 2.26–27. *Part. or.* 96.

reducing his art to a fatuous swirl of words that could have no credibility and was deserving only of ridicule. Cicero repeatedly emphasizes the primacy of matter over words in the attainment of eloquence. Mastery of the *res* not only gave speech maturity and value but carried with it the inspiration for a rich and consummate style. He summarizes this view in a statement of Crassus in the *De oratore:* "Rerum enim copia verborum copiam gignit." It was not a new idea among Roman orators. Cato the Censor had long before expressed a similar sentiment in the words "Rem tene, verba sequentur."[63]

As a political attribute, therefore, eloquence needed the backing of the knowledge that pertained to the craft of politics—in other words, the knowledge underlying *prudentia civilis*. Since Cicero regarded politics as the primary and natural domain of the orator, this was also the knowledge to which he gave the greatest emphasis in all discussions of the orator's education, and it is a recurrent subject in the *De oratore*. Orators and statesmen were not wholly separable in Cicero's mind, nor were their educational requirements. The same *doctrina,* with philosophy at its center, was essential to both, the fountainhead alike of *prudentia* and *eloquentia*.[64]

The other components of Cicero's conception of political *virtus* were

---

63. *De or.* 1.5, 17, 20, 50–51; 2.1–5, 101, 148; 3.54–55, 125, 142–43. Julius Victor 374, Halm. Cf. Horace, *AP* 311. M. Orban, "Rehabilitation de la parole dans le *De oratore* de Cicéron," *AC* 19 (1950), 27–44. E. Gibson, "Eloquence et sagesse selon Cicéron," *Phoenix* 7 (1953), 1–19. G. Calboli, "La formazione oratoria de Cicerone," *Vichiana* 2 (1965), 3–30. P. H. Meador, "Rhetoric and Humanism in Cicero," *Phil. and Rhet.* 3 (1970), 1–12. R. Mueller, "Die Wertung der Bildungsdisziplinen bei Cicero," *Klio* 43 (1965), 77–173. G. M. A. Grube, *The Greek and Roman Critics* (London, 1965), 168–92.

64. *De or.* 1.33, 46–47; 3.57–59, 123, 142. Modern discussions of Cicero's views on the orator and oratory have concentrated heavily on *Quellenforschung,* and, as often, with uncertain results. See W. Kroll, "Studien über Ciceros Schrift *De oratore*," *RhM* 58 (1903), 552–97. H. von Arnim, *Leben und Werke des Dio von Prusa* (Berlin, 1898), 97–114. H. K. Schulte, *Orator: Untersuchungen über das Ciceronische Bildungsideal,* Frankfurter Studien zur Religion und Kultur der Antike 11 (1935). F. Solmsen, "The Aristotelian Tradition in Ancient Rhetoric," *AJP* 62 (1941), 35–50, 169–90. A. Michel, *Rhétorique et philosophie chez Cicéron* (Paris, 1960), 81–149. A. M. Guillemin, "Cicéron entre le génie grec et le mos maiorum," *REL* 33 (1955), 209–30. U. Knoche, "Cicero, ein Mittler griechischer Kultur," *Hermes* 87 (1959), 57–74. S. E. Smethurst, "Cicero and Isocrates," *TAPA* 84 (1953), 262–320. W. Steidle, "Einflüsse römischen Lebens und Denkens auf Ciceros Schrift De oratore," *Mus Helv* 9 (1952), 10–41. A. E. Douglas, "The Intellectual Background of Cicero's Rhetorica: A Study in Method," *ANRW* 1.3 (1973), 95–137.

the qualities of character that he considered necessary to meet the challenges and responsibilities of political life. He believed that these qualities consisted in the moral traits that derived from adherence to what he termed the *pristina severitas,* the ascetic sternness that marked the moral outlook of the early Romans. This pristine ethic placed the primary emphasis on duty and success and demanded unsparing effort in meeting the demands of both. This entailed the safeguarding and promotion of one's family's interests, but, above all, it meant the diligent pursuit of notable achievements in the service of the state. The old morality was preoccupied with *laus, honor, dignitas,* and *gloria,* and made a driving ambition to achieve them a cardinal virtue and a leading characteristic of the exemplary statesman.[65]

This impulse to great political endeavors Cicero sometimes calls *virtus,* but the term by which he most fully described it was *magnitudo* or *elatio animi.* In his strictest use of this term he presents it as a subdivision of the cardinal virtue of *fortitudo,* signifying a loftiness of spirit manifested in an energetic courage that arouses to action and welcomes difficult and dangerous undertakings for worthwhile ends. He seldom makes any real distinction, however, between the *magnus animus* and the *fortis animus,* and generally his use of *magnitudo animi* implies, in addition to courageous pursuit of strenuous and noble ends, the other main features of *fortitudo,* namely, a strength of spirit that despises pain and death and rises above the fears, passions, and vicissitudes of fortune that oppress weaker minds. This quality of high-souled ambition and unshakable fortitude Cicero considered essential to success in political life, providing the stimulus and resolution necessary to enable men to forgo the many allurements of *otium* and to confront and endure the many labors and stresses of political leadership.[66]

But *pristina severitas* represented a range of other associated virtues that Cicero considered equally necessary to good statesmanship. Those most prominently mentioned by him are *pietas, gravitas, labor* and *industria,* and *frugalitas.*

Pietas was a benevolent sense of duty and of devoted attachment toward all benefactors. It was founded in justice, which required above

---

65. *Cael.* 39–40, 42, 72–76. *Verr.* 2.2.7. *Arch.* 14. *Par. st.* 12. *Off.* 2.64.
66. *Arch.* 29. *Rab.* 24. *Pis.* 27. *Rep.* 1.1; 5.9. *Sest.* 99, 139, 141. *Har. resp.* 43. *Mil.* 1, 61, 69. *Phil.* 12.2. *Tusc.* 2.32. *Fin.* 4.17. *Par. st.* 12. *Off.*1.13, 15, 61–73; 3.100. See U. Knoche, *Magnitudo Animi. Ph* Supplbd. 27.3 (Leipzig, 1935).

all that each receive his due, and was closely related to *gratia*, the virtue of gratitude.[67] Cicero regarded it, in fact, as a particular manifestation of *gratia*, representing the sense of obligation and the desire to serve that came from a grateful consciousness of favors received. It was widely used to describe this sense of duty based on an appreciative recognition of indebtedness. Cicero says, for instance, that *pietas* was one of the reasons for his support of Pompey in the fifties and the motivation for his defense of clients, such as Sestius and Milo, who had done him great service. He also uses the term to describe the obligation of the state to honor its dead soldiers.[68] *Pietas* applied particularly, however, to the special attachment and sense of loyalty that people felt toward their greatest benefactors, namely, parents and kinsmen, country, and the gods.[69]

Gravitas was a seriousness of mind and strength of character that engendered a sense of responsibility and a vigor and steadfastness in defense of one's beliefs and in pursuit of one's objectives. *Constantia*, meaning firmness and consistency, and its corollary quality of *fides*, in the sense of integrity or trustworthiness, are the concepts that Cicero most commonly joins with it.[70] He also frequently uses it alongside *severitas* with many of the connotations of the latter: seriousness, sternness, rigid adherence to principle, and an austere concern for dignity and propriety.[71] He associates it too with *fortitudo* and sometimes gives it a similar sense of a resoluteness superior to ordinary human concerns and independent of the unsettling effects of passion or emotion.[72]

Cicero considered *gravitas* a particular characteristic of the *optimates* or *boni,* whom he viewed above all as statesmen who were unswerving in their loyalty to the institutions of the *respublica* and ready to face any

67. *Inv.* 2.161. *Leg.* 1.43. *ND* 1. 116. For justice in the sense of giving each his due, see *Off.* 1.15.

68. *Planc.* 80–81. *Sest.* 3. *Mil.* 100. *Phil.* 14, 29, 35. *Fam.* 1.1.1; 1.8.2.

69. *Rep.* 6.16. *Inv.* 2.66, 161. *Sest.* 7, 68, 146. *Off.* 2.11, 46; 3.41. *Rosc.* 37. *Cael.* 4. *Mur.* 12. *Verr.* 2.2.97–98. *Planc.* 29, 80. *Phil.* 2.99; 9.12; 13.46. *ND* 1.116. *Fin.* 3.73. *Top.* 90. See J. Lengle, "Pietas," *Römische Wertbegriffe* (Darmstadt, 1967), 229–73. J. Ferguson, *Moral Values,* 164–72.

70. *Fin.* 3.1. *Tusc.* 1.2; 4.57, 60; 5.12–13. *Off.* 1.23, 72, 112. *Sen.* 33. *Par. st.* 16. *Acad.* 2.53. *ND* 1.1. *Sest.* 88, 129, 139, 141. *Sulla* 82–83. *Cluent.* 196. *Phil.* 7.7, 14, 27; 8.19. *Flacc.* 36. See W. Kroll, *Kultur der Ciceronischen Zeit* (Leipzig, 1933), 27ff. On *fides,* see Hellegouarc'h, *Le vocabulaire latin,* 23–40.

71. *Mur.* 6, 66. *Cael.* 29, 33, 35. *Off.* 1.137. *Am.* 66.

72. *Tusc.* 2.32; 4.57. *Off.* 1.72, 137.

danger or hardship to safeguard them. *Populares,* on the other hand, were especially lacking in *gravitas,* characterized instead by a *levitas* that pandered to popular whims and shifted in accordance with the capricious mutability of the mind of the mob.[73]

Gravitas, therefore, conferred qualities of leadership that Cicero considered of foremost importance in the good statesman. He also saw it as a trait that gave authoritativeness to those who possessed it, an important additional benefit in a system that hoped for strong and harmonious government by the few.[74] He believed that it was a peculiarly Roman characteristic and, like so many other noble qualities, especially prominent among the earlier Romans. He admitted, with a typical leaning toward flexibility and moderation, that it needed to be tempered by good sense and humanity, but he still regarded it as the attribute that could insure resolute protectors for the *respublica* and a respected, authoritative political leadership.[75]

Labor and *industria* together described the capacity for work and the industry necessary for success in the pursuit and in the administration of high political office in the republican system. *Labor* represented the quality that enabled a person to endure toil. It implied both a devotion to hard work and an ability to tolerate it. It was akin to the general term for endurance, *patientia,* and is often used by Cicero in association with it to indicate a willingness and capacity to undergo hardship.[76]

Industria signified a dynamic energy and spirit of initiative that looked for challenging undertakings and pursued them vigorously and aggressively. Cicero often joins it to *virtus,* the latter in these contexts meaning worth or all-round ability, *industria* meaning the energetic exercise of that ability.[77]

Cicero repeatedly stresses the need for these qualities of energy and

73. *Sest.* 101, 105, 139, 141. *Har. resp.* 43. *Prov. cons.* 18. *Phil.* 2.24; 11.17. *Att.* 1.20.2; 2.1.6.

74. *Gravitas* in Cicero often carries a meaning close to prestige or authoritativeness and sometimes is nearly equivalent to power or influence. See *Har. resp.* 2, 45. *Sest.* 119, 130. *Leg. agr.* 2.87. *Leg.* 3.17.

75. *Sest.* 130, 141. *Cael.* 33. *Flacc.* 36. Cicero believed, however, that an excessive preoccupation with *gravitas* could lead to barren and imprudent rigidity. He accuses Cato the Younger of such rigidity on several occasions. *Mur.* 66. *Att.* 1.18.7; 2.1.8.

76. *Planc.* 62. *Mur.* 34. *Verr.* 2.2.7; 2.3.103. *Cael.* 13. *Cat.* 1.26. *De or.* 1.260. *Brut.* 233. *Off.* 1.122; 2.36. *Inv.* 2.163.

77. *Verr.* 2.5.39, 181. *Mur.* 16. *Sest.* 137. *Phil.* 13.24. *Off.* 1.122; 2.36. *Ad Quir.* 24.

dynamism in aspiring statesmen. They were highly prized by the electorate and essential in establishing a candidate's fitness for political responsibility. This was particularly true in the case of new men, who had to overcome the resentment or active opposition of an exclusive *nobilitas* and the prejudice of a public that largely accepted the idea of hereditary excellence and viewed political ambition in a *novus homo* with scepticism or hostility. The political drawbacks imposed by obscure birth could be offset only by a convincing display of *virtus* through unusual effort and enterprise.[78]

Cicero believed that the successful administration of high political office also required exceptional energy and vigor. He saw the institutions and traditions of republicanism under constant threat from the reckless designs of those who, for reasons of desperation, derangement, or misguided ambition, were intent on radical change. The defeat of these *audaces* and *improbi* entailed unfailing vigilance and tireless, unwavering dedication to strengthening the defenses of the Republic. These were the means, Cicero asserts, by which he himself had saved the state in 63.[79]

Frugalitas and the adjective of closely similar meaning, *frugi*, derived from *frux* and had basic connotations of worth and usefulness. The words also sometimes indicated honesty or moral uprightness. The antithesis of this positive sense of the terms was *nequitia*, meaning the absence of anything good, a total worthlessness.[80] In Cicero, *frugalitas* and *frugi* frequently retain their positive nuances of goodness and moral integrity, but their central meaning is most commonly a sobriety and self-discipline that rejects all forms of excess. Even this more negative sense, however, implied the presence of certain positive traits, and *frugalitas* is often joined by Cicero to such words as *labor, industria, patientia, diligentia,* and *parsimonia*. The man who was *frugi* could also be expected to possess qualities of industriousness, toughness, carefulness, and thrift.[81]

Cicero only once discusses directly the precise meaning of *frugalitas*.

78. *Planc.* 62. *Off.* 2.36. *Mur.* 34. *Sulla* 5. *Man.* 2. *Cael.* 47, 74. *Verr.* 2.3.7; 2.5. 180–81. *Sest.* 136.

79. *Sest.* 98–102, 138–43. Cf. *Rep.* 1.4–8. For Cicero's own *labores* in 63, see *Leg. agr.* 2.100. *Cat.* 2.14; 3.1. *Sulla* 5, 83. *Mur.* 3. *Off.* 1.77–78.

80. *Tusc.* 3.16–18; 4.36. *Fin.* 2.25. *Planc.* 62. *Verr.* 2.1.101; 2.4.39. *Sest.*21. *Phil.* 8.32. *Cluent.* 47. *De or.* 2.248. Cf. Quintilian, *Inst.* 1.6.29. Horace, *Sat.* 2.7.3.

81. *Deiot.* 26. *Font.* 40. *Verr.* 2.2.7; 2.3.7, 67; 2.4.39. *Phil.* 2.69. *Flacc.* 71. *Planc.* 62.

In a lengthy analysis of the term in the *Tusculan Disputations* he emphasizes its positive overtones of moral probity and asserts that, in its fullest sense, it encompassed all the cardinal virtues since no one who was deficient in any of them had ever been called *frugi*. He acknowledges, however, that the word generally had a narrower and more negative significance, which he represents as *omnis abstinentia, omnis innocentia*, self-restraint in all things and abstention from all wrongdoing. He equates *frugalitas* in this sense with the Greek virtue of σωφροσύνη, and describes its special function as the control and assuagement of the appetitive part of the soul and the preservation of a constant moderation resistant to inordinate desire.[82]

The meaning of *frugalitas* can be further illustrated from three other terms, *temperantia, moderatio,* and *modestia,* that Cicero also used to translate σωφροσύνη, and often listed as partial equivalents or subdivisions of *frugalitas*.[83] *Temperantia* had the widest meaning of the three and became Cicero's favorite word for σωφροσύνη. It was formed from the verb *temperare,* which had a basic sense of mixing in due measure, harmonizing different elements. It also contained from its earliest appearances in extant Latin an idea of restraint or moderation, a meaning not far distant from the primary force of the verb.[84]

Temperantia retained these connotations of measured blending and restraint. Cicero provides a number of general definitions of the term, all of which present as its central meaning the control and moderation of the appetites and of all impulses of the soul by reason.[85] Strictly speaking, it included the ideas represented by Cicero's two other terms for σωφροσύνη, *moderatio,* and *modestia. Moderatio,* the observance of *modus,* the proper measure, was an integral aspect of the chief sense of *temperantia,* since it was the quality by which the appetites were kept in a correct relationship to reason and prevented from running ahead or lagging behind.[86] *Modestia* is specifically listed by Cicero in the *De inventione* as a subdivision of *temperantia.* It was related to *modus,* but had

82. *Tusc.* 3.16–18; 4.36. See H. North, *Sophrosyne: Self-Knowledge and Self-Restraint in Greek Literature* (Ithaca, N.Y., 1966), 266–70.

83. *Deiot.* 26. *Font.* 40. *Tusc.* 3.16, 18; 4.36.

84. *Off.* 3.119. A. Ernout and E. Meillet, *Dictionnaire etymologique de la langue latine* (Paris, 1951), s.v. *temperare.* M. B. Ogle, "Horace, Epistle 1.19. 28–29," *AJP* 43 (1922), 55–61. North, *Sophrosyne,* 262.

85. *Part. or.* 76. *Inv.* 2.164. *Fin.* 1.47; 2.60.

86. *Off.* 1.15, 93, 96, 102, 141, 152; 3.96, 116. *Part. or.* 76. *Cael.* 42. *Inv.* 2.164.

the special meaning of restraint based on *pudor*, the quality that gave a sense of decency and propriety and shrank from any form of unbecoming behavior. Very often, however, *modestia* simply denoted a general quality of restraint that exercised a moderating influence on the passions, and its meaning was virtually indistinguishable from that of *temperantia*.[87]

This idea of a balanced regulation of the appetitive soul by reason which *temperantia* represented is most fully dealt with by Cicero in the *De officiis*, where he links it to the notion of *decorum*, an aesthetic concept that had first been converted into an ethical doctrine by Panaetius. *Decorum* in its widest sense meant that which was consistent with or appropriate to the higher aspects of human nature that differentiated man from the other animals. More specifically, it meant the presence in human actions of order, consistency, and moderation arising out of a state of soul in which the appetites and impulses were in harmony with each other and with the soul's controlling power, reason. This orderly regulation of the *motus animi* was demanded by the nature of man, which gave him an appreciation of beauty and harmony and impelled him to achieve in the world of the spirit the beauty, consistency, and order that he saw and admired in the world of sense. In specific terms, this entailed moderating and calming the appetites and rejecting the lure of sensual pleasure in the recognition that the excellence and dignity of human nature was designed for serious and important tasks and a style of life marked by thrift, restraint, austerity, and sobriety. The soul thus harmonized with man's true propensities through the balanced rule of reason had an energetic dedication to duty and achievement and possessed freedom from all mental disturbances and a calm deliberateness and firm constancy in behavior. It was endowed with *gravitas* and *constantia*, the qualities that most befitted the nature of man.[88]

Cicero, again following Panaetius, goes on to state in the *De officiis*

---

87. *Inv.* 2.164. *Pis.* 9. *Mur.* 87. *Sulla* 15. *Planc.* 56. *Fin.* 2.60, 73. *Off.* 1.15, 93; 2.48. *Tusc.* 3.16. Cf. *Herr.* 3.3. *Modestia* was also used by Cicero to translate εὐταξία, the proper ordering of affairs so as to do the right thing at the right time. *Off.* 1.142.

88. *Off.* 1.13–14, 93–106, 120, 125, 137. See M. Pohlenz, *Antikes Führertum: Cicero de Officiis und das Lebensideal des Panaitios* (Leipzig, 1934), 55ff. M. van Straaten, *Panetius, sa vie, ses écrits, et sa doctrine* (Amsterdam, 1946), 160ff. E. V. Arnold, *Roman Stoicism* (Cambridge, 1911), 312–14. J. M. Rist, *Stoic Philosophy* (Cambridge, 1969), 186–200. P. Fedeli, "De Officiis di Cicerone," *ANRW* 1.4 (Berlin, 1973), 357–427. L. Labowski, *Die Ethik des Panaitios* (Leipzig, 1934), 112ff. R. Philippson, "Das Sittlichschöne bei Panaitios," *Philologus* 85 (1930), 357–413.

that, in addition to the general nature that he shares with all human beings, man also has a particular nature that gives him his own physical, mental, and moral traits. Each person has, besides, been placed in particular circumstances by virtue of such factors as birth, family fortune, and occupation. *Decorum* meant not only conforming to one's general nature but also to one's individual character and particular situation. Each person must, therefore, carefully evaluate his own special nature and the conditions in which chance has placed him, and must attempt to live in harmony with that nature and those conditions. This determination of what was right and proper for men, not only on the basis of their talents but also of their backgrounds and general circumstances, fitted well with Cicero's antipathy toward ideas of political and social equality. It provided an argument for the rule of the few best suited to govern, and gave sufficient importance to external circumstances in the calculation of what a man could properly seek or expect, to justify hereditary class divisions.[89]

Cicero also extended the range of *decorum* from the realm of morals to that of manners. He argues that nature has implanted in us a desire not only to avoid doing wrong but also to avoid giving offense in any aspect of our relations with others. This latter impulse gives rise to the virtue of *verecundia*, a sense of respect or reverence for the feelings of others and for how they regard us that causes us to seek approval by eschewing all that is unseemly and displeasing.[90] The means to this end is to observe in our social behavior and in the image of ourselves that we present to the world the same order and moderation that determines our moral conduct. *Decorum* in this sense was summarized for Cicero in the phrase *species liberalis*, a gentlemanly posture. He described what this entailed toward the end of the first book of the *De officiis*. It included modesty and dignity in dress and deportment, a pleasing mode of speech, ease and charm in conversation that showed respect and consideration for the other participants, a restraint in expressing emotion consistent with *gravitas* and *constantia*, a sensible and moderate way of life and a respectable occupation, a sense of tact and timing, observance of established customs and conventions, cultivation of all that contributed to social harmony and

89. *Off.* 1.110–21.
90. *Off.* 1.98–99, 105, 127, 148. *Part. or.* 79. *Rep.* 5.6. *Leg.*1.50. *Fin.* 4.18. *Tusc.* 5.74. *Am.* 82. *Marc.* 1. *Quinct.* 39. *Phil.* 5.7; 10.13.

human fellowship. In much of this, Cicero was, no doubt, reproducing Panaetius, but the picture accurately reflects his own often evident preoccupation with social proprieties and external appearances, and it highlights, especially in its emphasis on adherence to established *mores,* his pervasive conservatism.[91]

Another term that he mentions in connection with the social significance of *decorum,* and the concept that most fully epitomized for him not only the social but also the cultural attributes and mentality befitting the nature of man, was *humanitas.* This was the word by which he described the refining or humanizing effects of a broad education in the liberal arts. It represented the nature of man at his most civilized, when he had been molded and polished by the studies appropriate to his human qualities and capacities.[92]

The specific attributes of *humanitas,* in Cicero's conception of it, were first of all a cultural and intellectual sophistication and savoir faire that showed themselves especially in wit and elegance of speech and in the urbane gentility and social gracefulness of erudite *litterati* such as the patrons of his youth and their associates, particularly Lucius Crassus, the Catuli, and Caesar Strabo.[93] Scipio Aemilianus and C. Laelius he considered earlier examples of *humanissimi,* men who combined eloquence and intellectual brilliance with a deep graciousness and civility.[94]

But *humanitas* meant more to Cicero than high culture or refined manners. It also implied a developed moral sense, reflected in lofty aspirations and high ideals that prized dignity and moral worth and placed honor and virtue before the pleasure and gain that preoccupied boorish

91. *Off.* 126–51. For the extent to which this aspect of the *De officiis* represents Cicero's own ideas, see P. A. Brunt, "Dio Chrysostom and Stoic Social Thought," *PCPS* 19 (1973), 26–33. M. I. Finley, *The Ancient Economy* (London, 1973), 42–58.

92. *Rep.* 1.28; 2.35. *Fin.* 5.54. *Tusc.* 5.66. *De or.* 1.32; 2.40, 72, 154; 3.58, 94. *Mur.* 61. *Flacc.* 62. *Cael.* 24. *Arch.* 2, 4. *Humanitas* was also used by Cicero as the equivalent of the Greek παιδεία, to describe training in the *bonae artes,* a usage derived, according to Aulus Gellius (*NA* 13.17.1–2), from the fact that this training was reserved for man alone. See R. Reitzenstein, *Werden und Wesen der Humanität im Altertum* (Strasbourg, 1907). K. Büchner, "Humanum und Humanitas in der römischen Welt," *Studium Generale* 14 (1961), 636–46. M. L. Clarke, *The Roman Mind* (London, 1956), 135–45. O. E. Nybakken, "Humanitas Romana," *TAPA* 70 (1939), 396–413. W. Schadewaldt, "Humanitas Romana," *ANRW* 1.4 (1973), 43–62.

93. *De or.* 1.27; 2.40, 72. *Off.* 1.133, 144–45. *Phil.* 2.7. *Urbanitas* was an integral aspect of *humanitas* in this sense. Cf. *Rosc.* 120–21. E. S. Ramage, *Urbanitas: Ancient Sophistication and Refinement* (Norman, Okla., 1973), 56–64.

94. *De or.* 2.154. *Mur.* 66. *Verr.* 2.4.98.

and uneducated minds. It further represented the social spirit that came from a maturation of man's innate sense of fellowship and gentleness, and that extended beyond social graces, good manners, and humanism to a broader humaneness, humanitarianism, and sociability that made possible a secure and civilized way of life in a just and harmonious society. Cicero goes so far as to present *humanitas* as the difference between primitive, ill-ordered societies with brutish concerns and brutish habits of violence and aggression, and those where moral idealism had a place and where unity and order prevailed, protected by justice, laws, courts, rights, and a concern for peace. With reference to political leaders, he saw it as the quality that put a human face on *gravitas* and *severitas,* tempering the forceful exercise of power with a gentleness and good nature that removed harshness and cruelty and insured that those who were ruled desired no other ruler. It was, therefore, to his mind, a most important force in the creation and administration of a proper political community and stood as another major benefit of a wide education and the acquisition of *doctrina.*[95]

But, although these social and cultural ideas contained in *decorum* and *humanitas* came broadly within Cicero's conception of *temperantia* and had great importance for him, it was with the more basic and more strictly moral senses of the term that he was primarily concerned when he considered *temperantia* purely as a political virtue. In relation to statesmen he used the word most particularly to describe an austere and strong-willed self-discipline that kept all immoderate desires at bay.[96] He often identifies it with *continentia* in political contexts, and the latter concept would seem to have incorporated for him the main political force of *temperantia. Continentia* was the equivalent of the Greek ἐγϰράτεια, and indicated a general mastery over the passions. In its political uses in Cicero it appears as a spirit of asceticism that set little value on physical gratification or comfort or on material possessions and was, in consequence, immune to the allurements of pleasure and wealth. This resulted in an incorruptibility that insured loyal dedication and efficiency and prevented misuse of the state's resources and the oppression of subjects and

---

95. *Part. or.* 90. *Div.* 1.2. *De or.* 1.33. *Leg.* 2.36. *Rep.* 2.27. *Off.* 3.32. *Cael.* 26. *Sest.* 92. *Mur.* 65–66. *Leg.* 3.1. *Q.F.* 1.1.21. *Fam.* 12.27. *Humanitas* is commonly linked in Cicero to *clementia, mansuetudo, comitas, facilitas. Q.F.* 1.1.25. *Off.* 1.90. *Rep.* 2.27. *Mur.* 66. *Man.* 36, 42. *Fam.* 13.24.2; 13.65.1. Cf. *Herr.* 2.50.

96. *Man.* 40–41. *Verr.* 2.4.98. *Leg. agr.* 2.64. *Cat.* 2.25.

allies. This freedom from self-interest and self-indulgence Cicero considered an integral part of the *vetus disciplina* and a hallmark of great Roman leaders such as M. Camillus, C. Fabricius, M. Curius, and Scipio Aemilianus. In his speech for the Manilian law he attributes these aspects of *temperantia* and *continentia* to Pompey also, and emphasizes their importance in insuring dedication and success.[97]

The vice most directly opposed to these political virtues was *luxuria*, the term that described an immoderate attachment to physical pleasures and to material splendor. Cicero presents it as a product of excessive wealth and of a common accompanying desire to use and display it in extravagant ways. *Luxuria* showed itself in an addiction to opulent surroundings such as the sumptuous villas and other ostentatious symbols of wealth for which many of Cicero's contemporaries became notorious. This spirit of extravagance extended to matters of food, drink, and dress, and ultimately resulted in a general sensuality preoccupied with pleasure and unwilling to place any limit on self-indulgence. Cicero gives many specific examples of the licentiousness and prodigality that resulted— lavish banquets, drinking parties, adulterous love affairs, and the beach and boat parties and orgiastic revels associated with notorious resorts such as Baiae. *Libido* and *licentia* held sway in such a life-style, and there was no place for the moderate rule of reason.[98]

Cicero ascribed a variety of political evils to such preoccupation with material possessions and physical gratification. It brought an erosion of the desire and capacity to undertake the serious responsibilities appropriate to the true nature of man. *Luxuria* abhorred toil and hardship and drew men to *desidia*, a spirit of idleness that was the antithesis of the vigorous courage and initiative fundamental to political *virtus*.[99] A further consequence was fiscal irresponsibility, reckless spending of money that led to indebtedness and disregard for a primary concern of the *prisci mores*, the protection and careful management of one's patrimony. Cicero attributes

97. *Inv.* 2.164. *Leg.* 3.30. *Cael.* 39, 72. *Verr.* 2.2.10; 2.4.115. *Planc.* 3, 9. *Cat.* 2.25. *Off.* 2.76–77, 86; 3.116. *Sen.* 55. *Tusc.* 5.99. *Par. st.* 12, 48. *Prov. cons.* 11. *Flacc.* 28. *Man.* 41, 67. *Phil.* 9.13. *Q.F.* 1.1.32. Cicero often joins *continentia* to *abstinentia* and uses the two words with virtually the same force. See *Off.* 2.77. *Q.F.* 1.1.32.

98. *Fin.* 2.21–23, 30, 70. *Mur.* 13, 76. *Cael.* 35, 43–44. *Balb.* 56. *Cat.* 2.25. *Rosc.* 6.39. *Verr.* 2.2.134; 2.5.87. *Flacc.* 71. *Pis.* 66–77. *Leg. agr.* 2.95. *Off.* 1.106, 140. *Leg.* 2.2; 3.30–31. *Att.* 1.18.6; 1.19.6; 1.20.3; 2.17.

99. *Rep.* 2.8. *Flacc.* 71. *Verr.* 2.2.7, 76. *Cael.* 45–47.

many of these vices to the upper-class youth of his day, attacking their licentiousness and presenting them as foppish and affected, heroes of the symposium and the boudoir, their wit and smartness attuned to such frivolous diversions but feeble and absurd when faced with the tough demands of real life.[100]

But the most serious effect of *luxuria,* in Cicero's opinion, was the growth of *avaritia,* a greed for money that inevitably accompanied addiction to the things that money could buy. Cicero considered avarice the commonest cause of wrongdoing; it was a vice that inevitably generated *audacia* in the sense of a reckless and irresponsible daring receptive to any form of criminality. *Avaritia* was the direct antithesis of the indifference to money and of the cleanhandedness inherent in his concept of *continentia,* and it unleashed all the evils that the latter held in check. Cicero provides a long list of illustrations from recent Roman history— the trials, fears, and divisions that had become commonplace since the mid-second century, the destructive injustices perpetrated on citizens during the proscriptions of lawless eras such as that of Sulla, the emergence of generals who misused public resources and brought ruin wherever they went and of rapacious governors such as Verres and Gabinius, whose depredations and abuse of power were transforming Roman rule from a benevolent protectorate into an oppressive despotism.[101]

In general, Cicero, like many of his contemporaries, tended to see in *luxuria* and in the greed for money that it fostered the chief cause of the social and political upheavals of the late Republic. He considered these vices the source not only of the particular evils mentioned above but also of the broader and more continuous instability afflicting his generation. They provided, in his opinion, the main impetus for the radical schemes and revolutionary movements of the *improbi,* and were the foremost impediment to responsible and forceful government by the *boni.*[102]

Moreover, he saw in the growth of *luxuria* among the ruling class and in the accompanying breakdown in self-restraint and moral rectitude a

100. *Rosc.* 6,39. *Cael.* 17, 38, 42, 44, 67. *Off.* 1.92; 2.64. *Rep.* 2.8. *Pis.* 82. *Att.* 1.14.5; 1.16.1, 11; 1.18.2; 1.19.8; 2.7.3; 7.7.6.

101. *Off.* 1. 24–25, 35; 2.26–30, 75–77. *Tusc.* 4.24–26. *Par. st.* 10–13. *Leg.* 1.51. *Verr.* 2.1.87, 128; 2.2.134, 192; 2.3.217–21; 2.5.24, 38–39, 189. *Man.* 37–40. *Quinct.* 26. *Rosc.* 75, 87–88, 101, 118. *Pis.* 86. *Prov. cons.* 11. *Fin.* 3.75. *Sulla* 72. *Dom.* 43.

102. *Sest.* 99. *Leg. agr.* 102. *Cat.* 2.10–11, 18–23. *Att.* 1.18.6; 1.19.6; 1.20.3; 2.1.7. *Leg.* 3.29–30. See T. N. Mitchell, "Cicero on the Moral Crisis of the Late Republic," *Hermathena* 136 (1984), 22–41.

serious threat to the moral health of the entire state. Political leaders, he maintained, set the moral tone of a society; their character was represented in the character of the state to its benefit or detriment. Moral decadence in high places tended therefore to infect the whole body politic and to produce, in addition to corrupt government, a corrupt society. A virtuous ruling class, of course, tended to have the opposite effect, a fact which, Cicero emphasizes, made it incumbent on statesmen not simply to avoid any appearance of moral laxity but to show positive virtue and make their lives an expression of the moral law and a model for imitation by their fellow citizens.[103]

The high virtue that Cicero sought in political leaders could, he believed, be restored and maintained at Rome only by a revival of the *mores* of earlier days that gave the foremost place to *laus* and *dignitas* and encouraged diligence and self-denial in pursuit of great achievements. To achieve such a regeneration he looked partly to laws and institutions of the state and to strict supervision of the conduct of public officials. He was aware, however, of the limited effect of regulations and sanctions on morality, and it was once more to education that he looked for the real solution.[104]

The inculcation of moral excellence he considered a central goal and consequence of a good education. He maintained that even the instinctively virtuous needed the formative benefits of *doctrina* to realize the full potential of their native qualities. He believed that all liberal studies contributed to the process of moral development and that this was an important part of their intent, and he considered it a natural expectation that those who had received extensive training in the liberal arts would have a high sense of moral responsibility and reflect it in their behavior. He reminds his brother of this in a lengthy letter in 60, when he exhorts him to govern Asia with integrity and self-restraint as befitted a man "doctrina atque optimarum artium studiis eruditus."[105]

Although Cicero frequently deplored the moral standards of his time, he nonetheless clearly believed that the virtues represented by *frugalitas*

103. *Leg.* 3.30–31. *Rep.* 1.52, 54; 2.69. *Off.* 1.140. *Phil.* 8.29. *Fam.* 1.9.12.

104. *Rep.* 3.41; 5.1. *Par. st.* 10–13. *Leg.* 3.29.

105. *De or.* 3.57–58. *Arch.* 15. *Rep.* 3.6. *Q.F.* 1.1.22. Cicero made his most extravagant claim about the moral value of *doctrina* after the death of his daughter, Tullia, when he declared that the nature of the learned is closest to the nature of god and assigned Tullia a place in heaven as the most learned of her sex. Lactantius, *Div. inst.* 1.15.20; 3.19.6.

and its subdivisions were still highly regarded by the society as a whole and were valuable assets in the pursuit of political office. On several occasions he directly asserts that they were a sure means of winning goodwill and of making an impression on the public. The lengths to which he was prepared to go to show that those he was defending or praising possessed these qualities, and that those he was attacking did not, also indicate a belief that *frugalitas* and all it implied remained a cherished component of Roman *mores*. The bulk of the *Pro Caelio*, for example, is designed to prove that, whatever peccadilloes Caelius may have committed, he had not violated the laws of *moderatio* and surrendered to *luxuria*. Roscius, the Sicilians, Fonteius, Cluentius, Deiotarus were other clients that Cicero sought to commend by praising them as models of sobriety and moderation.[106]

His attacks on his opponents show a similar concern to discredit them by dwelling on their rejection of the old morality and on their subservience to *libido*. Verres, Catiline, Clodius, L. Calpurnius Piso, Mark Antony are all portrayed as representative of an intemperance foreign to the Roman spirit, incompatible with the dignity of a Roman leader, and a bar to the fulfillment of one's duty to the state. In general, Cicero rarely omits an opportunity to highlight the moral rectitude of friends and the licentiousness of opponents; the rhetoric of praise and blame continued, in his hands, to find its dominant themes in the virtues and vices associated with *frugalitas* and its opposites.[107]

One further aspect of political *virtus* is given great prominence by Cicero, namely, the motives that should govern all actions and ambitions of political leaders. He strongly insists that *virtus* must never have as its purpose any personal ends such as wealth or power. Its aim must be the benefit of others. In the case of the statesman, that entailed for Cicero the promotion of the common safety and the common good in a spirit of justice and selflessness so as to produce for citizens what he called the *beata vita*, by which he meant a life that was secure, prosperous, esteemed, and honorable. He repeatedly belabors the point that political leaders must be governed by a sense of righteousness and patriotic al-

---

106. *Planc.* 30, 62. *Off.* 2.46, 48, 77. *Mur.* 76. *Cael.* 44–47, 76–77. *Rosc.*75. *Verr.* 2.2.7. *Font.* 40. *Cluent.* 133. *Flacc.* 28. *Deiot.* 26.
107. See *Verr.* passim. *Cat.* 1.13–14; 2.25. *Cael.* 13. *Dom.* 115–16. *Prov. cons.* 6–12. *Pis.* 66–71. *Phil.* 2.44–47, 61–63.

truism; their capacity to see what is expedient for the state must be joined to a purity of motive and concern for justice, sufficient to make them seek to achieve it without regard for personal considerations.[108] Without the moral anchor provided by this selfless commitment to the just pursuit of the common good, the potentially noble impulses and attributes represented by *virtus* became perverted and were inevitably misdirected to evil ends. *Prudentia* became *calliditas* or *astutia,* political expertise and acumen converted to an unscrupulous cunning concerned only with personal gain. *Eloquentia* became a dangerous weapon capable of manipulating the multitude and arousing strife and tumult ruinous to the state.[109] *Magnitudo animi* and *fortitudo,* which were by their nature close neighbors of arrogance and excessive ambition, easily degenerated into *audacia* and *pertinacia,* a reckless determination to satisfy immoderate desires for power and prominence without regard for the common good. Qualities of industry and endurance and disciplined restraint became instruments for the promotion of the pernicious designs of a Catiline or a Caesar. Other aspects of *virtus,* such as *pietas,* were inseparable from justice and the desire to serve others, and were wholly incompatible with goals of personal aggrandizement.[110]

These perversions of *virtus* Cicero saw exemplified in varying degrees in popular politicians. He ascribed motives of personal power, or gain to all *populares* and an indifference to the true welfare of the state. The most dangerous of them, such as Julius Caesar, combined these misguided ambitions with ability, industry, and skill in the manipulation of the public, and further possessed an *audacia* that generated a willingness to go to extreme lengths and, if necessary, subvert the state to advance personal ends. *Populares,* to Cicero's mind, were a threat to sound government precisely because many of them were part of the talented few from which the state's leadership should be drawn, but they had perverted their instincts and abilities and misdirected them to ends that threatened also to pervert the system of rule by a virtuous and benevolent aristocracy that was his ideal.[111]

---

108. *Att.* 8.11.1. *Rep.* 1.3; 2.51, 70; 5.5; 6.29. *Sest.* 23, 139, 143. *De or.* 1.211. *Off.* 1.22–29.
109. *Off.* 2.34; 3.113. *Inv.* 1.1.4. *De or.* 3.55.
110. *Off.* 1.62–65, 90, 157. *Cael.* 13. *Cat.* 1.26; 3.16–17. *Phil.*2.116.
111. *Sest.* 96, 99–100, 139. *Leg. agr.* 2.10, 15, 102. *Cat.* 2.10–11, 18–23. *Off.*

Cicero's insistence that the goal of *virtus* must always be the promotion of the common interest did not, however, preclude all forms of personal reward. The statesman had a right to seek a personal recompense for his services in the form of *gloria,* a word which, in Cicero's use, meant the acclaim of right-minded citizens and of posterity in acknowledgment of virtuous achievement. The desire for praise Cicero considered not only an honorable motivation but a desirable one, reinforcing the good citizen's natural urge to great accomplishments and his desire to serve the common good with the prospect of an immortality of fame and the grateful commemoration of future generations.[112]

Cicero's discussions of all the various aspects of *virtus* are liberally illustrated with *exempla* from the actions and opinions of the great figures of Roman history. He was, like so many of his contemporaries, a *laudator temporis acti,* who deeply admired the tough, straightforward moral code of a simpler society governed by a rural ethos committed to hard work and simple living.[113] Yet the rugged men of rustic *mores,* such as M.' Curius and C. Fabricius, that he so often cites as exemplars of the moral soundness of earlier times did not fully match his concept of *virtus* in its widest sense. They lacked some of the important benefits of *doctrina,* most notably the attributes that comprised *humanitas.* Military heroes in the main, they had few of the gentler qualities that Cicero considered central to the tasks of peace, and they were deficient in the social and intellectual polish that he prized so highly as an expression of the true dignity of human nature. The demands of Cicero's concept of *virtus* could not be met without *scientia* and *doctrina,* and his highest admiration was reserved for those statesmen whose intellectual training and attainments were exceptional. Two such leaders in particular received his unqualified approval and came close to representing his ideal of political *virtus* in all its aspects. They were P. Scipio Africanus and the chief patron of his youth, L. Licinius Crassus.

1.25–26; 3.82–83. *Att.* 7.3.4–5; 7.7.6; 7.13.1; 8.11.2; 10.4.2, 4; 10.7.1. *Phil.* 2.116. See Ch. Wirszubski, "Audaces: A Study in Political Phraseology," *JRS* 51 (1961), 12–22. E. Badian, "Manius Acilius Glabrio and the *audacissimi,*" *AJP* 96 (1975), 62–75. E. Gabba, "Per un' interpretazione politica di *De Officiis* di Cicerone," *RAL* 34 (1979), 117–41.

112. *Tusc.* 3.3. *Inv.* 2.166. *Brut.* 281. *Arch.* 14, 29. *Rep.* 5.9. *Phil.* 29–30, 33; 2.115; 14.32. *Sest.* 139, 143. *Mil.* 97. *Rab.* 29–30.

113. *Sen.* 55. *Off.* 2.26–27, 75–76, 85. *Rep.* 3.41; 5.1. *Leg.* 3.31. *Cael.* 33–34, 39–40. *Phil.* 9.13. *Verr.* 2.27. *Flacc.* 28. *Man.* 11–12.

Scipio gets frequent mention in all of Cicero's writings, and always in laudatory terms. He belonged to the first generation of Romans to benefit from the influx of Greek teachers and Greek educational ideas into the Roman world in the second century B.C. Through the efforts of his father he received a liberal education on the Greek model from a variety of Greek tutors, and he continued throughout his life to seek the company of learned Greeks, and to expand the range of his knowledge. Cicero gives him the title *doctissimus* and saw him as an example of the unique excellence that resulted when great native ability and instinctive goodness were combined with wide learning.[114]

Scipio possessed, in Cicero's estimation, all the attributes that went to make the good statesman. As a devoted student of philosophy and political science, he had unrivaled expertise in the workings of states, and he had quickly added to his theoretical knowledge wide experience in the highest spheres of government. His good judgment and foresight had been tested and vindicated in a variety of public crises, especially in the two great wars he had successfully conducted against Carthage and Numantia. He ranked among the foremost of Roman orators and used his eloquence as a powerful aid to his other political skills.[115]

Cicero's portrait adds to these abilities the qualities of character most strongly favored and promoted by the old morality. Scipio had the high-souled seriousness and eagerness to give distinguished service to the state that were the hallmark of the *pristina severitas,* and saw the pursuit of the praiseworthy and the glorious as the foremost goal of life. This desire to achieve political greatness was backed by *industria* and governed by a resolute consistency and the highest moral integrity. Cicero ascribes to Scipio the qualities of *gravitas, constantia,* and *fides,* the virtues that represented especially the sincerity and unwavering steadiness of purpose that Cicero considered characteristic of the true optimate politician and the antithesis of the fickleness and unreliability of *populares.*[116] He gives still greater emphasis to Scipio's moral uprightness. He had the purity of purpose that led him always to pursue justice and the welfare of the state. He was a model of *temperantia* and *abstinentia,* who despised

114. *Verr.* 2.4. 81, 98. *Mur.* 66. *Tusc.* 1.5, 110. *Acad.* 2.5. *Top.* 78. *Arch.* 16. *Rep.* 1.34. *De or.* 2.154. *Am.* 104. Cf. Plutarch, *Aem.* 6.5.
115. *Rep.* 1.34–37, 71; 6.12. *Am.* 96. *Off.* 1.76, 116. *De or.* 1.211, 215; 3.28. *Brut.* 82–84. *Inv.* 1.5. *Mur.* 58.
116. *Par. st.* 12. *Off.* 1.108. *Am.* 95–96. *Mur.* 58. *Verr.* 2.4.81. *Top.* 78. *Inv.* 1.5.

luxuria and resisted all temptations to enrich himself from his great victories. Cicero also cites him as an exemplar of scrupulous fairness and honesty, and, most significant of all, as one committed to equability and rationality in all circumstances. He had the spirit of reasoned moderation that was the foundation of steadfast virtue.[117]

But Scipio also had *humanitas*. Cicero gives considerable prominence to this aspect of his character. Sometimes he is referring merely to Scipio's cultural interests and attainments. Scipio was *doctissimus*, and Cicero asserts that Rome had produced no better representative of the cultured refinement that *doctrina* bestowed.[118] But he also emphasizes that Scipio had other, more politically important attributes of *humanitas*. His *gravitas* and *severitas* were leavened by a gentleness and affability that endeared him to those he ruled and that extended even to his disagreements with political opponents. Cicero also mentions that he was an eager student of Xenophon's *Cyropaedia*, which portrayed Cyrus as a model of the just ruler because he had combined the highest *gravitas* with exceptional *comitas*. There is a clear implication that Scipio was greatly attracted by the idea of such a combination and sought to achieve it.[119]

The historical accuracy of certain features of Cicero's portrait of Scipio might be questioned, but there can be no doubt that his admiration for him was genuine. He felt a kinship with many aspects of the man, and found much in him that he wished to imitate. He was also in accord with Scipio's political views, and fully approved his domestic statesmanship.[120]

It was L. Crassus, however, who provided the greatest inspiration for Cicero's political life and who must stand as the Roman statesman that he most admired and most wished to emulate. I have discussed his estimate of his patron in some detail elsewhere and need only repeat here that there was no important aspect of his concept of *virtus* that he did not ascribe to him. His admiration for his skills and qualities of character was further increased by the fact that Crassus, unlike Scipio and very much like Cicero himself, had worked his way to political success by skillful and

117. *Verr.* 2.2.29, 86–87; 2.4.73, 81. *Off.* 1.90; 2.76. *Cluent.* 134. *Am.* 11. *De or.* 1.211.
118. *Verr.* 2.4.98. *De or.* 2.154.
119. *Mur.* 66. *Off.* 1.87. *Am.*11, 77. *Q.F.* 1.1.23. *Verr.* 2.2.86.
120. *Verr.* 2.4.81. *De or.* 1.211; 2.106. *Mil.* 8. *Leg.* 3.37–38. *Am.* 96. Astin, *Scipio Aemilianus,* 23ff. and 302ff., doubts the accuracy of some aspects of Cicero's portrait.

energetic use of his great oratorical talents and by his uncommon political prudence and good sense. He was, for Cicero, the great exemplar of the arts of peace, the civilian statesman par excellance, whose ultimate position as a *princeps* of the highest *auctoritas* in a dominant Senate was Cicero's own fondest ambition.[121]

The Social and Political Implications of Cicero's Concept of Virtus

As already indicated, Cicero argued that *virtus* must be recognized and utilized in the sphere of government.[122] Its recognition gave rise to the notion of *dignitas,* which, as a political term, denoted the esteem and standing enjoyed by an individual because of the merit that was perceived to exist in him.[123] Any concept of political egalitarianism that failed to have regard for *dignitas* was, to Cicero's mind, pursuing an equality that was fundamentally inequitable. Justice demanded that society recognize *gradus dignitatis* to take account of the differing abilities of men, and these gradations should be reflected in a structure of government based on the precept that the greatest power should not be given to the greater number but to those whose *virtus* and resultant *dignitas* indicated their greater capacity to exercise it.[124]

Dignitas, therefore, represented for Cicero the crucial modifier of extreme egalitarian notions of political freedom that presupposed an equal share for all in the exercise of political power. It precluded radical democracy with its attendant evils of license, capriciousness, and instability, and made possible an enduring political order based on a just balance between the claims of *libertas* and *dignitas* that insured equality of basic rights and liberties but gave effective control of the state to those who stood foremost in the public's esteem. Cicero variously describes

---

121. *De or.* 2.1–4, 6; 3.2–7, 74–77. *Brut.* 143, 159. *Off.* 2.47. Mitchell, *Ascending Years,* 42–44.

122. *Sest.* 136–37. *Balb.* 15, 19. Asconius 22, Clark. *Leg. agr.* 2.3. *Planc.*62. *Verr.* 2.4.81; 2.5.180. *Ad Hirtium* fr. 3, Purser.

123. *Inv.* 2.166. *Phil.* 1.34; 2.38; 10.20. *Sest.* 89, 128–29, 137. *Planc.* 7, 50. *Mur.* 76. *Dom.* 9, 14, 86. *Marc.* 19. *Att.* 7.11.1. H. Wegehaupt, *Die Bedeutung und Anwendung von Dignitas in den Schriften der republikanischen Zeit* (Breslau, 1932). T. C. Piscatelli, "Dignitas in Cicerone. Tra semantica e semiologia," *B Stud Lat* 9 (1979), 253–67. Hellegouarc'h, *Le vocabulaire latin,* 362–424.

124. *Rep.* 1.43, 53; 2.39.

this balance as *temperamentum, temperatio iuris, moderatus et concors civitatis status, moderate permixta conformatio,* applying to his concept of a just political order the same principles and terminology by which he identified and defined the spiritual disposition of the virtuous man. The just society required the same harmonious blending of elements that was achieved by *temperantia* in the ordering of the impulses of the soul.[125]

Cicero's concept of a political society that blended the idea of equal liberty for all with that of a hierarchical political structure based on merit and implying full upward mobility for men of talent and industry tended to be considerably modified in practice, however, by his social prejudices and readiness often to associate *virtus* and *dignitas* with factors not directly related to an individual's personal worth. The idea, already noted, which he promotes in the *De officiis,* that an individual's aspirations and way of life should be determined to a degree by the circumstances into which he is born, limits significantly the role of merit in determining social and political advancement and indicates a certain predilection for fixed social divisions. Cicero also shows a frequent incapacity to separate ideas of ability, uprightness, and overall worthiness from the environment and way of life of the affluent and socially respectable. *Virtus* and *dignitas* did not seem to him compatible with the world of the poor and the humbly employed. Those who had to sell their labor, the artisans tied to their workshops, those, such as cooks and entertainers, who served the pleasures of others, the petty traders and retailers, the usurers and tax collectors and others like them whose work aroused odium—all such were caught in sordid and demeaning occupations and existed in a boorish milieu that precluded the development of the mentality and attributes necessary in leaders of the state. The lower classes as a whole he considered totally unsuited to political responsibility and untrustworthy in their political judgments and reactions. He saw them preoccupied with slavish concerns of survival and material sufficiency and believed that they were forever manipulable and undependable, their character and aspirations matching the baseness of their lives and occupations. He could see no scope for virtuous achievement and nothing to justify any claim on the public's esteem in the activities and environment of those sections of society, and he would abhor the notion of anyone from such a background being entrusted with political power.

125. *Rep.* 1.65–69; 2.65, 69. *Leg.* 3.24, 28.

Even those who made a living from skills such as medicine or architecture, which involved great expertise and conferred great benefits on society, he would refuse to classify among the state's most worthy citizens.[126]

Virtus and *dignitas* belonged for him in the loftier ambiance of those whose wealth liberated them from the necessity of pursuing banausic activities or hiring their services. They alone were the truly free, the *liberi* or *ingenui*. They alone could be expected to acquire the training and *doctrina* essential to great political leaders; they alone could cultivate the *species liberalis* and develop the *humanitas* and *urbanitas* so important to *decorum* and civilian statesmanship. For Cicero, therefore, wealth was a good and a reasonable measure of it indispensable to true freedom and to the development of the full excellence and dignity of human nature. He fully approved the pursuit and accumulation of wealth, provided the means employed were intelligence, diligence, and thrift, with no recourse to base or offensive forms of gain, and provided possessions were used in a spirit of generosity and in the common interest and not converted to the service of *libido* and *luxuria*. Particularly to be desired was wealth derived from agriculture, an activity that he considered totally honorable and in every respect worthy of the free.[127]

Cicero tended to associate wealth and *virtus* also for the reason that he considered high prosperity a powerful aid to nature in making men loyal and responsible citizens. It provided a stake in the state's safety and welfare that insured a steadfast commitment to its defense and an invulnerability to the allurements of radical social or political change. With the exception of the aberrant few who were dominated by misguided ambition or revolutionary madness, Cicero saw the well-to-do, and particularly the landed rich, as the stable nucleus of a political community, the dependable bulwark of the state against the malcontents and subversives

126. *Off.* 1.150–51. Cicero's contempt for the lower classes is evident in many places. See *De or.* 1.83; 3.128. *Brut.* 2.97. *Rosc.* 134. *Cluent.* 138. *Phil.*7.4. *Sest.* 103. *Dom.* 89. *Flacc.*17–18. *Tusc.* 5.104. Cf. Seneca, *Ep.* 88.21–23. Brunt, *PCPhS* 19 (1973), 26–33. Finley, *The Ancient Economy*, 41–61. D. Norr, "Zur sozialen und rechtlichen Bewertung der freien Arbeit in Rom," *ZRG* 82 (1965), 67–105. Wood, *Cicero's Social and Political Thought*, 90ff.

127. *Off.* 1.21, 25, 42, 92, 106, 115, 150–51; 2.64, 87; 3.22–26. See Finley, *The Ancient Economy*, 35–41. For Cicero's loftiest praise of agriculture, see *Sen.* 51–60. His concept of *frugalitas* did not extend to any exaltation of poverty. In *Pis.* 67 he goes so far as to say there is a form of *luxuries* which is "ingenuo ac libero dignior."

constantly threatening the harmony and security of every society. They were the *boni* in his broadest use of that term, and he not only considered them the source of the leaders of government but he also favored a decisive role for them in any political decision-making assigned to the people.[128]

Cicero further diluted the idea that personal worth should be the sole determinant of social distinction and political prominence by the degree to which he was prepared to link the credentials for political leadership to family pedigree. He largely accepted the prevailing republican sentiment, institutionalized in the formal recognition of a *nobilitas,* that *dignitas* was inheritable and derived not only from a person's own merits but from the status of his family as well. He did not, of course, accept the view that high birth was a necessary or sufficient qualification for high office. His own position as a *novus homo* and his pride in his success despite a lack of noble ancestry led him frequently to proclaim the primacy of intrinsic *virtus* in the evaluation of politicians and to point to his own career as proof that talent and industry were more potent political possessions than the number of *imagines* of illustrious forebears adorning a candidate's *atrium.*[129] His resentment of any slights or spiteful allusions to his lineage from his noble associates also led him on occasion to decry the hostility of the aristocracy toward new men and their readiness to impede and isolate them in order to maintain an exclusive ascendancy.[130]

But despite his insistence that the highest reaches of government should be open to all who showed superior qualities of leadership, he did not disapprove the unequal process of evaluation produced by the idea of hereditary *dignitas* and by the general partiality toward those of noble birth still prominent in his day. He often notes as a matter of course that *dignitas* derives from *genus* as well as from personal worth, and he takes it for granted that the fame of a father should redound to the credit and political advantage of his children. He confidently expected that his own success in 63 would insure high standing for his son.[131]

128. *Phil.* 10.3; 13.8.16. *Sest.* 97, 103. *Rep.* 2.39–40. *Flacc.* 16–18. *Att.* 1.19.4; 2.19.4; 8.1.3.

129. *Fam.*3.7.5. *Sest.* 136–37. *Balb.*18, 51. *Verr.*2.4.81. *Mur.* 16–17. *Cluent.* 111. *Sulla* 24. *Ad Hirtium* frag. 3, Purser. *Man.* 2. *Leg. agr.* 2.3. *Pis.* 2. Asconius 22, Clark. Cf. *Rep.* 2.24.

130. *Verr.* 2.5.180–81. *Sulla* 23–24. *Balb.* 15, 19. *Leg. agr.* 2.5.

131. *Mur.* 15, 18. *Phil.* 13.7, 15. *Cat.* 4.23. *Off.* 1.78. Cf. *Q.F.* 1.1.44.

Such favoritism toward those of illustrious parentage he considered defensible and indeed beneficial to the state. The children of noble houses inherited, in addition to inbred excellence, a tradition of public service and an incentive to emulate or surpass the achievements of their ancestors and to prove themselves worthy of the family into which they were born. It was in the interests of the state to have a pool of such well-motivated aspirants to public office, and the circumstances of their background and upbringing justified a certain presupposition that they had a suitability and capacity for political leadership. Provided this favorable prejudice was not reinforced by a marshalling of aristocratic resources to exclude new blood, Cicero saw no injustice in the politically privileged position of the *nobilitas*.[132]

In short, Cicero's conception of a government drawn from the few who demonstrated exceptional *virtus* and as a result stood foremost in *dignitas* was considerably modified in practice by a number of social prejudices that caused him virtually to exclude the lower classes from consideration and to approve a degree of preferment for the highborn that insured the dominance of an hereditary ruling elite. The way to political distinction would remain open for new men of proven ability from the broader body of respectable well-to-do citizens, but they would rightly carry a heavier burden of proof in their efforts to convince the electorate of their fitness for high political responsibility.

Cicero's Political Ideas and the Republican Constitution

Cicero found in the institutions and traditions of the Republic a political system that was wholly compatible with his social and political instincts and beliefs. He saw in it a practical embodiment of the political and economic principles that he considered the foundations of efficient and stable government, and he was convinced that no other form of political organization was superior to it in its constitution, in its classification of citizens, or in the discipline it imparted.[133]

In his theoretical analysis of it in the *De republica* he presents it, in imitation of Polybius, as a model of the "mixed constitution," a bal-

132. *Sest.* 21, 136. *Rab. Post.* 2. *Mur.* 15. *Off.* 1.116.
133. *Rep.* 1.70; 2.2–3, 66.

anced combination of the basic forms of monarchy, aristocracy, and democracy, but when he speaks more specifically of its functioning and of how he wished to see it function, his description diverges significantly from the scheme of the mixed constitution. The greatest discrepancy appears in his treatment of the monarchical element. Like Polybius, he identifies the consuls as the representatives of monarchy, but assigns them a role that is far from regal and that merges into the managerial and deliberative functions of the Senate. Only in the field does he allow them any real independent power. In domestic affairs they are restrained by the tribunes and to an extend overshadowed by the censors, whose important role in civil government Cicero enlarges by giving them the power to review and appraise the conduct in office of all magistrates. But more important, Cicero presents the consuls as wholly subordinate to the Senate in decision making. Even while he describes their *potestas* as *regia* in the *De republica,* he states that the Senate controlled the state and directed all the highest affairs of government. In the *De legibus,* though he continues to speak of the *regium imperium* of consuls, he makes no mention at all of a three-way division of power in the constitution. He continues to emphasize the importance of a balanced distribution of rights and duties, but it is explicitly a two-way division between Senate and people. Consuls have no independent or counterbalancing function, their *potestas* merely an adjunct to the Senate's *auctoritas,* to insure implementation of senatorial decisions.[134]

This view of the consulship as a subsidiary element of senatorial government is still more clearly expressed by Cicero outside the political writings. In the *Pro Sestio* he asserts that the founders of the Republic intended that magistrates should make full use of the Senate's authority

---

134. *Rep.* 2.55–56, 58–59, 61. *Leg.* 3.6, 8, 10, 11, 24, 28, 47. Cicero repeatedly defines republicanism in terms of *libertas* for the people and *auctoritas* for the Senate. See *Div.* 1.27. *Fam.* 10.6.2. *Dom.* 130. The suggestion of C. W. Keyes, "Original Elements in Cicero's Ideal Constitution," *AJP* 42 (1921), 317–18, that one of Cicero's provisions in relation to the consuls that stated "ollis salus populi suprema lex esto" was designed to give consuls extralegal powers in emergencies and make them independent of the Senate is wholly inconsistent with Cicero's general purpose. The provision seems clearly to refer to consuls' duties in the field where they have *summum ius.* For the sources of Cicero's ideas in his political writings, see F. Solmsen, "Die Theorie des Staatsformen bei Cicero de republica I," *Philologus* 81 (1933), 326. V. Pöschl, *Römisches Staat und griechisches Staatsdenken bei Cicero* (Berlin, 1936). F. Cauer, *Cicero's politisches Denken* (Berlin, 1903), 67ff. O. Seel, *Cicero* (Stuttgart, 1961), 386–93. P. L. Schmidt, "Cicero de Republica" (with extensive bibliography) *ANRW* 1.4. (Berlin, 1973), 262–333.

as the state's highest deliberative council and should act as its *ministri* in the affairs of government. The same view recurs in other speeches where attempts by consuls to act without the advice and consent of the Senate are decried and treated as violations of the constitution.[135]

The idea, already well established, that the Roman state could be represented as a living example of an ideal acclaimed by the great minds of Greece naturally appealed to Cicero, but he did not attempt to bend the realities of the republican system as he saw them into strict conformity with the schematic structure of the mixed constitution. The feature of the latter that chiefly interested him was the idea that stable government depended on a carefully balanced distribution of rights and powers between different elements of the society. He saw these elements as two, however, corresponding to what he considered the two great natural divisions in every body politic: the mass of the people, and the few whose abilities and standing set them apart and entitled them to a position of leadership. A just and effective balance of power, a *temperatio iuris*, between these two segments of the state was, to Cicero's mind, the true touchstone of the good constitution, and he believed such a balance had been realized through the wisdom of many in the long and unique evolutionary process that gave rise to the final political structures of the Roman Republic.[136]

As far as the people were concerned, the republican constitution, in Cicero's opinion, guaranteed them all the rights and liberties inherent in the definition of *respublica* and necessary to satisfy the political needs inherent in the nature of man. It was a system based on law and committed to strict equality in the administration of justice. It demanded that all, even magistrates and judges, should be equally subject to the law, which was to stand as an impersonal master over all so that all might be free. It renounced any idea of arbitrary or unchecked power and even removed from the trappings of magistrates any symbol of their authority that might seem a threat to liberty. It also provided more concrete safeguards against injustice and abuse of power by recognizing the right of appeal against the sentences of all magistrates and by developing laws to protect it. It gave further protection against oppression in the office of the tribunate,

135. *Sest.* 137, 143. Cf. *Pis.* 7–9. *Phil.* 2.11, 15–17, 23. *Post red. in sen.* 17. *Sulla* 21.
136. *Rep.* 2.2, 41, 69. *Leg.* 3.24, 28.

which Cicero saw as a powerful guarantee of freedom that was a major advance toward the necessary *temperamentum* between the power of the people and the ruling aristocracy.[137]

The right of all citizens to a say in the management of the state was also, Cicero believed, fully met by the republican system. It recognized the assemblies of the people as the only law-making and electoral bodies. The people were therefore constituted as the highest authority in the state and the ultimate source of the power not only of magistrates but also of the Senate, since the latter consisted of ex-magistrates and was, therefore, indirectly chosen by the people. Finally, it recognized another basic principle of political equality, the equal right of all citizens to seek political office. Cicero was fond of proclaiming that the *mos maiorum* prescribed *virtus* and *industria* as the true criteria in the selection of candidates for public office and made it possible for the most lowly born to achieve *nobilitas,* provided his ability and industry showed him worthy of it. He found proof of this in the many new men who had reached the highest rank by their merits alone, and he emphasized that nowhere else was talent welcomed and rewarded in this way and class distinctions leveled by excellence.[138]

Admittedly, his emphasis on this feature of republicanism was, to some extent, disingenuous. He knew well from personal experience the unequal contest facing even the most talented newcomers in republican politics and, as I indicated earlier, he accepted and indeed approved the de facto exclusion from public life of the lowest classes, but what mattered to him and to his idea of the good constitution was the absence of any de iure obstacle to political participation that would create castes rather than classes and abjure the principle of *aequa libertas,* that fundamental claim of defenders of the people's rights that freedom, if it was to have any meaning, had to be the same for all.[139]

The second essential feature of his ideal constitution, namely, the concentration of power in the hands of those of greatest *dignitas,* he

137. *Cluent.* 146. *Planc.* 33. *Leg. agr.* 2.102. *Rep.* 1.53; 2.53–55.
138. *Leg.* 3.33–39. *Rep.* 1.47. *Sest.* 137 and n. 129 above.
139. *Rep.* 1.47. The contention of C. Nicolet, *The World of the Citizen in Republican Rome,* trans. P. S. Falla (Berkeley, Calif., 1980), 3ff., that from the beginning of the Republic there was a property qualification for all magistracies and for membership in the Senate, runs contrary to the evidence of Cicero and seems untenable. See D. R. Shackleton Bailey, *Cicero: Epistulae ad Familiares* (Cambridge, 1977), 2.460. I. Shatzman, *Senatorial Wealth and Roman Politics* (Brussels, 1975), 45–46.

found equally well established and safeguarded in the laws and traditions of the Republic. This he believed had been achieved above all by the emergence of a dominant Senate. Cicero conceived the Senate as the state's highest deliberative body, comprising those chosen from all the citizens for their *virtus* and *industria,* and he viewed it as the linchpin of republicanism, the ideal machinery of government by which to insure aristocratic ascendancy without infringement of the people's freedoms.[140] It brought together those of the highest political ability and broadest experience and fully utilized their talents and expertise by providing them with a permanent forum in which to develop public policy and work for its implementation. Its procedures gave the greatest prominence to those who had achieved the highest distinction, namely, the *consulares,* and gave full scope for the exercise of the skills of civilian statesmanship most admired by Cicero, *prudentia* and *eloquentia.* It was therefore an institution that gave full recognition to *gradus dignitatis* and made the fullest use of *virtus.*[141]

But the Senate's greatest constitutional merit for Cicero derived from his conviction that the collective *dignitas* of its members, when combined with dedication to the pursuit of the public interest and to the preservation of the dignity of the orders closest to it and of the liberty and welfare of the common people, produced a degree of *auctoritas,* based on respect and trust and goodwill, that insured the compliance of magistrates and willing acceptance of senatorial decisions by all. Thus was able government by the talented few with the free consent of the masses achieved and the formula for the successful political system so frequently

140. *Sest.* 137. *Leg.* 3.28. Cf. *Dom.* 130. *Fam.* 10.6.2. *Div.* 1.27. *Am.* 41. *Rep.* 2.55–56. The strengthening of the Senate's authority was always a central aim of Cicero's statesmanship. See *Leg. agr.* 1.27. *Planc.* 93. *Pis.* 7. *Phil.* 2.11–12. *Att.* 1.18.3; 1.20.3. *Fam.* 1.9.12. See W. W. How, "Cicero's Ideal in the *De Republica,*" *JRS* 20 (1930), 32ff. M. Gelzer, *Cicero: Ein biographischer Versuch* (Wiesbaden, 1969), 212–19. M. Fuhrmann, "Cum dignitate otium. Politisches Program und Staatstheorie bei Cicero," *Gymnasium* 67 (1960), 497–500. S. E. Smethurst, *TAPA* 84 (1953), 283–317.

141. The Senate ideally suited Cicero's own talents, which, no doubt, increased his attachment to the notion of senatorial rule. He had looked forward to playing a leading role in its affairs. See *Fam.* 1.8.3–4. *Q.F.* 3.6.4. *Brut.* 7–9. P. Martin, "Cicéron *Princeps,*" *Latomus* 39 (1980), 850–78, stretches the evidence in arguing that Cicero favored the idea of a single dominant *princeps togatus,* and sought such a position for himself. It is a new variation on the thesis put forward most notably by E. Meyer, in *Caesars Monarchie und das Principat des Pompeius* (Stuttgart, 1922), that Cicero favored a principate along the lines of that established by Augustus. See R. Reitzenstein, "Ciceros 'Staat' als politische Tendenzschrift," *Hermes* 59 (1924), 73–94.

repeated by Cicero—namely, *libertas* for the people, and *auctoritas* for the *principes*—implemented.[142]

This view of the Senate's character and functioning, with its presupposition of a membership that was unified and sufficiently able and admirable to command public confidence and support, contained, of course, a considerable measure of naivete and idealization, and has often brought dismissal of Cicero's political ideas as myopic conservatism or wishful thinking. He believed, however, that his view corresponded to the intended position of the Senate and to its historical position in pre-Gracchan times, before the moral decline of the aristocracy undermined its unity and authority.[143] Moreover, he was not unaware of the fragility of a power based on moral influence alone, nor did he believe that the Senate's position had been or should be entirely dependent upon it. He found several other effective props of aristocratic control in republican law and tradition, and he looked to them to provide the necessary additional assurances of senatorial supremacy.

One of the most important of these aids to oligarchic government he considered the auspices and the powers of the College of Augurs, a body drawn almost exclusively from the highest rank of the aristocracy. The regulations governing the auspices and the right of augurs to invalidate enactments of the assemblies made it possible to prevent the holding of unwanted assemblies, to force the adjournment of those taking an unwelcome direction, or to set aside measures whose obstruction proved impolitic or impractical. Cicero regarded these controls as a valuable weapon of the aristocracy against maverick magistrates and popular caprice, and states that the auspices had often been the means of suppressing unjust eruptions of popular unrest.[144] The principle of *par maiorve potestas,* which allowed any magistrate to veto any action of other magistrates of equal or lesser power, he saw as a further safeguard against rebellious officials who might seek to thwart or ignore senatorial wishes. Even the tribunes' right of veto he regarded as, on balance, a benefit, since at least one member of the college could generally be counted on to

---

142. *Sest.* 137. *Rep.* 2.55–56. See n. 134.
143. *Rep.* 1.31–32; 2.59. *Off.* 2.85. *Leg.* 3.25. *Acad.* 2.15.
144. *Rep.* 2.16. *Leg.* 2.32–33; 3.27. See L. R. Taylor, *Party Politics in the Age of Caesar* (Berkeley, Calif., 1964), 80–85.

use the power to prevent the passage of measures harmful to the Senate's interests.[145]

The development of public religion and a code of religious law under the control of public priests, who were selected, like the augurs, from members of the *nobilitas,* he presents as another source of aristocratic control. Belief in the gods and the celebration and regulation of the rites of worship by the state not only made the people more tractable and dependable, but also subject to the priests in matters of religious law, and, in Cicero's words, "Dependence by the people on the advice and authority of the *optimates* binds a people together."[146]

Such dependence he found further increased by another institution that got his full approval, *clientela,* the arrangement whereby poorer citizens became clients of the *principes* and received advice and material assistance from them. This munificence by the upper class toward the needy, which Cicero considered the chief answer to poverty, obviously created goodwill toward the aristocracy and increased its hold over the common people. But Cicero saw an additional benefit in the institution in that clients repaid their benefactors by assisting them in their canvass for office and by voting according to their wishes in the assemblies. This capacity to render worthwhile political service gave ordinary citizens a feeling of political power that contributed to political contentment and stability.[147]

One other feature of republicanism that Cicero believed added strength to the position of the aristocracy was the broad acceptance of the idea that increased political power was a natural and unobjectionable consequence of wealth. *Clientela* as it functioned in Cicero's day gave a certain sanction to this view, as did many other aspects of Roman political life, especially electoral procedures that permitted generous gifts and favors by candidates to members of their tribe and to the voters in general. More important, the idea had formal recognition in the structure of the *comitia centuriata,* which gave a disproportionate number of votes to the wealthiest class. These timocratic tendencies clearly favored the ascendancy of a ruling class that possessed a high proportion of the nation's wealth. They also, Cicero believed, rightly gave a greater say in the

145. *Leg.* 3.11, 24, 42.
146. *Rep.* 2.26–27. *Leg.* 2.15–16, 20, 30. Cf. Polybius 6.56. St. Augustine, *CD* 4.27, 31. Dionysius 2.18.
147. *Rep.* 2.16, 59. *Mur.* 70–71.

affairs of the state to those who had the greater stake in its safety and well-being, and had the further effect, especially when joined with the corollary and traditionally republican belief in the sanctity of private property and free enterprise, of producing a powerful and united army of the prosperous committed to the defense of the status quo.[148]

Cicero therefore considered that the power of the Senate to control political affairs had abundant safeguards, the *auctoritas* of its members reinforced by a variety of political privileges and indirect sources of political influence. He saw no insuperable bar to senatorial rule; for him it was an entirely practical as well as desirable political ideal.

The depth and permanence of his attachment to the republican constitution as a whole is further—and perhaps most strikingly—evidenced in the detailed code of law for his ideal state contained in the *De legibus*. Although written late in his career when the republican system had come close to collapse and the hopes of 63 had vanished utterly, it has few departures, as Cicero states himself, from Roman statutory law and custom and makes no attempt to confront the many inadequacies of the republican constitution that had become glaringly evident in the fifties in relation to such basic problems as political violence and control of the military. Such changes as are proposed show a conservative, not a reforming, spirit; they look backward, seeking to restore or strengthen, not alter, the traditional regime.

Religious law gets extensive treatment and the importance of religion in the life of the state is strongly emphasized, but the laws themselves are by and large a reaffirmation of traditional structures and rituals, to the extent that Quintus remarks that they differ little from the laws of Numa and existing practices.[149] The main innovative aspect would appear to be a greater insistence on the moral nature of the gods and a closer link between religion and morality. The gods are to be seen as benevolent

---

148. *Planc.* 45. *Mur.* 77. *Rep.* 2.40. See n. 128 above.

149. *Leg.* 2.23. A. du Mesnil, *Cicero: De Legibus* (Leipzig, 1879). E. Rawson, "The Interpretation of Cicero's De Legibus," *ANRW* 1.4 (1973), 334–56. M. van den Bruwaene, "Précisions sur la loi religieuse du de legibus II 19–22 de Cicéron," *Helikon* 1 (1961), 40–93. R. J. Goar, *Cicero and the State Religion* (Amsterdam, 1972), 78–96. P. L. Schmidt, *Die Abfassungszeit von Ciceros Schrift über die Gesetze* (Rome, 1969). K. Buchner, "Sinn und Entstehung von De Legibus," *Atti del Primo Congresso Internazionale di Studi Ciceroniani* (Rome, 1961), 81–90. Wood, *Cicero's Social and Political Thought*, 168 ff.

lords and directors of all things, who carefully observe the character and behavior of each individual and punish the impious. They demand purity of spirit from worshippers and cannot be placated by gifts that are offered by the unrighteous. Heroes of great virtue may be recognized as having found a place in heaven, and may be worshipped as gods, as may the qualities that give access to heaven, but vices or evil forces must not be deified or worshipped. Modes of worship must be free of material extravagance and under the control of the public priests, and any practice or ritual, especially in connection with nocturnal or alien rites, that might encourage superstition or lead to excesses of any kind is to be abolished.

Cicero's concern here is plain enough. He saw religion as a potent moral force that could produce a more upright and responsible citizenry strong in the social virtues essential to a stable society. The closer its links to morality, the greater he believed would be its civilizing and stabilizing effects. If men believed that the gods were not merely all-powerful but also moral beings who observed the behavior of mortals and punished wrongdoers while offering even heaven itself to the truly virtuous, they would have a powerful incentive to right conduct and noble endeavors in both their public and private lives. Cicero was, therefore, intent on promoting a form of religion that was centered on moral deities and on compliance with the moral law. The urgent need for moral regeneration in his time, which he so often enunciates, no doubt increased his interest in a strongly moralistic religious code.[150]

The other noteworthy aspect of his religious laws is the dominant position assigned to the colleges of priests. The pontiffs retain their traditional control of the interpretation of religious law and the determination of forms of worship. But they also receive extensive powers to deal with crimes of sacrilege, and their involvement in the performance of all private rites is required. Augurs are given still greater prominence. All their traditional powers are reasserted and Cicero's desire to see them fully exercised is shown by a provision, which is probably new, that makes disobedience to an augur a capital offense. Finally, the full powers of fetials, most if not all obsolete by Cicero's day, are revived and possibly extended. All matters relating to the declaration and conduct of

---

150. *Leg.* 2.15–43. *ND* 1.3–4. *Har. resp.* 18–19. See n. 146 above. J. Vogt, *Ciceros Glaube an Rom* (Stuttgart, 1935), 77.

war and the making of peace are to be subject to their adjudication to insure that justice and good faith are maintained.[151]

In all of this Cicero was clearly seeking to strengthen the considerable benefits, alluded to earlier, that he saw in religion as an instrument of senatorial supremacy. A strong aristocratic priesthood would increase the general influence of the aristocracy. Augury, fully controlled by an exclusive body of *nobiles,* would restrict the capacity of rebellious magistrates to dictate the course of domestic politics, while fetial law would similarly limit the independence of powerful and ambitious commanders in matters of war and peace.

In book 2 of the *De legibus* Cicero goes on to deal with the constitutional role of magistrates, Senate, and people. Two of the magistracies, the quaestorship and censorship, undergo significant change. The quaestorship becomes a minor magistracy with the same status as the vigintivirate. It is also displaced by the aedileship as the first formal step in the *cursus honorum* and as the office that gave access to the Senate.[152] These innovations would mean a less unwieldy and more experienced Senate, a development consistent with Cicero's strong oligarchic views and concern for high expertise at this level of government. They would also mean a more exclusive Senate, since many new men would not be able to advance beyond the quaestorship, but this too Cicero would most likely consider a benefit, since he wished to see only newcomers of exceptional ability entering the ruling elite.[153]

The changes in the censorship represent the most novel aspect of the *De legibus.* The office is made continuous and given greatly increased powers, especially with regard to the supervision of the behavior of senators and magistrates. In addition to their traditional responsibility to

151. *Leg.* 2.20–22, 29–34. See Rawson, *ANRW* 1.4 (1973), 346–47. Goar, *Cicero and the State Religion,* 86–88.

152. *Leg.* 3.6–7. Keyes (*AJP* 42 (1921), 313) doubts that Cicero was making the holding of the aedileship a necessary qualification for admission to the Senate, but surely the major downgrading of the quaestorship meant it was being placed on exactly the same level as the other minor magistracies and no longer carried the important benefit of qualifying its holders for the Senate. See K. Sprey, *De M. Tulli Ciceronis politica doctrina* (Amsterdam, 1928), passim. Rawson, *ANRW* 1.4 (1973), 350–51.

153. The aedileship was not an essential part of the republican *cursus* and was often bypassed in favor of the tribunate. See T. P. Wiseman, *New Men in the Roman Senate* (Oxford, 1971), 159–62. Part of the purpose of Cicero's innovation in relation to the aedileship may have been to decrease the role of the tribunate by decreasing the number of politicians who would seek it.

safeguard public morality and to expel senators found guilty of moral wrongdoing, the censors are to have the task of guarding the laws, an assignment that apparently involved insuring that the texts of laws were properly presented and interpreted and that the actions of magistrates accorded with them. They are further commissioned to review the conduct in office of magistrates on the expiry of their term and to give a preliminary judgment about their administration.[154]

This expanded role for the censors, partly modeled on Greek practices and on ideas of Greek philosophers, was an attempt to secure in the ruling class the moral probity and political integrity indispensable to Cicero's oligarchic ideal by subjecting the private and public lives of politicians to rigorous and continuous scrutiny and the threat of swift retribution for depravity or malfeasance. Cicero further sought to promote high standards among the aristocracy by a series of injunctions setting forth specific obligations of senators. They were to attend regularly, to be fully informed about public affairs, and to serve as a model of right conduct for the rest of the citizens. These provisions had more the character of hortatory prescriptions than enforceable laws, but they would have the effect of making explicit the standards of dedication and uprightness demanded of senators and of providing criteria by which censors could judge a senator's fitness for his high station.[155]

The other main innovations in the *De legibus* relate to the position of the Senate. Its powers are augmented in two important respects. It acquires the right to create a dictator, a power formally belonging to the consuls under republican law, and its decrees are to have binding effect. Both provisions reflect Cicero's concern that the Senate should be seen as the state's highest deliberative body and have control of all important decisions of government, and that the magistrates should regard themselves as its *ministri*. He believed that this was the status intended for the Senate by the framers of the constitution and he would undoubtedly see his assertions of the Senate's primacy in decision making in these two statutes as mere affirmations in law of well-established features of the *mos maiorum*.[156]

The provision dealing with senatorial decrees in no way affected the

154. *Leg.* 3.7, 11, 46–47.
155. *Leg.* 3.10–11, 28–32, 40.
156. *Leg.* 3.9–10. Cf. *Sest.* 137. *Rab.* 3. Keyes, *AJP* 42 (1921), 312–13. How, *JRS* 20 (1930), 31–34.

critical balance between the powers of Senate and people. Its concern was with the relationship between Senate and magistrates, and it involved no curtailment of the legislative functions of the assemblies. The people remained the highest authority in the state, the supreme legislature. Cicero goes to considerable lengths in the *De legibus* to insure that all the ingredients of *libertas,* including the full powers of tribunes, are retained. In fact, he increases the role of the people in the administration of justice, reverting to the system of *iudicia populi* in place of the jury courts. [157] In one provision relating to the secret ballot, he does attempt to limit the independence of the ordinary citizen by prescribing that the *optimates* should have a right to see the ballots and the voters to show them. He believed, however, that this modification, designed to maintain the influence of the aristocracy over clients and beneficiaries, retained *species libertatis* and would cause no contention. [158]

All of the innovations of the *De legibus* show one overriding concern: the reestablishment of an effective and respected Senate in firm control of the business of government. Its members were to be fewer and more experienced, and were to be required, under penalty of expulsion, to show dedication and the highest standards of personal and professional integrity. Its constitutional position as Rome's *summum consilium* was to be confirmed in law to remove any dispute about the duty of magistrates to consult and obey it. Its control of domestic and foreign affairs and its overall *auctoritas* were to be strengthened by the resources of religion and by the threat of censorial sanctions against recalcitrant magistrates.

At the same time the powers and liberties of the people were to be carefully safeguarded, even to the extent of retaining potentially troublesome institutions such as the tribunate. Senatorial rule was not to be imposed at the cost of traditional popular prerogatives but achieved with the aid of popular acquiescence and goodwill. Cicero was still pursuing the formula on which he believed traditional republicanism was based, a harmonious balance between the claims of *dignitas* and *libertas.* Nothing had changed from the goals and outlook of 63.

---

157. *Leg.* 3.6, 10–11, 24–25, 27. See A. H. M. Jones, *The Criminal Courts of the Roman Republic and Principate* (Oxford, 1972), 2–3.
    158. *Leg.* 3.10, 33–39.

2: THE EUPHORIA FADES

Cicero left the consulship convinced that he had securely laid the foundations for a revival of the traditional form of republican government that he equated with the ideal constitution. The *improbi* had been checked and discredited, the *boni* had been united in defense of the state and its institutions, the authority of the Senate had been strengthened. In short, power had been restored to the aristocracy with the goodwill and support of all right-minded citizens, producing again the ideal political arrangement whereby government was in the control of the state's *principes*, but in a free society that accepted and supported their ascendancy.[1]

Cicero looked forward to a continuing position of prominence in this revitalized Republic. He was now at the top of the political pyramid, a *consularis*, member of that select group which dominated senatorial decision making and, in times of senatorial supremacy, controlled the government of Rome. He hoped that his talents and achievements would secure him a leading place in this elite coterie. He saw himself as a *princeps* of proven ability, foresight, and mature oratorical skill, endowed with the high favor, prestige, and influence that had come from his labors in the courts and from a brilliant political career crowned by the achievements of 63. These achievements he placed on a par with those of Pompey. He states that on the day he left office and swore the oath that he had saved the state and the city, he was *Magnus Praetextatus*. In his varied talents and in the high standing and favor won by his successes, he

1. *Att.* 1.14.4; 1.16.6; 1.18.3; 4.18.2. *Fam.* 1.9.12. *Pis.* 4–8. *Leg.* 3.37.

believed that he possessed the ideal and the only valid skills and resources for the role of the authoritative senior statesman, and was entitled to a commanding voice in the administration of the Republic.[2]

Cicero's expectations both for the Republic and for his own place in its government were ill-founded. The shortcomings in his view of republicanism and in his perception of the problems of his time have often been recited and need only brief reference here. There was little hope for a permanent revival of unified and effective senatorial government in a political world where the scramble for office was becoming ever more intense and where electoral corruption, encouraged by the opportunities provided by provincial governorships for the recovery of squandered fortunes, was eroding the basic institutions of the Republic. There were now too many powerful families, formerly props of senatorial authority, whose allegiance to traditional republicanism was lukewarm at best and who were willing to subordinate the proper functioning and stability of the system to the achievement of personal objectives.[3]

The possibility of strong senatorial rule was further diminished by continuing class tensions and alienation of the lower orders because of economic hardship and the widening gulf between rich and poor. The ruling class continued to amass wealth from the spoils of empire and investment of their gains, while the lower classes bore the brunt of the adverse economic consequences of the long series of wars that had afflicted the Roman state since 90. The large and varied constituency that had initially supported Catiline was an indication of the size and seriousness of the problem of the impoverished. The condition of the Catilinarian sympathizers remained unaltered after 63 and their disaffection undiminished.

Nor was there much hope for a union of the well-to-do to safeguard senatorial authority. The structure of government gave limited opportunity to the Italian upper class to participate actively in political decision making, and the *publicani* and financiers, who were in a position to influence the course of political events, were unstable allies, their political responses too often dictated by personal interests.[4]

---

2. *Att.* 1.16.8; 1.17.6; 1.19.6; 3.10.2; 6.1.22. *Q.F.* 1.3.6; 3.6.4. *Fam.* 1.8.3–4; 4.13.2. *Pis.* 6. *Brut.* 7–9. Cf. *De or.* 3.7.

3. The Aemilii, Claudii, and Metelli provide examples. See R. Syme's great chapter on the Roman oligarchy in *The Roman Revolution* (Oxford, 1939), 10–27.

4. See Mitchell, *Ascending Years,* 203–04. P. Brunt, *Italian Manpower 225 B.C.–*

Cicero also overestimated the appreciation and prestige his achievements would bring him from his peers and from the public. The acclaim that came from the Senate after the exposure of the conspiracy proved temporary. The *nobilitas* reacted enthusiastically in relief at the ending of an alarming crisis, but it was not disposed to be moved and directed on a permanent basis by the exhortations and often vainglorious rhetoric of a parvenu from a *municipium*. Cicero was to feel more keenly than before the force of *invidia* and to experience the fragility of *dignitas* unbacked by a revered name or by *potentia* based on political compacts, or money, or rawer forms of power.

The applause of the people proved equally ephemeral. Cicero had little to offer the Roman proletariat. He had never won their hearts, nor did he genuinely seek to do so. His claims to be a *popularis* consul were specious, and he made little effort to sustain them. His hopes for political supporters and for defenders of republicanism lay elsewhere, and his great themes of stable oligarchic rule in a state safe for private property and the fruits of enterprise were directed elsewhere and unlikely to win any lasting favor from the populace. The drama of the Nones of December enveloped the common people in a general patriotic fervor and mood of relieved celebration, but once the excitement subsided they were easily led to view Cicero's conduct of his consulship in a different light.

The Reaction to the Executions

Even before he left office, signs of renewed dissension and of personal difficulties for Cicero himself were building. The execution of the Catilinarian conspirators, which was an unprecedented assertion by the Senate of powers of life and death over citizens who had committed no overt act of hostility against the state, evoked a strong reaction and brought charges of repression and of violations of fundamental citizens' rights. The issue was volatile. It raised the same question which had underlain the trial of Rabirius earlier in 63—whether an ultimate decree of the Senate could justify the killing of citizens who were not in arms without recourse to the judicial procedures prescribed by the laws. Basic and cherished principles of liberty were involved, the right to a formal

A.D. 14 (Oxford, 1971), 108–09, 289, 309–12. E. S. Gruen, *The Last Generation of the Roman Republic* (Berkeley, Calif., 1974), 425–28.

trial and the right to appeal against judgments of magistrates in relation to the lives and property of citizens. Cicero himself called these rights liberty's true mark and safeguard, and Caesar, in his speech in opposition to the executions, had shown how failure to observe them, even in the case of evil men and even in the exceptional conditions created by the ultimate decree, could be seen as alien to republican tradition and a dangerous breach of constitutionality that could pave the way for a recurrence of Sullan-style proscriptions of citizens.[5] These were issues and concerns likely to stir public feeling and to be fully aired in the climate of confrontation that prevailed in post-Gracchan politics.

Attacks on the handling of the Catilinarian crisis by Cicero and the Senate began quickly, led by one of the new tribunes, Q. Metellus Nepos, brother of Metellus Celer, a praetor in 63, and half-brother of Pompey's third wife, Mucia. Nepos had served as a *legatus* of Pompey in the East from 67 to 64, and had returned to Rome in the spring or summer of 63 to stand for the tribunate. He was a well-trained and talented orator of the demagogic variety, and already had a reputation for unpredictability and capriciousness sufficient to make Cato, on hearing of his candidacy, reverse an earlier decision and run for the tribunate to check anticipated radical behavior by him in office. The *boni* as a whole had similar expectations of trouble from Nepos and fully approved Cato's candidacy.[6]

Their concern was well founded. Even before he entered office and before the executions, Nepos showed himself intent on using his tribunate to attack the status quo, and as early as November he was using the *contio* for that purpose. The events of December 5 gave him fresh grounds for assailing the rule of the oligarchy, and in conjunction with another tribune, L. Calpurnius Bestia, he launched a campaign to highlight the unconstitutionality of the action of Cicero and the Senate in condemning citizens without trial. The campaign was directed against the Senate as a whole, but, as the magistrate who had referred the issue to

5. *Dom.* 33, 43, 77. *Rep.* 3.44. *De or.* 2.199. *Leg.* 1.42; 3.6. Sallust, *Cat.* 51. Cf. Livy 3.45.8; 3.55.4. Wirszubski, *Libertas,* 24–26. The sensitivity of the issue is also shown by the fact that it continued to be raised by Cicero's enemies to the very end of his life. Clodius, Piso, Gabinius, Vatinius, and Antony all attempted to exploit it. See *Ad Brut.* 1.17.1. *Att.* 1.16.1. *Pis.* 14. *Post red. in sen.* 12. *Sest.* 28, 133. *Vat.* 23. *Phil.* 2.18.

6. Appian, *Mith.* 95. Florus 1.41. Josephus, *AJ* 14.29; *BJ* 1.127. *Brut.* 247. Plutarch, *Cat. min.* 20–21; *Cic.* 26.6. Asconius 63–64, Clark.

the Senate and had implemented its decision, Cicero bore the brunt of the criticism. Nepos singled him out in his public denunciations of the executions and threatened to bring about his impeachment, and, in collaboration with Bestia, used his power of veto to prevent him addressing the people on the day he left the consulship on grounds that he who had punished citizens without a hearing should not himself be heard.[7]

Nothing survives of the actual speeches of Nepos and Bestia, but the tone and substance of their attacks are clear enough from the allusions to them in the sources and from the many rehearsals of the same accusations by Cicero's enemies during the remainder of his life. The main theme of the attacks was *regnum*, a common catchword in the language of political invective in the late Republic, used to signify excessive official or unofficial power that made its holders independent of the law and of all constraint. Cicero stood accused of the most odious and extreme manifestation of this form of tyrannous power, the arrogation of powers of life and death over citizens and the subversion of all the safeguards of liberty. Added, to reinforce the *invidia* attached to such charges of despotic oppression of citizens of Rome, were disparaging allusions to Cicero's non-Roman origins; he was not only a tyrant, but a foreign tyrant, lately grafted on the city but lording it in the Senate as if he belonged to the highest nobility.[8]

Cicero was sufficiently concerned about the rhetoric and designs of Nepos, which he feared might increase the danger from the remnants of the conspiracy, to retain the quaestor Sestius, whom he had summoned from Capua with his army, in the neighborhood of Rome during the final days of 63. He also made several attempts through Clodia, the wife of Metellus Celer, and Pompey's wife, Mucia, and other common friends to

7. *Mur.* 81. *Fam.* 5.2.6–8. *Sest.* 11. *Pis.* 6. *Sulla* 31, 34. Asconius 6, Clark. Plutarch, *Cic.* 23.1–2. Dio 37.38, 42. *Schol. Bob.* 82, 127, Stangl. Nepos and Bestia placed their benches on the rostra and allowed Cicero to come forward only to take the customary oath of a retiring magistrate that he had upheld the laws. Cicero considered this an unprecedented affront, but believed he had turned it splendidly to his advantage by substituting for the usual formula an oath that he had singlehandedly saved the Republic and the city.

8. *Sulla* 21–25. *Vat.* 23, 29. *Dom.* 75. *Pis.* 14. *Att.* 1.16.10. *Fam.* 7.24.1. The near-contemporary invective against Cicero attributed to Sallust and the speech attributed to Fufius Calenus in Dio 46.1–28 provide the fullest illustration of the range and character of the accusations to which Cicero was exposed as a result of the executions. For the meaning of *regnum*, see W. Allen, Jr., "Caesar's *Regnum* (Suet. *Jul.* 9.2)," *TAPA* 84 (1953), 227–36. Wirszubski, *Libertas*, 62–64.

deter Nepos, and when these failed he determined to fight back openly, vehemently attacking the tribune in the Senate on January 1. When Nepos made further attacks and threats at a *contio* on January 3 he responded with another hard-hitting speech, which he subsequently published in 61 and entitled *Contra contionem Q. Metelli*. The Senate meanwhile lent its support by granting immunity to all who had been involved in the suppression of the conspiracy and by decreeing that anyone who dared bring a prosecution against any of them would be considered an enemy of the state. Cato was also active in defense of the handling of the conspiracy, and he harangued the populace on the merits of Cicero's consulship with such success that Cicero was again saluted as *pater patriae*.[9]

But there was another aspect of Nepos's activities that was causing still greater disquiet. In addition to his criticisms of the executions, he had put forward a proposal that Pompey should be recalled with his army to restore order and end the threat from Catiline. The ancient evidence does not identify the precise terms of the bill, but considered as a whole and in conjunction with the circumstances in which the proposal was made, it points clearly to the conclusion that sweeping powers were being advocated for Pompey that would have given him not only command of the military operations against Catiline in Italy but also military authority in Rome itself to deal with any elements of the conspiracy still operative within the city.[10] According to Dio, the bill offered Pompey a general commission to rectify the existing state of things. Plutarch has two accounts, both of which imply that Pompey was to be given control of the city, though they variously describe the reason as an ending of Cicero's tyranny and the protection of the city against Catiline. Cato understood the bill to mean that Pompey could enter Rome with armed troops, and the Senate as a whole viewed the measure with a degree of alarm that suggests it entailed more than a command against Catiline's meagre forces in Italy. Even Cicero, normally well-disposed toward extraordi-

---

9. *Sest.* 11. *Fam.* 5.2.6, 8. *Att.* 1.13.5. Quintilian, *Inst.* 9.3.50. Gellius, *NA* 18.7.7. Dio 37.42. Appian, *BC* 2.7. Plutarch, *Cic.* 23.3.

10. The danger within Rome was by no means considered ended by the elimination of the leading conspirators. See *Sest.* 11. Sallust, *Cat.* 52.14, 35. There were ongoing investigations and a general nervousness, and arrests and prosecutions continued well into 62. *Sulla* 6, 21. Dio 37.41. Suetonius, *Caes.* 17.

nary commissions for Pompey, considered defeat of the proposal a matter of high importance.[11]

It is further evident that the bill was linked to the controversy over the executions. Plutarch's remark that Cicero's alleged tyrannical behavior was raised as a justification for the measure indicates as much, and Cicero himself testifies that Nepos's attacks on him at *contiones* continued into January, the time when Nepos was most vigorously promoting his legislation. This linkage between the charges of misgovernment in the handling of the conspiracy in Rome and Pompey's recall again suggests that control of remaining aspects of the crisis inside as well as outside the city was being proposed for the general.[12]

Finally, a command confined to the military operations against Catiline's forces in the field would have had little point or justification by January 62. By then two armies, one led by Nepos's own brother, were hemming in Catiline, whose troops had been greatly depleted by desertions in the wake of the arrests at Rome. It was not a situation that offered much prospect of further military glory for Pompey.[13]

There are therefore good grounds for supposing that Pompey's responsibilities under the bill were to extend beyond the military effort in Italy to insuring the security of Rome itself and that the justification offered for his appointment was not merely the fading threat from Catiline's army but conditions in the capital, where, it was being claimed, the crisis had been grievously mismanaged by Cicero and the Senate. The bill was therefore to a large extent a continuation and intensification of the dispute concerning the executions and of Nepos's broader effort to discredit the rule of the oligarchy.

11. Dio 37.43. Plutarch, *Cic.* 23.2; *Cat. min.* 26.2–4. The Senate considered Nepos's activities madness, extreme enough to cause serious harm. For Cicero's view, see *Sest.* 62. The *Scholia Bobiensia* (134, Stangl) states that Nepos attempted to carry *plerasque leges* and lists two, one to recall Pompey *adversus arma Catilinae*, a second to have Pompey elected consul in his absence. There is no mention of a proposal to give Pompey a consulship in the detailed accounts of Plutarch and Dio, an omission that must cast doubt on the scholiast's veracity.

12. Plutarch, *Cic.* 23.2. *Fam.* 5.2.8.

13. Sallust, *Cat.* 57. Appian, *BC* 2.7. Dio 37.39. Catiline may well have been defeated before Nepos's bill came to a vote. See G. V. Sumner, "The Last Journey of L. Sergius Catilina," *CP* 58 (1963), 215–19. Sumner's contention, however, that Nepos, anticipating imminent defeat for Catiline, attempted to force his bill through the assembly on January 3 is not supported by the evidence.

At the beginning of 62 Nepos acquired a powerful political ally in Julius Caesar, who, as soon as he entered on his praetorship, resumed the strategy he had consistently followed earlier in the sixties of building influence by espousing popular causes and garnering any popularity to be gained by promoting the interests of Pompey. On January 1, when the Senate's leaders were attending ceremonies on the Capitol to mark the entry into office of the new consuls, he summoned a *contio* in connection with the restoration of the temple of Capitoline Jupiter, which the Senate had placed under the supervision of Catulus in 78. The work was still unfinished, and Caesar demanded an accounting from Catulus and put forward a proposal to transfer control of the project to Pompey. But when Catulus's friends rushed to the meeting and showed their determination to block the proposal, he did not press the matter further. He had aired another instance of optimate incompetence and possible malfeasance and had advertised again his support of Pompey. These, it would appear, were his main objectives.[14]

He continued, however, to support Nepos's legislative initiative to recall Pompey, and the issue gave rise to a major political storm culminating in serious disorder. Cato led a determined optimate drive to prevent passage of the bill and, in an attempt to offset the popularity of his opponents and especially of Caesar, he went so far as to persuade the Senate to take the uncharacteristic step of extending the corn dole at a cost to the treasury of thirty million sesterces. When he failed to dissuade Nepos from his course in a senatorial debate, he strongly attacked him and made clear his intention to veto his proposal. On the day of voting he duly appeared and forbade the reading of the bill. Nepos tried to force it through with the help of armed supporters. A riot ensued, in which Cato was in danger of his life until rescued by the consul Murena. The opponents of the bill prevailed, however, and prevented its passage. The Senate responded to the disorders by passing the ultimate decree and suspending Nepos and Caesar from office. Nepos, after summoning another *contio* and delivering a final tirade against the oligarchy, left for Asia to lay his complaints before Pompey. Caesar defended Nepos and

14. Suetonius, *Jul.* 15. Dio 37.44. *Att.* 2.24.3. Caesar, of course, had a personal reason for seeking to humiliate Catulus because of the latter's attempts to implicate him in the Catilinarian conspiracy. Sallust, *Cat.* 49. Plutarch, *Caes.* 7.3. A further unsuccessful attempt to link him to the plot was made early in 62, another episode, no doubt, in the ongoing feud between him and leading *optimates*. Suetonius, *Jul.* 17.

himself in the Senate, but, once he realized that the consuls intended to enforce the Senate's wishes, he gave up his lictors and emblems of office and retired quietly to his house. The Senate quickly reinstated him, however, following public demonstrations on his behalf. It also reversed its suspension of Nepos and, on the advice of Cato, refrained from any punitive action against him.[15]

The events of Nepos's tribunate have led many historians to conclude that Nepos was an agent of Pompey dispatched from the East to promote the general's interests, and that his proposed legislation represented an attempt by Pompey to crown his foreign victories and repeat the manner of his return from Spain in the seventies by crushing a domestic uprising.[16] But the policy of aggressive hostility toward the Senate persistently followed by Nepos was unlikely to benefit Pompey, and does not accord with the latter's evident concern on his return to avoid undue antagonism of the *boni*. Besides, it is not clear why Pompey in the early part of 63, when Nepos must have set out for Rome, should have seen any particular need for a henchman in the tribunate in 62. Mithridates was still alive and entrenched in the Crimea, and the settlement of Syria and adjoining regions and a resolution of the troubles in Palestine had yet to be achieved. It seems unlikely that Pompey was at this point envisaging an early return to Italy, and there were no signs of impending crisis in the early half of 63 that might have encouraged him to hurry home. Nor can he have had the opportunity, once the threat from Catiline did come to light, to send any directive about it to Nepos. It was not until October 21, when Cicero informed the Senate of information he had received about a conspiracy and secured passage of the ultimate decree, that any definite evidence about Catiline's designs emerged. Even then there was considerable scepticism about the existence of the plot until Manlius took the

15. Plutarch, *Cat. min.* 26–29; *Caes.* 8.4; *Cic.* 23.3. Suetonius, *Jul.* 16, 55. Dio 37.43. *Sest.* 62. For the terms of Cato's grain proposal, see G. Rickman, *The Corn Supply of Ancient Rome* (Oxford, 1980), 168–70.
16. See T. Rice Holmes, *The Roman Republic,* vol. 1 (Oxford, 1923), 266, 285–86, 467. W. E. Heitland, *The Roman Republic,* vol. 3 (Cambridge, 1909), 109–10. E. G. Hardy, "The Catilinarian Conspiracy in Its Context: A Re-Study of the Evidence," *JRS* 7 (1917), 223–26. W. E. Gwatkin, Jr., "Cicero *In Catilinam* 1.19—Catiline's Attempt to Place Himself in *Libera Custodia*," *TAPA* 65 (1934), 271–81. M. Gelzer, *Caesar: Politician and Statesman,* trans. P. Needham (Oxford, 1968), 56. Gruen, *Last Generation,* 83. Ch. Meier, "Pompeius' Ruckkehr aus dem Mithridatischen Kriege und die Catilinarische Verschwörung," *Athenaeum* 40 (1962), 103–25.

field openly in Etruria on October 27 and Catiline left Rome to join him in early November. Pompey was at that time in Amisus in Pontus, and for news of the conspiracy to reach him there and for instructions from him to get back to Rome would have taken close to three months. This would seem to rule out any idea that Nepos was acting on instructions from him in proposing his recall.[17]

Nepos's candidacy for the tribunate of 62 and his behavior in office can be far more easily and plausibly explained in terms of his own political leanings and aspirations and the political circumstances of the time. He had served in the East since 67, and by 63 had successfully completed his assignment in Syria. It was time for him to resume his political career, and a tribunate or aedileship was the next logical step for him on the way to the praetorship. For a talented demagogic orator who was already known for his radical temperament, the tribunate was the natural choice, and, like many before him, he proceeded to use it to advertise himself and his dissatisfactions with the status quo. The executions gave him a fertile issue with which to promote the antisenatorial campaign he had already begun, and his proposal to summon Pompey, in part at least, to remedy another manifestation of senatorial misrule, enabled him to dramatize further his general criticism of the oligarchy and win besides the benefits attached at this time to any association with the name and interests of Pompey. His course was closely similar to Caesar's and so, no doubt, were his motives. The great difference between him and his ally was that Caesar was more temperate and knew better the point beyond which demagoguery brought no profit.[18]

Despite the failure of the Pompeian proposal, the activities of Nepos and Caesar had a considerable effect. The issue of *senatoria potentia* and its abuse had been effectively thrust once more into the forefront of Roman politics, and the Senate had been forced into drastic measures that

17. An indication of the time it took for dispatches from Rome to reach the interior of Asia Minor can be found in *Att.* 5.19, in which Cicero expresses surprise that a letter from Atticus at Rome reached him at Cybistra in southwestern Cappadocia in 45 days. See *Att.* 6.2.6. D. R. Shackleton Bailey, ed. and trans., *Cicero's Letters to Atticus,* vol. 3 (Cambridge, 1968), 222–23.

18. The only ancient evidence to suggest that Nepos was Pompey's agent or was using his tribunate to promote Pompey's interests is a suspicion of Cato reported in Plutarch, *Cat. min.* 20.2. But Cato was notoriously distrustful of Pompey and an opponent of all *potentes.* Florus 2.13.9. Dio 37.22. Besides, the main reason for Cato's decision to stand for the tribunate in opposition to Nepos was the latter's radical reputation.

exposed it to further charges of repression and abuse of power. The results can be seen in the public demonstrations that followed the suspensions of Nepos and Caesar and brought their speedy reinstatement, and in allusions in Cicero to particular public resentment at this time of what was seen as excessive and oppressive senatorial power.[19]

Cicero's own position also deteriorated sharply in 62, another indication of a sudden change in public attitudes toward the events of late 63. He encountered a predictable hostility from those who had supported Catiline and from the class of politicians generally that he termed *improbi*.[20] But there is evidence also of a more widespread antipathy against him in the aftermath of the events of early 62. At the trial of P. Sulla, whom Cicero defended in the first half of 62 on a charge of complicity in the Catilinarian conspiracy, the young prosecutor L. Torquatus, who had been an active supporter of Cicero in 63, found it expedient to denounce the executions and repeat the charges of tyranny initiated by Nepos and Bestia, obviously confident that such sentiments would find sympathy with the jurors. Cicero himself confirms that he was out of favor in 62 with what he terms the parasitic rabble that peopled the *contiones,* and he writes to Atticus that his unpopularity with the masses diminished only after his influence seemed to wane and he developed friendlier relations with Pompey in the course of 61.[21]

The glory of the Nones had quickly dimmed. The Senate's firm control backed by a popular consensus had given way to disorder and violence in the Forum and hostile demonstrations against senatorial decisions. For Cicero himself the tributes and public acclaim had been replaced by vilification and broad popular disfavor. The *improbi* had not gained all their ends, but they had provided a telling demonstration of the fragility of the republican revival achieved in 63.

19. Suetonius, *Jul.* 16. *Att.* 2.9.1–2.
20. *Fam.* 5.2.1; 5.6.2. *Att.* 1.15.1; 1.19.6; 2.19.4. *Sulla* 29.
21. *Sulla* 21–35. *Att.* 1.16.11. Cf. *Att.* 2.3.4. It would appear that Cicero was also meeting criticism from the *iuventus,* the *adulescentes* of the upper classes, many of whom had supported Catiline's bid for the consulship and program of reform in 63. *Cael.* 10–12. *Mur.* 49. Sallust, *Cat.* 14. Though they had shied away from his violent methods, they retained their sympathies for his aims and their antagonism toward the policies and outlook of the conservative *nobilitas.* Cicero had a very uneasy relationship with them in the years following his consulship. *Att.* 1.14.5; 1.16.1; 1.18.2; 1.19.8. Sulla's prosecutor, Torquatus, was of course one of the *iuventus,* but it is unlikely that he was a Catilinarian sympathizer (*Sulla* 34), and his attacks on Cicero were doubtless dictated by what he saw as the interests of his case.

Cicero and Pompey in the Late Sixties

Cicero suffered a further major setback in the first half of 62. At the end of his consulship he had written Pompey a voluminous account of his *res gestae*. The letter was sent in the midst of the confrontations of late December and January and, as Cicero himself testifies, it had an important political purpose—to secure a congratulatory response that would give the sanction of Rome's most authoritative leader to Cicero's achievements and the controversial actions of December 5 and counteract the damaging criticism of his detractors. Cicero apparently circulated the letter, so that it amounted to a public invitation to Pompey to take a stand in support of senatorial authority and the optimate cause. But Pompey pointedly declined the invitation, and his reply not only omitted all reference to Cicero's consulship, but showed a studied coldness toward Cicero himself.[22]

Pompey's frosty silence was a serious blow to Cicero, and he did not conceal his disappointment. In a well-known letter he made a stiff but dignified response, which made clear his sense of injury at the failure to requite his services, but expressed the hope that Pompey would yet come to appreciate the importance of his achievements and that the welfare of the state, if nothing else, would unite them in personal and political friendship in the tradition of Scipio and Laelius.[23]

The correspondence with Pompey in early 62 confirms that Cicero was actively seeking an open political association with the general at this time and entertaining the hope that he could win him as a supporter of the *status reipublicae* established in 63. There were several factors prompting his efforts and expectations. He was keenly aware of the benefits that Pompey's enormous popularity and influence would confer on any cause or party to which he lent his support, but he was also drawn to him by a genuine admiration for his overall abilities and qualities as a leader.[24] His extraordinary career and outstanding military successes had demonstrated many of the attributes central to Cicero's concept of political *virtus*. The *Pro Lege Manilia* had listed and extolled them—high intelligence, good judgment, courage, initiative and energy, trustworthiness,

---

22. *Fam.* 5.7.2. *Sulla* 67. *Planc.* 85. *Schol. Bob.* 167, Stangl. The letter was in circulation in the early half of 62. Torquatus was able to quote from it at the trial of Sulla.

23. *Fam.* 5.7. 2–3.

24. Cicero's awareness of Pompey's value as a political ally can be seen in *Att.* 1.19.7; 1.20.2; 2.1.6.

consideration and clemency, cleanhandedness and self-control. Cicero especially admired his disciplined moderation and restraint and overall moral uprightness. He saw exemplified in both his private and public life the *temperantia* and *continentia* that he regarded as fundamental elements of the old morality and essential attributes of the good statesman. These were the qualities that he found sadly lacking in so many of his contemporaries, including leading *boni,* and whose decline he believed was precipitating a moral crisis and threatening the traditions and stability of the Republic.[25]

Cicero found other reasons also to admire Pompey's qualities of leadership. He believed that he had the bearing and personality befitting a leading statesman. He emphasizes his commanding presence and great personal dignity along with a kindliness and affability of manner. These were important aids to prestige and influence and they were also qualities that Cicero associated with *decorum,* the virtue that extended the dictates of *temperantia* to manners and social relations.[26]

Finally, there is every indication that, prior to Pompey's return from the East, Cicero regarded him as a *bonus civis,* dedicated in time-honored fashion to the pursuit of glory in the service of the Republic. He saw nothing sinister in his succession of extraordinary commands or in the manner in which he had secured them. He presents them as a product of a unique talent and of a willingness in the state's leaders to use it for the good of the state. He further considered that Pompey had discharged his tasks with brilliance and responsibility. He had shown *gravitas,* in the sense of a seriousness and steadfastness of mind that resulted in principled and responsible behavior. Cicero was later to question more than once his estimate of this aspect of Pompey's character, but he never wholly abandoned his original conviction, and in the terse obituary that he wrote to Atticus following news of Pompey's death, it was this quality that he chose to emphasize along with the private virtues of moral blamelessness and chastity.[27]

25. *Man.* 10, 27–29, 36–42, 64–67. *Balb.* 9–16. *Phil.* 2.69. *Att.* 11.6.5. Cf. Plutarch, *Pomp.* 1.3; 18.2; 36.6–7; 53.1–2; *Ant.* 21.2. Velleius 2.29.3.

26. *Brut.* 239. *Man.* 42. *Q.F.* 2.3.2. Pompey had *facilitas* (*Man.* 41). In general Cicero found him personally most agreeable, and he had a remarkably strong affection for him. See *Att.* 1.16.11; 2.19.2; 7.23.2; 8.2.4; 9.10.2; *Fam.* 1.8.3; 1.9.6, 11. Plutarch, *Pomp.* 1.3.

27. *Man.* 60–63. *Att.* 11.6.5. *Gravitas* is a recurring term in Cicero's allusions to Pompey. *Man.* 61. *Balb.* 13. *Phil.* 13.2. *Fam.* 3.10.10.

There are omissions in Cicero's catalogue of Pompey's political virtues, and his most generous appraisal does not attribute to him the all-round excellence ascribed to Scipio. Pompey was especially deficient in *doctrina* and *eloquentia*. From an early stage his energies had been directed elsewhere and as a result he lacked distinction in the skills of civilian statesmanship that Cicero associated with learning and eloquence.[28] But this was no great deterrent to Cicero since it was precisely in these skills that he believed he himself excelled, and he considered that he had exercised them with a distinction that rivaled Pompey's military fame. An alliance between them would therefore bring together a range of complementary talents and combine *auctoritas* derived from celebrated achievements in complementary areas of statesmanship. The result would be mutually advantageous and would insure able and authoritative leadership for the republican cause that could effectively counteract the designs and influence of the *improbi*.[29]

Cicero had helped further to pave the way for the cooperation he was seeking by what he regarded as loyal and devoted service to Pompey's cause. He believed, and with considerable justification, that he had strong claims on Pompey's friendship. From his praetorship, when he first began to speak publicly on political issues and gave his support to the Manilian law, he had continued to advertise himself as a supporter of Pompey sufficiently to allow him at the beginning of his consulship to claim a special status as a protector of Pompey's *dignitas*. The *Commentariolum petitionis* confirms his close attachment to Pompey's cause in the mid-sixties and speaks of his zealous devotion to the enhancement of Pompey's fame. Even after he reached the consulship and was no longer equally concerned with the electoral benefits of friendship with Rome's leading military hero, he had carefully maintained a pro-Pompeian stance. In his speeches against the Rullan land law he presented himself as a continuing champion of Pompey and watchdog of his interests, and later in the year, when news arrived of the death of Mithridates and the end of the Mithridatic War, he proposed and secured passage of an unprecedented ten-day *supplicatio* to celebrate the victory and the victor.

28. *Brut.* 239. See A. E. Douglas, *M. Tulli Ciceronis Brutus* (Oxford, 1966), 176.
29. For Cicero's comparisons of his achievements with Pompey's, see *Att.* 6.1.22. *Off.* 1.77–78. *Pis.* 72–75. *Phil.* 2.20. He would have considered that he had much more to offer Pompey than Laelius had offered Scipio, in that his civilian achievements were greater and his skills more needed.

He had, moreover, in all his promotions of Pompey exploited to the full the varied resources of the rhetoric of praise. He had sought to embellish and, as he tells Atticus, he had, like an Apelles, used all the colors of his art to embroider and polish his subject.[30]

Neither his services nor his achievements, however, proved sufficient to win him a political partnership with Pompey. The latter's behavior on his return from the East quickly dispelled any such hope. Pompey made no move toward public association with Cicero or his political views and showed no inclination to exert his influence in support of the *via optimas*. He was not prepared to play the role of optimate *princeps* that Cicero had envisaged for him or to embrace publicly the rigidly conservative brand of republicanism such a role entailed.

This did not mean that he had any wish to disassociate himself from the conservative *nobilitas* or any plans to undermine its traditional ascendancy. Cicero's estimate of his basic political character was broadly accurate; he was at heart in tune with the optimate ideal. There were radical aspects to his character but there was no radicalism in his political thinking. He had no designs to overthrow or fundamentally alter the political or social structure of the Republic or to impose an ascendancy based on

30. *Leg. agr.* 2.49–54. *Com. pet.* 5, 14. *Fam.* 1.9.11. *Dom.* 27. *Prov. cons.* 27. *Att.* 1.14.3; 2.9.1; 2.21.4. *Orator* 102. Despite his disappointment at Pompey's refusal to commend his consulship, Cicero determined to continue his role as a prominent supporter of the general, and when about this same time a final communiqué arrived from Pompey announcing an end to all wars by land and sea, he proposed another ten-day *supplicatio*. *Fam.* 5.7.1. *Prov. cons.* 27. See Shackleton Bailey, *Ad Familiares*, 1.279. Cicero's defense of the poet, A. Licinius Archias, who was accused in 62 of falsely claiming Roman citizenship, has been seen as an indication by Cicero that he was moving to the side of Pompey's opponents. See Heitland, *Roman Republic*, 3.113ff. Archias was a long-time client of the Luculli, leading enemies of Pompey at this time, and he had recently celebrated in an epic poem the achievements of L. Lucullus in the Mithridatic War. His prosecution may therefore well have been part of ongoing efforts by friends of Pompey to discomfit the Luculli in the mid-sixties, but there are no grounds for assuming that Cicero's defense of the poet had any special political significance or made any statement about his political affiliations. Archias had been his boyhood teacher and remained a close friend, and at this very time Cicero was attempting to persuade him to write an epic about his consulship. He had therefore abundant personal reasons for defending him. The obligations of *amicitia* were well defined and well respected at Rome, and one of the clearest of them was the duty to help an *amicus* when his vital interests were threatened by a prosecution. See Mitchell, *Ascending Years*, 164. For the political implications of the trial, see J. H. Taylor, "Political Motives in Cicero's Defense of Archias," *AJP* 73 (1952), 62–70. T. A. Dorey, "Cicero, Pompey, and the Pro Archia," *Orpheus* 2 (1955), 32–35. Gruen, *Last Generation*, 268.

force. What he sought was a leading and honored place within the system; he wished for power freely given and for acclaim gratefully bestowed by a reverential public for glorious achievements in the service of the state. His drive for primacy and fame sometimes moved him to uses of *potentia* that stretched legality and bordered on what Cicero would call *audacia,* but he preferred to operate behind a screen of constitutionality and respect for the *mos maiorum* and to be seen as a reluctant receiver rather than an aggressive pursuer of honors and offices. His political strategy therefore favored conciliatory tactics and the amassment of broad-based support and general esteem and popularity, rather than factional or confrontational politics or resort to strong-arm expedients.[31]

The strategy is reflected in his meteoric rise to the position of dominance conferred by the great commands of the mid-sixties. From the beginning he had sought to establish close links with the inner circles of the *nobilitas.* His important services to the Sullan cause had given him claims to a favored place within the Sullan oligarchy, and he had quickly moved to strengthen it by the familiar device of the marriage connection. In 82 he had married Aemilia, daughter of Sulla's wife Metella and of Aemilius Scaurus, the great *princeps senatus* of the nineties. When Aemilia died in childbirth in 81, he had immediately formed another dynastic union, this time with Mucia, daughter of Q. Mucius Scaevola, consul of 95, and half-sister of the Metellan brothers Celer and Nepos, sons of the consul of 98. The marriage with Mucia not only cemented Pompey's links to the powerful Metelli, but gave him a connection with other prominent *nobiles* as well, notably the consuls of 79, Servilius Vatia and Appius Claudius, both of whom had ties to the family of Celer and Nepos.[32]

31. Velleius 2.33 gives an astute analysis of Pompey's character. Pompey's political style is well illustrated by his elaborate efforts in 59 to justify his behavior and avoid responsibility for any breaches of constitutional procedure perpetrated by his allies. See *Att.* 2.16.2; 2.21.3. His feigned reluctance to accept various commissions in the fifties was also typical. See *Att.* 4.1.7; 4.9.1. *Fam.* 1.1.3; 1.2.3; 1.5b.2. *Q.F.* 2.2.3; 3.8.4. Biographies of Pompey in English have recently multiplied. They include John Leach, *Pompey the Great* (London, 1978). R. Seager, *Pompey: A Political Biography* (Oxford, 1979). P. Greenhalgh, *Pompey, the Roman Alexander* (London, 1980); *Pompey, the Republican Prince* (London, 1981).

32. *Fam.* 5.2.6. B. Twyman, "The Metelli, Pompeius and Prosopography," *ANRW* 1.1 (1972), 836. Mitchell, *Ascending Years,* 122ff. Some uncertainty surrounds the parentage of Celer and Nepos and their precise relationship to Mucia. See T. P. Wiseman, "Celer and Nepos," *CQ* 21 (1971), 180–82. G. V. Sumner, *The Orators in Cicero's*

His efforts to maintain supporters and general goodwill within the *nobilitas* had continued even after his military successes and relentless pursuit of further commands and high distinction inevitably brought hostility and opposition from his peers. His behavior in relation to his command against the pirates provides a good illustration. During debate on the bill he tried to lessen the animosity of the oligarchy by staying in the background and feigning reluctance to take such a commission, and after the measure became law he made still more determined efforts to counteract *invidia* by choosing a high proportion of *legati* from distinguished noble houses. The great campaigns of the mid-sixties were conducted with the aid of no less than thirteen representatives of consular families, ten of them patricians. They shared the glory and the political and material gains and owed the opportunity to Pompey.[33]

Aristocratic friendships, however, represented only one aspect of Pompey's power-building designs. His ambition extended to a level of eminence and influence that required, in the complicated political world of the first century, a far wider nexus of friends and clients and, in addition, a high degree of public renown and popularity. These he had determinedly pursued, alongside his cultivation of friends in the oligarchy, by the route of military glory. He had learned early on in the service of Sulla the value of his military talents, and thereafter had aggressively seized every opportunity to exercise them and had worked to extract from every assignment and success the maximum political gain. As a result, he had amassed by the end of the seventies a formidable array of political resources additional to his aristocratic *amici*—wealth, new friends derived from appointees to his staffs, clients abroad in the form of favored provincials and at home in the form of loyal veterans, and the high prestige and public favor attached to virtue displayed in war. The consulship had followed and, not long afterwards, the powerful commands against the pirates and Mithridates.[34]

Brutus: Prosopography and Chronology (Toronto, 1973), 132. D. R. Shackleton Bailey, "Brothers or Cousins," *AJAH* 8 (1983), 191.

33. Dio 36.24–26. For Pompey's *legati,* see T. R. S. Broughton, *The Magistrates of the Roman Republic,* vol. 2 (New York, 1952), 148–49.

34. See E. Badian, *Foreign Clientelae* (Oxford, 1958), 268–84; *Roman Imperialism in the Late Republic* (Oxford, 1968), 77–84. Pompey always sought to maximize the glory of his victories, whether by triumphs or other forms of advertisement. Typical of his efforts was his construction of a temple to Hercules, most likely in 70, and of a great trophy in the Pyrenees after the Sertorian War. Pliny, *NH* 7.96. Sallust, *Hist.* 3.89, 145,

It is noteworthy that throughout this entire period Pompey had avoided to a very large degree direct participation in political disputes or unequivocal association with particular political movements or ideologies. Only once had he become centrally involved in a political controversy when, following his election to the consulship for 70, he had declared his support for the restoration of tribunician powers and reform of the courts, and on entering office, had enacted, in cooperation with his colleague M. Crassus, legislation to reestablish the tribunes' prerogatives. But even on that occasion, though he had undoubtedly welcomed the opportunity to reap the benefits of implementing a popular reform, he had moved with tact and restraint, avoiding any demagogic exploitation of the issues and assuming the role of mediator between *plebs* and *patres*. After his consulship he had continued to eschew explicit partisan alignments or embroilment in political controversies, keeping out of the political limelight and aloof from the public.[35]

Pompey obviously saw no gain in prominent involvements in the disputes of domestic politics, and had no relish for the political infighting and oratorical jousting of Senate and forum. The nature of his ambition, centered on the lofty role of the preeminent *princeps* broadly supported and broadly revered, led him away from narrow partisan associations and divisive political stands. The wide influence and general acclaim essential for such a role could not easily be acquired by espousal of contentious principles or crusades, and was better built on high connections and on the varied political rewards of military glory.

His behavior in the eastern campaigns and on his return to Rome followed familiar lines. The goals and tactics had not changed. In the war against Mithridates he stretched his mandate under the Manilian law to the limit and extended his area of military operations over the entire Near East. After he gained control of the region he reorganized it on his own initiative, enlarging existing provinces, creating new ones, founding

---

Maur. See B. Rawson, "Pompey and Hercules," *Antichthon* 4 (1970), 30–37. R. E. A. Palmer, "C. Verres' Legacy of Charm and Love to the City of Rome: A New Document," *Rendiconti della Pontificia Accademia Romana de Archeologia* 51–52 (1978–79, 1979–80), 111–36. B. Marshall, "Pompeius' Temple of Hercules," *Antichthon* 8 (1974), 80–84.

35. *Verr.* 1.45. Plutarch, *Pomp.* 21.4–5; 23.3. Sallust, *Hist.* 4.45, Maur. See Mitchell, *Ascending Years*, 117–18. The speech of Licinius Macer in Sallust, *Hist.* 3.48, Maur., shows that Pompey had successfully avoided definite identification with any side or with any particular set of political views.

cities, establishing a network of client kings. In the process he amassed immense wealth and a vast clientela throughout the area. He also made certain of the loyalty of his soldiers by giving each man a donative of six thousand sesterces, and he increased further his claims on the *amicitia* of his officers by dividing among them one hundred million sesterces. Altogether, he diverted almost half of the immediate financial profits of his conquests to the purpose of augmenting his own *potentia*.[36]

He took further steps to maximize the political benefits of his victories by elaborate advertisement of his achievements. At his first *contio* after his arrival at Rome in January 61, he dwelt in grandiose terms on victories that had brought the defeat of twenty-two kings and made the proud boast that he had transformed Asia from an outpost into the heartland of the empire.[37] But his chief efforts to magnify his fame and popularity centered on his triumph, which was celebrated on the last two days of September 61, after eight months of preparation. Banners proclaimed the nations conquered, fourteen in all, and recorded the military highlights of the campaigns and the massive new revenues that would accrue to the Roman people. Captives, booty, tableaux, and trophies, representing all phases of the victory, gave life and substance to the statistics. One trophy at the end dominated, a lavishly adorned representation of the inhabited world, recalling Pompey's triumphs on three continents. Pompey him-

36. For Pompey's settlement of the East, see D. Magie, *Roman Rule in Asia Minor* (Princeton, 1950), 1:351–78; 2:1220–47. A. H. M. Jones, *The Cities of the Eastern Roman Provinces*, vol. 2 (Oxford, 1971). A. Dreizehnter, "Pompeius als Städtegrunder," *Chiron* 5 (1975), 213–45. For his payments to his soldiers and to the treasury, see Appian, *Mith.* 116. Pliny, *NH* 37.16. Strabo 11.14.10. Plutarch, *Pomp.* 45. Badian, *Roman Imperialism*, 81. Shatzman, *Senatorial Wealth*, 391.

37. Pliny, *NH* 7.99. Orosius 6.6.4. His final communiqué to the Senate in early 62 probably made similar boasts which, as I have argued elsewhere (*Historia* 24 [1975], 618–22), were most likely the source of Cicero's statement (*Fam.* 5.7.1) that the dispatch had offered "tantam spem oti quantam ego semper omnibus te fretus pollicebar," a sentiment echoed in another allusion to the communiqué in *Prov. cons.* 28; "confectis omnibus maritimis terrestribusque bellis." The idea that the words *spem oti* referred to internal peace and to a pledge in Pompey's dispatch to abide by the law and the constitution is hard to maintain. It assumes a widespread fear in Rome in 62 that Pompey would use his army to establish a military dictatorship and further assumes that Cicero, who singles out the *spem oti* as the most notable and praiseworthy aspect of Pompey's communiqué, shared the general concern. But there is no contemporary evidence for such fears, and certainly none in Cicero. Events such as Crassus's departure from Rome at the time of Pompey's return, which have been seen as evidence that a coup d'état was feared, have been plausibly explained on other grounds. See E. Ciaceri, *Cicerone e i suoi tempi*, vol. 2 (Milan, 1941), 18–19. E. J. Parrish, "Crassus's New Friends and Pompey's Return," *Phoenix* 27 (1973), 357–80.

self rode in a chariot set with precious stones and wore a cloak reputed to have belonged to Alexander the Great. It was an exhibition of unequaled magnificence that typified Pompey's yearning for glory and primacy, and his energy and thoroughness in their pursuit.[38]

His careful efforts to exploit every opportunity for political gain presented by his military success were accompanied by a characteristic concern to maintain connections and influence within the nobility. He had recently divorced Mucia, an action common opinion attributed to her infidelities during his absence.[39] But Pompey gave no reasons, and cold political calculations may have played their part as well. In any event, soon after his return he sought a new alliance with leading families of the oligarchy, proposing to marry himself the elder of two marriageable nieces of Cato and to marry his son to the younger. The proposed brides were daughters of D. Junius Silanus, consul of 62, and of the powerful and ambitious Servilia, daughter of Q. Servilius Caepio and of Livia, the sister of M. Livius Drusus. But their relationship with Cato was, perhaps, of greater importance to Pompey. Cato was connected by marriage with several prominent nobles and was also emerging in his own right as a leading voice of the conservative *nobilitas*. Moreover, he had recently stood forth as a persistent critic of Pompey and had shown himself a formidable adversary.[40] A bond of *adfinitas* with him might therefore not only ease Pompey's relations with many of the Senate's *principes* but also disarm a troublesome opponent. Cato upset these calculations by refusing to sanction the marriages, but the scheme reveals Pompey's ongoing desire to bolster his primacy with aristocratic friendships.[41]

38. Plutarch, *Pomp.* 45. Appian, *Mith.* 116–17. Dio 37.21. Pliny, *NH* 7.95–97; 33.151; 37.11. Pompey also planned an elaborate building program to provide permanent commemoration of his achievements, including a theater and temple to Venus Victrix and a shrine to Minerva (Pliny, *NH* 7.97). Diodorus 40.4 records an inscription summarizing Pompey's Asian achievements, which most likely came from the Temple of Venus. See M. Gelzer, *Pompeius* (Munich, 1949), 123.

39. Plutarch, *Pomp.* 42.7. Suetonius, *Jul.* 50. Caesar's name figured among her lovers. Cicero says the *boni* approved the divorce, no doubt believing it portended bad relations between Pompey and Caesar (*Att.* 1.12.3).

40. Plutarch, *Pomp.* 44; *Cat. min.* 30. For Cato's powerful connections, see Plutarch, *Cat. min.* 1.1, 24.3, 25, 41.2, 54.1; *Lucullus* 38.1. Syme, *Roman Revolution,* 21, 23–24.

41. Pompey also showed his concern to minimize aristocratic *invidia* by refusing any further titles or formal honors. Even the right to wear triumphal dress at the games, granted in 63 by a law of the tribunes, Balbus and Labienus, who were backed by Caesar, he exercised only once. Given Pompey's fondness for glory, this showed considerable determination to conciliate the oligarchy. Dio 37.21. 3–4. Velleius 2.40.4.

He was not prepared, however, to woo the favor of the oligarchy by open espousal of optimate causes. He continued to maintain his earlier cautious approach to partisan disputes and political controversies, intent on safeguarding the broad-based support and general popularity that had always been his principal political concern. His refusal to respond to Cicero's obvious play for his support in the Catilinarian controversy reflected this abstentionist posture, and his subsequent behavior after his arrival at Rome showed a similar wariness of open or unambiguous political stands.[42] His first *contio* disappointed the expectations of many by steering clear of political pronouncements and undertakings. Cicero's unflattering assertion that it held "no comfort for the poor, no interest for the unprincipled, no attraction for the well-to-do, no substance for the right-minded" attests its noncommittal character in circumstances where commitments were clearly expected. Pompey also persisted in his public silence about the Catilinarian crisis and Cicero's achievements, though typically he tried hard in his personal relations with Cicero to win his friendship, and from the outset privately praised his consulship in the most generous terms.[43]

His response to another heated political imbroglio that developed in early 61 in relation to the prosecution of P. Clodius on a charge of *incestum* followed similar lines. Clodius was alleged to have entered the house of Caesar disguised as a woman during celebration, in December 62, of the rites of the Bona Dea, from which men were excluded by religious law. He was supposedly keeping a tryst with Caesar's wife Pompeia. The matter was brought to the attention of the Senate by a former praetor, Q. Cornificius. The Senate referred it to the Vestals and College of Pontiffs, who determined that sacrilege had been committed. The Senate then decreed that Clodius should be charged with the crime and that a special court should be established to try the case, the jury to be chosen by the court's president, contrary to the normal practice of selec-

42. Cicero correctly perceived Pompey's concerns when he attributed his refusal to commend the suppression of the Catilinarian conspiracy to a desire not to offend anyone (*Fam.* 5.7.3).

43. *Att.*1.14.1. For Pompey's personal friendliness toward Cicero, see *Att.* 1.13.4; 1.16.11. In *Phil.* 2.12 Cicero says that Pompey, when he first saw Cicero on his return, embraced and thanked him and said it was thanks to him that he would see his country again. Cf. *Off.*1.78.

tion by lot. The consuls were instructed to promulgate a law constituting the special tribunal.[44]

A concern to maintain respect for religion and to curb licentiousness in the younger generation may have helped prompt the Senate's decision, but there can be little doubt that political considerations were also at work.[45] The names of the prime movers in the affair have been preserved for us by Cicero, and they were all leading conservatives: L. Lucullus, Q. Hortensius, Q. Catulus, C. Piso, M. Cato and his great imitator, M. Favonius, three Cornelii Lentuli, and the consul M. Messala. The defendant, on the other hand, had radical leanings that had brought him into conflict with prominent *optimates* and marked him as a foe of optimate interests. He had crossed swords with Cato in 73, when he had launched a broad attack on religious officialdom and accused the Vestal Fabia, half-sister of Cicero's wife, Terentia, of *incestum*. During his service on the staff of his brother-in-law, L. Lucullus, in the Mithridatic War he had helped instigate the mutiny that had crippled Lucullus's military efforts in 67. After his return to Rome he had become associated with Catiline and was believed to have acted as a collusive prosecutor in the latter's trial for extortion in 65. The association had persisted to an extent that allowed Cicero to accuse him routinely of being a member of the conspiracy and to repeat a common suspicion that he had tried to join Catiline's camp in Etruria. In 61 he was a quaestor, a resourceful rising young *nobilis,* whose record made him highly suspect to the oligarchy and whose downfall would please many of its leading figures.[46]

The prosecution would also embarrass Caesar, whose household was deeply involved in the scandal and who had already attempted to distance himself from the affair by divorcing Pompeia. Men like Catulus and Piso,

44. *Att.* 1.13.3; 1.14.1–2, 5; 1.16.1–6. Plutarch, *Cic.* 28–29; *Caes.*9–10. Velleius, 2.45.1. Suetonius, *Jul.*6.2. Appian, *BC* 2.14. Dio 37.45. Livy, *Per.*103. *Schol. Bob.* 85–91, Stangl. See J. P. V. D. Balsdon, "Fabula Clodiana," *Historia* 15 (1966), 65–73.

45. *Att.* 1.18.2. *Leg.* 2.35–37. *Severi* like Cicero were genuinely concerned to preserve the old moral standards and beliefs.

46. Plutarch, *Cat. min.*19.3; *Luc.*34.1–2. Dio 36.14.4, 17.2–3. *Har. resp.* 42. *Pis.* 23. *Att.* 1.2.1. Asconius 9, 50, 87, 92, Clark. *Mil.* 55. Plutarch's statement (*Cic.* 29.1) that Clodius had given Cicero active support during the Catilinarian crisis can hardly be right in light of Cicero's open accusations that he was involved in the conspiracy. Clodius's personality and moral reputation also most likely did not endear him to conservative elements of the oligarchy. He was seen as arrogant and reckless and morally depraved. Charges of incest with his sisters abounded. *Har. resp.*43. *Mil.*73. *Pis.*28. *Cael.*32, 36, 78. *Att.* 2.1.5. *Fam.*1.9.15. Velleius 2.45. Plutarch, *Luc.* 34; *Caes.*9.

who had tried so hard to damage Caesar by somehow linking him to the Catilinarian conspiracy, were not likely to let pass an opportunity to expose him to ridicule and to any unfavorable feeling generated by disclosure of sacrilegious immorality at the home of the *pontifex maximus* himself.[47]

Clodius responded to the Senate's action by marshalling gangs of roughs and his friends among the more radical elements of the *iuventus* and, with the cooperation of his *amicus,* the consul and presiding officer M. Pupius Piso, he used them at the *comitia* to gain control of the gangways and prevent the distribution of affirmative ballots. The *boni* realized what was happening and, led by Cato, invaded the platform and forced dismissal of the *comitia.* The Senate was summoned and, by an overwhelming majority of 400 to 15, directed the consuls to urge the people to accept the bill. Clodius then took to the Forum and extended the conflict in a series of fiery *contiones,* in which he lambasted his leading opponents and resurrected again Cicero's consulship and the executions. This drew Cicero into the middle of the dispute. He had initially favored the prosecution, eager to chastise the moral degeneracy of the young, but had quickly lost his enthusiasm as he contemplated the risks of an all-out conflict with the *improbi.* Clodius's attacks changed all that. His personal *dignitas* and the Senate's *auctoritas* were now at stake, and he responded with all the energy and vehemence at his disposal, reviling the fecklessness of Clodius's older supporters and the licentiousness of the *iuventus.*[48]

The upshot of this expanded war of words was a concession by the Senate's leadership, on the urging of Hortensius, who believed Clodius could not escape conviction, to allow the jury to be selected in the normal way. The bill establishing the court was then passed and the case came to trial in early May.[49] Cicero gave crucial testimony, which placed Clodius

47. *Att.* 1.13.3. Plutarch, *Caes.*10.6. Suetonius, *Jul.*6.2,74.2. Appian, *BC* 2.14. Dio 37.45. It would appear that Caesar had left for his province before the trial took place and that he had no further part in the affair. See H. Strasburger, *Caesars Eintritt in die Geschichte* (Munich, 1938), 111, n.55.

48. *Att.* 1.13.3; 1.14.5; 1.16.1; 1.18.2. See W. M. F. Rundell, "Cicero and Clodius: The Question of Credibility," *Historia* 28 (1979), 301ff. W. C. McDermott, "Curio Pater and Cicero," *AJP* 93 (1972), 381–411. Plutarch's story that Cicero became involved at the instigation of Terentia, who jealously suspected Clodia wanted to marry Cicero, smacks of idle gossip (*Cic.* 29.2).

49. *Att.* 1.16.2. The terminus ante quem is established by *Att.*1.19, which refers to a meeting of the Senate on the Ides of May, apparently not long after the trial.

in Rome on the morning of the day on which the rites were celebrated and undermined the cornerstone of his defense that he had been ninety miles away at Interamna.[50] In the end, however, the issue was decided by bribery, not evidence. Clodius purchased an acquittal, the money, by all indications, supplied by Crassus.[51]

The affair had developed into a major test of the Senate's authority and of the capacity of its conservative *principes* to control political events. It was the dominant issue in Roman politics in February and early March 61, and even brought the suspension for a time of all other senatorial business.[52] Pompey's position in a dispute of these dimensions was naturally a matter of the greatest interest, and both sides quickly attempted to involve him, each hoping, no doubt, for a sympathetic reaction. He was pressed for his views at a *contio* by one of Clodius's foremost defenders, the tribune Q. Fufius Calenus, and later in the Senate by an active supporter of the prosecution, the consul M. Messala. On both occasions Pompey avoided a specific response and took refuge in vague and verbose generalizations about the Senate's authority and his respect for its decrees. His words had an aristocratic air and expressed the irreproachable sentiments of a loyal statesman of the Republic, but in relation to the issue at hand represented an exercise in studied evasion. Cicero contrasted his performance in the Senate with a speech by Crassus at the same meeting in which the latter, no doubt seeking to highlight the emptiness of Pompey's generalities, extravagantly praised the actions of Cicero and the Senate in 63. This was the sort of specific and unequivocal

50. Plutarch, *Cic.* 29.1. *Schol. Bob.* 85. *Att.*2.1.5. *Dom.* 80. Quintilian, *Inst.* 4.2.88. Balsdon's contention (*Historia* 1966) that Cicero's testimony did not prove Clodius's alibi was false, since Clodius could have attended Cicero's *salutatio* and still have reached Interamna by nightfall of the same day, assumes an incredibly fast rate of travel. See A. M. Ward, *Marcus Crassus and the Late Roman Republic* (Columbia, Mo., 1977), 207–08.

51. *Att.* 1.16.5, 9–10, 13. *Schol. Bob.* 86, 91, Stangl. Plutarch, *Cic.* 2.9.5. The identity of the source of the money, referred to by Cicero as *Calvus ex Nanneianis,* has been endlessly debated. Many signs point to Crassus, however, who about the same time was buying Caesar's support by going surety for his debts. Suetonius, *Jul.* 18. Plutarch, *Caes.* 11.1; *Crass.* 7.6. A seldom-mentioned passage in the *Paradoxa Stoicorum* (45–46), in which Cicero mentions bribery of juries as one of Crassus' many shady activities, provides yet another sign. For a recent discussion with bibliography, see A. Ward, *Marcus Crassus,* 227–30.

52. *Att.* 1.14.5. The suspension had ended by March 15, when Cicero informs us (*Att.* 1.15.1) that one of the suspended items of business, the allocation of praetorian provinces, had been decided and that Asia had fallen to Quintus.

pronouncement on a controversial matter that Pompey conspicuously avoided on his return; he would not be drawn into declaring political positions that would imply narrow factional affiliations or partisan political views and that might alienate any element of support or affect the general acclaim and popularity that he believed his victories had gained him.[53]

Cicero had begun to revise his estimate and expectations of Pompey by January 61. His first contacts with him after his return had done nothing to relieve the disappointment he had felt when Pompey had refused to commend his consulship almost a year earlier. Pompey was outwardly friendly and complimentary, but Cicero sensed that the cordiality was a façade and a cloak for envy. He obviously found in it no sign of the public support and political friendship that he was so eagerly seeking. His disenchantment and frustration are vividly represented in a letter to Atticus in late January in which he describes Pompey in scathing terms as a man "without grace, directness, political finesse, integrity, fortitude, candor." The criticism continued, though in more muted tones, in later letters. Pompey's first *contio* and his responses to the Clodian controversy are reported with a mixture of plain disapproval and peevish ridicule.[54] The elections brought new grounds for reproach. Pompey attempted to secure the consulship for a henchman of low birth and ability, L. Afranius, using bribery on a scale that provoked a series of fresh attempts to curb electoral corruption and resulted in the postponement of the elections. But none of the proposals found their way into law, and Afranius was eventually elected. Cicero shared a widely felt resentment of Pompey's tactics. He viewed the election of Afranius as an insult to the office of consul and regarded the whole affair as a damaging blow to the system.[55]

No complimentary reference to Pompey's statesmanship in 61 survives anywhere in Cicero. Only in their personal relationship did he find any cause for satisfaction. They remained on cordial terms and had

53. *Att.* 1.14.1–4. In comparison with Crassus, Cicero considered Pompey had spoken *aperte tecte*. Plutarch reports that Pompey believed he had the general favor and support of the body politic (*Cat. min.* 30.1). He was doing nothing to endanger that position, and he maintained his cautious posture into 60. *Att.* 1.18.6.

54. *Att.* 1.13.4; 1.14.1–4.

55. *Att.* 1.16.12–13; 1.18.3. Plutarch, *Pomp.* 44.3; *Cat. min.* 30.5. For the bribery proposals, see Gruen, *Last Generation,* 223–24.

frequent contact, and Cicero greatly enjoyed the association.[56] It was a far cry, however, from the political partnership by which he had hoped to enlist Pompey's influence and resources in active defense of the objectives of 63.

Cicero Takes a New Road

Alongside his disillusionment with Pompey's political performance, Cicero felt a general despondency about the course of political events in 61. The Clodian affair he regarded as a major calamity. He saw its results as a clear-cut victory for the *mali* and *improbi* that was damaging not only to religion and morals but to the integrity of the courts and the authority and morale of the Senate. He had reacted to it in the spirit and style of his consulship, assuming a foremost role and using the full power of his oratory to overwhelm the *improbi* with abuse and ridicule and to arouse the *boni* to a sense of their dignity and responsibility and to the realization that *consensio bonorum* still existed and would prevail. He was highly pleased with his performance and its reception, but he remained discouraged by the signs of weakness in the Senate and in the courts that the trial revealed. The structure of republicanism built in 63 had been shaken and was beginning to seem ramshackle.[57]

Other developments in the latter part of 61 disturbed him even more. On the motion of Cato and in the absence of Cicero, the Senate decreed that legislation should be enacted to make equestrian jurors subject, like their senatorial counterparts, to prosecution for accepting bribes. The law which was promulgated in response to the decree did not carry, but the *equites* had been angered, and Cicero believed that serious damage had been done to the union of the orders cemented in his consulship. He expressed his disapproval of the action of his colleagues in a vigorous speech in the Senate, but this ex post facto intervention could do no more than protect his own standing with the equestrian order.[58]

Soon afterwards the *publicani* who had contracted to farm the taxes of

56. See *Att.* 1.16.11.

57. *Att.* 1.16.6–9. Cf. 1.18.2–3; 1.19.6.

58. *Att.* 1.17.8; 1.18.3; 1.19.6; 2.1.8. For the immunity of equestrian jurors from prosecution, see *Cluent.* 145–56. *Rab. post.* 16–19. U. Ewins, "*Ne Quis Iudicio Circumveniatur,*" *JRS* 50 (1960), 94–107. The decree was likely inspired by Clodius's acquittal and represented one of many attempts by Cato at this time to confront various forms of corruption. He was also behind the bribery proposals. *Att.* 1.16.12.

Asia asked the Senate to set aside their contract on grounds that they had bid too high a sum for it. Cicero considered the request disgraceful, but he took the lead in supporting it, convinced that the concession was necessary to prevent complete estrangement of the equestrian order. The Senate, however, acting once again on the urging of Cato, left the matter unresolved for months and eventually refused the request.[59]

These two clashes between the Senate and the *equites* largely ended Cicero's great hope for a lasting union of the upper classes sustained by mutual self-interest in the preservation of traditional republicanism. The *equites* had shown that their support would carry a price, and the Senate that it lacked the capacity to deal with such mercenary allies with any measure of diplomacy or foresight.[60]

In the midst of all this Cicero began to lose all confidence in his chief political allies, the conservative *principes* of the Senate. They were failing to provide the energetic and steadfast leadership that he considered necessary to defeat the *improbi* and sustain the authority of the Senate. All around him he saw incompetence or indifference, politicians "who did not count or did not care."[61] His severest criticism was reserved for those who had succumbed to the allurements of wealth and its trappings, and whose sense of values had become so perverted that they showed more concern for their fishponds than for the welfare of the state. But the *boni* as a whole were included in his censure; he could not find the ghost of a statesman anywhere.[62]

Cicero had good cause for his disenchantment with his noble associates. The Senate of the late sixties could boast few *principes* of high ability or achievement. Its body of *consulares* was unusually small and the bulk of them lacked sufficient distinction or influence to merit more than an occasional mention in our sources.[63] Of those whom Cicero

---

59. *Att.* 1.17.9; 1.18.7; 2.1.8. Cf. *Off.* 3.88. *Schol. Bob.* 157, Stangl. Ward, *Crassus*, 211. E. Badian, *Publicans and Sinners* (Oxford, 1972), 100–101.

60. *Att.* 1.17.8–9; 1.18.3; 2.1.7–8. In *Q.F.* 1.1.32 Cicero set out the difficult dilemma in dealing with the *equites*.

61. *Att.* 1.20.3. He quotes Rhinton to describe the politicians he saw around him ὅτι μὲν παρ' οὐδέν εἰσι, τοῖς δ'οὐδέν μέλει.

62. *Att.* 1.18.6; 1.19.6; 1.20.3; 2.1.7.

63. The repeated consulships of Cinna and Carbo and deaths in the civil wars of the eighties, together with the fact that many of the consuls of the seventies reached the office at a relatively advanced age, had reduced the number of *consulares* alive in 61. Only 24 can be listed with any certainty. See P. Willems, *Le sénat de la république romaine*

would classify as *optimates,* the most authoritative figures were Q. Catulus, consul in 78, L. Lucullus, consul in 74, Q. Hortensius, consul in 69, and C. Piso, consul in 67. But Catulus, whom Cicero admired more than any other statesman of his generation, died in 61, and Piso, another active and committed conservative, most likely died in the same year.[64] The remaining two, Lucullus and Hortensius, though they both had remarkable careers behind them and possessed outstanding gifts of leadership, had lost much of their vigor and zest for the rigors of Forum and Senate, and were becoming increasingly addicted to the life of luxury and urbane grandeur for which they both, though preeminently Lucullus, became notorious. They were the foremost exemplars of the fishpond fetish and the chief targets of Cicero's attacks on the extravagant frivolities and self-indulgence of leading *boni.*[65]

The oligarchy raised to power by Sulla was in sad decline in the late sixties, and it is indicative of the dearth of talent and initiative among its leaders that one of the most prominent and influential conservative voices of the period was a mere *tribunicius,* M. Cato. But even Cato did little to relieve Cicero's gloom about the leadership of the optimate cause. Cicero admired him for his integrity and dedication, but he considered his virtues fatally flawed by excessive rigidity and a lack of political sense, and he regarded him, on balance, as a liability rather than an asset to the *respublica.*[66]

Cicero's dissatisfaction with the statesmanship of the Senate's *principes* was compounded by a growing belief that they resented his own position and were jealously denying him due support and recognition. He had discovered early on that his consulship had not removed the stigma of

---

(Louvain, 1878), 1:423–555. E. J. Parrish, "The Senate on January 1, 62 B.C.," *CW* (1972), 160–68. R. J. Evans, "The *Consulares* and *Praetorii* in the Roman Senate at the Beginning of Sulla's Dictatorship," *Athenaeum* 62 (1983), 521–28.

64. *Att.* 1.20.3. Piso receives no mention in the sources after 61.

65. Macrobius 3.15.6. *Leg.* 2.1; 3.30–31. *Off.* 1.140. *Par. st.* 38. *Brut.* 320. Varro, *RR* 3.6.6, 13.2, 17.5–7. Plutarch, *Luc.* 38–42. The great houses of the Metelli and Claudii, which had earlier been the mainstay of the Sullan oligarchy, had no elder statesmen of real authority in this period. Q. Metellus Creticus, who, after a wait of several years, had finally been allowed to celebrate a triumph over the Cretan pirates in the middle of 62, took an active part in opposing ratification of Pompey's *acta,* as did Lucullus, but, apart from this crusade against a personal enemy, was apparently inactive. Velleius 2.40.5. Florus 2.13.9. See Syme, *Roman Revolution,* 22–23. Gruen, *Last Generation,* 50–53.

66. *Att.* 1.18.7; 2.1.8; 2.9.1–2; 2.21.1. *Off.* 3.88.

novitas or won him acceptance into the high nobility. He had endured a variety of sneers and insults relating to his birth in the attacks connected with the execution of the Catilinarian conspirators, and had received a further reminder of the pervasiveness and persistence of class distinctions in Rome when his purchase of a house on the fashionable Palatine from Crassus in 62 had brought a barrage of critical comment and spiteful jibes from his enemies.[67] But the *invidia* that most acutely troubled him came from his optimate colleagues and was related to politics. He had tried hard in 62 and 61 to continue the leading role he had assumed in 63 and to promote further the twin props of republicanism, *auctoritas senatus* and *concordia ordinum,* that he believed he had established in that year. He considered that he had been left largely unsupported in his endeavors especially since the death of Catulus, and he saw the reason as not simply the general apathy and indolence that he ascribed to the Senate's leadership in this period but envy of himself. He had not attained the authoritative status among the state's *principes* that he had hoped for in the wake of his consulship, and he had not been able to consolidate the gains of 63. The *boni* were not rallying to the leadership of the *novus* who was presumptuously seeking to direct the ways of the old nobility. They did not accept his generous estimate of his achievements and merits, nor did they share his enthusiasm for cooperation with the order from which he sprung. Socially and politically he was still on the periphery of the *nobilitas,* and he was gradually coming to realize that he was unlikely ever to be able to step beyond.[68]

The many disappointments, personal and political, that Cicero experienced in 61 led him toward the end of the year to a radical reappraisal of all his political hopes and aspirations. He still had an honored place in public life, and took satisfaction in the crowds that thronged his house for the *salutatio* and accompanied him to the Forum. His services as an advocate were eagerly sought, and he continued to work hard in the courts to maintain his influence and high standing. In the Senate he

67. Cicero bought the house for three and a half million sesterces and had to borrow heavily to pay for it. Some of the money came from P. Sulla, the man he defended in the middle of 62. He also got a loan from C. Antonius, his consular colleague in 63, arranged through an agent referred to as Teucris. *Att.* 1.12.1; 1.13.6; 1.16.10; 4.5.2. *Fam.* 5.6.2. Gellius, *NA* 12.12.2.

68. See *Att.* 1.16.1; 1.17.10; 1.19.6; 1.20.3; 2.1.7. Cicero also had little personal rapport with his noble colleagues. He longed for the company of Atticus or Quintus, both abroad since early 61. See *Att.* 1.18.1.

remained a prominent voice, the second speaker in debates, and he persisted in his efforts to promote his political ideas and objectives.[69]

But much had changed from the triumphal days at the end of his consulship. He now saw the state as weak and unstable, foundering through lack of leadership and disunity between its highest orders, the salutary effects of 63 dissipated. He had little hope left that he could effect a remedy, and increasingly he felt isolated and vulnerable in the position he had adopted, separated by a wall of jealousy from those who should have been his friends and allies, and exposed to the enmities incurred by his uncompromising devotion to the *vetus respublica* and hostility toward its enemies.

These gloomy assessments of the state's situation and his own brought a drastic change in Cicero's political posture and priorities. Faced with the collapse of his hopes for the *respublica,* alienated from the optimate *principes* and concerned for his political future and even for his safety, he decided that he must take a new road in Roman politics and seek greater resources and protection. By the end of 61 he was already committed to his new policy and was beginning to adumbrate its components and rationale in the letters to Atticus. His chief purpose now was to maintain a more restrained middle course that would balance steadfastness in serving the welfare of the Republic with a measure of concern for his private interests. This specifically involved moderating his aggressive stand as a foremost adversary of the *improbi* and adopting a more conciliatory attitude toward other elements, notably the upper-class *iuvenes,* who had been frequent targets of his outspoken censure in the past.[70]

But there was a more positive and important aspect to his new *ratio,* a new affiliation which he styled *novae amicitiae* and which moved him away from association with the persons and objectives of the conservative *nobilitas* toward a closer form of friendship and cooperation with Pompey. The new connection was easily made, facilitated by Pompey's particular needs at the end of 61. The latter was making careful prepara-

69. *Att.* 1.17.6; 1.18.1; 1.20.7. In January 61 he had lost his place as first speaker in the Senate (*Att.* 1.13.2). It is clear that Cicero was very involved in the courts, but the only known cases in which he appeared in the period 62–60 are those of Sulla and Archias in 62, and Metellus Scipio Nasica (*Att.* 2.1.9) in 60.

70. *Att.* 1.17.7–10; 1.18.2–3; 1.19.6–8; 1.20.3; 2.1.7. Cicero's concern with his own position and resources increased at the beginning of 60, when moves began to get plebeian status for Clodius to enable him to stand for the tribunate. *Att.* 1.18.4; 1.19.5; 2.1.4–5.

tions to resolve in the following year the pressing question of land for his veterans. He had gone to great lengths to insure that he had a loyal adherent in the consulship, and had also apparently secured a friendly College of Tribunes. But he badly needed friends in the Senate, where he faced powerful opposition from the men with whom he had clashed in the pirate and Mithridatic wars, L. Lucullus and Metellus Creticus, and an uncertain response from the optimate leadership as a whole. The support of a figure of Cicero's stature and abilities and conservative credentials would be enormously valuable, and Pompey's eagerness to secure it is shown by the fact that at the beginning of 60 he was willing for the first time to speak publicly in praise of the achievements of 63.[71]

Cicero's purpose in seeking the new association was, no less than Pompey's, plain self-interest. His estimate of the general had not changed. He continued to describe him to Atticus, who fully shared his opinion, in bitter and derogatory terms. Pompey remained in his eyes a self-serving politician devoid of greatness or high-mindedness, who had the resources and prestige to stabilize the *respublica* but refused to do so, repaying the favors of the state with silence instead of leadership. But he was offering friendship to Cicero where others offered envy, and he had besides the popularity and influence to guarantee prominence and security as certain concomitants of that friendship.[72]

Cicero did hope, however, that he could maintain a close relationship with Pompey and draw strength from the public's knowledge of their friendship without compromising his political ideals. Later on in 60, deluded by his own vanity and spurred by the misgivings of Atticus, who saw his new course as an abandonment of old allies and ideals for the camp of the enemy, he went so far as to claim that his intimacy with Pompey was dictated by patriotism and was bringing more benefit to the state than to himself. His sole basis for the claim, however, proved to be Pompey's praise of 63, which Cicero egotistically reckoned as a major gain for the Republic and from which he extrapolated that Pompey was becoming a better citizen and more willing to forgo the unprincipled pursuit of popular favor. But these were largely efforts to embroider a policy based on expediency, and were typical of Cicero's penchant for

71. *Att.* 1.17.10; 1.19.7; 1.20.2; 2.1.6. Cicero uses the phrase *novae amicitiae* in *Att.* 1.19.8.

72. *Att.* 1.18.6; 1.20.2. See E. Badian, ''The *Auctor* of the *Lex Flavia*,'' *Athenaeum* 55 (1977), 233–38.

specious justifications whenever he chose the *utile* over the *honestum*. He was, however, genuinely determined to insure that his *novae amicitiae* did not enforce compromise of his old beliefs and objectives, but the difficulty of achieving even that was soon to become apparent.[73]

At the beginning of 60 a tribune, L. Flavius, introduced the agrarian bill by which Pompey hoped to provide land for his veterans. The bill proposed to distribute remaining public land in Italy, including controversial property such as the *Ager Campanus* and the lands confiscated by Sulla. It also proposed to purchase additional land with the money accruing from the new revenues over the following five years. The measure was ambitious, designed to provide land for the urban poor as well as for Pompey's soldiers. Its broad scope would increase its appeal and also help alleviate the problems of overcrowding and unemployment in Rome, drawing off, in Cicero's words, "the dregs of the city." It was also highly contentious, containing again the idea, anathema to the Senate, of distributing the rich, high-revenue-bearing *Ager Campanus* and raising the explosive issue of the legitimacy of Sullan grants and confiscations. The sums of money it proposed to divert from a hard-pressed treasury, amounting, by Pompey's own calculations, to seventeen hundred million sesterces, were also certain to arouse opposition.[74]

It was clear where Cicero's record as an opponent of agrarian legislation and fervent defender of property rights and of a healthy treasury dictated he should stand in regard to this proposal. He found himself compelled, however, in his new circumstances, to take account of the wishes of Pompey and the general public and to give qualified support to the bill, opposing only the provisions that posed a threat to private interests. He believed this was a popular stance, but it was an odd posture for the victor over Rullus, and it set him sharply apart from his senatorial colleagues, who, led by L. Lucullus, Cato, and the consul Metellus Celer, strongly opposed the entire measure, their traditional hostility toward agrarian laws reinforced by personal enmity toward Pompey and a jealous suspicion that he was in pursuit of some new power. Cicero did not fully satisfy Pompey either, who was determined to get the full proposal passed into law.

73. *Att.* 1.19.7; 1.20.2–3; 2.1.6–7.
74. *Att.* 1.18.6; 1.19.4. Dio 37.50. For Pompey's estimate of the value of the new revenues, see Plutarch, *Pomp.* 45.3.

The awkwardness of Cicero's position was alleviated, however, by the fact that, after some sharp clashes, during which Flavius went so far as to imprison Metellus, the issue quickly faded into the background. There were several reasons for this turn of events. Pompey's main allies, Afranius and Flavius, proved totally inept, and the Senate's leaders totally hostile. The unexpected and vigorous opposition of Metellus, a former *legatus* of Pompey, dealt a further damaging blow to the bill's prospects. In addition, the threat of a serious war in Gaul emerged in March and began to monopolize the attention of politicians and public. The agrarian debate began to lose momentum, and by June it was moribund.[75]

Pompey had suffered a serious reverse and had learned the limits of his power when exercised within the conventional framework of the republican system. He had failed to mitigate the enmities and suspicions of begrudging noble colleagues, characteristically hostile, in the manner of oligarchies, to the exceptionally eminent, and he had failed to control the political process over their opposition. But his needs were too pressing and his desire for predominance too strong to allow him meekly to accept the defeat of his designs, and he determined to find stronger allies for 59 and to bring the force of his *potentia* more directly to bear on the political decision making. His search for allies turned him to Julius Caesar, who had recently returned from a successful governorship of Further Spain and was seeking the consulship. He was an obvious choice for Pompey. He was a rising star, who would bring to an alliance proven ability and high popularity as well as the advantages of high office. He had, besides, been a frequent supporter of Pompey's interests in the sixties and could reasonably be expected to respond favorably to the idea of a coalition. Caesar had, in fact, particular reason to welcome such a proposal in 60. As he began his campaign for the office that would place him permanently among the state's *principes,* he began to experience the full force of the enmity that had been building against him in the oligarchy throughout the sixties, and he became, like Pompey, a special target of Cato's hostility, who saw it as his great mission to bring down those he consid-

---

75. *Att.* 1.19.4; 2.1.6. Dio 37.49–50. Plutarch, *Luc.* 42.6; *Cat. min.* 31.1. Pompey was also seeking ratification by the Senate of his eastern *acta* about this time, though no allusion to this issue is made in Cicero's letters. Ratification was blocked by Lucullus, Cato, Metellus Creticus, and, it would appear, Crassus. Plutarch, *Luc.* 42.6; *Cat. min.* 31.1; *Pomp.* 46.3. Dio 37.49. Appian, *BC* 2.9. Velleius 2.40.5. Florus 2.13.9. It would appear that Cicero took no part in the debate.

ered to have excessive power.[76] Caesar got a foretaste of the strength and determination of his optimate foes when, to avoid crossing the *pomerium* and thereby surrendering his *imperium* and the triumph for his successes in Spain already granted him, he sought an exemption from the regulation requiring candidates to submit their nominations in person and was denied it through the machinations of Cato. He was forced to give up his triumph and the opportunity to parade the full measure of his exploits and to enhance the military fame that he so eagerly coveted. It was a forceful indication that, if he was to fulfill his high ambitions in the face of such formidable opposition, he would need powerful friends.[77]

The oligarchy had to be content, however, with depriving him of his triumph. They could not keep him from the consulship, though they did succeed in installing as his colleague a brother-in-law of Cato and a tenacious traditionalist, M. Calpurnius Bibulus. Caesar could expect the maximum obstruction from Bibulus in 59 and, as the year approached, he took further steps to expand his resources. By December 60 he was moving to bring together his new ally, Pompey, and his long-time associate, Crassus, intent on uniting behind him the full *potentia* of these two former enemies. He also tried to draw Cicero into the coalition, no doubt encouraged to do so by the latter's changed political posture in 60. Cicero weighed the advantages—intimacy with Pompey and Caesar, reconciliation with his enemies, peace with the mob, and a restful old age. They were essentially the benefits that had led him into closer cooperation with Pompey a year earlier, only now they were being offered in even greater degree. But this time he drew back, well aware that the proposed association could not be reconciled with his political beliefs or past behavior.[78]

76. For Cato's well-known hostility toward *potentes*, see n. 18 above. It may be that Pompey also sought to woo the Claudii in 60 and that it was at this time he married his eldest son to the daughter of Appius Claudius. According to Plutarch, he also secured Clodius as an ally. He did, however, oppose in 60, no doubt in deference to his friendship with Cicero, the adoption of Clodius into a plebeian family. *Har. resp.* 45. *Fam.* 3.4.2. Dio 39.60.3. Plutarch, *Cat. min.* 31.2; *Pomp.* 46.4. See T. W. Hillard, "P. Clodius Pulcher 62–58 B.C.: 'Pompeii Adfinis et Sodalis'," *PBSR* 1 (1982), 34–44. Shackleton Bailey, *AJAH* 8(1983), 191.
77. Plutarch, *Caes.* 13; *Cat. min.* 31.2–3. Appian, *BC* 2.8. Dio 37.54.1–2. Suetonius, *Jul.* 18.
78. *Att.* 2.3.3–4. Scholars have failed to reach agreement about the precise time at which Pompey and Caesar formed their alliance, but most of the ancient accounts place the compact before the elections, and Pompey's need for a strong ally in the consulship strongly supports this version. One of the other candidates, L. Lucceius, was later a close

Cicero was now traveling a lonesome and uncertain road in Roman politics. He had moved away from his natural political allies, the *boni*, convinced that they lacked the capacity and the will to govern effectively and that he could not find among them the support and friendship necessary to insure his own standing and safety. He had soon discovered, however, that his alternative course, based on the naive hope that he could somehow have the best of both worlds and pursue his old policies while maintaining friendship with those most likely to collide with them, was untenable, and he had promptly abandoned it also. He was left without firm attachment to any political faction and had neither the inherited resources or the accumulated *potentia* to give him significant independent influence. As a result, despite his spectacular rise and successes as consul, he found himself, at the beginning of 59, without a firm place or clear purpose in Roman politics, and a decade and a half would elapse before he recovered either.

---

friend of Pompey (*Att.* 13.41; 13.42. Caesar, *BC* 3.18.3), but politically and socially he was an obscure figure, and it is unlikely that Pompey, after his experience in 60, was building his hopes around another nonentity. (See W. C. McDermott, "*De Lucceis*," *Hermes* 97 (1969), 233–46.) There is no reason, however, to reject the evidence of Cicero and conclude that the triple alliance of Pompey, Caesar, and Crassus had been sealed before the end of 60. The question of the formation of the so-called First Triumvirate has inspired a massive amount of writing. See G. M. Bersanetti, "La tradizione antica e l'opinione degli storici moderni sul primo triumvirato," *Riv. Indo-Grec.-Ital. Filol.* 11 (1927), 1–20, 185–204; 12 (1928), 21–42. Gruen, *Last Generation*, 88ff. R. Hanslik, "Cicero und das erste Triumvirat," *RhM* 98 (1955), 324–34. Meyer, *Caesars Monarchie*, 59–60. H. A. Sanders, "The So-Called First Triumvirate," *MAAR* 10 (1932), 110–13. G. R. Stanton and B. A. Marshall, "The Coalition between Pompeius and Crassus, 60–59 B.C.," *Historia* 24 (1975), 205–19. Ward, *Crassus*, 213–17.

3: DISILLUSIONMENT BECOMES DESPAIR

Cicero's casual report to Atticus in December 60 of an emerging coalition between Pompey, Caesar, and Crassus showed no inkling of the far-reaching consequences for the *respublica* that were to ensue from it. Informal compacts for mutual political gain were a commonplace in Roman political life, and there was nothing especially surprising or sinister about such a compact between Pompey and Caesar, or the inclusion in it of Caesar's friend and benefactor Crassus. Cicero recognized that the political ends and outlook of the new partnership were at variance with his own, and that honor and consistency precluded association with it, but beyond that he found no cause for concern.

The Events of Caesar's Consulship

The early months of 59 quickly changed this perspective. The manner of government ushered in with Caesar's accession to the consulship set the new alliance sharply apart from the standard *coniunctio* of republican politics, and showed the state in the grip of a powerful clique ready to subvert the constitution and make force, not law, the controlling element in political life. Caesar's first legislative initiative starkly revealed the new state of things. Early in January he turned his attention to solving Pompey's most urgent problem, the settlement of his veterans, and brought forward another agrarian proposal. Like the Flavian law, it was a comprehensive measure that was designed to provide land not only for the veterans but also for the poor of Rome, in an attempt to return the burgeoning urban proletariat to useful employment on the land and re-people deserted areas of Italy.[1]

It was more carefully drawn, however, and sought to eliminate the controversial features that had stirred broad resistance to the Flavian bill and to the earlier law of Rullus. It proposed to distribute land owned by the state in Italy, but unlike the Flavian bill, it exempted the *Ager Campanus* and land confiscated by Sulla, and may well have adopted a provision of the Rullan proposal to give clear legal title to grantees and possessors of the Sullan territories.

Additional land for distribution was to be purchased with funds from the new revenues, but only from those willing to sell and only at prices that accorded with the valuations in the registers of the censors.[2] The scheme was to be administered by a large commission of twenty to avoid the appearance of control by a few, and, as a denial of any motives of self-interest on the part of the bill's author, Caesar was disqualified from membership.[3]

The bill had undeniable merits and had been so carefully trimmed of

1. Dio 38.1.3. Plutarch, *Pomp.* 47.3; *Caes.* 14.1; *Cat. min.* 31.4.

2. The most reliable accounts of the bill and its passage are to be found in Dio 38.1–6 and Suetonius, *Jul.* 20. Cf. Plutarch, *Caes.* 14; *Pomp.* 47–48; *Cat. min.* 31–32. Appian, *BC* 2.10–11. Velleius 2.44. Velleius and Appian mention only one law, as does Plutarch in his *Pompey* and *Caesar*, and strangely, until the last half-century, modern scholars were divided on the question of the number of Caesar's land acts. For a summary of the arguments in this surprising dispute, see M. Cary, "The Land Legislation of Julius Caesar's First Consulship," *JP* 35 (1920), 174ff. There is some uncertainty as to what the agrarian law specified with regard to lands appropriated by Sulla, but Cicero's statement in *Fam.* 13.4.2 that in 59 Caesar "agrum Volaterranum et oppidum omni periculo in perpetuum liberavit" clearly implies that the territory of this city, which had been confiscated by Sulla, was not only exempted from distribution at this time, but was further confirmed as the property of those then holding it. All other such lands were presumably treated in the same way. The Rullan law, in which Caesar was deeply involved, had confirmed as private property the lands being held by Sullan colonists and *possessores*, and it would not be surprising if Caesar's own law had a similar provision. Brunt's arguments to the contrary (*Italian Manpower*, 318, 323, 325) are based on highly inconclusive texts.

3. Dio 38.1. *Dom.* 23. *Att.* 2.6.2; 2.7.3. *Schol. Bob.* 161, Stangl. There was also an inner commission of five, which presumably formed an executive committee. *Att.* 2.7.4. *Prov. cons.* 41. An inscription (*ILS* 46) describes M. Valerius Messala (consul 61) as *Vvir a(gris) d(andis) a(ssignandis) i(udicandis)*, which indicates that at least the members of the inner board had powers similar to those proposed for the commissioners in the Rullan proposal.

the objectionable features of earlier agrarian proposals that, when Caesar laid it before the Senate, no one could find any substantive grounds on which to oppose it. But the general hostility of the oligarchy toward agrarian laws remained and the fear that such measures, if implemented, would give dangerous power to their authors. Cato as usual took the lead in voicing the objections of the *boni* and adopted his favorite obstructive tactic of talking out the session. Caesar, with typical intolerance of such forms of opposition, resorted to his powers of *coercitio* and ordered him imprisoned. This merely brought a show of support for Cato, and Caesar quickly reversed his order and then dismissed the Senate, declaring that the people would decide the issue.[4]

At a subsequent *contio,* after Bibulus resolutely refused to approve the bill, Caesar brought forward Pompey and Crassus and asked their views. Pompey argued the merits and justice of the proposal and made his celebrated statement that if anyone threatened to raise a sword in opposition to it, he would come armed with sword and shield. Crassus supported Pompey's belligerent stance, and a gathering of veterans in Rome drove home the point. The intentions of the three potentates had been made plain.

Bibulus, however, was undeterred and, supported by three tribunes, he was determined to prevent passage of the bill. His first tactic was to declare all comitial days religious holidays, and when Caesar, probably with some justification, ignored this pronouncement and fixed a day for the voting, he fell back on two other common devices for controlling assemblies, the announcement of unfavorable omens (*obnuntiatio*) and the veto.[5] But Caesar secured the Forum with armed supporters, and Bibulus was unable to get through in time to exercise *obnuntiatio,* which

4. Dio 38.3. Gellius 4.10.8. Suetonius, *Jul.* 20.4. Cf. Val. Max. 2.10.7 (mistakenly associates Cato's arrest in the Senate with opposition to the claims of the *publicani*).

5. Dio reports that Bibulus declared a ἱερομηνία for all the remaining days of the year, which must mean that he attempted to make all comitial days *feriae.* This could be done by placing moveable feasts or thanksgivings, both of whose dates were fixed by the consuls, on such days. The number of feast days could be greatly increased by compelling the repetition of festivals on grounds that a mistake in ritual had been made. The consuls of 56 successfully employed these devices to eliminate comitial days (*Q.F.* 2.4.4). It seems unlikely, however, that one consul could thus manipulate festivals in defiance of his colleague, and Caesar was probably justified in ignoring Bibulus's action. See L. R. Taylor, "The Dating of Major Legislation and Elections in Caesar's First Consulship," *Historia* 18 (1968), 173–93. Shackleton Bailey, *Letters to Atticus,* 1.380, 407.

had to be delivered before a meeting began. When he finally forced his way to the platform to use his veto, he and his followers were attacked and forcibly driven from the Forum.[6] The bill was then passed. Next day Bibulus tried to have the law annulled by the Senate, but he found no support in a meeting thoroughly cowed by the recent turn of events. He responded by retiring to his house, where he remained in seclusion for the rest of the year, issuing abusive edicts against the triumvirs and attempting to prevent further legislation by announcement, whenever assemblies were called, that he had observed unfavorable omens.[7]

Caesar disregarded this extreme attempt to maintain a running *obnuntiatio* through edicts, and he passed into law a variety of further measures during the first half of 59.[8] By April Ptolemy Auletes had been confirmed

6. The evidence indicates Bibulus attempted to use both *obnuntiatio* and veto. Suetonius, *Jul.* 20.1, 30.3. *Dom.* 39–40. *Har. resp.* 48. *Vat.* 5, 15, 21. *Att.* 2.16.2. In *Phil.* 2.81 Cicero says it was forbidden *per leges* (presumably referring to the Leges Aeliae et Fufiae) to announce "de caelo servasse" in the course of a *comitia*. For a full discussion of *obnuntiatio*, see I. M. J. Valeton, *"De iure obnuntiandi comitiis et conciliis," MN* n.s. 19 (1891), 75–113, 229–70.

7. The form of announcement was "de caelo servasse." For its precise meaning, see R. G. Nisbet, ed., Cicero, *De Domo Sua* (Oxford, 1939), 202–03. The date of Caesar's first agrarian law and of Bibulus's retirement continue to be debated. See M. Cary, *JP* 35 (1920), 174–90. L. R. Taylor and T. R. S. Broughton, "The Order of the Two Consuls' Names in the Yearly Lists," *MAAR* 19 (1949), 3–14; "The Order of the Consuls' Names in Official Republican Lists," *Historia* 17 (1968), 166–72. L. R. Taylor, "On the Chronology of Caesar's First Consulship," *AJP* 72 (1951), 254–68; also *Historia* 17 (1968), 173–93. J. Linderski, *Historia* 14 (1965), 424–42. Ch. Meier, "Zur Chronologie and Politik in Caesars ersten Konsulat," *Historia* 10 (1961), 68–98. Shackleton Bailey, *Letters to Atticus,* 1.406–08. Gelzer, "Die *Lex Vatinia de imperio Caesaris," Hermes* 63 (1928), 113–37; *Caesar,* 72–74. The studies of Taylor and Broughton have shown that the consul listed first in the *fasti* was the consul who had first been declared elected, and that this priority of election brought with it priority in holding the *fasces*. Caesar is named first in the *fasti* and in all consular datings and would therefore have held the *fasces* in January. There is no reason to doubt that he would have moved immediately to introduce the agrarian law, which was already in preparation in December 60 (*Att.* 2.3.3) and whose speedy implementation was of crucial interest to Pompey. Further, in view of the summary manner in which he overrode all forms of opposition, there is every likelihood that the bill had been passed into law by the end of January. Our most reliable accounts (Dio 38.6.6 and Suetonius, *Jul.* 20.1) indicate Bibulus retired after passage of the first agrarian law. The only evidence to the contrary is Plutarch's statement (*Pomp.* 48.4) that Bibulus shut himself in his house for eight months, but this is most likely an error derived from Plutarch's telescoping of the first and second land bills.

8. J. Linderski ("Constitutional Aspects of the Consular Elections in 59 B.C.," *Historia* 15 [1965], 425ff.; see also *HSCP* 89 [1985], 207–34) has argued that Bibulus's declara-

as king of Egypt and friend and ally of Rome, the contracts of the Asian tax farmers had been reduced by one third, and Pompey's eastern settlement had been ratified.[9] In May came a more provocative proposal, a supplementary agrarian law to distribute the highly valued *Ager Campanus*. It contained a qualification that only those who had three or more children would be eligible for allotments. Not many veterans would have satisfied this requirement, which would indicate that the bulk of them had already been provided for under the first law, and that the new bill was chiefly concerned with Caesar's second objective, the reduction of the numbers of urban poor. The earlier law had evidently failed, or appeared likely to fail, to make available sufficient land to meet this objective, so Caesar fell back on the large Campanian possessions of the state and also narrowed his aims, concentrating on aiding the larger families of the proletariat, whose conditions of life must have been by far the most desperate.[10]

---

tions "de se caelo servasse" were not sufficient to invalidate comitial proceedings and that the announcement had to be made in person to the presiding magistrate. But this was clearly a very controversial point at the time. Cicero (*Dom.* 39–40) relates that the augurs, when questioned about it at a public meeting, replied that it was unlawful to hold "comitia, cum de caelo servatum sit." Bibulus and the three tribunes who imitated him surely hoped to gain something by their action, and much was made of Bibulus's stand in subsequent attacks on the validity of the legislation of 59. (*Har. resp.* 48. *Dom.* 40. *Prov. cons.* 45–46.) The references in Cicero that can be adduced to show *obnuntiatio* had to be announced in person all refer to incidents subsequent to Clodius's modification of the procedure in 58. (See esp. *Att.* 4.3.3–4. *Sest.* 78.) It may well be therefore that Clodius's bill first explicitly stated in law that notice of unfavorable omens had to be delivered in person to the presiding officer, and that this represented, in fact, his famous modification of the *Leges Aeliae et Fufiae*. The requirement, which had always applied to *intercessio*, may have been implicit in earlier legislation governing *obnuntiatio*, but have become overlaid with a convention that the mere declaration "de caelo servasse" or "de caelo servaturum" was sufficient to prevent the holding of *comitia*. Caesar refused to be bound by the convention, creating a bitter constitutional row, in which the legalities were far from clear. For a full discussion, see T. N. Mitchell, "The *Leges Clodiae* and *Obnuntiatio*," *CQ* 36 (1986), 172–76.

9. *Att.* 2.16.2. Caesar, *BC* 3.107. Suetonius, *Jul.* 20.3, 54.3. Dio 38.7.4–5. Appian, *BC* 2.13. There is no certain evidence for the date at which Pompey's eastern *acta* were ratified, but the allusion in *Att.* 2.9.1 to the lavishing of kingdoms on tetrarchs and in *Att.* 2.16.2 to revenues from Mt. Antilibanus must refer to these *acta*, which would mean that they had been ratified by April. It should also be noted that the new agrarian law was being financed from the proceeds of the eastern settlement, which made its validation a matter of urgency.

10. The shortage of land available for distribution is alluded to in *Att.* 2.15.1. For the terms of the *Lex Campana*, see *Att.* 2.16.1. Dio 38.7.3. Suetonius, *Jul.* 20. Velleius 2.44.4. Appian, *BC* 2.10. Plutarch, *Cat. min.* 33.1. The commission of twenty was also

Other laws were meanwhile being enacted by Caesar's chief adherent among the tribunes, P. Vatinius,[11] and it was he who was the agent of the most important legislation of the entire year, the law that conferred on Caesar for a period of five years the governorship of Cisalpine Gaul and Illyricum with command of three legions. This replaced the provincial assignment decreed by the Senate before the consular elections for 59 and described by Suetonius as *silvae callesque*. The precise nature of that assignment is unknown, but there is broad agreement that it represented some form of minor administrative task in rural Italy. Certainly, it was a most unusual consular *provincia,* and, in view of the inveterate hostility between Caesar and the *optimates,* its selection must surely be seen as another attempt by the conservative *principes* to discomfit their enemy and frustrate his ambitions.[12] The *Lex Vatinia* negated that attempt and put Caesar in control of an important province and a sizeable army.[13]

---

to have charge of the distributions in Campania (Varro, *RR* 1.2.10). The area involved was about 200 square miles. See M. A. Levi, "Una pagina di storia agraria romana," *Atene e Roma* 3 (1922), 239–52. For the history of the region, see Brunt, *Italian Manpower,* 315–17. The only other law known to have been passed by Caesar in 59 was an elaborate extortion measure. See Gruen, *Last Generation,* 239–43. He also arranged to have the *acta diurna* of both the Senate and the people compiled and published. Suetonius, *Jul.* 20.1.

11. Vatinius passed a bill relating to the challenging of jurors (*Vat.* 27), and other measures described by Cicero as involving treaties with states, kings, tetrarchs, and the expenditure of public funds. *Vat.* 29. Cf. *Att.* 2.9.1. Taylor (*AJP* 72 [1951], 263) believes these measures took the place of senatorial transactions with foreign embassies, which could not have taken place in the usual way in February, since Bibulus, who had the *fasces* in that month, was in retirement and would not have summoned the Senate. It seems more likely, however, that these laws related to aspects of the settlement of the East not covered in the bill ratifying Pompey's *acta.*

12. This was the opinion of Suetonius (*Jul.* 19.2). Balsdon's contention ("Consular Provinces under the Late Republic," *JRS* 29 [1939], 180ff.) that the Senate acted so as to leave the consuls of 59 free for reassignment to Gaul if fresh trouble erupted there, seems far-fetched. At the time of the Senate's decision the Gallic crisis appeared to be over and, besides, major steps had already been taken to deal with any threat from that area. *Att.* 1.19.2–3. Balsdon's idea has resurfaced recently in P. J. Rhodes, "Silvae Callesque," *Historia* 27 (1978), 617–20, and Seager, *Pompey,* 83. A more reasoned discussion occurs in J. W. Rich, *"Silvae Callesque," Latomus* 45 (1986), 505–21.

13. For ancient references to the law, see Dio 38.8.5. Suetonius, *Jul.* 22. Plutarch, *Caes.* 14.6; *Pomp.* 48.3. Velleius 2.44.5. Appian, *BC* 2.13. Orosius 6.7.1. *Vat.* 35–36. *Sest.* 135. *Prov. cons.* 36–37. The date of the *Lex Vatinia* remains disputed. It was passed before July, when Cicero was offered the position of *legatus* on Caesar's staff (*Att.* 2.19.5). The only other significant evidence is an allusion in a letter of Cicero from the end of April (*Att.* 2.16.2) to Caesar's army, which must refer to the Gallic army, and this would seem to favor a date prior to that time. March was very likely the month when

Soon afterwards his provincial mandate was extended further. On the motion of Pompey, the Senate, aware that a *lex* would secure whatever it refused to grant, and anxious, no doubt, to preserve as far as possible its traditional control over the allocation of provinces, added Transalpine Gaul to Caesar's jurisdiction with an additional legion. The action was not, however, as surprising or significant as might first appear. The two Gauls had been administered by a single governor in the recent past, and growing threats to the security of the area from migrations and internal squabbles in free Gaul made a return to a single administration at this time militarily desirable. In any event, since the main Roman forces on the northern frontier were concentrated in Cisalpine Gaul, the primary responsibility for the entire region would inevitably devolve in any major crisis on the governor of that province. Caesar was exultant after securing the provinces, and a few days later made the triumphalist and provocative remark in a full Senate that he would henceforth dance on the heads of all his enemies.[14]

The early show of force and evident superiority of the *potentia* of the dynasts enabled the rush of legislation put forward by Caesar and Vatinius to pass easily into law. But the position of the alliance was by no means totally secure or its long-term control assured. An active opposition continued and, as the oppressive character of the regime became more apparent and the traditional Roman antipathy toward any man-

provincial appointments were normally considered by the Senate (see Balsdon, *JRS* 29 [1939], 66) and would therefore be an appropriate time for the introduction of any special provision regarding the provinces. See Gelzer, *Hermes* 63 (1928), 113–37. Taylor, *AJP* 72 (1951), 264–66; *Historia* 17 (1968), 182–88. Meier, *Historia* 10 (1961), 68–98.

14. Suetonius, *Jul.* 22.1–2. *Att.* 8.3.3 shows that Pompey was behind the motion. C. Piso had governed both Gauls in 66–65. Dio 36.37.2. *Att.* 1.1.2. The grant of Transalpine Gaul by the Senate meant it could be reassigned annually in accordance with the *Lex Sempronia. Fam.* 1.7.10. *Prov. cons.* 36–37. It is surprising that the *Lex Vatinia* did not include Transalpine Gaul in the first place. The answer may be related to the death in April 59 of Metellus Celer, who had been assigned the province by special decree of the Senate in 60. *Att.* 1.19.2; 2.5.2. Caesar may not have wanted to antagonize this powerful family by taking over a province to which Celer had not yet even set out. Broughton's argument ("Metellus Celer's Gallic Province," *TAPA* 79 [1948], 73–76) that Metellus was prevented by the tribune Flavius from going to his province in 60 and thereby lost it altogether, is very tenuous. Metellus badly wanted the command (*Att.* 1.20.5) and clearly expected to have it even after the main confrontation with Flavius was past. Even if he had been kept from going to his province in 60 by Flavius, he would still have expected to hold it as a proconsular command.

ifestation of despotic power began to take effect, a more general and increasingly more visible hostility toward the triumvirs emerged.

The active opposition encompassed many elements of the aristocracy, which reacted strongly, in characteristic oligarchic fashion, to a threat to its collective domination of the political process and managed, despite the lack of a strong, unified leadership and a coordinated response, to provide a sustained resistance of various forms that proved highly troublesome and disquieting for the triumvirs. In the forefront were Bibulus and Cato. The former waged an unremitting war of propaganda by means of edicts and speeches posted in the Forum. He evidently had, like so many of his countrymen, considerable skills in invective, and he used them to good effect to produce Archilochean denunciations of the careers and characters of Pompey and Caesar. His pasquinades were eagerly read and copied, and he became something of a heroic figure, praised as if he were a Fabius who had delivered the state.[15]

Cato offered a more conventional but no less vehement challenge. He followed his efforts to obstruct the first agrarian bill with a refusal to take the oath to abide by its terms, which Caesar, in accordance with the precedent established by Saturninus in 100, had included in the provisions of the bill as a requirement for all senators. He was finally prevailed upon to swear, but only after numerous appeals from relatives and friends, including Cicero, and only after dramatizing his dissent by waiting until the last day of the period allowed for the taking of the oath. Subsequently, he continued to show defiance and opposition by refusing to attend meetings of the Senate and by speaking out in the most trenchant terms against the legislative initiatives and general behavior of the dynasts. He attacked the *Lex Campana* at a *contio* and, if Plutarch is to be believed, to such effect that Caesar once more ordered his imprisonment and once more saw the strategy misfire as demonstrations of support quickly compelled his release. He also condemned the grants of the Gallic provinces, warning the people that they themselves by their votes were setting a tyrant in the citadel of Rome. New marriages contracted by Pompey and Caesar near the middle of 59, when Pompey married Caesar's daughter, Julia, and Caesar married Calpurnia, the daughter of

---

15. *Att.* 2.19.2,5; 2.20.4, 6; 2.21.3–5. *Vat.* 21–22. Suetonius, *Jul.* 9.2, 49.2. Plutarch, *Pomp.* 48.4. See C. Meier, *Res Publica Amissa* (Wiesbaden, 1966), 282–85.

L. Piso, a consular candidate for 58, provided him with another occasion for denunciation of their actions and purposes, as he accused them of intolerable trafficking in power through the use of women.[16]

But there were many others who also stood in open opposition to the triumvirs, among them several *consulares*. L. Lucullus, on at least one occasion, presumably in connection with the bill ratifying the eastern settlement, angered Caesar sufficiently by the outspokenness of his criticism that he resorted to threats to silence him. Metellus Celer continued the stance in opposition to Pompey and to land legislation that he had adopted as consul in 60 and joined Cato in initially refusing to swear the oath to uphold the agrarian law. The aged Gellius Publicola, despite a long association with Pompey, could not accept the implications of the *Lex Campana* and pledged, as long as he lived, to resist its implementation.[17]

Numerous less senior opponents are recorded. M. Petreius, an ex-praetor who had won high distinction during more than thirty years of military service, some of it almost certainly under Pompey, forcefully indicated his disapproval by walking from the Senate in support of Cato, after Caesar had ordered the latter imprisoned, and flatly declaring that he would prefer to be in prison with Cato than in the Senate with Caesar.[18] Three tribunes, Domitius Calvinus and C. Fannius, both *nobiles*, and Q. Ancharius of praetorian family, supported Bibulus in his efforts to block the first agrarian bill and later, again following the lead of the consul, tried to prevent further legislation by declaring that they were watching the heavens.[19] The younger Curio became a caustic and celebrated critic of the triumvirs as the year progressed, delivering vitriolic attacks on

16. Plutarch, *Cat. min.* 32–33; *Caes.* 14.5; *Pomp.* 48.4. Dio 38.7.1–2. Appian, *BC* 2.12, 14. *Att.* 2.21.1. Cicero makes clear in *Sest.* 63 that Cato refused to attend the Senate in 59.

17. Suetonius, *Jul.* 20.4. Plutarch, *Luc.* 42.6. Dio 38.7.1. Plutarch, *Cic.* 26.3. The elder Curio might be added to this list. Around the mid-fifties he published a dialogue vilifying Caesar with emphasis on the events of 59. *Brut.* 218–19. Suetonius, however, speaks of attacks by Curio in speeches (*Jul.* 9.2, 49.1, 50.1, 52.3). Whether these were speeches contained in the dialogue or separate attacks delivered in 59 cannot be determined, but Cicero's description of the elder Curio in *Vat.* 24 as an unremitting foe of all *improbi* and a particularly outspoken defender of liberty whom Vatinius wanted to destroy along with his son in 59 suggests he may have been an open critic of the dynasts in that year.

18. Sallust, *Cat.* 59. 4–6. Dio 38.3.2.

19. *Sest.* 113. *Vat.* 16. Dio 38.6.1. *Schol. Bob.* 135, 146, 151, Stangl.

Pompey and Caesar.[20] Another young *nobilis*, M. Juventius Laterensis, publicly registered his dissent by giving up his candidature for the tribunate rather than take the oath demanded of all candidates for office by the *Lex Campana*.[21] Other open dissenters included Cato's foremost *aemulatores*, M. Favonius and P. Servilius Junior, steadfast backers of their idol in all things in this period and consistent opponents of the triumvirs in succeeding years.[22]

Behind these individual acts and expressions of opposition there was a general mood of indignation in the Senate at the behavior of the dynasts and the state to which they had reduced the *respublica*. It was muted for the most part, its expression confined chiefly to talk on the social circuit and at dinner parties. But occasionally it broke forth in demonstrations of support for men like Cato and Curio or was more indirectly signaled by boycotting of senatorial meetings. All in all, the triumvirs were made sufficiently aware that they retained scant goodwill anywhere within the senatorial order.[23]

They were further having difficulty in holding the loyalty of even close allies. Q. Arrius, a loyal adherent of Crassus, was alienated by the refusal of the alliance to back him for the consulship of 58. Two of Pompey's strong supporters in the sixties, C. Memmius and Metellus Nepos, had become disenchanted with the direction of events as early as April 59. Memmius's estrangement persisted, and as praetor in 58 he initiated with Domitius Ahenobarbus a movement to overturn Caesar's *acta*. The ex-

20. *Att.* 2.7.3; 2.8.1; 2.12.2; 2.18.1; 2.19.3; 2.24.2–3. Suetonius, *Jul.* 50.1. Cf. *Vat.* 24.

21. *Att.* 2.18.2. *Planc.* 52–53.

22. Dio 38.7.1. *Att.* 1.14.5; 1.19.9; 2.1.10. Cf. *Q.F.* 2.3.2. Servilius was married to Cato's niece Junia. Other likely opponents of the triumvirs may be derived from the list of those named by L. Vettius in the late summer of 59 as parties to a plot to murder Pompey. See *Att.* 2.24.2–3 and discussion of Vettius affair.

M. Terentius Varro is sometimes included among the open critics of the alliance on the basis of a statement in Appian (*BC* 2.9) that he wrote a monograph about the triumvirate in which he labeled the alliance and presumably the book Τρικάρανος, "the three-headed monster." But the date and character of this work are unknown, and our other evidence suggests Varro was a firm friend of Pompey in this period. He was a member of the land commission (Pliny, *NH*, 7.176. Varro, *RR* 1.2.10) and Cicero considered him very influential in 59. *Att.* 2.25.1. See W. S. Anderson, *Pompey, His Friends and the Literature of the First Century B.C.* (Berkeley, Calif., 1963), 45. R. Astbury, "Varro and Pomepy," *CQ* 17 (1967), 403–07.

23. *Att.* 2.18.1–2; 2.19.2; 2.20.3; 2.21.1; 2.23.2; 2.24.4. Dio 38.3.2. Plutarch, *Cat. min.* 33.2; *Caes.* 14.7–8.

tent and duration of Nepos's discontent remain uncertain.[24] The dynasts also lost many of their younger supporters. It would seem that much of the *iuventus* was initially favorably disposed toward Pompey and Caesar. The latter's social aims and program would have appealed to them. But they would not accept the despotic and self-serving aspects of his regime. Soon, like Curio, they saw the members of the alliance as *reges superbi* and reacted with appropriate anger and hostility.[25]

But most notable were the troubles of the triumvirs with their most mercurial ally, P. Clodius. Caesar, in his capacity as *pontifex maximus,* had passed a *lex curiata* in the early part of 59 sanctioning the adoption of Clodius into a plebeian family. Pompey had publicly associated himself with Caesar's action by assisting as augur at the taking of the auspices. The adoption was a major favor to Clodius, and the dynasts had every reason to expect that their enactment of it would insure them his loyalty and support.[26]

But the relationship did not run smoothly. Clodius took offense when he failed to win a place on the land commission and a promised *legatio* to Alexandria did not materialize, and by the end of April his relations with the dynasts had deteriorated to the degree that he was pursuing the tribunate as an enemy of Caesar and declaring his intention of using it to rescind Caesar's *acta*. The latter responded by disavowing the adoption.[27] A total and permanent rupture seemed in the offing. That did not happen, but neither was there any firm reconciliation. During the remainder of 59 Clodius avoided open confrontation with Pompey and Caesar and showed a ready willingness to attack their enemies in the oligarchy. But there was a marked ambivalence in his public attitude toward the dynasts and in general an independence and unpredictability

---

24. *Att.* 2.5.2; 2.7.3; 2.12.2. There were rumors of dissent even among the Board of Five (*Att.* 2.7.4). By August Cicero reports that all backers of the alliance had lost their enthusiasm (*Att.* 2.23.2). For Memmius's activities in 58, see Suetonius, *Jul.* 23.1. *Sest.* 40. *Schol. Bob.* 130, 146, Stangl.

25. *Att.* 2.7.3; 2.8.1.

26. *Att.* 2.7.2; 2.9.1; 2.12.1; 8.3.3. *Dom.* 37–41. *Har. resp.* 45. *Prov. cons.* 42. Dio 38.12.1–2. Plutarch, *Cat. min.* 33.3. Suetonius, *Jul.* 20. Velleius 2.45.

27. *Att.* 2.7.3; 2.9.1; 2.12.2; 2.15.2. The *legatio* to Alexandria was a commission to the court of Ptolemy Auletes chiefly for the purpose of exacting the money Ptolemy had agreed to pay for his recognition by Rome. *Att.* 2.7.3. Clodius was offered instead a *legatio* to Tigranes, king of Armenia. *Att.* 2.4.2; 2.7.2.

in his political responses that made him as much a threat as a support to the coalition.[28]

The difficulties of the triumvirs were not confined, however, to the ruling class. They faced growing antagonism in all segments of the society. The *equites,* despite the concessions to the *publicani,* were not yet ready to countenance a *regnum* and freely indicated their hostility.[29] The people as a whole, influenced, no doubt, by the vigorous protests and effective propaganda of enemies of the alliance as well as by their natural aversion to despotic government, soon replaced the early support generated by the land legislation with shows of indignation and dissent. They thronged to read Bibulus's edicts and extolled their author. At a gladiatorial show given by Gabinius, and at the Ludi Apollinares in early July, they cheered opponents of the coalition and greeted its members and their minions with stony silence or with catcalls and hisses. Passages in the plays that could be directed against Pompey as insults or reproaches were given emphasis by the actor Diphilus and brought thunderous applause and demands for encores. In the municipalities of Italy a similar mood prevailed and was given even freer expression. There was a feeling that *regnum* had settled on Rome and it was not to be endured.[30]

Pompey and Caesar reacted strongly to this varied opposition, a further indication of its extent and seriousness. Pompey, who was unused to insult or ridicule or public disfavor and was obsessed with his standing and reputation, found the situation especially disturbing. He had tried, after his initial declaration of support for Caesar, to keep as distant as possible from the irregularities and repressive practices of Caesar's regime and to abjure responsibility for them, but he had found himself at the center of the controversies they provoked and a leading target for the

28. *Att.* 2.22.1. It is clear from this letter that Clodius stopped short of openly attacking the triumvirate, but kept open the possibility that he would do so. The *boni* were more centrally his targets, and he deprived Bibulus of the opportunity for a final grand attack on Caesar's regime, when he prevented him addressing the people on the expiry of his consulship. Dio 38.12.3.

29. *Att.* 2.19.3. Shackleton Bailey, *Letters to Atticus,* 1.391 rightly dismisses the idea that Cicero was referring to the *equitum centuriae* rather than the entire equestrian order.

30. *Att.* 2.13.2; 2.19.2–3; 2.20.4; 2.21.1, 4–5. Cicero is sometimes accused of making too much of these popular reactions out of a natural desire to see the dynasts founder, but any such desire was tempered by his constant fear in 59 that strong opposition would bring greater repression, and there are no grounds for supposing that he significantly exaggerated the hostility and opposition experienced by the triumvirs.

abuse of the optimate opposition. Bibulus's edicts concentrated heavily on him and so enraged him that he attempted (pathetically and ineffectually, according to Cicero) to use the *contio* to offset their obviously high popular appeal and impact. He became increasingly disconcerted and exasperated by the extent of his unpopularity as the year progressed, and Cicero was in constant fear that he would use direct force to strike back at his enemies and secure his position.[31]

Caesar was also disquieted by the opposition, as his efforts to deal with it clearly show. Besides his use of force and intimidation to suppress any interference with the passage of his legislation, he was driven on several other occasions into angry or extreme responses. He reacted to the expression of disaffection by the *equites* and the general public with threats to repeal the Roscian law and the corn dole. When Bibulus postponed the elections to October, he went so far as to try with inflammatory rhetoric to incite a *contio* to march on the house of the consul. On another occasion his chief henchman, Vatinius, had Bibulus actually dragged from his home in an act of violent intimidation that was ended only by the intervention of other tribunes.[32]

The marriage alliance in May was another major initiative to discourage and defend against the rising tide of opposition. Sudden and unexpected, and requiring the breaking of an engagement between Julia and a loyal partisan of Caesar, Q. Servilius Caepio, it was evidently prompted by a freshly recognized mutual need for the added security of closer ties. The new commitment to full cooperation was underlined by the simultaneous displacement of Crassus by Pompey as the speaker first called on by Caesar in the Senate. Caesar's own marriage to Calpurnia about the same time linked him to a prominent candidate for the consulship of 58, creating a second ally for the coalition among the consular candidates alongside Pompey's longtime adherent, A. Gabinius. The determination of the dynasts to maintain their domination and safeguard it for the future was being firmly demonstrated.[33]

---

31. *Att.* 2.16.2; 2.19.2; 2.21.3–4; 2.22.6; 2.23.2.
32. *Att.* 2.19.3; 2.21.5. *Vat.* 22. Dio 38.6.6.
33. *Att.* 2.17.1. Suetonius, *Jul.* 21. Plutarch, *Caes.* 14.4–5; *Pomp.* 47.6. Dio 38.9.1. Appian, *BC* 2.14. Munzer (*RE* 2A.1776ff.) puts forward the view that Julia's fiancé, Caepio, was in fact M. Brutus, Caesar's future assassin, who was adopted into the family of the Servilii Caepiones, but the identification is not generally accepted. Pompey's *legatus* in the eastern wars is a more likely candidate. Plutarch, *Pomp.* 34.5. Florus 1.41.10.

In the late summer there occurred an event which perhaps best illustrates the bitter, confrontational character of Roman politics in 59 and the nervousness and insecurity of Pompey and Caesar. L. Vettius, an *eques* who had acted as informer during the Catilinarian crisis, tried to involve the younger Curio in a plot to murder Pompey. Curio told his father, who in turn told Pompey. When the matter came before the Senate, Vettius alleged that a group of young men, including Aemilius Paulus, M. Brutus, and L. Lentulus (the last acting with his father's knowledge), had formed a conspiracy under Curio's leadership and with help from Bibulus and had planned to attack Pompey in the Forum during Gabinius's gladiatorial show. The Senate did not believe the story and decreed that Vettius be imprisoned. The next day Caesar brought him to the Rostra and had him tell his tale again. What he produced was a much amended version, however, that omitted Brutus and added the names of Lucullus, C. Fannius, Domitius Ahenobarbus, Cicero's son-in-law C. Piso, and M. Laterensis. He implicated Cicero indirectly by saying an eloquent *consularis* had said a Servilius Ahala or a Brutus needed to be found. Vatinius then promulgated a bill to establish a special *quaestio* to investigate the charges, but the proposal was not well received. Soon afterwards Vettius was found strangled in prison and the matter was dropped.[34]

Cicero shared the *communis opinio* of the time and believed the whole affair was a scheme by Caesar to implicate Curio in criminal activity that would expose him to prosecution, the original plan being that Vettius, armed and accompanied by armed slaves, would be arrested in the Forum and would then offer to turn informer. That was foiled by the action of the Curios, and Caesar then primed Vettius to produce his expanded list of conspirators at the *contio*.

Modern scholars have been loath to accept Cicero's version of the affair and have produced a bewildering array of speculative variations on it.[35] Cicero too was speculating to some extent, an inevitable exercise in any attempt to unravel conspiracies, but he was doing so as a well-placed

---

34. *Att.* 2.24. *Vat.* 24–26. *Sest.* 132. *Flacc.* 96. Cf. Suetonius, *Jul.* 20.5. Dio 38.9. Appian, *BC* 2.12. Plutarch, *Luc.* 42.7–8. *Schol. Bob.* 139, 148, Stangl.

35. W. C. McDermott, "Vettius ille, ille noster index," *TAPA* 80 (1949), 351–67. L. R. Taylor, "The Date and Meaning of the Vettius Affair," *Historia* 1 (1950), 45–51. W. Allen, "The Vettius Affair Once More," *TAPA* 81 (1950), 153–63. Meier, *Historia* 10 (1961), 88ff. R. Seager, "Clodius, Pompeius and the Exile of Cicero," *Latomus* 24 (1965), 519–31. Gelzer, *Caesar*, 90–92. D. Stockton, *Cicero: A Political Biography* (Oxford, 1971), 183–86. Ward, *Crassus*, 236–42.

and well-informed contemporary observer, and his conclusions cannot easily be disregarded unless obviously flawed by errors of fact or major improbabilities. In the event few such flaws can be discerned in his basic contention that the affair was a Caesarian strategem to damage or remove important political opponents. All of those named by Vettius are known to have opposed or to have had reason to oppose one or more members of the coalition.[36] The suborning of witnesses as a means of contriving criminal prosecutions against political enemies was by no means unheard of in this era, as events during the Catilinarian crisis and the activities of the self-same Vettius at that time illustrate. Nor were such tactics inconsistent with the general approach and disposition shown by Pompey and Caesar in dealing with their opponents in 59. Cicero in fact had long been expecting them to produce some such pretext for oppression and accurately predicted that efforts to institute prosecutions would follow the disclosures.[37]

In the final analysis, only one aspect of Cicero's version raises any serious question. Vettius's differing stories in the Senate and at the *contio* are hard to understand if the same hand was guiding him from the start. This difficulty, unexplained by Cicero, must cast some doubt on the notion that Caesar was the initial instigator of the affair, and it may well be that Vettius, a notorious intriguer, was originally an independent agent or was acting in collaboration with lesser figures in Caesar's coterie.[38] In any event, it is certain that Caesar took control after the initial revelation and suborned Vettius to accuse a wide range of opponents of the triumvirate as a prelude to their prosecution through a special *quaestio*. It was a feeble and transparent maneuver and quickly foundered, but it was symptomatic of hardening hostilities that were fostering extreme expedients and creating conditions of fear and uncertainty.[39]

36. See McDermott, *TAPA* 80 (1949), 363ff. Seager, *Latomus* 24 (1965), 525ff.

37. For the activities of informers during the Catilinarian crisis, see Sallust, *Cat.* 48.3–9, 49. Dio 37.35.1–2, 41.2–4. Suetonius, *Jul.* 17.1. Appian, *BC* 2.6. For Cicero's fears, see *Att.* 2.22.6; 2.24.4.

38. There were other rumors of plots against Pompey's life in 59. Bibulus had sent Pompey a warning of one on May 13 (*Att.* 2.24.2). In such circumstances it is not inconceivable that men like Vettius were seeking to find or to create an opportunity to ply their informer's trade.

39. It is commonly urged that one of Caesar's purposes in promoting the scheme was to scare his unhappy and wavering ally, Pompey, into closer association with himself and away from any thought of rapprochement with the *optimates*. But there is no evidence that

This troubled atmosphere persisted to the end of 59. The elections were finally held in October, and friends of the dynasts, L. Piso and A. Gabinius, secured the consulship.[40] But two well-known dissidents, Domitius Ahenobarbus and C. Memmius, gained election to the praetorship, and a high level of opposition and of tension continued. Cicero recounts an incident from near the end of the year that he felt typified the dire state of things and betokened a defunct Republic. A young activist, C. Porcius Cato, attempted to prosecute Gabinius on a charge of bribery. The praetor in charge of the *quaestio,* who was obviously a friend of Pompey, refused to make himself available to hear the *postulatio.* Cato then addressed a *contio* and called Pompey an unofficial dictator. He was attacked and came within an ace of losing his life. Gabinius was later to boast that he had been rescued from prosecution by armed gangs.[41] Caesar's consulship was ending as it had begun, in a climate of confrontation and lawless violence.

Cicero's Political Posture in 59

In the letter to Atticus in December 60 which contained news of Caesar's projected alliance with Pompey and Crassus, Cicero, engaging, as he described it, in an exercise in Socratic dialectic, had considered all sides of his own situation and the varied implications of the options available to him. He could offer vigorous resistance, which would mean a fight, but one rich in glory. He could keep quiet, which would be

Pompey's discontent put any strains on his relations with Caesar or turned his mind to the unlikely hope of reconciliation with his chief attackers. On the contrary, as Cicero's evidence makes plain, the likeliest consequence of his frustration was a more extreme posture and the oppression rather than conciliation of his optimate foes. *Att.* 2.14.1; 2.19.2; 2.20.5; 2.21.1, 4; 2.22.6. A related idea (Allen, *TAPA* 81 [1950], 158–62) that Caesar was especially aiming to sow distrust between Pompey and Cicero again assumes an imminent rift in the coalition and misreads Cicero's place and concerns in 59.

40. Bibulus was the consul who had charge of the elections in 59, a duty apparently determined by lot. He had postponed them in an edict in April (*Att.* 2.15.2), presumably in the expectation that the popularity of the triumvirs would decline. In July he issued another edict fixing October 18 as the date (*Att.* 2.20.6). Whether he left his house to preside over the elections or allowed Caesar to preside is unknown. See Linderski, *Historia* 14 (1965), 423–42. Taylor and Broughton, *Historia* 17 (1968), 166–72.

41. *Q.F.* 1.2.15. C. Cato, though a relation of M. Cato, did not belong to the latter's circle. A demagogic and turbulent opportunist, described by Cicero as "adulescens nullius consili," he emerged in the mid-fifties as an ally of Clodius and Crassus. See Shackleton Bailey, *Letters to Atticus,* 2.201.

equivalent to retiring to an Italian backwater, or he could lend assistance as Caesar wished and expected him to do, which would bring him powerful friends and a peaceful old age. The conclusion of his Socratic exercise was that, in accordance with the admonishments of his own poem *De consulatu,* he must hold fast to the course he had pursued from his youth through his consulship and continue to court fame and good men's praises. That meant choosing the path of resistance and upholding the principle that the foremost duty is to fight for the fatherland.[42]

This high-minded commitment to his former policies and the spirit of 63 does not seem, however, to have survived the first major confrontation of 59—the dispute in connection with Caesar's first agrarian law. There is no indication anywhere in Cicero's own writings or in any other ancient source that he associated himself in any way with the opposition to that proposal, or offered any form of independent dissent. Leadership of the optimate resistance fell to Cato and Bibulus, and it must be assumed that Cicero declined the *dimicatio plena laudis* he had spoken of to Atticus in December and stood with the many *principes* who, in Dio's account, registered neither opposition nor approval. The one mention of his name in connection with the land law, his efforts to persuade Cato to take the oath prescribed in the bill for all senators, is a further sign that his role was passive. There is similarly no record of involvement by him in any form of resistance to the other laws enacted by Caesar and Vatinius in the early part of the year, a silence that affirms he had suffered a quick change of heart when faced with the grim realities of Caesar's regime, and had turned toward the option of quiescence.[43]

He did on one occasion, in the course of his defense in February or March of his former colleague in the consulship, C. Antonius, make certain remarks critical of the state of the *respublica.* He later claimed in the *De domo* that it was in reaction to these criticisms that Caesar and Pompey, at a meeting of the *comitia curiata* held only three hours after the remarks were spoken, enacted the adoption of Clodius. The claim is commonly accepted without question, and on its basis Cicero is often presented as an early opponent of the triumvirate who fell victim to his

---

42. *Att.* 2.3.3–4.

43. Dio 38.2.2. Plutarch, *Cat. min.* 32.4–6. There is one positive indication in a letter from the end of April or beginning of May (*Att.* 2.16.3) that Cicero had offered no opposition prior to that time. He writes: "Quodsi in eam me partem incitarem, profecto iam aliquam reperirem resistendi viam."

penchant for outspokenness and incurred, in consequence, the dynasts' disfavor and ultimately the penalty of exile. Yet there is much that is questionable about the statement of the *De domo,* and the deductions from it are difficult to reconcile with the overall evidence for Cicero's political stance and outlook throughout 59. The trial has been given undue prominence in accounts of Cicero's political life, and the facts surrounding it deserve further scrutiny.[44]

After his consulship Antonius had governed Macedonia, which had been ceded to him by Cicero in 63 to secure his cooperation. Complaints about his administration were already being made in the Senate before the end of 62, and Pompey, who was then nearing the end of his journey home from the East, was adding his voice to the criticism and declaring his intention to seek Antonius's recall. Antonius, however, somehow managed to delay his return until the end of 60, but the feeling against him had not abated, and a prosecution had been set in motion even before he reached the city.[45]

It is uncertain whether the charge was treason or extortion, but the bulk of the evidence favors the former. Antonius had engaged in military adventurism with disastrous results and had almost certainly violated Sulla's *lex de maiestate,* which imposed strict controls on a governor's right to leave his province or wage war.[46] Charges of involvement in the conspiracy of Catiline also figured prominently in the prosecution's case and, on the evidence of Cicero, were the decisive factor in the jury's decision to convict. These charges also came within the purview of the *quaestio de maiestate,* and their inclusion and centrality in the case are consistent with the practice in Roman courts of adducing all violations of the law in question that could be alleged against the defendant, in the hope that the jury would find him guilty of at least one of them. In a trial

44. *Dom.* 41. Cicero's claim is repeated in Suetonius, *Jul.* 20.4. Dio (38.10.1, 4) asserts that Cicero attacked Caesar at the trial, but does not connect this with the adoption of Clodius. For modern opinions, see J. L. Strachan-Davidson, *Cicero and the Fall of the Roman Republic* (London, 1896), 216–17. R. E. Smith, *Cicero the Statesman* (Cambridge, 1966), 148–49. Stockton, *Cicero: A Political Biography* (Oxford, 1971), 168. D. R. Shackleton Bailey, *Cicero* (New York, 1971), 50–51. Gelzer, *Caesar,* 70; *Pompeius,* 135. J. van Ooteghem, *Pompée le grand* (Brussels, 1954), 311.

45. *Pis.* 5. Plutarch, *Cic.* 12.3. *Fam.* 5.6.4. *Att.* 1.12.1; 2.2.3.

46. Dio 38.10.1–3. Livy, *Per.* 103. Cf. the trial of Gabinius in 54 on a charge of *maiestas* and Cicero's catalogue of his violations of the *Lex Cornelia maiestatis* in *Pis.* 50. Antonius's military failures are a far more likely cause of the complaints and high feeling against him than reports of extortion, which seldom caused a major stir in Rome.

for extortion, accusations relating to a conspiracy would have been irrelevant to the law under which the defendant was being charged and, while they might have been introduced to damage the character and credibility of the accused, they could not have formed a legitimate basis for conviction.[47]

But whatever the charge, the case was reasonably routine, with no special features or implications to lend it particular political significance. It is likely that Pompey, in view of his earlier promotion of Antonius's recall, favored conviction. Caesar, who was an old enemy of Antonius and whose lackey, Vatinius, was collaborating with the prosecution, probably did also. But it would be wrong to deduce that the prosecution was therefore expressly a triumviral enterprise or that Cicero in taking the defense was coming into direct collision with the dynasts.[48] The hostility of Pompey and Caesar toward this notoriously corrupt and much-despised proconsul was shared by many of varying political hues, and the prime movers in the prosecution had, in fact, closer ties to Cicero than to any of the dynasts.[49] The most active instigator of the trial was P. Nigidius Figulus, a respected senator renowned for his learning, who was a close friend of Cicero and had collaborated with him in the suppression of Catiline.[50] The chief prosecutor, M. Caelius Rufus, had been placed under Cicero's tutelage on assuming the *toga virilis* and had forged a lasting friendship with his patron. His motive in undertaking the prosecution was a common and personal one: he was seeking in accordance with ancient practice and the example of earlier eminent statesmen to show his

47. *Cael.* 15, 74, 78. Dio 38.10. *Schol. Bob.* 94, Stangl. See R. G. Austin, *M. Tulli Ciceronis Pro M. Caelio Oratio*, 3d ed. (Oxford, 1960), 158–59. M. Alexander, "Repetition of Prosecution, and the Scope of Prosecutions, in the Standing Criminal Courts of the Late Republic," *Classical Antiquity* 1 (1982), 141–66. The only evidence to suggest the charge was extortion is the reference in *Schol. Bob.* 94, Stangl. An allusion in Quintilian, *Inst.* 4.2.123, referring to a description by the prosecutor M. Caelius of Antonius's drunken condition before a battle, provides no help in determining the charge.

48. Caesar had prosecuted Antonius for extortion in 76. Asconius 84, 92, Clark. Plutarch, *Caes.* 4.1–2. For Vatinius's involvement, see *Vat.* 27–28. E. S. Gruen ("The Trial of C. Antonius," *Latomus* 32 [1973], 301–10), greatly stretching the evidence, presents the prosecution as a joint initiative of the triumvirs and the first instance of their collaboration in the courts. See also his *Last Generation,* 287–89.

49. Cicero indicates that the *boni* as a whole were hostile to him (*Att.* 1.12.1). Even the Catilinarian sympathizers hated him, seeing him as a renegade. *Flacc.* 95.

50. *Att.* 2.2.3. *Fam.* 4.13.2. *Sulla* 42.

industry by means of an *illustris accusatio*.[51] As for Cicero, he shared the general antipathy toward the accused and undertook his defense with reluctance but for the compelling reason that he was in Antonius's debt and was bound in honor to aid his benefactor in a crisis involving his vital interests.[52] The reasons for the trial and the motives of the participants were therefore commonplace and uncomplicated, and warrant no assumptions of unusual political ramifications.

Cicero's criticism of the state of the *respublica* did introduce a political note, but his story of its effects in the *De domo* is replete with improbabilities and can hardly be taken at face value.[53] Even assuming that the members of the College of Pontiffs and the lictors representing the thirty *curiae* could have been contacted and assembled in so short a time, the idea that Caesar and Pompey took so important a step with such impetuous haste in response to remarks made by an advocate in the special circumstances of a criminal defense itself stretches credibility.[54]

Besides, the conspicuous flouting of established procedures entailed in such a hurried enactment of a *rogatio* would surely have been unacceptable to Clodius as an unnecessary endangerment of the validity of the

51. *Cael.* 9–10, 73. Caelius had links to Crassus also, but there is no reason to believe he was an active ally of Crassus at this time or collaborating with him in any way in this trial.

52. See *Att.* 1.12.1. *Fam.* 5.5. That the loan which Cicero had been trying to negotiate with Antonius had come through is clear from *Att.* 1.14.7. Gruen's contention (*Latomus* 32 [1973], 303ff.) that Cicero undertook the defense because he saw it as an attack on the man officially credited with the defeat of Catiline's army and thus indirectly an attack on himself, has little to commend it. It is based on efforts by Cicero later in 59 in his defense of Flaccus, who had also been prominent in the suppression of the conspiracy, to link the two cases and present them as part of a scheme by evil men to destroy all who had led the struggle against the conspirators. Cicero was fond of parading dangers, real or imagined, from the *improbi*, and it was besides a useful argument to present his client as the target of a spreading threat to the saviors of the state in 63. But the fact was that in the trial of Antonius, as Cicero himself later emphasized, the accused was portrayed as the collaborator rather than the conqueror of Catiline, and was damaged by that association, and his conviction, therefore, vindicated rather than threatened the suppressors of Catiline.

53. The precise nature of the criticism can only be guessed. Cicero's description is as follows: "Questus sum . . . quaedam de republica, quae mihi visa sunt ad illius miseri causam pertinere."

54. For the procedure of the *comitia curiata* in relation to *adrogatio*, the form of adoption involved in the case of Clodius, see Gellius, *NA* 5.19. *Dom.* 34–38. Tacitus, *Hist.* 1.15. G. W. Botsford, *The Roman Assemblies* (New York, 1968), 160–61.

adoption that could lead to its future annulment.[55] Finally, the implied, and only conceivable, reason for the precipitate response—to give a dramatic warning to Cicero to stay silent—was largely, if not completely, negatived by the fact that Pompey gave Cicero immediate and repeated assurances that the adoption was not aimed against him and that he had, in fact, before consenting to it, exacted a pledge from Clodius that he would not use his tribunate to harm Cicero.[56]

It should also be emphasized that only once did Cicero link Caesar's enactment of the adoption to the criticisms made at the trial of Antonius. On other occasions when he alludes to Caesar's action, he is far less certain about the reasons for it, and advances several suggestions such as pressure from Clodius and the opposition of the *principes*. He retains anger with himself as a further possibility, but when he gives grounds for the anger he attributes it not to his remarks at the trial, but to his persistent refusal to accept Caesar's favors and join his side.[57]

These explanations of the background to the adoption more likely represent the truth than the statement of the *De domo*. Clodius was determined to become tribune. The office, as his use of it in 58 demonstrated, was crucial to his political plans. He had tried hard in 60 to secure his transference to the *plebs,* and he is likely to have intensified his efforts with the emergence of the triumvirate. He had claims on the friendship of at least two of its members and had much to offer them besides.[58] His political abilities and influence had been shown in the Bona Dea affair. He was emerging as the clear leader of the Claudian clan with the capacity and determination to exploit the family's great resources to maximum effect. Caesar and Pompey badly needed such friends in the face of the

55. Most obviously the *Lex Caecilia Didia*, which prescribed a *trinum nundinum* between promulgation and voting, would have been violated. See *Dom.* 41. But there would also not have been time for the examination of the case by the pontiffs and the passage of a pontifical decree approving the adoption, which, according to Cicero (*Dom.* 34–38) and Gellius (*NA* 5.19.5) was a necessary preliminary to the *lex curiata*. See Quint. 2.4.35. It is also worth noting that the *optimates* accepted the validity of Clodius's adoption and the legality of his tribunate (*Dom.* 42. *Prov. cons.* 45), and that Cicero, in his many allusions in the letters of 59 to the adoption and to ways in which he might ridicule it, never raises the issue of its legality.

56. *Att.* 2.9.1; 2.19.4; 2.20.2; 2.21.6; 2.22.2; 2.23.3; 2.24.5; *Sest.* 15.

57. *Sest.* 16. *Har. resp.* 45. *Prov. cons.* 42.

58. See n. 26 above. He was an *adfinis* of Pompey (*Har. resp.* 45. Cf. Plutarch, *Cat. min.* 31.2; *Pomp.* 4.6.4), and the Bona Dea affair had allied him with Crassus and, according to Dio (38.12), disposed him to friendship with Caesar.

growing opposition in 59, and it was an obviously sensible step for them to seek to cement Clodius's support by conferring on him a major *beneficium.*[59] This does not mean that anger with Cicero played no part in their decision. It is clear that both of them valued and diligently cultivated Cicero's friendship in this period, and for good reasons.[60] Though the orator had lost his place as the leading voice of the *optimates,* he remained a respected figure who commanded wide influence among the great body of the prosperous that he liked to call his army and had, besides, the support of the large *clientela* that he had built and was continuing to build by his labors in the courts.[61] His refusal of Caesar's earnest bids for his cooperation did give offense and, no doubt, made the wooing of his archenemy a simpler step. But the purposes of that decision extended far beyond the figure of Cicero and so, it must be accepted, did the causes.[62]

What then lay behind the statements of the *De domo?* In that speech Cicero was seeking to marshall all possible arguments to prove that Clodius's adoption was illegal and all the *acta* of his tribunate accordingly invalid. The coincidence in time between the trial and the adoption and the seeming plausibility of a causal connection between the two events enabled him to link them with a measure of reasonableness and to postulate a procedure in relation to the adoption that provided additional grounds for his assault on its validity. Cicero was a skilled contriver of arguments and seldom scrupled to exploit all the rhetorical opportunities afforded by every aspect and circumstance of his case.[63]

But even in the *De domo* he did not claim that his criticisms of Caesar's regime were a declaration of open opposition to the coalition. On the contrary, he emphasized that the sole purpose of his complaints was to

59. For Clodius's early career and political resources, see A. W. Lintott, "P. Clodius Pulcher—Felix Catilina?" *Greece and Rome* 14 (1969), 157–69. E. S. Gruen, "P. Clodius: Instrument or Independent Agent?" *Phoenix* 20 (1966), 120–30. E. Rawson, "The Eastern Clientelae of Clodius and the Claudii," *Historia* 22 (1973), 219–39, and *Historia* 26 (1977), 340–57.

60. *Prov. cons.* 41. *Pis.* 79.

61. *Att.* 2.18.3; 2.19.4; 2.22.3; 2.25.2. *Q.F.* 1.2.16.

62. It is clear from *Att.* 9.2a.1 that Caesar did not take kindly to Cicero's rejection of his offers.

63. Such an argument might seem to have little point in a speech before the College of Pontiffs, who would have known the true facts, but the published version of the speech, as we have it, was aimed at a wider audience, and at posterity, and the arguments of this section could, of course, have been added in revisions for publication.

draw attention to aspects of the political situation that he considered prejudicial to his client, and he maintained that the import of his remarks was misrepresented by the villainous men who reported them to Pompey and Caesar. Cicero never made any pretense to being, at any time in 59, an open opponent of the triumvirs, and even if one accepts the statements of the *De domo* at face value, they provide no grounds for assuming that he was.[64]

Certainly by April he had moved far away from any thoughts of opposition and was totally committed to a policy of quiescence. His letters to Atticus during a stay in the country that extended through April and May make plain his thinking and his plans. He was glad that he had remained true to his principles and had rejected the offer to join the coalition. He expected that other offers would come his way, including the highly desirable *legatio* to Alexandria, but fears that he would seem to have been bribed into political apostasy and would draw the wrath of the *optimates* or, worse still, incur the opprobrium of history, made him reluctant to accept any favors from the dynasts. The same concerns a fortiori precluded any form of open support for the alliance.[65]

But his anxiety for his reputation no longer drove him to the state's defense in glorious opposition to those oppressing it. He had lost all appetite for the political fray and had even come to regard his earlier achievements as hollow. His disillusionment and weariness had reached the stage where he preferred to live under tyranny than to fight with the greatest hope of success. His wish was not only to withdraw from political activity but to banish all thought of politics from his mind and turn his entire attention back to intellectual pursuits, which he was convinced offered the greatest reward and which he now felt he ought never to have abandoned. He intended to cultivate a stoical indifference and to view political developments with philosophic calm from behind his books.[66]

He was less than successful in his pursuit of this scholarly retirement and detachment. Even as he disclaims interest in political affairs, he eagerly seeks and dissects every morsel of news from Rome.[67] His protestations of indifference are intermingled with expressions of hate for

64. *Dom.* 41: "Haec homines improbi ad quosdam viros fortes longe aliter atque a me dicta erant detulerunt."

65. *Att.* 2.4.2; 2.5.1. Cf. *Prov. cons.* 41. *Pis.* 79.

66. *Att.* 2.4.4; 2.5.2; 2.6.1–2; 2.7.4; 2.9.3; 2.13.2; 2.14.1; 2.16.3; 2.17.1–2.

67. *Att.* 2.4.4; 2.5.2; 2.11.1; 2.12.20.

the dynasts and of spiteful satisfaction at signs of their unpopularity and the prospect of their ultimate failure and downfall.[68] His cultivation of activities of the mind ended in a growing concentration of his efforts on a polemical history of recent events that he did not intend to publish and that served mainly to give vent to his hatreds and frustrations.[69] But though he proved temperamentally incapable of a mental withdrawal from politics or a dispassionate acceptance of the current political situation, his aversion in this period to the political life and determination to stay removed from it were real and deep-rooted.

His return to Rome at the beginning of June brought no significant change in his political stance or outlook. There was renewed pressure for his cooperation from the dynasts. Offers to join Caesar's staff or to accept a *libera legatio* came about immediately and, when one of the land commissioners died in July, his position was added to the list of inducements. Cicero was especially tempted by the *legatio* in the service of Caesar, which would have relieved him of any anxieties about Clodius, but he remained keenly aware that any such association with the dynasts would be a negation of his past endeavors and achievements, and in the end he accepted none of the offers.[70] But neither could he bring himself to join the opposition. He stood devoid of party or policy, and responded by holding fast to the abstentionist course to which he had so fervently committed himself in April and May. His perseverance in this passive stance is attested in several letters to Atticus and confirmed by the absence of any record of any political action by him throughout the entire second half of 59, with the exception of an inconsequential involvement in the consular elections as the chief overseer for his *adfinis,* C. Calpurnius Piso, of the voting tablets of the *centuria praerogativa.*[71] Legal activity preoccupied him instead, as he threw himself with renewed energy into the cases that always came his way in abundance and that he

---

68. *Att.* 2.6.2; 2.7.4; 2.9.1–2; 2.12.1–2; 2.17.2.

69. On the urging of Atticus, he planned to write a geography, but made little headway. *Att.* 2.4.3; 2.6.1; 2.7.1. Cf. 2.12.3; 2.14.2. He gave more time to the polemical history (*Att.* 2.6.2; 2.8.1), which he alludes to as ἀνέκδοτα and which is generally believed to be the *De consiliis suis.* Cicero was still working on it in 44, and it was most likely not published before his death. *Att.* 14.17.6; 16.11.3. Dio 39.10. Plutarch, *Crassus* 13. K. Büchner, *RE* 7A.1267ff. R. Syme, *Sallust* (Berkeley, Calif., 1964), 62–64.

70. *Att.* 2.18.3; 2.19.2, 4–5. *Prov. cons.* 41–42. *Pis.* 79. *Att.* 9.2a.1.

71. *Att.* 2.19.2; 2.22.3; 2.23.3. For his part in the consular elections, see *Pis.* 11. *Post red. in sen.* 11.

especially relied on in times of political uncertainty or mishap as a means of maintaining his popularity and safeguarding his *dignitas*.[72]

Cicero's sustained policy of quiescence during this pivotal and eventful year in the history of the late Republic highlights the dramatic change that had taken place in his political outlook and expectations. He had lately seen himself as the Republic's saviour and foremost champion of its institutions and ideals and had aspired to a commanding place among its *principes* as an inspiring unifier of the *boni* and relentless foe of the *improbi*. Yet in this year, when the survival of the Republic was more seriously threatened than at any time since the eighties, and when significant and spirited opposition to its oppressors was being offered by many elements, he opted for silence and inaction, retreating from any responsibility to defend the beleaguered constitution and at times even renouncing concern for its fate. He had moved a long way from the proud hopes of his consulship and its immediate aftermath.

The main reasons for this remarkable mental turnabout and dispirited subsidence into virtual retirement from politics had their roots in the disillusionment with optimate policies and in the sense of personal alienation from the Senate's *principes* that Cicero had begun to experience in the final years of the sixties. The developments of 59 deepened this broad disillusionment with his erstwhile allies. The collapse of the Senate's rule and the domination of the dynasts he saw largely as a consequence and an almost inevitable culmination of the ruinous course of the *boni* in the preceding years, when, led by Cato, they had scorned his advice and, in a series of blunders, had alienated the *equites* and brought an end to the

72. *Att.* 2.22.3; 2.23.3. Cf. *Att.* 1.17.6. Three criminal cases in which he acted for the defense are recorded, two involving an otherwise unknown A. Minucius Thermus (*Flacc.* 98), and the case of L. Valerius Flaccus, who came to trial in August on a charge of extortion arising out of his governorship of Asia in 62. Gruen (*Last Generation,* 289–91) also presents this trial as a contest in the courts between the triumvirs and their opponents, and once again unduly stretches the evidence. Flaccus was supported by several enemies of the coalition, and the chief prosecutor D. Laelius was a friend of Pompey and was, apparently, backed by him in the prosecution (*Flacc.* 14). But, as so often, these lineups can be explained on grounds of *amicitia.* Flaccus had been a trusted ally of Cicero in the Catilinarian crisis and had been given the crucial task of arresting the Allobrogian envoys (*Cat.* 3.5). His other supporters P. Servilius Isauricus, Q. Metellus Creticus, and Cn. Domitius Calvinus were also *amici.* He had served under Servilius and Metellus, and Domitius had been his *legatus* in Asia. Pompey's opposition can be explained by the fact that he had unusually close ties to Asia (*Flacc.* 14) and he had a duty to look out for the interests of his clients. It is gratuitous to read political significance into the trial, and the case has no bearing on Cicero's political position or outlook at this time.

concordia he had so carefully established as the great prop of senatorial government.[73]

His sense of personal grievance against the Senate's leaders grew alongside this confirmation of his misgivings about their statesmanship. They had shown no greater regard for him than for his political objectives, and had denied him the place of honor and influence to which he believed his achievements entitled him. He was left disheartened and resentful and wholly disinclined to further political effort. A letter to Atticus at the end of April plainly shows his feelings. He complains bitterly that the *boni* had never, even in word, made him any return or shown him any gratitude for his devotion to their cause and declares that it was this denial of due recognition by his optimate colleagues more than any fear of the power of the dynasts that accounted for his abstentionist course in 59. Elsewhere he asserts that he now preferred to watch the ship of state founder under another pilot than to guide it aright with such ungrateful passengers, and he emphasizes that he had grown weary of the helm long before the emergence of the coalition took it from his hand.[74]

The new friendship with Pompey that he had cultivated in late 61 or 60 in reaction to his deteriorating relations with the *boni* was also inclining him toward a policy of inaction. Pompey worked hard throughout 59 to preserve that friendship and to minimize any offense that his role in the coalition might cause Cicero. He made much of the pledge he had exacted from Clodius before consenting to his adoption and continued to give Cicero assurances that he would hold Clodius to his promise whatever the cost. In general, he went out of his way to maintain a close and cordial relationship with Cicero and to persuade him that he valued their friendship most highly and was determined to meet the obligations it imposed on him to protect Cicero's interests.[75]

Cicero was by no means wholly convinced or placated by Pompey's assurances and cordiality. He had little faith left in the general's political or personal integrity. He considered him the real power behind the triumvirate and held him fully responsible for the extremism of Caesar's regime and its damaging effects on the constitution. He believed that nothing would deter him from the achievement of his ambitions, and it

---

73. *Att.* 2.9.1–2. Cf. *Att.* 1.18.3, 7; 1.19.6; 2.1.8.
74. *Att.* 2.7.4; 2.9.3; 2.16.2.
75. *Att.* 2.9.1; 2.19.4; 2.20.1–2; 2.21.6; 2.22.2; 2.23.3; 2.24.5. *Q.F.* 1.2.16.

was a violent reaction from him rather than Caesar that he especially feared when opposition to the coalition hardened in the course of 59. He also had doubts about the sincerity of his professions of friendship. His participation in the adoption of Clodius rankled deeply and left a lingering unease about his response in any future clash between the claims of friendship and political expediency.[76]

But despite his disapproval of Pompey's general course and distrust of his motives and character, Cicero was reluctant to stand against him and end their friendship. He was still powerfully drawn to him by the liking and affection he had always felt for him, and he wanted to believe the best of him even while he feared the worst. He was also still beguiled by the greatness of his name and achievements and, to an extent, by an idealized image of him that he had himself created. The result was a perplexing ambivalence that was to cloud his judgment and complicate his political decisions while Pompey lived, and it strongly disposed him in 59 to follow the path of quiescence.[77]

Other considerations reinforced these personal antipathies to political involvement in this period. Cicero believed that the triumvirs could not be successfully opposed in 59. They had established a *dominatio*. They controlled everything and were prepared to use their power to enforce their wishes. In such circumstances resistance, though honorable and understandable, could only provoke greater oppression that would tighten the grip of the oppressors and inflict more serious and more permanent damage on the institutions of the Republic. The more prudent course was to allow the political wheel to turn as smoothly as possible and effect, through the natural revolving movements of political affairs, the erosion of the power of the dynasts and the restoration of the old order. Early in 59 Cicero hoped dissension between the triumvirs and their supporters would hasten this process and bring a speedy end to the *dominatio*. Later in the year he abandoned such hopes and no longer expected a quick remedy, but he held to the belief that this political storm

76. *Att.* 2.9.1; 2.14.1; 2.16.2; 2.17.1; 2.20.1; 2.21.4,6; 2.22.2, 5–6. *Q.F.* 1.2.16. Cicero had made a final effort to restrain Pompey's *popularis* leanings by advising him against coalition with Caesar (*Fam.* 6.6.4. *Phil.* 2.2.3), but after that failed and the alliance became firmly established, all indications are that he abandoned any hope that Pompey would become a *bonus civis*.

77. *Att.* 2.19.2; 2.20.1; 2.21.3–5.

would pass and could be weathered with less danger and damage by patient endurance than by any attempt to arrest its course.[78]

Finally, the threat from Clodius that emerged with the latter's adoption and consequent eligibility for the tribunate is often seen as a major influence on Cicero's political posture in 59. The prospect of a tribunate for his militant adversary did distract him to some degree from other political issues and added to his political caution, but the extent of his anxiety can be easily exaggerated. Until the latter part of April it was not clear that any threat existed or that Clodius would even seek the tribunate for 59. He was showing interest in an embassy to the East, where his family had extensive *clientelae,* and seemed likely to accept an offer from the dynasts of a *legatio* to the court of Tigranes, king of Armenia. In the event he declined the offer, but simultaneously his relations with the triumvirs became severely strained, and, as already noted, when, around the middle of April, he finally declared his intention to stand for the tribunate, it was as the enemy of the dynasts and with the avowed purpose of overturning their enactments.[79]

Cicero, who was receiving almost daily bulletins from Atticus about Clodius and his plans, was highly pleased by these developments, hoping they portended a wider disaffection among supporters of the coalition. He found himself even welcoming Clodius's candidature as the state's best hope for a speedy end to the *dominatio.* The danger to himself became subordinate to this most pleasing prospect of an embattled alliance crumbling from within. Besides, he saw no great cause for disquiet. He reasoned that, if Clodius remained in favor with the dynasts, he would be unable to launch a credible *popularis* crusade against the allegedly tyrannous regime of 63, whose odious power had now passed to his own allies, and if he broke with them, it would be absurd for him to follow such a course. At this stage the threat from Clodius was neither sufficiently clear or pressing to affect Cicero's political attitudes and decisions. Other considerations were dictating his abstentionist policy.

---

78. *Att.* 2.6.2; 2.7.3; 2.9.1–2; 2.12.2; 2.14.1; 2.15.2; 2.18.1–2; 2.19.2–3; 2.20.3; 2.21.1–2; 2.22.6. Cicero never expressed wholehearted admiration for opponents of the triumvirs, such as Cato, Bibulus and M. Laterensis. See *Att.* 2.15.2; 2.19.2; 2.21.1, 4. *Planc.* 52. For other instances of his use of the metaphor of the political wheel, see *Planc.* 93. *Rep.* 2.45.

79. *Att.* 2.4.2; 2.7.2; 2.12.1–2.

Any impact from Clodius was in the future and even then, as Cicero saw it in early 59, unlikely to cause more than a temporary interruption of his retirement.[80]

By mid-year the situation had changed considerably. Clodius was no longer threatening the triumvirate and was openly and aggressively threatening Cicero. An all-out confrontation in 58 began to seem inevitable. Cicero was now forced to take notice and he started to count his defenses. He insisted to Atticus, however, that he was only slightly concerned and felt fully confident that he could resist Clodius's attacks without danger to his safety or *dignitas*. He found support and goodwill everywhere. His consular army of all loyal citizens was holding firm. Crowds thronged his house and declared their approval of his consulship and backing for his cause. He felt protected by a depth of goodwill that made him eager to fight. Pompey's assurances also brought him comfort, though he put limited faith in them and relied mainly on the friends and clients won by his work in the courts and on the wider favor derived from his many achievements. His confidence eliminated any pressure to change his political course. He felt an added concern to confirm his support and safeguard it by avoiding political controversy, but the effect of this was merely to reinforce his already firm determination to eschew political involvements in 59.[81]

His optimism persisted to the end of the year. A letter to Quintus in the final months summarized his view of the situation as follows:

> It is clear that our cause will not lack supporters. People are giving assurances, offering personal help, making promises in a remarkable fashion. I have the highest hopes and even higher spirits—hopes that we will prevail, high spirits from the fact that in this state I have no fear of even an accidental mishap. In any event, the situation is as follows. If he gives notice of a prosecution, all Italy will unite and we will come away with redoubled glory; if on the other hand he tries to proceed by force, I am hopeful that we will resist with force through the support not only of friends but also of strangers. All are pledging themselves along with their friends, clients, freedmen, slaves, and even their money. Our old band of loyalists are fired with zeal and affection for us. Those who were

80. *Att.* 2.7.3; 2.9.1,3; 2.12.1; 2.15.2.
81. *Att.* 2.19.1,4–5; 2.20.2; 2.21.6; 2.22.2–3; 2.23.3; 2.24.5; 2.25.2.

previously inclined to be unsympathetic or indifferent are now ally-
ing themselves with the loyalists through hatred of the tyrants.
Pompey is full of assurances, as is Caesar, but I do not trust them
sufficiently to relax any of my own preparations. The tribunes are
friendly, the consuls are creating an excellent impression, and we
have very friendly praetors and highly energetic citizens in
Domitius, Nigidius, Memmius, and Lentulus. The others are also
loyal citizens, but these outstandingly so. You should therefore
have courage and good hope.[82]

Exile

This sanguine assessment of his situation by Cicero was soon to be
disproved by the events of early 58. After entering the tribunate Clodius
quickly emerged in a commanding position, skillfully using the prerogatives of his office and exploiting the tensions created in 59 along with
endemic weaknesses of the *respublica* to achieve a level of power that
upset all Cicero's calculations and confounded his supporters. By early
January the signs of the new tribune's rising dominance were already in
evidence. Four major bills, which he had promulgated immediately on
taking office, were passed into law with maximum speed and with no
recorded opposition.[83] A *lex frumentaria* abolished the charge of 6⅓
asses per *modius* for the monthly ration of grain issued by the state to the
plebs frumentaria.[84] A second bill permitted the enactment of legislation
on all *dies fasti* and modified the regulations governing *obnuntiatio*.[85] A

82. *Q.F.* 1.2.16.
83. Cicero reports that Clodius's bills were passed three days after the Ludi Com-
pitalicii that accompanied the festival of the Compitalia, which took place on January 1
(*Pis.* 8). A. Michels (*The Calendar of the Roman Republic* [Princeton, 1967], 205) has
pointed out that, since the Ludi almost certainly did not begin until the day after the
festival and according to Festus (304L) lasted three days, and since January 5 and 6 were
dies fasti, Clodius's bills cannot have been voted on before January 7.
84. *Sest.* 55. *Dom.* 25. Asconius 8, Clark. *Schol. Bob.* 132, Stangl. Dio 38.13. For
the implications of the law, see Brunt, *Italian Manpower*, 379 ff. and Rickman, *Corn
Supply*, 172ff.
85. *Post red. in sen.* 11. *Sest.* 33, 56. *Har. resp.* 58. *Vat.* 18. *Prov. cons.* 46. *Pis.* 9–
10. Asconius 8, Clark. Dio 38.13. The precise nature of the changes introduced by
Clodius in relation to *obnuntiatio* has been endlessly discussed. See especially A. H. J.
Greenidge, "The Repeal of the *Lex Aelia Fufia*," *CR* 7 (1983), 158–61. W. McDonald,
"Clodius and the *Lex Aelia Fufia*," *JRS* 19 (1929), 164–79. S. Weinstock, "Clodius and

lex de collegiis restored the clubs suppressed by a decree of the Senate in 64 and authorized the establishment of new ones.[86] The fourth bill prohibited the use of the *censoria nota* unless the alleged offender had been given a formal hearing and had been condemned by the verdict of both censors.[87]

The success of these far-reaching legislative initiatives was based on popular support and skillful moves by Clodius to forestall opposition and strengthen his political base. The nature of the laws insured them the backing of the *plebs*. The grain bill came at a time of particular economic hardship, and the high value placed on the concession it bestowed can be seen in two of its effects—increased migration of the rural poor to Rome and increased manumissions to make those freed eligible for the *frumentatio*, the benefit going ultimately to the former masters, who were entitled to claim the labor of their freedmen to the extent it was not required to provide the latters' livelihood.[88] The *lex de collegiis* restored an ancient right of association established in the Twelve Tables and a form of local organization among those who shared a common profession or religious cult that was an important part of the life of the lower classes.[89] The other two laws safeguarded the powers of the people by removing restrictions on the legislative process and reducing the capacity

---

the *Lex Aelia Fufia*," *JRS* 27 (1937), 215–22. J. Balsdon, "Roman History 58–56 B.C.: Three Ciceronian Problems," *JRS* 47 (1957), 15–16. G. V. Sumner, *"Lex Aelia, Lex Fufia,"* *AJP* 84 (1963), 337–58. R. Gardner, *Cicero Pro Sestio and In Vatinium* (Loeb edition, 1958), 309–22. No agreement has emerged and the main hypotheses advanced— that the right of *obnuntiatio* was taken from curule magistrates, or was abolished altogether in the case of legislative assemblies, or that the people were empowered to disallow it on any given occasion, or that it was wholly eliminated but soon restored through senatorial annulment of Clodius's law—have all been shown to be incompatible with later allusions to *obnuntiatio* and Clodius's laws, notably *Sest.* 78–9, 129. *Phil.* 2.81. *Prov. cons.* 46. *Att.* 4.3. See n.8 above and Mitchell, *CQ* 36(1986), 172–76.

86. *Sest.* 34,55. *Post red. in sen.* 33. *Pis.* 9. *Att.* 3.15.4. Asconius 8, Clark. Dio 38.13.2. For the Senate's decree, see *Pis.* 8. Asconius 7, Clark. *Mur.* 71. J. Linderski, "Der Senat und die Vereine," in M. N. Andreev et al., *Gesellschaft und Recht in griechisch-römischen Altertum* (1968), 94–132.

87. *Sest.* 55. *Pis.* 9–10. *Prov. cons.* 46. Asconius 8, Clark. Dio 38.13. *Schol. Bob.* 132, Stangl. This law was repealed in 52 by the consul Q. Scipio. Dio 40.57.

88. For evidence of grain shortages, see *Dom.* 11. For Clodius's bill see Brunt, *Italian Manpower*, 379ff. Rickman, *Corn Supply*, 172ff. S. Treggiari, *Roman Freedmen during the Late Republic* (Oxford, 1969), 16.

89. See P. A. Brunt, "The Roman Mob," *Past and Present* 35 (1966), 25ff. Treggiari, *Freedmen*, 168ff. A. W. Lintott, *Violence in Republican Rome* (Oxford, 1968), 77ff.

of the oligarchy to take punitive action through the censorship against popular dissidents.

But the support of the *plebs* was not sufficient to guarantee legislative success in the Roman system, and Clodius had taken other steps to insure passage of his laws. He had averted a veto by Cicero's supporters among the tribunes by promising not to take action against the orator.[90] He had further managed to make an agreement with the consuls, L. Piso and A. Gabinius, under which he undertook to secure them by plebiscite the provinces of Macedonia and Cilicia in return for their cooperation. His pact with the consuls was a vital step in his rise to power, removing the most powerful potential source of official opposition to his designs and the main vehicle for the implementation of any senatorial moves against him. Cicero constantly harps on the critical consequences of the development in his many later analyses of the causes of Clodius's easy domination of political events in early 58.[91]

But behind the consuls were the still more important figures of their political overlords, Pompey and Caesar, and they too fully acquiesced in Clodius's ambitious legislative initiatives. The obvious conclusion is that Clodius's alliance with the consuls extended to them also. Recent opinion, however, has tended to discount any such association and, in reaction against earlier assumptions that Clodius was a mere henchman of the triumvirs in 58, has sought to present the tribune as a wholly independent agent, who was tolerated by the coalition because they did not dare oppose him.[92]

---

90. Dio 38.14.1–2.

91. *Post red. in sen.* 9–18, 32. *Quir.* 13,21. *Dom.* 23, 55, 70, 91, 96, 124, 131. *Sest.* 17–18, 24–25, 33–34, 42, 52–55, 64, 69. *Pis.* 8–11, 15, 19, 23–24. 28, 31, 77–78. *Planc.* 86–87. Gabinius's province of Cilicia was later changed to Syria by another bill of Clodius (*Sest.* 55. *Dom.* 23). E. Badian ("M. Porcius Cato and the Annexation and Early Administration of Cyprus," *JRS* 55 [1965], 115ff.) links the change to the decision to send Cato to Cyprus, speculating that Gabinius was originally intended to carry out that commission from Cilicia and had to be given a more important province when Cato was appointed. It is an attractive hypothesis, though Cicero merely calls the change an increased bribe, and he is unlikely, in his careful cataloguing of every suspicion of jobbery and intrigue in 58, to have missed the connection with Cyprus. From *Sest.* 55 and *Vat.* 18 it is clear the consuls not only acquiesced in Clodius's designs, but lent positive support. Cf. *Sest.* 33. *Post red. in sen.* 11.

92. See Gruen, *Phoenix* 20 (1966), 120–30. Rundell, *Historia* 28 (1979), 301–28. Lintott, *Greece and Rome* 14 (1969), 157–69. The notion that Clodius was independent of Pompey and Caesar but an ally of Crassus has been recently argued by Ward, *Crassus,* 231–58. The most thorough and most recent study of Clodius is H. Benner, *Die Politik des P. Clodius Pulcher* (Stuttgart, 1987).

But revisionism, as often, has gone a step too far. It is true that the dynasts could ill afford in early 58 to antagonize or be seen to oppose a popular tribune promoting popular reforms. The opposition generated in 59 had not abated and positive moves were afoot to reverse all the enactments of that year and to prosecute their authors. At the beginning of 58 the praetors C. Memmius and Domitius Ahenobarbus brought the question of the *acta* of 59 before the Senate. An acrimonious three-day debate ensued, which had inconclusive results but showed that the *principes* and the Senate as a whole were unwilling to accept the validity of the legislation of Caesar's consulship and were seeking a way to overturn it.[93]

The courts became the next instrument of attack. First, Caesar's ex-quaestor was arraigned in a preliminary attempt to establish illegality in relation to the *acta* of 59. Soon afterwards came the main endeavor—the prosecution of Caesar himself, initiated by a tribune L. Antistius. But Caesar, in evident anticipation of such a move, had gone outside the *pomerium* and assumed his proconsular *imperium,* thereby securing the protection of the *Lex Memmia,* which gave immunity from prosecution to those who were absent *reipublicae causa.* He now asserted his right to immunity and appealed the matter to the College of Tribunes, which upheld his claim.[94] But the judicial offensive continued. Vatinius was the next target. He too had immunity, since he was at this time a *legatus* of Caesar, but he chose to waive it and returned to the city. When the day of the hearing arrived, however, he objected to the constitution of the court and appealed to the tribunes to prevent the trial taking place. Clodius responded and forcefully broke up the proceedings.[95]

93. Suetonius, *Jul.* 23.1; *Nero* 2.2. *Sest.* 40. *Schol. Bob.* 130, 146, Stangl. For the Lex Memmia see Val. Max. 3.7.9: "Quae eorum qui reipublicae causa abessent recipi nomina vetabat."

94. Suetonius, *Jul.* 23. E. Badian ("Two Roman Non-Entities," *CQ* 19 [1969], 198–204; "The Attempt to Try Caesar," in *Polis and Imperium: Studies in Honor of E. T. Salmon,* ed. J. A. S. Evans [Toronto, 1974], 145–66) argues that Caesar's indictment did not necessarily take place in 58, but as probably in 57 or 56. This, however, entirely misrepresents the force of the Suetonian passage: "Et statim quaestor eius in praeiudicium . . . arreptus est. mox et ipse . . . postulatus." The succession of *statim, praeiudicium, mox* clearly depicts a sequence of interconnected events that followed each other in rapid succession. See E. S. Gruen, "Some Criminal Trials of the Late Republic: Political and Prosopographical Problems," *Athenaeum* 49 (1971), 62–67.

95. *Vat.* 33–34. *Sest.* 135. *Schol. Bob.* 140, 150, Stangl. Vatinius's motive in waiv-

These determined attacks on the *acta* of 59 and their agents no doubt increased pressure on the triumvirs to avoid the added risks of opposing a determined and influential tribune, but there are many reasons to believe that their smooth relations with Clodius in early 58 had a more positive and solid basis than a policy of reluctant toleration dictated by political weakness.

The challenges to the coalition in 58 were a predictable sequel to the opposition that had been building throughout Caesar's consulship. Pompey and Caesar had, from an early stage, shown themselves keenly alert to the likelihood of such threats ahead, and they had striven to defend against them by working to insure they would have friends in the magistracies of 58. Clodius had figured prominently in that strategy from early 59, and there are many indications that the effort to woo him had persisted and had eventually succeeded.[96] Cicero, who was carefully monitoring relations between Clodius and the coalition in Caesar's consulship, reports no sign of friction after August. At the end of the year Clodius clearly showed himself a defender of Caesar's interests when he prevented Bibulus addressing the people on laying down his consulship, thus depriving him of a notable opportunity on a major official occasion to crown his campaign of vilification through his edicts with a final denunciation in person of Caesar's character and administration. Around the same time a *legatio* was given to a brother of Clodius in Caesar's army, which was then gathering in Italy.[97] The collaboration of both consuls, the main triumviral agents in office in 58, with Clodius in the passage of his laws in January continues the signs of an active alliance between tribune and dynasts.[98] Moreover, the laws themselves, while

---

ing his immunity was obviously to clear the way for his candidature for the aedileship later in 58. See Gruen, *Athenaeum* 49 (1971), 65–67. Badian, *Polis and Imperium,* 154–58. L. G. Pocock, *A Commentary on Cicero In Vatinium* (London, 1926), 186–90.

96. It was also, of course, very much in Clodius's interest to have the goodwill of the triumvirs as he prepared to launch his ambitious legislative programs, and he was shrewd enough to realize it and act accordingly. He had proved a difficult and erratic ally for the coalition in 59, but such unpredictability, which sometimes looked like caprice, was, as Cicero well recognized, generally based on hard-headed calculation, aiming to enhance the price of his cooperation or to exploit particular conditions. *Har. resp.* 46–50.

97. Dio 38.12.3. *Sest.* 41.

98. It is worth noting that the rewards of the consuls in the form of provinces which, though desirable, were unexceptional proconsular commands, are unlikely in themselves to have generated such close cooperation with a radical tribune. Triumviral backing for the consuls' stand seems a necessary assumption on many grounds.

they undoubtedly represented Clodius's concerns and were designed to serve his purposes, included one measure that offered substantial benefits to Caesar. The bill relating to *obnuntiatio,* whatever its precise terms, almost certainly placed the dubious form of obstruction attempted by Bibulus in 59 outside the law, which would further weaken the force of any challenge on that basis to the enactments of Caesar's consulship. Finally, the attempts to indict Caesar and Vatinius were thwarted in both cases with the aid of the College of Tribunes, rendered in the case of Vatinius through the agency of Clodius, in the case of Caesar at least with his consent. In short, the evidence for relations between Clodius and the dynasts in late 59 and early 58 reveals a catalogue of mutual favor that must surely have issued from a positive agreement for mutual cooperation.[99]

Clodius's next burst of legislative activity showed even closer cooperation between him and the triumviral faction and further confirms the likelihood that he was firmly allied with the coalition from the outset of his tribunate. In February he brought forward three new bills, proposing that Cyprus be annexed and the property of its king, Ptolemy, confiscated,[100] that Macedonia and Cilicia be assigned to Piso and Gabinius,[101] and that anyone who had put to death a Roman citizen without trial should be interdicted from fire and water. The last commenced his long-threatened attack on Cicero, cleverly framed to emphasize the principle at stake—the fundamental right of citizens to due process of law.[102]

The bill on Cyprus served an urgent purpose of Clodius, to insure funds were available to meet the cost of his grain law, but it also had much to commend it to the triumvirs.[103] Cyprus had been subject to the

99. None of the later ancient sources saw Clodius as independent of the coalition, though it is with Caesar that he is principally linked. See Dio 38.14–15. Appian, *BC* 2.14. Plutarch, *Cic.* 30.3; *Caes.* 14.9.

100. *Dom.* 20, 52. *Sest.* 57, 59–60. Dio 38.30.5. Appian, *BC* 2.23. Velleius 2.38.6. Plutarch, *Cat. min.* 34.2. *Schol. Bob.* 133, Stangl.

101. *Sest.* 25, 53–54. *Post red. in sen.* 18. *Dom.* 23. Plutarch, *Cic.* 30.1.

102. Velleius 2.45.1. *Sest.* 25, 53. *Dom* 62. *Att.* 3.15.5. Dio 38.14.4. Appian, *BC* 2.15. Plutarch, *Cic.* 30.4. The bills on the provinces and the execution of citizens were promulgated on the same day (*Sest.* 25, 53). The bill on Cyprus must have appeared somewhat earlier, since it had been passed and the subsequent proposal to appoint Cato promulgated before Cicero left Rome and the voting took place on the other two (Plutarch, *Cat. min.* 35.1. *Sest.* 53, 62. *Dom.* 20).

103. The economic motive is mentioned in Festus, *Brev.* 13.1 and Ammianus Marcellinus 14.8.15. Revenge for a failure by Ptolemy to rescue Clodius from pirates also occurs as a motive in Dio 38.30.5. Appian, *BC* 2.23.

kings of Egypt from the time of Ptolemy I, and, together with Egypt, had been bequeathed to Rome by a will of Ptolemy Alexander I, who had died in 87. Crassus and Caesar had made strenuous efforts to secure the annexation of Egypt in the sixties, and in 59 Caesar had extracted the massive sum of six thousand talents from the claimant to the throne, Ptolemy Auletes, as the price of keeping his kingdom.[104] A takeover of Cyprus and of the wealth of its king was in line with this Egyptian policy and was likely besides to draw particular support from Pompey, since possession of the island would round off the control of the eastern Mediterranean established by him and would safeguard the sea route to the new province of Syria.

Clodius's proposal had an additional appeal for the dynasts in that part of its design was to remove from Rome their most intractable and dangerous opponent, M. Cato, by appointing him to supervise the annexation. Cato was not named in the original bill, but after its passage Clodius introduced another measure proposing his appointment.[105] It was a skillful move that would not only enfeeble the optimate opposition by removing its most energetic and effective spokesman, but would also blunt Cato's opposition in any future challenges to the validity of the *acta* of either Caesar or Clodius, since the legitimacy of his own commission and achievements under it would be based on them.[106] Caesar wrote Clodius a letter after Cato's dispatch warmly congratulating him on the stratagem and clearly indicating, as Clodius was careful to publicize, complete approval of the entire enterprise.[107]

The attack on Cicero was the fulfillment of a long-standing threat from

104. Plutarch, *Crass.* 13.1. Suetonius, *Jul.* 11, 54.3. Caesar, *BC* 3.107.

105. *Sest.* 62 and *Dom.* 20 make clear that Cato was appointed by a separate law, introduced after the annexation had been approved. See S. I. Oost, "Cato Uticensis and the Annexation of Cyprus," *CP* 50 (1955), 99. The reason for the separate bill was most likely the fact that a proposal for a specific extraordinary command within the annexation bill would have violated the Lex Caecilia Didia. See *Dom.* 53, where Cicero defines the force of the law as "ne populo necesse sit in coiunctis rebus compluribus aut id, quod nolit, accipere, aut id, quod velit, repudiare." The delay in promulgating the second bill until after the first had been approved was probably an attempt to avoid inviting unnecessary opposition to the annexation from Cato. For Badian's suggestion (*JRS* 55 [1965], 16–17) that the choice of Cato was not part of the original plan but a happy afterthought, see n. 91 above. Clodius's bill appointing Cato added a further commission to restore certain exiles to Byzantium. *Dom.* 52–53. *Har. resp.* 59. *Sest.* 56. Plutarch, *Cat. min.* 34.4.

106. Plutarch (*Cat. min.* 40.1–2) tells how Cato later defended the legitimacy of Clodius's tribunate and laws to protect the legitimacy of his own *acta* in Cyprus.

107. *Dom.* 22. Cf. *Sest.* 60.

Clodius. He wanted his revenge and he was also eager to exploit an issue that could further promote his image as a defender of the people's liberties. But of all his undertakings in 58, his legislation against Cicero most clearly had the sanction of the dynasts and, to the extent necessary to insure its success, was supported by the weight of their authority and by the direct assistance of their chief collaborators, the consuls.

Cicero responded to Clodius's move against him by putting on mourning and directly supplicating the people. His supporters quickly rallied, and from many quarters. There were repeated pleas from senators and others to the consuls to take action on his behalf. A deputation of *principes* pleaded his case before Pompey and Piso. A large gathering of *equites* from Italy as well as from the city assembled on the Capitol and resolved to promote his defense by wearing mourning and by any other means at their disposal. Accompanied by Hortensius and the elder Curio, they then proceeded to the Temple of Concord, where the Senate was meeting, and entreated Gabinius to lend his assistance. The Senate itself, on the initiative of the tribune, L. Ninnius, followed the lead of the meeting on the Capitol and decreed that its members too should wear mourning. Further resolutions of support poured forth from the towns of Italy, from the companies of tax farmers, and from a variety of other forms of association.[108]

Cicero had received the broad and vigorous response from *boni* that he had so confidently predicted to Quintus toward the end of 59. But, contrary to his expectations, it proved woefully inadequate in face of the forces that showed themselves arrayed against him. Clodius was now a major power in his own right. His legislative successes in January had added considerably to his influence. His grain bill and general posture as a champion of the people's rights had given him a firm hold on the loyalty of the urban *plebs*. He had further used the *lex de collegiis* to acquire a more direct and formidable variety of political leverage. After passage of the law he had personally organized on a local basis a network of *collegia*, recruited mainly from craftsmen and shopkeepers, but with an admixture of slaves. More significant, the new clubs were structured

108. *Att.* 3.15.5. *Sest.* 25–26, 32. *Pis.* 77. *Post red. in sen.* 12. *Quir.* 8, 13. *Planc.* 87. Plutarch, *Cic.* 30.5–31.1. Dio 38.16.2–6. Appian, *BC* 2.15. Plutarch says 20,000 *iuvenes* joined Cicero in supplicating the public, but this number most likely refers to the demonstration on the Capitol. *Quir.* 8. There is no other indication that Cicero was accompanied by large numbers in his pleas to the people.

along paramilitary lines. They were divided into *decuriae*, they had *duces* to command them, and, if Cicero can be believed, they were supplied by Clodius with money and arms. This reconstitution of the system of *collegia* further tightened Clodius's political control of the lower classes and also provided him with his notorious *operae*, armed gangs which he freely used to attack opponents and intimidate voters in the assemblies.[109] Cicero's side soon experienced the effects of his new resource. Cicero himself was harassed as he went around seeking support. Hortensius was almost killed in an attack by a band of Clodius's hirelings, and Cicero's leading defenders among the *equites*, after they had been summoned by Clodius to a public hearing, were set upon by his gangs with stones and swords.[110]

But once again Clodius's own *potentia* was powerfully augmented by the support of both consuls, who, on this occasion, backed him with the full authority of their office. They rejected all pleas to deflect Clodius from his purpose, and, when the *equites* and Senate took their decision to wear mourning, Gabinius summoned a *contio,* denounced their action, and warned the *equites* they would pay for their part in the execution of the Catilinarian conspirators. To drive home his point, he issued a proclamation at the meeting banishing one of Cicero's staunchest equestrian adherents, L. Lamia, to a distance of two hundred miles from Rome. Soon afterwards both consuls issued a decree directing senators to resume normal dress. They also lent their aid to Clodius's efforts to revive and exploit the controversial issues associated with the Catilinarian executions, both of them declaring at a *contio* their disapproval of the punishment of citizens who had not been condemned in a court of law.[111]

It was the attitude of the dynasts themselves, however, that proved most decisive in insuring the success of Clodius's campaign against Cicero. All three stayed silent when Clodius repeatedly claimed at his

109. *Att.* 3.15.4. *Post red. in sen.* 33. *Quir.* 13. *Dom.* 5, 13, 45, 54, 79, 89, 129. *Sest.* 34, 38, 53, 55, 59, 65, 85, 95, 106, 112. *Har. resp.* 28. *Pis.* 9, 11, 23. *Par. st.* 30. Asconius 7, Clark. See Treggiari, *Freedmen,* 173ff. Brunt, *Past and Present* 35 (1966), 23ff. F. M. de Robertis, *Il diritto associativo romano dai collegi della reppublica alle corporazioni del basso impero* (Bari, 1938), 96ff. J. M. Flambard, ''Clodius, les collèges, la plèbe et les esclaves. Recheches sur la politique populaire au milieu du Iᵉʳsiècle,'' *MEFR* 89 (1977), 115–56.

110. *Sest.* 27. *Mil.* 37. Plutarch, *Cic.* 30.5. Dio 38.16.5. Appian, *BC* 2.15.

111. *Sest.* 25–33. *Post red. in sen.* 12–17, 32. *Quir.* 13. *Dom.* 91, 96, 131, *Pis.* 11, 13–14, 17–19, 77. *Planc.* 86–87. Plutarch, *Cic.* 31.1. Dio 38.16.5–6.

daily *contiones* that he had not only their approval for his measures but their commitment to provide, if necessary, the backing of their military might. Crassus and Pompey, when formally asked to help Cicero, took refuge behind constitutional niceties, asserting that it was the responsibility of the consuls to take up the case, and that they could only act on the consuls' lead. When confronted with personal pleas from Cicero himself, Pompey found further excuses for inaction in his obligations to Caesar.[112] The latter did not seek to equivocate or dissemble. He not only allowed the threat of his Gallic army to be paraded at Clodius's *contiones,* but gave a positive show of support by reaffirming at a special *contio,* summoned by Clodius outside the *pomerium* to enable him to attend, his condemnation of the executions of 63.[113]

The stance of the coalition was dictated by the same fears for the *acta* of 59 that caused Caesar to approve the removal of Cato. Cicero represented another gifted and prestigious optimate *princeps* around whom the considerable senatorial opposition could rally. Caesar in particular was determined to forestall such a possibility. His various offers to Cicero in 59 clearly had such a purpose in view. Their rejection had angered him and added further to his anxiety about the orator's future role and impact. In the tense political atmosphere of 58, Cicero and his ambiguous political posture became a still more worrisome threat, and the extent of Caesar's unwillingness to leave him a free agent and accept the risks of active opposition from him can be seen in his later refusal to consent to his restoration until he received guarantees that he would not attack the coalition.[114]

To all appearances Caesar's view had the full support of his partners.

---

112. *Sest.* 39–42, 52. *Dom.* 66. *Har. resp.* 47. *Pis.* 77. *Planc.* 86. *Att.* 3.15.4; 10.4.3. *Q.F.* 1.44. Plutarch, *Cic.* 30.2–3; *Pomp.* 46.5. Dio 38.17.3. Plutarch says Pompey avoided seeing Cicero, but *Att.* 10.4.3 makes clear that there was a meeting.

113. *Sest.* 39–42, 52. *Post red. in sen.* 32–33. *Dom.* 131. *Har. resp.* 47. *Prov. cons.* 18, 43. *Att.* 10.4.1, 3. Plutarch, *Cic.* 30.4; *Caes.* 14.9. Dio 38.17.1–2. Dio says that Caesar, though he condemned the executions at the *contio,* expressed disapproval of the idea of retroactive legislation to punish those responsible for them. But Plutarch (*Cic.* 30.4) presents Caesar's appearance at the *contio* as an act of unequivocal support for Clodius's course, and it seems very unlikely that Clodius would have called a special *contio* for Caesar's benefit if such support were not assured. Certainly, Cicero never doubted that Caesar wanted him exiled. See *Prov. cons.* 18, 43. *Att.* 3.15.3; 3.18.1; 10.4.1.

114. *Att.* 9.2a.1; 10.4.1. *Sest.* 40–41, 52, 71. *Pis.* 79. *Prov. cons.* 41–43. *Fam.* 1.9.9, 12.

Pompey's situation was complicated by his friendship with Cicero and by the many pledges of protection he had given him in 59, but in early 58 he had particular fears for his own position and particular suspicions of Cicero that did not dispose him to take much account of his previous ties and commitments to the orator. There were fresh rumors of plots against his life and persistent allegations that Cicero was involved in them. Pompey was prone to believe such reports, and in this instance they had sufficient effect to insure his cooperation with his associates in foreclosing any potential threat from Cicero to the interests of the coalition.[115]

The open alignment of consuls and dynasts with Clodius sealed Cicero's fate. His support quickly dissolved in face of such overwhelming odds. The praetors, among whom he had numbered several friends, abandoned him. The *publicani* grew fearful. No voice was raised in his defense at the daily *contiones.* The leaders of the *optimates,* notably Hortensius and Cato, gave up the fight and advised him to yield, softening the advice with assurances that he would soon be recalled with glory.[116]

Cicero was easily persuaded to capitulate. The attitude of the consuls and especially the defection of Pompey had taken him by surprise and had completely unnerved him. He had expected, and with some reason, that Piso, an *adfinis,* and Gabinius, the adherent of Pompey whom he had supported and praised in 66, would be well disposed toward him, and, though he had put limited faith in Pompey's pledges, he had never anticipated that he would be so abruptly and totally abandoned by him.[117]

---

115. *Dom.* 28. *Sest.* 41, 133. *Pis.* 76. For Pompey's nervousness about plots and strong reaction to threats to his life, see *Sest.* 69. *Har. resp.* 49. *Mil.* 18, 65ff. Asconius 36, 50, Clark. As usual, the evidence for Crassus's attitudes is scanty, but his relations with Cicero were consistently hostile and, by all indications, remained so in the early 50s. *Fam.* 14.2.2; 1.9.9, 20. *Att.* 3.15.3. *Phil.* 2.7. Plutarch, *Cic.* 30.2. Dio 38.17.3.

116. *Sest.* 42. *Q.F.* 1.3.10; 1.4.4. *Quir.* 13. *Att.* 3.7.2; 3.9.2; 3.15.2. *Fam.* 1.9.13–14. Plutarch, *Cic.* 31.4; *Cat. min.* 35.1. Dio 38.4. Cicero's statement in *Att.* 3.15.2 that he regrets Cato's *fides* had not had more influence with him than the *simulatio* of others might seem to contradict the evidence of Plutarch and Dio that Cato took the lead in advising capitulation, but in view of what Cicero says elsewhere (see *Sest.* 60–61) about Cato's attitude toward resistance to Clodius, it is likely that the statement to Atticus is merely exempting Cato from the charges of *simulatio* and *invidia* that he is leveling against other *boni* and regretting that in general he had not cultivated a closer political relationship with him.

117. *Q.F.* 1.2.16. *Pis.* 11–13. *Post red. in sen.* 17. *Sest.* 20. Dio 38.15.6. For Cicero's reaction to Pompey's refusal of help, see *Q.F.* 1.4.4. *Att.* 3.15.4. Plutarch, *Cic.* 31.3.

The successive shocks of these unexpected desertions effectively quashed his earlier optimism and eagerness to fight and made capitulation seem the only course. His despair at the unexpected turn events had taken brought him to the brink of suicide, but the calmer counsels of Atticus and the pleas of his family prevailed, and around the third week in March, on the day of the voting on Clodius's bill, he quietly left Rome escorted by a group of friends.[118] One of his final acts before leaving was to carry a statue of Minerva, which he kept in his house, to the Temple of Jupiter on the Capitol where he dedicated it with the inscription: "To Minerva, guardian of Rome." It was an important symbolic gesture. Minerva was *custos urbis,* the role in which Cicero especially liked to cast himself, and since his consulship he had sought to be closely identified with the goddess and seen as her favored ally in the fulfillment of that role. In departing voluntarily he believed he was saving Rome from civil war, and he wanted to present himself as again the protector of the city and again the coadjutor of Minerva.[119]

Immediately after his departure, his house on the Palatine was plundered and burned, and Terentia was forced to take refuge in the Temple of Vesta. His properties at Tusculum and Formiae were also looted and destroyed.[120] There followed another bill from Clodius which formally declared him an outlaw and fixed four hundred miles from Italy as the limit within which the outlawry would apply. It also prescribed penalties against anyone who harbored him within this limit, confiscated his property to the state and gave Clodius charge of its disposition, and forbade any proposals for invalidation or repeal to be brought before Senate or people.[121] After the bill became law, Clodius, acting on its authority,

118. *Q.F.* 1.4.4. *Fam.* 1.9.13. *Post red. in sen.* 32. *Quir.* 13. *Dom.* 96. *Sest.* 35–50. *Vat.* 6. *Planc.* 86–90. *Pis.* 19–21. *Mil.* 36. *Leg.* 3.25. Plutarch, *Cic.* 31.5. He alludes to his thoughts of suicide in *Q.F.* 1.4.4. *Att.* 3.3; 3.4; 3.7.2; 3.9.1–2. *Fam.* 14.4.5. *Sest.* 53 indicates he left on the day of the voting. The exact date of his departure is disputed. For a detailed discussion, see Shackleton Bailey, *Letters to Atticus,* 2:227–32.

119. *Sest.* 49. *Vat.* 7. *Dom.* 76, 92, 99, 144–45. *Leg.* 2.42. Plutarch, *Cic.* 31.5. Dio 38.17.5. Quintilian, *Inst.* 11.1.24.

120. *Sest.* 53–54. *Post red. in sen.* 18. *Dom.* 59, 62. *Pis.* 26. *Att.* 4.2.5,7. *Fam.* 14.2.2. Asconius 10, Clark. Plutarch, *Cic.* 33.1. Dio 38.17.6.

121. *Dom.* 47, 50–51. *Post red. in sen.* 8. *Sest.* 65. *Pis.* 30. *Planc.* 97. *Att.* 3.4; 3.12.1; 3.15.5–6; 3.23.2. *Fam.* 14.4.2. Plutarch, *Cic.* 32.1. Dio 38.17.7. For the constitutionality of Clodius's *lex de exsilio,* see A. H. J. Greenidge, *The Legal Procedure of Cicero's Time* (Oxford, 1901), 361–66. R. G. Nisbet, *De Domo Sua* (Oxford, 1939), XVII–XVIII and 204–05. Plutarch and Dio give the limits of the outlawry as 500 miles, but Cicero's evidence must surely be preferred.

demolished and rebuilt the Portico of Catulus on the Palatine and extended it onto the site of Cicero's house, which adjoined it. He then added, in a dramatic gesture highlighting the issue underlying Cicero's banishment, a shrine to Libertas and, to prevent future interference with these monuments, he had them both officially consecrated.[122]

Cicero's humiliation was complete. He had fallen victim to the polarizing and increasingly anarchic effects of the emergence of the triumvirate and the events of Caesar's consulship. The traditional power structure, with the Senate and its *principes* in a commanding role, and the stability afforded by strong, continuous leadership, had been permanently upset by the developments of 59, opening the way to demagogic opportunism and the politics of force. The Senate's authority had been critically damaged by Caesar's contemptuous disregard of its constitutional prerogatives throughout his consulship, and its *principes* had lost their controlling influence, their usual forms of manipulation and obstruction rendered obsolete by the raw power and extremism of their opponents. Unfriendly consuls in league with the coalition added to the Senate's impotence in 58.

But the dynasts themselves, though they had gained their ends in 59, had by no means established a stable and secure ascendancy. They were joined in a marriage of convenience that lacked the binding force of either personal friendship or shared political beliefs, and they had been forced into unwelcome excesses that gave dangerous scope for attack to their enemies. Individually and collectively they had a need to look carefully to their defenses at the beginning of 58.

In this nervous, confrontational, and unstable political climate, Clodius emerged as a formidable independent power. He was backed by the resources of a proud and powerful clan and had the qualities necessary to take full advantage of the troubled political conditions of the early fifties. He was, in Cicero's terms, the archetypal *audax,* ruthlessly ambitious, a highly effective demagogue dedicated to cultivating the populace and exploiting its power, but ready, when necessary, to bolster popular support by resort to the most flagrant violence. He made an uncomfortable and volatile ally, but the coalition needed his support in

122. *Dom.* 102–22, 131. *Par. st.* 30. *Leg.* 2.42. *Att.* 4.2.2–5. Dio 38.17.6. Plutarch, *Cic.* 33.1. See Nisbet, *De Domo,* 206–12.

58, and he exploited that need to build further his independent power base, reinforcing it with armed *operae* organized on a grand scale. He was a towering figure in his own right by early 58, and when he acted with the support or acquiescence of the triumvirs, he was unstoppable. He had at least the tacit support of the alliance in his attack on Cicero, and the orator's speedy and total defeat was an inevitable consequence.

After leaving Rome Cicero had traveled to the south of Italy, where he lingered trying to decide his ultimate destination. He had first headed for Brundisium, hoping to cross to Greece with Atticus. But he changed his mind in Campania and decided to go to the farm of a friend near Vibo in the toe of Italy. From there he planned to go to Sicily, which he considered a second home, but got word, presumably at Vibo, that the governor, C. Vergilius, though an old friend, was not prepared to admit him. He next thought of Malta, but news of Clodius's *lex de exsilio* and its four-hundred mile limit ruled out that possibility. Hopes of an early return had now faded, and he decided to settle in Asia, preferably the free city of Cyzicus, so he headed once more for Brundisium, which he reached on April 17. He was welcomed by a friend, M. Laenius Flaccus, who found him passage to Dyrrachium on April 29.

From Dyrrachium Cicero traveled eastwards through Macedonia, where he was met by the quaestor of the province, his friend Cn. Plancius, who escorted him to Thessalonica and established him in the quaestor's residence. Cicero intended to continue his journey to Cyzicus, but on the urgings of Atticus and Plancius and because there were good communications between Rome and Thessalonica, he remained with Plancius until November, when the imminent arrival of Macedonia's new governor, his enemy Cn. Piso, consul of 58, forced him to leave the province. By then he had some hope of an early restoration, and decided to move closer to Italy and accept Atticus's long-standing invitation to stay in his well-fortified home at Buthrotum in Epirus. He went first to Dyrrachium, however, a free city with which he had close ties and where he could most readily get news from Rome. He remained there at least until the beginning of 57, when the extant correspondence from exile ceases. This, combined with the earlier statements of his intentions, suggests that early in the new year he may finally have gone to Epirus and joined Atticus there. But in any event, he was back in Dyrrachium when the bill for his restoration was finally passed on August 4, and on the very same day he sailed for Italy.[123]

His exile was therefore relatively short, about sixteen months in all, but the experience proved traumatic in the extreme, and brought him at times to the verge of mental collapse. His sufferings are vividly portrayed in the letters to Atticus, Terentia, and Quintus, and tell much about Cicero the man and also something about the potential severity of exile in antiquity as a form of public penalty.

Cicero was fortunate in one respect, in that he had loyal friends who saved him from any great physical hardship or danger. In the early stages he had the strains of long journeys in Italy and Greece, and he faced some danger from old enemies, especially Catilinarian exiles, but after he reached Thessalonica on May 23, he was able to live in reasonable comfort and security. He had more than enough money for his needs. Before he left Rome Atticus had given him the generous sum of 250,000 sesterces, and he had also received from the treasury money owed to Quintus in connection with his governorship of Asia. Quintus later offered to send him additional funds, but he indicated there was no need. During the five months he spent at Thessalonica he had accommodation in the quaestor's official residence and the comfort of Plancius's devoted friendship. The Greek cities also showed him goodwill and vied with each other in sending deputations to greet him. At Dyrrachium he was again in friendly surroundings in which he felt completely safe, and he had the further haven of Atticus's home in Buthrotum, to which he could have resorted at any time.[124]

But none of this did much to relieve the acute mental distress that overwhelmed him as soon as he left Rome. He was overcome by a sense of the suddenness and completeness of his change of fortune. He saw himself, lately blessed in brother, children, wife, and wealth, and in talent, influence, and the support of all good citizens, abruptly cast ignominiously into the life of a homeless fugitive, a reversal he bewailed

---

123. *Planc.* 95–100. *Post red. in sen.* 35. *Fam.* 14.1–4. *Att.* 3.1–27. *Q.F.* 1.3–4. *Schol. Bob.* 153, Stangl. Plutarch, *Cic.* 32. *Leg.* 2.7, which appears to indicate that Cicero had never seen Atticus's place in Epirus, must cast doubt on the idea that he spent the last months of his exile at Buthrotum.

124. Nepos, *Att.* 4.4. *Q.F.* 1.3.7. *Att.* 3.19.1; 3.22.1,4; 4.3.6. *Fam.* 14.1.3,7. *Planc.* 99–100. Plutarch, *Cic.* 32.4.

as more calamitous than any in the history of man.[125] It separated him from his wife and two children, a grief aggravated in the early stages by fears for their safety. It brought the loss of the properties on the Palatine and at Tusculum that he valued most of all, and of a style of living to which he was especially devoted.[126] Cicero's attachment to the political, social, and intellectual life of Rome, which caused him to remark on a later occasion that all life abroad meant obscurity and drudgery, made enforced absence in the circumstances of exile especially hard to bear.[127]

But his greatest pain came from feelings of dishonor and blighted *dignitas*. Exile had connotations of disgrace and rejection from which he could not escape. He was later to argue that *exsilium* carried no infamy unless joined to wrongdoing and that, in his case, it was a consequence of virtue, not vice, and therefore a source of glory more than shame.[128] But his perceptions were very different in the course of the exile itself. Banishment seemed then a fall from honor and a cruel negation of all his achievements. It laid in ruins his proud conception of himself as a uniquely gifted *princeps* who, by *virtus* and *industria,* had won his way from obscurity to the highest limits of *dignitas, auctoritas,* and *gratia.*[129] It also shattered the hopes he had entertained for the future of his children and brother, turning the anticipated social and political benefits to them of his ascent to *nobilitas* into a legacy of hatred and shame.[130] The undeserved character of his misfortune, far from offering consolation, brought increased bitterness at the ingratitude of gods and men.[131]

His grief was further compounded by a conviction, which took firm hold in the early weeks of his exile, that his voluntary departure was a catastrophic mistake and the result of treacherous advice from optimate

125. *Att.* 3.7.2; 3.8.4; 3.10.2; 3.12.1; 3.13.2; 3.15.2; 3.20.1; *Q.F.* 1.3.6.

126. *Fam.* 14.1.1,5; 14.2.1–3; 14.3.1–2, 5; 14.4.1, 3. *Q.F.* 1.3.1,3. *Att.* 3.19.3; 3.20.1; 3.22.3. *Quir.* 2–4. *Dom.* 96–98.

127. *Fam.* 2.12.2. Cf. *Fam.* 2.11.1. Dio 38.23.1.

128. *Dom.* 72ff. The prejorative connotations of *exsilium* are evidenced by the fact that enemies of Cicero (e.g., Clodius, *Dom.* 72; Crassus, Dio 39.60.1; Gabinius, *Q.F.* 3.2.2) continued to taunt him with it, and he himself carefully avoided it in references to his banishment, preferring words such as *aerumna, calamitas, maeror, discessus, mea tempora.*

129. *Att.* 3.15.8; 3.20.1. *Q.F.* 1.3.1, 6. *Dom.* 98.

130. *Fam.* 14.1.1, 5; 14.2.1; 14.3.1; 14.4.3. *Q.F.* 1.3.1, 10; 1.4.1. *Att.* 3.19.3; 3.23.5. Cicero was especially troubled about Quintus, who was threatened with prosecution on his return from Asia. See *Att.* 3.8.3; 3.9.1, 3; 3.11.2; 3.13.2; 3.17.1; 3.19.3; 3.23.5. *Q.F.* 1.3.2.

131. *Q.F.* 1.3.1, 9. *Fam.* 14.4.1.

allies jealously seeking his downfall behind a mask of friendship. The misery and sense of humiliation that exile brought him made his unresisting acceptance of it seem both senseless and dishonorable. He began to think of the support expressed for him in the Senate and throughout Italy and to lament that he had not rallied it to defeat his attackers or at least insure, by a courageous fight and an honorable death, the preservation of his name and standing. Instead he had meekly surrendered to his enemies in shameful disregard of his own and his family's *dignitas* and had managed only to prolong an existence that was becoming daily more intolerable. His remorse was joined with fury against the *boni* for urging him to this ruinous course instead of leading the fight in his defense. He could see only motives of malice and envy in their advice and actions. He accused them of plotting his downfall under his own roof, in betrayal of his trust and friendship, inveigling him by simulated fears and false assurances, as he wavered in a welter of worry and grief, into accomplishing his own destruction. It was the crowning disillusionment with his optimate associates. The *invidia* that he had seen undermining his prestige and authority in the preceding years he now believed had extended its venomous influence to encompass his ruin.[132]

Cicero was temperamentally badly equipped to deal with adversity on this scale. He readily admitted that he lacked the toughness of spirit necessary to rise above the grief that assailed him, nor could he find the strength to sustain it in the teachings of any system of philosophy.[133] He succumbed utterly, finding excuses in the number and magnitude of his afflictions. He shunned crowds and all company, brooding in solitude, indulging his pain. His general aversion to life outside Italy further encouraged withdrawal and reinforced his longing for Rome. In Plutarch's words, he lived gazing toward Italy like a demented lover. Time brought no improvement. He kept his mind fixed rigidly on thoughts of restoration or death, and made no attempt to adapt to circumstances or to respond to the kindness shown him by so many. From beginning to end, his exile brought him unrelieved and harrowing misery, the memory and effects of which would not easily be erased.[134]

132. *Att.* 3.3; 3.4; 3.7.2; 3.8.4; 3.9.2; 3.10.2; 3.13.2; 3.14.1; 3.15.2, 4, 7; 3.19.3; 3.20.1. *Q.F.* 1.3.5–6, 8; 1.4.1,4. 4. *Fam.* 1.9.13; 14.1.2; 14.2.1; 14.3.1–2. 14.4.1, 5. *Quir.* 21.

133. *Dom.* 97–98. *Q.F.* 1.3.5. Cf. Plutarch, *Cic.* 32.5. Dio 38.18–29.

134. *Att.* 3.2; 3.5; 3.6; 3.7.1; 3.8.2, 4; 3.10.2; 3.12.1, 3; 3.13.2; 3.14.2; 3.15.2; 3.19.1; 3.25; 3.26. *Q.F.* 1.3.1. *Fam.* 14.1.7; 14.4.1. *Planc.* 101. Plutarch, *Cic.* 32.4.

4: COMPROMISE AND COEXISTENCE

Cicero was recalled from exile on August 4, 57, by a law passed by unanimous vote of a crowded *comitia centuriata* on the motion of the consul P. Lentulus Spinther and with the support of all magistrates except Clodius's brother Appius who was a praetor, and two tribunes.[1] The restoration was achieved with an impressive show of unity and determination by the state's leaders and the nation as a whole, but it had been slow in coming. Clodius had made sure of that. He had remained a dominant political force throughout 58 and had continued aggressively to use his office and his formidable *potentia* to promote his interests and thwart opponents. Not long after Cicero's departure he had come into conflict with Pompey by securing the release of Tigranes, son of the king of Armenia, whom Pompey was holding as a hostage and had placed for safekeeping in the house of the praetor L. Flavius. The incident involved a bloody clash between Flavius and his followers and the forces of Clodius, in which Flavius was worsted and a friend of Pompey, a *publicanus* named M. Papirius, was killed. It was an extraordinary affair, a massive affront to Pompey, and thought likely at the time to produce major political reverberations.[2]

1. *Post red. in. sen.* 27. *Quir.* 17. *Dom.* 75, 87, 90. *Sest.* 109, 128. *Pis.* 35–36. *Att.* 4.1.4. Dio 39.8.2. Plutarch, *Cic.* 33.4.
2. Asconius 47, Clark. *Dom.* 66. *Mil.* 37. Dio 38.30. Plutarch, *Pomp.* 48. 6. Cicero

Clodius's motives are unclear, but his action fits into a series of interventions during his tribunate in the affairs of various areas of the East, a region where his family had extensive *clientelae* and where the financial rewards for political favors were especially tempting.[3] Besides his annexation of Cyprus, his legislation included measures to restore exiles to Byzantium and to grant control, with the title of king, of the sanctuary-principate of Pessinus to Brogitarus, the tetrarch of Trocmi. These initiatives, which Cicero later described to his brother as matters involving piles of money, betoken a definite drive by Clodius to use his tribunate to build his wealth and expand his family's eastern connections. The release of Tigranes, who was the son-in-law of the king of Parthia and the single direct heir to the throne of Armenia, could greatly advance these aims. Clodius, with typical arrogance and daring, was prepared to risk the wrath of Pompey to promote a personal political end.[4]

Pompey's initial reaction was muted, so much so that the news Cicero was receiving in May led him to believe the whole affair had blown over. It soon became apparent, however, that it had not. As May progressed, Pompey made clear that any friendship or cooperation between him and Clodius was at an end, and he began to speak in opposition to the tribune and to criticize his *acta*. About the same time, and almost certainly as a consequence of Pompey's new position, Cicero's supporters began to press more actively for his restoration. On June 1 a full Senate unanimously approved a motion for recall introduced by the tribune L. Ninnius. The resolution was vetoed, but support for Cicero was building and was beginning more aggressively to show itself. Soon after the senatorial debate Quintus, lately thought likely to face vigorous prosecution for extortion on his return from his governorship of Asia, was welcomed home from the province by large, supportive crowds. Friends of Clodius who found themselves arraigned in the criminal courts were condemned. The *equites* began to hold meetings in support of Cicero, and his son-in-

speaks of "motus in republica" that were expected as a result of the release. *Att.* 3.8.3; 3.13.1. *Q.F.* 1.4.2. Cf. *Att.* 3.10.1.

3. See E. Rawson, "The Eastern *Clientelae* of Clodius and the Claudii," *Historia* 22 (1973), 219–39. The wealth to be made can be illustrated by the enormous sums that Pompey received from kings such as Tigranes and Ariobarzanes. See Appian, *Mith.* 104–05. Dio 36.53. *Att.* 6.1.3. Badian, *Roman Imperialism*, 82ff.

4. *Sest.* 56–57. *Har. resp.* 28–29, 58. *Dom.* 129. *Mil.* 73. *Q.F.* 2. 8 (7), 2. For the younger Tigranes, see Appian, *Mith.* 104. Dio 36. 53. Plutarch, *Pomp.* 33. 5. Magie, *Roman Rule in Asia Minor*, 1.358.

law, C. Piso, began a campaign to pressure his kinsman, the consul L. Piso, into action.[5]

The elections gave further encouragement to Cicero's backers. One of the consuls-elect was P. Lentulus Spinther, who, as aedile in 63, had become a confidant of Cicero and had served as his loyal ally during the suppression of the Catilinarian conspiracy. The new tribunes gave even stronger grounds for hope. At least five of them were considered friendly to Cicero, among them P. Sestius, another ally of the orator in 63 and described by Cicero to his brother as *amicissimus*. The elections were quickly followed by a fresh initiative to press for restoration. There were renewed calls to the consuls to put a motion to the House. Senior figures such as Scribonius Curio, consul of 76, spoke in favor. One of the praetors of 58, L. Domitius Ahenobarbus, a longtime supporter of Cicero, threatened that he would himself bring a motion. Finally, the Senate indicated it would transact no further business until the consuls responded to the demands for action in Cicero's case.[6]

Pompey played an active part in at least some of these developments. He now had many reasons to work for Cicero's return. It is reasonable to assume he was anxious to redress the injury done to an *amicus* now that the need to accommodate Clodius was at an end. It was also to his advantage to promote a cause that was broadly popular and the most likely to bring Clodius a political defeat and weaken his overall political control. He could expect other benefits in improved relations with the general body of the Senate, which was strongly committed to achieving Cicero's restoration, and in renewed friendship with the orator himself, who remained a valuable ally, particularly in matters of senatorial politics.

A change in Pompey's attitude toward Cicero's exile was becoming evident by the end of May. Cicero was by then making direct approaches to him, and Atticus was sending optimistic reports of his goodwill. According to Dio, he was the real author of Ninnius's motion in the

5. *Att.* 3.8.3. *Post red. in sen.* 3. *Sest.* 67–68. *Pis.* 27. Dio 38. 30.

6. For Lentulus's ties to Cicero, see *Quir.* 15. Sallust, *Cat.* 47.3. He was also a friend of both Pompey and Caesar. *Att.* 3.22.2. Caesar, *BC* 1.22. For the hope offered by the elections and the new College of Tribunes, see *Sest.* 70. *Att.* 3.13.1. *Q.F.* 1.4.3. The debate in the Senate is mentioned in *Sest.* 68. *Pis.* 29. *Att.* 3.15.3, 6; 3.24.2. The chronology of events can be roughly determined from *Sest.* 67–68 and from Cicero's letters, allowing close to three weeks for letters to reach Thessalonica from Rome. Occasionally letters took as little as two weeks. *Att.* 3.8.2

Senate on June 1. By early July he was giving Atticus and Varro firm assurances of his support and was promising definite action in the Senate after the elections. The senatorial initiative duly happened; Pompey was clearly a prime mover in it, and he had plans to follow it with the selection of a magistrate to introduce the actual legislation for recall.[7]

Pompey was pursuing his efforts at this stage, however, mainly behind the scenes. He did not participate in either of the main senatorial debates nor did he otherwise publicly campaign for Cicero's recall.[8] Cicero in fact felt unsure of his support at many points throughout the period. Pompey's caution, however, was due not to any lack of commitment to Cicero's cause but to a desire to avoid offending Caesar, who had firmly favored the orator's banishment and might well object to his return. Pompey wanted to be assured that the movement for restoration would not alienate his partner, and early in the campaign he wrote to Caesar seeking his views. He made clear to Cicero's friends that he would openly work for Cicero's recall and begin the process of legislation only after he received Caesar's reply. That reply was expected, however, to be favorable and was being awaited toward the end of July. Optimism remained high among Cicero's supporters.[9]

Clodius had meantime reacted with characteristic vigor and resourcefulness to Pompey's opposition and the growing support for Cicero. He centered his attack not on Pompey but on the interests of the coalition as a whole, resurrecting the charges of illegalities in the enactment of the legislation of 59. In the Senate and at *contiones* he highlighted the violations of the auspices, producing Bibulus and certain of the augurs to attest that the heavens had been watched during passage of the Julian laws, and that, under augural law, legislation passed in such circumstances was null and void. Clodius sounded the theme for months, with calls for the Senate to rescind Caesar's laws.[10]

7. Cicero reports he is in correspondence with Pompey in *Att.* 3.8.4; 3.9.3. Atticus's contacts and reports are mentioned in *Att.* 3.8.3; 3.9.2; 3.13.1; 3.14.1; 3.18.1. For Pompey's part in Ninnius's proposal, see Dio 38.30.

8. See *Q.F.* 1.3.9. *Att.* 3.15.1.

9. *Att.* 3.18.1. The coalition was holding firm in 58. There are several allusions in Cicero's letters to *motus* and *discordia,* often taken to indicate strain in the alliance, but even if one assumes they refer to possible trouble within the coalition, and not to conflict between Clodius and Pompey, they were clearly no more than rumors. *Att.* 3.8.3; 3.10.1; 3.13.1. *Q.F.* 1.4.2. The optimism of Cicero's main supporters and correspondents is indicated in *Q.F.* 1.4.2. *Att.* 3.18.1.

10. *Dom.* 40. *Har. resp.* 48.

Clodius's assault on the *acta* of 59, one of which was the measure ratifying his own adoption as a plebeian, has puzzled many historians and provoked extensive debate about his real intentions.[11] The evidence, however, can be taken at face value and shows a strategy both sensible and unsurprising. Clodius was facing opposition from the dominant partner in the coalition. He responded by returning to the form of attack that had been strongly pressed by optimate foes of the dynasts earlier in 58 and that he himself had previously and profitably pursued in 59, when he had threatened to use his tribunate to rescind all the legislation of Caesar's consulship.[12] The illegalities of 59 remained a troublesome problem for the triumvirate and the obvious avenue of attack for its opponents.[13]

Clodius could also count on gathering support for his anticoalition campaign from hardline *optimates* eager to embrace any opportunity to embarrass their archenemies. According to Cicero, a new alignment with leading *boni* to dilute the strength of his opposition was a central part of his strategy. There is certainly abundant evidence that he established close cooperation with leading conservatives at this time, at least in relation to the attacks on the dynasts. The appearance of Bibulus and the augurs at *contiones* to assist in highlighting the nature and extent of the illegality in 59 signaled the beginning of the collaboration.[14] There followed a concerted effort to insure the challenge to Caesar's laws could not be used to cast doubts on the legitimacy of Clodius's own tribunate. Certain *principes civitatis,* as Cicero called them, made repeated public statements affirming that Clodius had the legal right to transact business with the people, which was, in effect, a declaration that he had been validly elected tribune. They also maintained that all due process had been observed in the passage of his laws, leaving no reason on any

11. See F. B. Marsh, "The Policy of Clodius," *CQ* 21 (1927), 30–35. L. G. Pocock, "Publius Clodius and the Acts of Caesar," *CQ* 18 (1924), 59–64. Rundell, *Historia* 28 (1979), 301–28. Lintott, *Greece and Rome* 14 (1969), 157–69. Gruen, *Phoenix* 20 (1966), 120–30. Ward, *Crassus*, 246ff. H. Benner, *Die Politik des P. Clodius Pulcher* (Stuttgart, 1987), 133ff.

12. See discussion in Chapter 3 of Clodius's posture in 59.

13. Caesar's concerns in 58 and 56 to insure Cicero would not attack the *acta* of 59 show how important this matter was. See *Fam.* 1.9.9,12.

14. *Har. resp.* 48, 50. *Dom.* 42. *Prov. cons.* 45–46. *Fam.* 1.9.10. See Meier, *Res Publica,* 286ff; *MH* 32, 197–208. Hortensius and Lucullus were augurs (see Broughton, *MRR* 2.254–55) and were very likely active with Bibulus in aiding Clodius's attack on the coalition.

grounds for contesting their validity.[15] The strength of Clodius's ties to conservative leaders was to become even more apparent in 57, when optimate intervention protected him from a prosecution for violence and helped him win election to the aedileship. Clodius had skillfully exploited the divisions in Roman politics to forge a new alliance of the coalition's foes that would clearly show the dynasts his continuing capacity to threaten their position.[16]

In early August, stirred perhaps by signs that decisive action to recall Cicero was imminent, he intensified his attacks on Pompey, resorting to another great prop of his dominance in 58, his armed gangs. It became unsafe for Pompey to attend the Senate or the Forum. Gabinius rallied to the assistance of his longtime ally and attempted to oppose Clodius. There followed daily clashes in which the consul distinctly fared the worse. He had his *fasces* broken; he was himself wounded, and he suffered the further indignity of having his property consecrated. Finally, Clodius organized an attempt to assassinate Pompey on August 11. The plot was uncovered when a slave dropped a dagger in the Temple of Castor, where the Senate was meeting, and confessed he had been posted there by Clodius to kill Pompey. The latter reacted by retiring to his house on the Carinae, and for the remainder of Clodius's tribunate he avoided the Senate, the Forum, and all involvement in public life.[17] There was no investigation, no attempt to institute proceedings against Clodius. The tribune had reasserted full control.[18]

Pompey's complete and sustained withdrawal from public affairs was an extraordinary turnabout. It is sometimes attributed to his well-documented fear of assassination, but more likely represents a decision by the

---

15. *Prov. cons.* 45–46. *Dom.* 42. *Har. resp.* 50. The threat to Clodius's tribunate from the attacks on Caesar's laws was, in any case, less serious than is sometimes alleged. It is highly improbable that permanent repeal of Caesar's laws was ever seriously contemplated. The enemies of the coalition were concerned to safeguard the integrity of the auspices and establish illegality that would expose its perpetrators to prosecution. They were less concerned about the substance of the laws, with the possible exception of the *Lex Campana*, and there was a standing offer from the Senate to reenact them once due regard had been paid to the auspices. *Prov. cons.* 46.

16. See *Att.* 4.3.3,5. *Fam.* 1.9.10. *Har. resp.* 50. *Sest.* 85, 89, 95.

17. *Sest.* 69. *Dom.* 67, 124. *Har. resp.* 49. *Mil.* 18, 37. *Pis.* 16, 27–28. Asconius 46, Clark. Dio 38.30. Plutarch, *Pomp.* 49.2.

18. *Mil.* 18–19. Clodius continued his attacks even after Pompey's retirement, threatening to take over the latter's house on the Carinae and built a second portico to match the one he had built on the site of the houses of Catulus and Cicero. *Har. resp.* 49.

coalition as a whole to avoid further conflict with Clodius in 58.[19] The latter had again effectively shown his political resourcefulness and his capacity to dominate political events when backed by the powers of the tribunate. The triumvirs had determinedly backed away from confrontation with him in 59; they had more reason than ever to do so in the middle of 58. It is further evident that Caesar had no wish at this time to provoke a conflict with Clodius over the issue of Cicero's restoration. He did not yet share Pompey's enthusiasm for the orator's recall, as is evidenced by the fact that Cicero's closest friend among the tribunes-elect, P. Sestius, thought it necessary to make a special trip to Cisalpine Gaul in early November to try to win him to Cicero's side. The trip, on Cicero's evidence, was largely unsuccessful. Caesar's consent to restoration appears, in fact, to have come only after extensive consultations, involving pledges by Pompey, for which Quintus went guarantor, that Cicero would not attack the *acta* of 59. It seems certain that Caesar did not give the expected immediate endorsement of Pompey's plans that was being awaited in late July. That response most likely counseled instead a general retreat from Pompey's course of opposition to Clodius. Pompey, anxious as he was in 58 to act only with the cooperation of his partner, changed course, the threat of assassination doubtless serving to confirm his decision.[20]

The events of early August ended all hope of restoration in 58. By early September Cicero had accepted that all activity for the year was over. One final initiative did emerge in late October, a bill for restoration promulgated by eight tribunes. It was strongly supported by Lentulus but was never considered to have any chance of passage, its purpose being to show continuing support for Cicero and to set guidelines for tribunician action in 57.[21] Toward the year's end the mood of Cicero and his friends

19. For Pompey's fear of assassination, see Asconius 36, 50, 51–52, Clark. *Sest.* 69. *Mil.* 65–66. *Q.F.* 2.3.3.

20. *Sest.* 71. Cf. *Att.* 3.23.5. *Pis.* 80 suggests Caesar's consent coincided with Pompey's campaign for restoration in spring of 57. For the pledges he exacted as a condition of his consent, see *Fam.* 1.9.9, 12. Crassus may also have been opposed to restoration in 58, though his attitude, as always, is difficult to determine because of the almost total lack of evidence. The few mentions of him suggest, however, that he was showing no support for Cicero. *Fam.* 14.2.2. *Att.* 3.15.3; 3.23.5. Cicero's attitude toward Crassus after his return points to the same conclusion. *Fam.* 1.9.20. *Att.* 4.13.2. Ward (*Crassus*, 244ff.) finds reason to argue otherwise.

21. *Att.* 3.19.1; 3.23.1. *Sest.* 70. *Post red. in sen.* 29.

was mixed. There were grounds for hope in the stance of the new magistrates. Lentulus Spinther remained strongly supportive, and the other consul-elect, Metellus Nepos, though an old enemy of Cicero, declared he would not oppose restoration. The new tribunes held even greater promise. They seemed fully united and were pledging quick action on Cicero's behalf. But there were reasons also for disquiet. The attitude of the triumvirs remained uncertain, and Cicero had fears that even out of office Clodius would be able to sway public gatherings and would find someone to veto any legislation. The orator's future still seemed uncertain as the year closed.[22]

Early in 57 the consuls and tribunes launched their expected initiatives supported by deputations from the Italian communities. On January 1 Lentulus placed the question of restoration before the Senate. Nepos indicated support, declaring that he was ending his feud with Cicero in the interests of the state. L. Cotta, consul of 65, was asked to open the debate, and he argued that the law under which Cicero had been banished was invalid and that he should be recalled by a simple decree of the Senate. Pompey spoke next and expressed agreement with the views of Cotta, but recommended that a decision of the people should accompany the Senate's decree to exclude the possibility of popular agitation. All the subsequent speakers rivaled each other in supporting Cicero, but when a division was about to take place, a tribune, Atilius Gavianus, asked for one night to consider, a modified form of veto and a clear signal that Clodius had succeeded, as Cicero had feared, in securing an ally among the tribunes. Atilius persisted in his course of obstruction, and though all of the remaining senatorial meetings in January were devoted to discussion of Cicero's case, no resolution was passed.[23]

In the meantime, the tribune Q. Fabricius had promulgated a bill to recall Cicero and it came before the *concilium plebis* for voting on January 23. Clodius did not rely on any constitutional mode of obstruction on this occasion, but used a contingent of gladiators borrowed from his brother Appius, who was preparing funeral games for a relative, to drive Fabricius and his followers from the Forum. It was a bloody encounter that claimed many lives and almost brought the death of Cicero's brother. No further attempt was made to pass Fabricius's bill; the tribuni-

---

22. *Att.* 3.23.4; 3.24.2; 3.25. *Fam.* 14.1.2; 14.2.2; 14.3.3. *Sest.* 70, 72. *Q.F.* 1.4.3.
23. *Sest.* 72–77. *Quir.* 12. *Dom.* 68–69, 84. *Pis.* 34.

cian initiative on which Cicero had placed such high hopes in late 58 had faltered.[24]

Clodius had quickly shown that his capacity to dominate political events had not ended with his departure from the tribunate. He remained a formidable force, his power derived from several sources. The tactics of force that he had developed at the beginning of his tribunate had not yet been countered by his opponents and were devastating in their impact. He retained his popularity with the urban populace and continued to have access through his brother Appius, who was a praetor in 57, to the *contiones* that he was so skilled in turning to his purposes.[25] Two tribunes, Sex. Atilius Serranus Gavianus and Q. Numerius Rufus, had defected to him, providing him with the enormously important obstructive power of their office. He also had other supporters of high rank and influence. Nepos, an old ally, remained his loyal adherent in 57, though he was unwilling actively to assist him in preventing Cicero's restoration. Gellius Publicola, brother of Lucius, the consul of 72, and stepbrother of L. Marcius Philippus, consul of 56, was a prominent leader of his gangs. P. Sulla, kinsman of the dictator, was another notable collaborator in his campaign of violence.[26] There were, besides, many *principes* of the Senate who, though not openly supportive of his actions and though unwilling, like Nepos, to cooperate with him in any attempt to prevent Cicero's return, remained ready to tolerate his extremism and protect him from its consequences, so long as his overall course threatened embarrassments and setbacks for Pompey.[27]

Clodius no longer possessed, however, the varied prerogatives of the tribunate so important to his strategy of intimidation and demagoguery, which gave a powerful inducement to his enemies to renew opposition and persist in it. He also faced some determined new opponents among

24. *Sest.* 75, 78. *Post red. in sen.* 22. *Mil.* 38. Dio 39.7.

25. See *Att.* 4.2.3; 4.3.4. *Sest.* 126.

26. For the Clodian tribunes, see *Sest.* 72, 77, 82, 87. *Pis.* 35. *Quir.* 12. *Mil.* 39. Asconius 11, Clark. For Nepos's continuing friendship with Clodius, see *Sest.* 79, 89. *Att.* 4.3.3. *Fam.* 5.3.1. Dio 39.7. For Clodius's other supporters, see *Att.* 4.3.3–4. *Sest.* 110. Shackleton Bailey, *Ad Att.* 2.174.

27. See n. 14 above. Gruen's idea (*Last Generation,* 294) that the leading *boni* combined with Pompey to defeat Clodius in 57 is untenable. Most of the *consulares* were not in the forefront of the movement for recall, and they showed no concern to weaken Clodius. Cicero felt he should name only two in his speeches of thanks after his return, Servilius Vatia and Gellius Publicola (*Quir.* 17).

the incoming magistrates, notably the tribunes T. Annius Milo and P. Sestius.[28] The former responded to the events of January 23 by arresting a number of the gladiators involved in the violence and bringing them before the Senate. They confessed and were put in chains by Milo, but the tribune Atilius forced their release. Clodius then turned his gangs on Milo, attacking his home and waylaying him in the streets. Milo resorted to the courts, launching a prosecution under the *Lex Plautia de vi*. Clodius's friends among the magistrates rallied to his support, and Nepos, Appius, and a tribune issued a decree suspending judicial proceedings.[29] Milo then decided to match force with force and assembled his own *operae*. He was most likely encouraged in this by some of Cicero's friends, who seem to have provided money for the gangs.[30] Cicero himself had no moral qualms about resorting to such violent extralegal methods to deal with a violent opponent, and the principle by which he later defended Milo's course—namely, that where *ius* and *iudicia* no longer prevail, *vis* must rule—was deeply rooted in the Roman tradition.[31]

Milo's new tactics were soon imitated by Cicero's other great supporter among the tribunes, P. Sestius. He, like Milo, had quickly found himself a target of Clodius's gangs, and he had narrowly escaped death when he had attempted to obstruct by *obnuntiatio* a meeting being conducted by Nepos in front of the Temple of Castor.[32] Soon afterwards he assembled an armed entourage that continued to attend him everywhere throughout his tribunate.[33] Clodius now had to deal with opponents

28. The consul Lentulus Spinther and seven of the eight praetors were opposed to him as well. See *Post red. in sen.* 22–23. *Mil.* 39.

29. *Sest.* 85–86, 88–90. *Post red. in sen.* 19. *Mil.*35. The exact nature of the decree remains obscure. Cicero calls it *novum,* but does not question its validity. It can hardly have been a *iustitium,* or Cicero would surely have said so. It applied only to the courts, a modified *iustitium,* perhaps, based on the general right of higher magistrates to suspend the functions of those of lesser power. See Greenidge, *Roman Public Life,* 175.

30. See *Att.* 3.23.5; 4.2.7. Shackleton Bailey, *Ad Att.* 2.173. One of Cicero's friends who made money available was the praetor Caecilius, who became a special target of Clodius's gangs. *Post red. in sen.* 22. *Mil.* 38.

31. *Sest.* 92, 127. *Mil.* 38. Cicero's attitude was not dictated by his special situation. He condoned extralegal violence in many instances in the history of the Republic. See Lintott, *Violence,* 60ff. Mitchell, *Ascending Years,* 86.

32. *Sest.* 79, 85. *Mil.* 38. *Q.F.* 2.3.6. The nature or subject of the meeting is not recorded. That Milo's gangs preceded those of Sestius is clear from *Mil.* 38 and the account in *Sest.* 86–90.

33. *Sest.* 78, 84, 92.

willing to match his own extremism, and he never again had the capacity to control by violence the course of decision making at Rome. The weapon of force that he had so effectively exploited had been badly blunted and a major obstacle to Cicero's restoration had been removed.

Clodius also had to contend in 57 with the full force of Pompey's opposition, which was no longer constrained by misgivings from Caesar. The latter had finally given his consent to Cicero's return, and Pompey, spurred no doubt by his humiliation in late 58, determined to use all his energy and influence to bring Cicero home in triumph and deal Clodius a decisive political defeat.[34] His speech in the Senate on January 1, the first time he had spoken publicly in favor of restoration, clearly signaled his full commitment to Cicero's cause and an end to the vacillation and timidity that had marked his dealings with Clodius in 58. After the failure of the first initiatives by the Senate and tribunes, he began elaborate preparations in cooperation with his close ally, the consul Lentulus, to insure success on the next occasion. His strategy was to rally all Italy in Cicero's support and by mobilizing the full citizenry of the state for the vote on restoration to offset the impact of the urban populace, which was firmly controlled by Clodius and was normally the dominant element in legislative assemblies. He used his position as *duovir* at Capua to secure passage of a decree by the local council calling for Cicero's restoration. He then took the campaign to the other *coloniae* and *municipia* of Italy and prompted a flood of similar resolutions.[35] Lentulus supplemented the effort by getting the Senate to decree that the consuls, using a traditional formula reserved for major crises, should call on all citizens in all Italy who wished for the safety of the state to assemble in support of Cicero's restoration. The Senate also decreed thanks to those in the provinces who had helped Cicero and commended him to foreign communities and to all Roman officials abroad.[36]

The Senate's action took place during games organized by Lentulus in honor of Marius's victory over the Cimbri and was well received by those attending the celebrations. Lentulus and the other senators were given a

---

34. See n. 20 above.

35. *Dom.* 30, 75. *Pis.* 25, 80. *Post red. in sen.* 29. *Mil.* 39. *Quir.* 10.

36. *Post red. in sen.* 24. *Dom.* 73, 85. *Planc.* 78. *Sest.* 116, 128. *Pis.* 34. The formal call to all who wished for the safety of the state to assemble had previously been issued in 100 (*Rab.* 20) and in 67 (Asconius 75, Clark). Cicero claims this was the first time it had ever been used in regard to a single citizen. *Post red. in sen.* 24.

standing ovation in the theater on the day of the meeting.[37] Other signs of broad public support for restoration also began to appear again. The corporations of *publicani* rallied once more and began to pass resolutions extolling Cicero's achievements and calling for his return. Similar decrees were passed by the *scribae* and by other associations in the city.[38]

The buildup to the introduction of a new bill for restoration reached its climax in early July. The final stage was carefully timed to coincide with the Games of Apollo, the period immediately preceding the elections when the greatest number of Italians could be expected to come to Rome. Around July 9, when the city was thronged with crowds, which had been augmented by the Senate's appeal, Lentulus called a meeting of the Senate in the Temple of Jupiter on the Capitol.[39] It was attended by 417 senators. Pompey was called on to speak first, and, using a prepared script to highlight the seriousness he attached to the occasion, he put forward a resolution describing Cicero as the saviour of his country and directing that legislation to recall him be introduced before the *comitia centuriata*. The motion was approved by everyone present with the single exception of Clodius. Even Nepos, who had previously maintained a neutral position on the issue, lent his support following a dramatic plea from Servilius Vatia.[40]

37. *Sest.* 116ff. *Planc.*78. *Schol. Bob.* 136, 166, Stangl. The meeting was held in the Temple of Virtus, built by Marius, Cicero's fellow townsman. Lentulus may have been seeking to exploit the connection by the timing and location of the debate on Cicero. The date of the meeting was most likely in May when Lentulus held the *fasces*. There were demonstrations of support for Cicero at other shows as well. Sestius was loudly applauded at a gladiatorial show. *Sest.* 124–26.

38. *Dom.* 74. *Pis.* 41.

39. The date can be approximately determined from the date of voting on the bill, which was August 4. The required *trinum nundinum* between promulgation and voting means the bill was published around July 10. Lentulus would not have delayed publication following the overwhelming vote in favor of the proposal in the Senate. He held a *contio* next day, which was very likely the beginning of the public discussion of the bill. The idea that promulgation of legislation was not permitted during the *trinum nundinum* preceding the elections must be discarded. See A. E. Astin, "Leges Aelia et Fufia," *Latomus* 23 (1964), 421–45. Michels, *Calendar*, 41. The date of the Senate's meeting is also indicated by the fact that the price of grain, high during the early stages of the Games of Apollo (Asconius 48, Clark), fell suddenly after the Senate's decree. *Dom.* 14.

40. *Post red. in sen.* 25–26,31. *Dom.* 30. *Sest.* 129–30. *Mil.* 39. *Pis.* 34–36. The prepared script showed the importance Pompey attached to the occasion. For other allusions to prepared scripts, see *Planc.* 74. *Phil.* 10.5. *Fam.* 10.13.1. *De or.* 1.152. The *comitia centuriata* was the most appropriate assembly to deal with an issue of civil rights (*Sest.* 73. *Rep.* 2.61. *Leg.* 3.44). Its voting structure would also lessen further the impact of the urban *plebs*.

The legislation was most likely promulgated at once. It was signed by all the magistrates except Appius and the two Clodian supporters among the tribunes.[41] Lentulus continued to maintain the momentum, and the day after the meeting on the Capitol he held a *contio* to appeal for restoration to the crowds assembled from Italy. Pompey again played the leading role, eulogizing Cicero and pleading for his recall. He was followed by the entire body of *consulares* and *praetorii,* all echoing the same sentiments.[42] Later the same day Lentulus again summoned the Senate and it was decreed, once more on the motion of Pompey, that no one should by any means obstruct the process of restoration, that anyone doing so would be regarded as a public enemy, and that, in the event of obstruction lasting more than five days, Cicero would be entitled to return with all his rights restored. The meeting also decreed thanks to those who had come from the *municipia* and asked them to return again for the voting.[43] The crowds duly reassembled on August 4 to assert the popular will in a rare show of unanimity. Even Appius decided to acquiesce in the decision at the end.[44] Cicero's cherished alliance of *boni,* rallied by strong leadership and freed from the threat of violence, had finally achieved the victory over Clodius that Cicero had hoped for in vain in early 58.

On the day of the voting, Cicero sailed from Dyrrachium and arrived in Brundisium on August 5. He was warmly welcomed, and had a joyous reunion with his beloved Tullia. As soon as he got word of the vote in the Centuries, he set out for Rome and had a triumphal journey through Italy, greeted everywhere by deputations from communities large and small. He reached the capital on September 4, where vast crowds had assembled to welcome him, and he was cheered by enthusiastic well-wishers as he made his way from the Porta Capena to the Capitol and on to the family home on the Carinae. The following day he delivered a speech in the Senate that combined thanks to those who had promoted his return with a

41. *Pis.* 35. Cicero explicitly indicates the bill was enacted *ex senatus consulto* and was in accord with Pompey's motion. *Sest.* 109. *Post red. in sen.* 31.

42. *Post red. in sen.* 26. *Quir.* 16–17. *Sest.* 107. *Pis.* 34, 80. Clodius continued to speak out in opposition. *Sest.* 108.

43. *Post red. in sen.* 27. *Sest.* 129. *Pis.* 35.

44. *Dom.* 75,87,90. *Post red. in sen.* 28. *Quir.* 17,25. *Pis.* 36. *Sest.* 109,112. *Att.* 4.1.4. Plutarch, *Cic.* 33.4. Dio 39.8. See Ciaceri, *Cicerone* 2:64ff. Gelzer, *Cicero,* 147ff.

carefully tailored version of the events of his exile and restoration that was designed to blot out any stain of ignominy or rejection and restore his position as defender and saviour of the true *respublica*. His departure into exile he presented as a selfless act to avoid useless bloodshed in conditions in which degenerate consuls and a violent tribune had brought the suppression of law and liberty; his restoration he acclaimed as an overwhelming endorsement of his views and actions by a Senate and public that had sought his return with a determination and unanimity unparalleled in the history of the state. The same sentiments were to be repeated frequently in the coming months and years.[45]

The list of those that Cicero singled out for special praise in his speech in the Senate is noteworthy. He says in the *Pro Plancio* that those he named were "causae nostrae duces." The consuls not surprisingly are prominent among them, as are Milo and Sestius. The six other tribunes and the seven praetors who signed the bill for restoration are also cited.[46] But out of all the *consulares* only two get mention, Pompey and P. Servilius Vatia, consul of 79. Pompey gets due recognition as the main architect of the great groundswell of support that built in the first half of 57. Cicero fully appreciated the extent and importance of Pompey's effort and he was fully prepared publicly to give him credit for it. Servilius he believed had also made an important contribution by his eloquent and successful plea to Nepos in the Temple of Jupiter. But there was no other *consularis* that he felt could be classified as a leader of his cause. The conservative *principes*, whom he could reasonably expect to be his strongest allies, had joined the chorus of support for restoration at the end, but they had waited for others to create the momentum. Their continuing flirtation with Clodius and hatred for Pompey doubtless explain their inertia but, whatever the cause, their behavior in 57 had done little to lessen the estrangement from them that Cicero had been feeling since late 61 and that had grown to paranoiac proportions during his exile.[47]

---

45. *Att.* 4.1.4–5. *Sest.* 131. *Pis.* 51–52. Plutarch, *Cic.* 33.5. The themes of the *Post reditum in senatu* were echoed in the *Ad Quirites*, which was probably delivered the same day, and in *De domo, Pro Sestio, In Vatinium, In Pisonem, Pro Plancio.*

46. *Planc.* 74. *Post red. in sen.* 18ff.

47. *Post red. in sen.* 25, 29, 31. *Quir.* 16–17. *Dom.* 30. *Har. resp.* 46. *Sest.* 74. *Pis.* 25, 35, 80. *Mil.* 39. Cicero gives one other *consularis*, L. Gellius Publicola, special

The Euphoria Fades Again

Cicero was given little time to bask in the glow of his triumphal return. He found himself immediately caught up in a political storm arising out of a serious shortage of grain that had pushed prices sharply higher. The scarcity was due mainly to poor harvests in the grain growing provinces, but it had been aggravated by the action of dealers, who were holding back supplies and selling to other markets. Cicero puts blame also on the system of procurement and distribution introduced by Clodius's grain law in 58.[48] By the middle of 57 the problem had become acute and there was rioting in early July at the Games of Apollo, a time when the shortages may well have been worsened by the crowds of Italians that had come to Rome in response to the Senate's appeal. There was a sudden drop in prices following the senatorial meeting in the Temple of Jupiter that decreed Cicero's recall, but it was short-lived and prices had soared again by early September.[49]

The Senate met for several days around the time of Cicero's return to discuss the crisis, and a general agreement was emerging, strongly backed by public opinion, that Pompey should be given a special command to oversee the entire grain supply. A further meeting of the Senate was held by Nepos in the Temple of Concord on September 7. A large crowd assembled to press for action, among them Clodius's *operae,* intent, according to Cicero, on stirring trouble. Clodius was seeking to throw the blame for the most recent rise in prices on Cicero, and his minions were inciting the mob to demand that Cicero come and take responsibility.[50] There was some stone throwing, and all the *consulares,* with the exception of two staunch Pompeian supporters, Messala and Afranius, used the threat of violence as a pretext for staying away al-

---

mention in *Quir.* 17. Both Servilius and Gellius, it is perhaps worth noting, had links to Pompey. Servilius was a prominent supporter of the Manilian law; Gellius had supported Pompey's interests as consul in 72. Both served under him in the sixties. See *Man.* 68. Plutarch, *Pomp.* 34.5. Appian, *Mith.* 95.

48. *Dom.* 11, 25. Dio 39.9.2. See Rickman, *Corn Supply,* 52ff.

49. Asconius 48, Clark. *Dom.* 14. *Att.* 4.1.6.

50. Shackleton Bailey (*Ad Att.,* 2.167) believes the meeting in the Temple of Concord took place on Sept. 6, and was not attended by Cicero, and that another meeting then followed on the Capitol on Sept. 7, at which Cicero made his proposal. The account in *Dom.* 6–7, 11–16 does not support this reconstruction. Cicero does speak of meetings in the Temple of Concord and on the Capitol, but is clearly referring to one and the same meeting, obviously regarding the Temple of Concord as located on the Capitol.

together.[51] Cicero waited until the trouble appeared to have ended, but then, though he was feeling unwell, he came and moved a proposal, which the Senate adopted, that Pompey be given full control of the entire grain supply for a period of five years and that a law to that effect be enacted. The next day the Senate, with all the *consulares* present, gave Pompey all the supplies and personnel he requested, including fifteen legates, among whom he named Cicero and Quintus. But a complication then arose when the tribune C. Messius produced a bill of his own that went well beyond the law that the consuls had drafted in accordance with the Senate's decree, adding ships, troops, control of funding, and *imperium maius* in the provinces. The *consulares* were fuming. Pompey professed to want the consular law but his friends said otherwise. Cicero kept silent, anxious to avoid offending any of the *consulares* who were pontiffs and who would soon be deciding the fate of his house. In the end it was the consular bill that was passed into law, but passions had been stirred and factional divisions exacerbated.[52]

The whole affair proved an uncomfortable experience for Cicero. He was thrust into the foreground of the crisis where he had little choice but to propose the new commission for his benefactor, though it was certain to offend the conservative *principes* whose friendship he would need if he was ever to rejoin the ranks of leading *boni*. Clodius highlighted and exploited the embarrassment of his position, mocking him as the supposed saviour of republicanism, the darling of the Senate and the much lamented exile whose first act on his return was to betray senatorial authority by taking the popular side and handing extraordinary power to Pompey.[53] The proposal of Messius aggravated the situation, increasing optimate resentment and forcing Cicero into a silent role unlikely fully to please either side. He was caught again in the difficulty of attempting to retain his position as a leading proponent of traditional republicanism and at the same time meet the claims of friendship with a man who so often strained republican orthodoxy and who had become a hated enemy of its most fervent guardians.

---

51. *Dom.* 8, 12–13. *Att.* 4.1.6. Messala had attached himself to the triumvirs in 59, becoming a member of the quinquevirate. ILS 46.

52. *Dom.* 15. *Att.* 4.1.6–7. Plutarch, *Pomp.* 49.4–6. Dio 39.9. Cf. Gelzer, *Pompeius,* 157. Van Ooteghem, *Pompée, 362.*

53. *Dom.* 4–5. Clodius's taunts hit home. Cicero felt compelled to offer an elaborate rebuttal (*Dom.* 4–31).

Cicero began to show signs of political strains and general unhappiness almost immediately after his return. His first letter to Atticus speaks of hidden resentment and open *invidia* among those who were supposedly his supporters. He expressed a strong need for Atticus's presence. His private affairs added to his worries. His finances were in chaos. Much money had been spent in efforts by his friends to achieve his restoration, and he had himself borrowed heavily from Quintus. To what extent confiscation of his property under Clodius's bill of outlawry had proceeded is not recorded, but there is evidence that costly precautions had had to be taken in regard to his slaves, and no doubt similar arrangements had been made in regard to other assets. Exile had also strained his relations with Terentia. Cicero gives no details, but he alludes to the problem in his first two letters to Atticus after his return. Overall, the homecoming had many sobering and depressing aspects to dim the glory of the generous welcome.[54]

On September 29 the pontiffs considered the question of Cicero's house and decided, in effect, that the site could be returned to Cicero without sacrilege. The Senate ratified this decision on October 2, following unsuccessful filibustering and obstructive efforts by Clodius and Atilius, and the consuls were assigned the task of assessing, with the help of a *consilium,* the amount of compensation to be paid to Cicero for damage to his properties. They recommended payments of 2 million sesterces for the house on the Palatine, 500,000 for the Tusculan villa, and 250,000 for the Formian. The valuations were sharply criticized as inadequate and did nothing to relieve Cicero's financial difficulties. He began rebuilding on the Palatine and at Formiae, but he was reluctantly forced to offer the Tusculan property for sale. He attributed the niggardly estimates directly to the jealous hostility he had long experienced from his noble associates, and he believed they were now intent on keeping him from recovering his former prominence. His alienation from the

54. *Att.* 4.1.8; 4.2.7; 4.3.6. *Fam.* 14.4.4 alludes to arrangements made to avoid his slaves being sold *sub hasta.* Cf. arrangements made in Milo's case in 52 (*Att.* 5.8.2). Money may have been part of the reason for the strained relations with Terentia. She had been in dire straits during Cicero's exile and had sold property against his wishes. See *Fam.* 14.1.5; 14.2.3. S. Dixon, "Family Finances: Terentia and Tullia," *Antichthon* 18 (1984), 78–101. Cicero's summation of his private affairs is "ut in secundis fluxae, ut in adversis bonae" (*Att.* 4.1.8). For Terentia's property holdings in general, see *Att.* 2.4.5; 2.15.4; 12.32.2; 15.17.1; 15.20.4; *Fam.* 14.1.15.

conservative *principes,* already becoming inveterate, was being continually reinforced.[55]

In November the menace of Clodius began again to loom large in Cicero's life. The workmen on the site on the Palatine were driven off by Clodius's *operae* on November 3, and Quintus's house, which adjoined the site, was bombarded with stones and set on fire. Cicero himself was attacked in the street on November 11 by a gang led by Clodius and had to take refuge in the vestibule of a house while his attendants fought off the attack. The next day Clodius attempted to burn down Milo's house and a pitched battle was fought in full view of everyone at eleven o'clock in the morning. The violence was reaching unprecedented levels as Clodius, perhaps encouraged by the absence of Pompey, who was away from Rome in November and December organizing the grain supply, and by the prospect of early election to the aedileship, threw off all restraint in an attempt to offset recent defeats and reassert control of the streets.

The Senate discussed Clodius's latest violent excesses on November 14, and the consul-elect, Cn. Lentulus Marcellinus, proposed that he stand trial for all the incidents before the aedilician elections. But Nepos, Appius, and an unnamed *familiaris* of Atticus talked out the session.[56] Milo proceeded, however, to launch a prosecution and to block by use of *obnuntiatio* all attempts to hold the elections. But the strategy failed when a new means of blocking the prosecution emerged with the departure of the quaestors from office on December 4. The quaestors assigned the jurors in cases *de vi,* and since quaestorian elections followed the aedilician and had accordingly been held up in 57, there were no new quaestors to enter office. Nepos ruled that no prosecutions *de vi* could therefore take place until quaestors had been elected. Marcellinus attempted to have the Senate authorize the *praetor urbanus* to select the jury, but a filibuster by Clodius and threatening demonstrations by his

55. *Att.* 4.2.2–5. *Fam.* 1.9.5. *Har. resp.* 12–13. The decision of pontiffs and consuls also involved rebuilding the portico of Catulus, which had been demolished by Clodius. Cicero considered the speech *De domo* a masterly effort, and he planned to publish it immediately. *Att.* 4.2.2.

56. *Att.* 4.3.3. Marcellinus was a longstanding opponent of Clodius, one of his prosecutors at his trial for *incestum* in 61 (*Schol. Bob.* 85, 89, Stangl). He had ties to Pompey and was his legate in the sixties. Appian, *Mith.* 95. The *familiaris* of Atticus was most likely Hortensius, commonly so described by Cicero. See *Att.* 2.25.1. Cicero remained very hostile to Hortensius in this period. *Att.* 4.6.3.

gangs caused the Senate to disband. Cicero expected no further action in the Senate in December, and apparently none took place. There was no prosecution and the aedilician elections were eventually held on January 20 and brought Clodius back into office.[57]

Cicero was understandably angered and alarmed by Clodius's escape from prosecution and election to the aedileship, and he put the chief blame for both on the support that leading *boni,* intent on insuring the survival of Pompey's most extreme and resourceful enemy, had given him in the Senate.[58] This latest collaboration between the *principes* and his archenemy was the crowning blow to any remnant of respect that Cicero retained for the conservative leadership. He was appalled by their continuing willingness to support, for reasons of narrow factionalism and personal spite, a lawless extremist who threatened all the institutions of republicanism, and he was personally affronted by their indifference to his own plight as the chief victim of Clodius's flagrant and repeated violence. He felt the *optimates* wanted him only partly restored, with his *caput* intact, but with the rest of his being left crudely incomplete.[59]

The new year brought further displays of factional jousting as a new controversy developed in connection with the restoration of Ptolemy Auletes. The latter, who had been given recognition as king of Egypt and friend and ally of Rome by a law of Caesar in 59, had been expelled by his subjects in 57 and had come to Rome seeking restoration. He stayed in Pompey's Alban villa and pursued his campaign by gross bribery and by the intimidation and, when necessary, the murder of envoys from Alexandria who came to argue against him. Toward the end of 57 Lentulus secured passage of a senatorial decree authorizing Ptolemy's restoration by the governor of Cilicia, a position Lentulus himself was about to assume. But Ptolemy and his backers wanted Pompey to get the job, as

57. *Att.* 4.3.2–5. *Q.F.* 2.1.2. *Har. resp.* 15. *Mil.* 40. *Sest.* 95. Gruen (*Last Generation,* 296) maintains the Senate at a subsequent meeting in late December decreed the elections should go ahead, basing this on Cicero's statement in *Sest.* 95 that Milo was prevented prosecuting Clodius *per senatus auctoritatem.* But this seems extremely unlikely, and Cicero probably means no more than that the influence of the Senate, or rather of some of its *principes,* was responsible for keeping Clodius from being brought to trial.

58. *Fam.* 1.9.15. *Har. resp.* 50. *Sest.* 95. The anxiety Clodius's election was causing him is apparent in *Q.F.* 2.2.3.

59. *Fam.* 1.9.15. *Prov. cons.* 47. *Har. resp.* 46–47, 50. *Att.* 4.3.2,5 shows his particular disillusionment with the *boni* at the end of 57.

undoubtedly did Pompey himself, and a bill to appoint him was introduced in December by one of the new tribunes, Caninius Gallus.[60]

The alliance of conservative *consulares* and Clodius swung into action again to thwart the ambitions of both Pompey and Lentulus, the latter out of favor with the *consulares* because of his close association with Pompey and his role in securing him the grain commission.[61] An oracle was produced by the keepers of the Sibylline books to the effect that Ptolemy should not be restored with an army. Clodius's chief ally among the new tribunes, C. Cato, brought the keepers of the books before the people and made public the pronouncement. This development reopened the entire question and brought a plethora of new proposals from the diverse factional interests. Lentulus's only friends among the *consulares,* Cicero, Hortensius, and M. Lucullus, proposed the job be left with the governor of Cilicia; Bibulus proposed a commission of three, to be chosen from among those not holding *imperium,* thus excluding both Lentulus and Pompey. He was backed by the great bulk of the *consulares.* Crassus also proposed a commission of three, but allowed the inclusion of those with *imperium.* Rutilius Lupus, one of the new tribunes, proposed Pompey. All observed the religious prohibition against use of an army.

The Senate debated the issue at three meetings on January 13, 14, and 15. Crassus apparently withdrew his proposal. Bibulus's was defeated. Procedural wrangles and filibustering kept the others from coming to a vote. The matter had then to be postponed to February since the days remaining in January were all comitial.[62]

The exercise did nothing to brighten Cicero's view of the political

60. *Fam.* 1.1.1–3; 1.4.1. *Rab. post.* 6,21. *Cael.* 23, 24, 51–55. Strabo 17.1.11. Plutarch, *Pomp.* 49.6. Dio 39.12–14. See P. T. Eden, "P. Cornelius Lentulus Spinther and Cn. Cornelius Lentulus Marcellinus. Cicero, *Ad Fam.* 1.1.2," *RhM* 105 (1962), 352–58. Meyer, *Caesars Monarchie,* 126ff. I. Shatzman, "The Egyptian Question in Roman Politics (59–54 B.C.)," *Latomus* 30 (1971), 363–69. For the king's bribery and efforts to have Pompey appointed, see *Fam.* 1.1.1, 4; 1.5b.2. *Q.F.* 2.2.3. Since Caninius's law was due to be voted on before January 20 (*Fam.* 1.4.1), it was promulgated soon after he entered office on December 10.

61. *Fam.* 1.1.3; 1.5b.2. Cf. *Fam.* 1.7.8.

62. *Fam.* 1.4.2 shows the oracle was believed to have been fabricated. The maneuvering in January is told in *Fam.* 1.1.3; 1.2.1–2; 1.4.1–2. *Q.F.* 2.2.3. Crassus's proposal was not debated at the meetings in January, and must have been withdrawn. In view of the fate of Bibulus's proposal, it probably had little support.

scene or his own place in it. He considered Lentulus's right to the commission unassailable and he gave vigorous support to his benefactor. But he found himself standing apart once more from the majority of his fellow *consulares,* whose spiteful machinations ranged them yet again with Clodius and seemed a renunciation of all that was represented by the *via optimas* and the *sensus bonorum.* Pompey too had proved, as often in the past, a difficult political associate. He pretended to favor Lentulus, but the activities of his friends told a different story. His reticence and penchant for dissembling left Cicero wondering to the end what his real wishes were, an awkward predicament in dealing with a friend and benefactor. Cicero reported to Quintus that he thought he had done well in the way he had discharged his obligations to Lentulus and Pompey, but it cannot have been a comfortable experience.[63]

Clodius's election to the aedileship on January 20 brought a fresh offensive against the enemies who had defeated him in 57. Milo became the first target. Clodius indicted him on a charge of public violence but, in order to dramatize the case and provide himself with a more tractable jury and the kind of popular forum in which he excelled, he bypassed the regular *quaestio* and used his aedilician powers to conduct a trial before the people, an antiquated procedure that involved three preliminary public meetings to hear the charges and rebuttals followed by a fourth hearing at which the prosecuting magistrate proposed a verdict, which was then voted on by the *comitia.*[64] The first hearing took place on February 2 and passed without incident. Clodius determined, however, to use the second hearing on February 6 publicly to embarrass Pompey, who with Cicero had rallied to Milo's defense. He posted his gangs to shout insults while Pompey was speaking, and during his own speech, which Milo's supporters proceeded in turn to interrupt, he taunted the general with mismanaging the grain supply and coveting the Egyptian commission. He also had his lackeys shout that they wanted Crassus to go to Egypt, a possible attempt to create or widen a breach between the coalition part-

63. *Fam.* 1.1.3–4; 1.2.3; 1.5b.2. *Q.F.* 2.2.3. Cf. *Fam.* 1.9.17.
64. For the legal procedure, see *Dom.* 45. Mommsen, *Strafrecht,* 164ff. It is the only known aedilician prosecution, but *Verr.* 2.1.12, where Cicero threatens Verres with a prosecution before the people, shows aediles had such powers. Gruen (*Last Generation,* 298) doubts if it was a trial before the people, but the procedure and the formal language used to describe it leave no doubt. Clodius's demagogic flair and influence with the urban *plebs* gave him many advantages in a trial before the people.

ners. The supporters on both sides eventually came to blows and the meeting ended in a riot.[65]

The Senate discussed the incident at two meetings on February 6 and 7, and condemned what had happened as an act against the state. Both occasions were used by the optimate diehards and the Clodian faction to press their campaign against Pompey, with Bibulus, Curio, Favonius, Servilius the Younger, and C. Cato all joining in the attack. Pompey reacted strongly. His general sensitivity and fearfulness of plots led him to believe he was now in a highly vulnerable position. He felt the Senate and public were unsympathetic and was convinced that his optimate foes were conspiring to kill him in conjunction with Clodius and C. Cato. He also believed Crassus had now joined the ranks of his active enemies. He began to take steps to protect himself and to import men from Picenum and Gaul. Clodius was also strengthening his gangs, and C. Cato began to use an armed bodyguard. Cicero expected serious repercussions.[66]

Clodius was meantime pressing attacks against other enemies. His associate C. Cato introduced a bill in early February to recall Lentulus from Cilicia, an unusual move to abrogate *imperium* with serious implications for Lentulus's *dignitas* and entire political future.[67] Sestius found himself next in line, indicted on February 10 on two separate counts, bribery and public violence. Clodius was not among the official prosecutors, but Cicero records his active involvement. The bribery

65. *Q.F.* 2.3.1–2. *Fam.* 1.5b.1. *Sest.* 95. *Mil.* 40, 68. Asconius 48, Clark. Dio 39.18. Crassus's position is, as always obscure. It seems certain that he had wanted a part in the restoration of Ptolemy, and Pompey's evident determination to get the command himself and his failure to back Crassus's proposal may well have strained relations between them. Clodius was very likely seeking to capitalize on any break. Schackleton Bailey (*Ad Quint.*, 176) thinks Crassus was present in support of Milo, taking *aderat* in its technical meaning, but this is hardly tenable in view of the overall description of Crassus's role and Pompey's response to it in *Q.F.* 2.3.

66. *Q.F.* 2.3.3–4. Gruen's conclusion (*Last Generation*, 229) that the Senate's condemnation of the violence was a rebuke to Clodius seems totally at variance with the thrust of Cicero's report. Pompey was the primary target of attack and the one who felt after the senatorial debate that his whole position was threatened. Clodius had decisively won the round, with the backing of the conservative *nobiles*. Cicero's phrase in this letter, "magnae mihi res iam moveri videbantur," is sometimes taken as a gleeful announcement that the triumvirate was breaking up. But Cicero makes it quite clear he is alluding to the prospect of serious violence between the forces being gathered by Pompey and the growing gangs of Clodius and C. Cato.

67. *Q.F.* 2.3.1, 4. *Fam.* 1.5a.2. *Sest.* 144. The recall was almost certainly a prelude to prosecution.

charge was apparently dropped, but the case *de vi* came to trial on March 11. Cicero defended and Pompey made a special appearance to speak in praise of Sestius. The verdict was acquittal and was unanimous. Cicero believed he had handled the case well and he reported to Quintus his particular satisfaction with the manner in which he had demolished during the trial one of Sestius's most bitter attackers, P. Vatinius, tribune of 59.[68]

There was one further prosecution around this time in which the Clodian *gens* was deeply involved and which is most likely linked to Clodius's sustained efforts in early 56 to destroy or discredit his main opponents. M. Caelius Rufus was indicted in March on a charge of involvement in the murder of Dio, the leader of the Alexandrine envoys. Pompey's name had been linked to that murder, and his open espousal of Ptolemy's restoration, combined with the vigorous efforts of his friends to secure the job for him, exposed him to suspicion of complicity in all the king's intrigues. The trial of Caelius could serve to air again the egregious misdoings associated with the Ptolemy affair and revive suspicions of unsavory intriguing and power seeking by Pompey.[69] Cicero again defended, helping a former protégé and seeking to defeat another Clodian-backed endeavor. He diverted attention from the charges and their political implications and presented the case as a personal vendetta orchestrated by Clodia, Caelius's rejected lover, whose life and morals he mocked and pilloried in a masterly display of the art of invective. He won another victory and again enjoyed the satisfaction of having publicly lacerated a hated enemy. The result, it can safely be assumed, was not what the Clodian *gens* had sought or expected.[70]

Despite the flurry of activity in the courts, the serious political turmoil anticipated by Cicero in the aftermath of Milo's second hearing did not

---

68. *Q.F.* 2.3.5; 2.4.1. *Fam.* 1.9.7. *Sest.* passim. See Gruen, *Last Generation,* 300ff.

69. *Cael.* passim. Dio 39.14. Quintilian, *Inst.* 4.2.27. There were other reasons also for the prosecution. The main accuser was a personal enemy of Caelius, and Clodia most likely encouraged the prosecution for her own reasons.

70. Cicero disliked Clodia almost as intensely as her brother. *Att.* 2.1. 5. *Q.F.* 2.3.2 shows Clodia was a target of obscene abuse from sources other than Cicero. See T. P. Wiseman, *Catullus: A Reappraisal* (Cambridge, 1985). J. Linderski, "Cicero Rede *Pro Caelio* und die ambitus und Vereingesetzgebung der ausgehenden Republik," *Hermes* 89 (1961), 106–19. M. B. Skinner, "Clodia Metelli," *TAPA* 113 (1983), 273–87. Gruen (*Last Generation,* 304) lists one other trial that he believes was linked to attacks on friends of Pompey in 56, the trial *de ambitu* of M. Cispius, a tribune of 57.

materialize. The situation was to some extent defused by the consul Marcellinus, a firm opponent of Clodius, who used thanksgivings and repetition of religious festivals to remove all comitial days. As a result, the proposals of C. Cato, which were certain to bring confrontation, and other tribunician bills proposing money and legates for Caesar could not be brought to a vote. Clodius does not appear to have sought any further direct conflict with Pompey, and the third stage of Milo's trial, which took place on February 18, was seemingly peaceful. Pompey's general political situation, however, did not improve. His defense of Milo had cost him support among the urban plebs, traditionally sympathetic to Clodius. He had also lost the goodwill of the *boni* as a whole. Even recent supporters such as Marcellinus had turned against him. His behavior in the Ptolemy affair formed part of the reason. The efforts of his friends to get him the Egyptian command were not popular, and were seen as a betrayal of his friendship with Lentulus. But Cicero speaks of a more general dissatisfaction among ordinary senators with Pompey's performance in this period; he had not come well out of the contest with Clodius and the conservative *principes*.[71]

Cicero's own position was also far from satisfactory. His private situation had shown some improvement and was a source of considerable satisfaction to him by early 56. He was no longer fretting about his finances. The rebuilding of his house on the Palatine was proceeding satisfactorily, and he was busily refurbishing all his other properties as well. He was also pleased by his general standing and popularity. His house was thronged. He was in high demand in the courts and had fully regained his old dominance there. His superior skills as a pleader gave him one arena in which he could confidently expect to outdo his enemies and continue to enhance his *dignitas* and *gratia*.[72]

But he faced no such prospect on the political front, where he remained paralyzed by conflicting loyalties in a hopelessly divided society. He was linked to Pompey not only by the latter's services in 57 but by the fact that they were fighting a common enemy in Clodius and defending common friends such as Milo and Sestius. He could not stand against him nor fail

71. *Q.F.* 2.5(4).2–4. For the tribunician proposals concerning Caesar, see *Fam.* 1.7.10. The final stage of Milo's trial was set for May 7 (*Q.F.* 2.6[5].4), but Luca intervened and the case was dropped. See Dio 39.20.

72. *Q.F.* 2.3.7; 2.4.2; 2.5(4).1, 4. His financial situation may have been helped by a loan from a banker, Vestorius. *Att.* 4.6.4.

to defend him, if asked for his opinion. But he realized that any public support of Pompey would distance him further from the conservative *boni* and, though he had scant regard for their statesmanship as a whole and was especially outraged by their attitude toward Pompey and Clodius, he still saw them as his natural political allies and was reluctant to sever all connection with them by an open, unequivocal commitment to Pompey's side. It was becoming increasingly difficult for him to reconcile old positions and affiliations with his present circumstances, and he began to resort again, as he had in 59, to a policy of quiescence, avoiding the Senate and to the extent possible all involvement in political affairs.[73]

The Conference at Luca

In April Pompey prepared to depart once more on the business of the grain supply. Before he left he obtained from the Senate at a meeting on April 5 the massive sum of forty million sesterces to fund his efforts. Whatever decline there had been in his general support in the Senate, no effort was being made to limit his capacity to make a success of his new commission. But there was concern about the depleted state of the treasury, and an acrimonious debate arose in the course of the meeting about Caesar's *Lex Campana*, which had not yet been fully implemented, but which threatened, if implementation continued, to aggravate further the chronic shortage of public funds. The issue was an old one, most recently raised in December 57 by the tribune Rutilius Lupus, who thoroughly aired the evil consequences of the law in a lengthy attack in the Senate. There were equally strong feelings expressed at the meeting on April 5, and among those who spoke was Cicero, who advanced a proposal, subsequently approved by the Senate, that the matter be brought before a *frequens senatus* scheduled for May 15. Soon afterwards, Pompey left Rome for Sardinia and Africa. On the way he met Caesar at Luca, and a new agreement was forged that recemented the alliance and altered drastically the existing alignments and power structure of Roman politics.[74]

73. *Q.F.* 2.5(4).3. After the violence at the trial of Milo he had decided not to attend the Senate to avoid offending the *boni* by defending Pompey. This typified his dilemma and his method of coping with it. *Q.F.* 2.3.2.
74. *Q.F.* 2.1.1; 2.6(5).1. *Fam.* 1.9.8. Plutarch, *Caes.* 21.3; *Pomp.* 51.4; *Cat. min.* 41.1; *Crassus* 14.5–6. Appian, *BC* 2.17. Suetonius, *Jul.* 24.

The Conference at Luca had far-reaching consequences, and the events and circumstances responsible for the timing and decisions of the meeting have generated extensive discussion and considerable controversy. The most common interpretation, and one still widely favored, links the conference to political maneuvering orchestrated by Pompey and Cicero in late 57 and early 56. It is argued that Pompey, faced with declining support, sharper opposition from his enemies, and the defection of Crassus, determined to put pressure on Caesar by highlighting the latter's vulnerability and his continuing need for Pompey's backing. He chose the *Lex Campana,* one of Caesar's most controversial laws, to make his point. He had a friendly tribune Rutilius Lupus raise the issue in the Senate in December 57 as a first indication of a willingness to break with Caesar. Cicero, responding to this and other signs of dissension within the coalition and eager to widen the breach, revived the issue in April 56, having earlier tested again Pompey's readiness to accept attacks on Caesar by delivering in his presence at the trial of Sestius a scathing denunciation of the events of 59. Caesar became alarmed by Pompey's evident withdrawal of support and convened the conference to reinstitute an active alliance that would secure the interest of all its members.[75]

The foregoing analysis, though inherently plausible, is to a great extent speculative, and is besides difficult to reconcile with the general thrust of the contemporary evidence for the political actions and concerns of both Pompey and Cicero in this period. No ancient source suggests that Pompey inspired or approved the senatorial discussions of the Campanian land or was otherwise intriguing to force a new agreement with Caesar. The first attack on the *Lex Campana* in December 57 can be linked to him only by the fact that its author was Rutilius Lupus, who later appeared as his supporter in the Ptolemy affair. But this provides no warrant for assuming he was a Pompeian lackey governed by Pompey's wishes in all his actions. By Cicero's account he was a highly independent and spirited tribune, and his first performance in the Senate was

75. The bibliography on Luca is immense. See especially M. Cary, *"Asinus Germanus,"* *CQ* 17 (1923), 103–07. D. Stockton, "Cicero and the *Ager Campanus,"* *TAPA* 93 (1962), 471–89. E. S. Gruen, "Pompey, the Roman Aristocracy and the Conference at Luca," *Historia* 18 (1979), 71–108. Balsdon, *JRS* 47(1957), 18–20. T. N. Mitchell, "Cicero before Luca (September 57–April 56 B.C.)," *TAPA* 100 (1969), 295–320. A. M. Ward, "The Conference at Luca: Did It Happen?" *AJAH* 5 (1985), 48–63. C. Luibheid, "The Luca Conference," *CP* 65 (1970), 88–94. Gelzer, *Caesar,* 121ff.

eagerly anticipated and brought an unusually large turnout. He lived up to expectations and gained a dramatic opening to his tribunate, advertising his *virtus* and *industria,* after the fashion of generations of ambitious tribunes, by grasping an issue of high controversy. No prompting from Pompey is necessary to explain his action.[76]

But there is further reason to dispute the notion of Pompey's involvement. The overall evidence for Pompey's relationship with Caesar in 57 indicates he remained anxious to preserve their friendship and cooperation. He had made sure to secure Caesar's consent to Cicero's restoration before he worked publicly for it, and in the autumn of 57 he supported, as did Cicero, a *supplicatio* of fifteen days in honor of Caesar's great victory over the Gauls on the banks of Sambre. Cicero commended his generosity in advocating a measure that exceeded the honor paid to himself in 63, when, on Cicero's motion, the Senate had decreed a *supplicatio* of ten days following the end of the Mithridatic War. There was no sign here of any loosening of links within the coalition.[77]

Further, Pompey had little reason to be unhappy with his political situation in December 57 or to resort to elaborate gambles to try to better his position. He had recently succeeded in forging in Italy an impressive consensus that had overwhelmed the forces of Clodius and achieved Cicero's restoration. His favorable standing with the Senate as a whole and his general popularity had been further shown by the broad support that emerged for his appointment to oversee the grain supply. He may have wished for the wider mandate proposed by Messius, but the bill voted gave him an important and powerful command, which was generously backed up by the Senate's allocation of all the supplies and legates he requested. It should also be noted that the grain commission took Pompey far from Rome for an extended period in November and December. He threw himself into his new assignment with his customary vigor, traveling, despite wintry weather, to Sicily, Sardinia, and Africa.

76. *Q.F.* 2.1.1. For Lupus's support of Pompey, see *Fam.* 1.1.3; 1.2.2. Pompey could not be accused of failing in his obligation to Caesar because of Lupus's action, as Shackleton Bailey (*Cicero,* 82) suggests. Pompey was out of Rome at the time. Lupus called for no particular course of action and did not raise the matter again. For all we know Pompey may well have silenced him.

77. *Prov. cons.* 26–27. *Balb.* 61. Caesar, *BG* 2.35.4. Dio 39.5. Plutarch, *Caes.* 21.1–2.

He therefore had little opportunity as well as reason at the end of 57 to initiate a new round of political intrigue in Rome.[78]

Political developments in early 56 did bring a sharp decline in Pompey's political fortunes and left him feeling isolated and threatened, but there is no sign he blamed Caesar for his predicament or saw a remedy in pressuring his ally by withdrawing support or encouraging attacks.[79] Caesar, like Pompey himself, did experience growing and more active hostility in 56, but it came from sources with which Pompey had no connection and over which he had no control. The tribunician bills, already mentioned, to give Caesar additional money and legates were blocked by Marcellinus, who was now an open opponent of Pompey. Various moves were being planned and bruited to allocate the Gallic provinces to the consuls of 55 and bring Caesar back to face trial for the illegalities of 59, but they all emanated from hardline *optimates,* Pompey's most intractable foes. The conclusion that emerges from this and from the rebuffs and harassment experienced by Pompey in the Senate in the same period is that the conservative *boni* were rallying strongly in 56 and were availing of every opportunity to strike at both Pompey and Caesar, their two most hated enemies since the late sixties, and especially since 59.[80]

The debate on the Campanian land on April 5 fits this pattern closely. By Cicero's account the debate arose in conjunction with a major payment from the treasury to fund Pompey's supervision of the grain supply and was closely linked to the depleted state of the public purse and the continuing high price of grain. The discussion does not appear, therefore, to have been prearranged by any side but to have been raised by critics of Caesar who were seizing the opportunity provided by the large disbursement and the ongoing grain crisis to denounce again the law that was

78. Pompey was out of favor with the bulk of the *consulares,* but Cicero's letters indicate he stood well with the general body of *boni* in 57. *Att.* 4.1.6–7. Plutarch (*Pomp.* 50) describes his energy in discharging his new responsibilities in late 57.

79. Pompey was confiding in Cicero at this time. He did blame Crassus for his worsening situation, but not Caesar, and the remedy he saw was a mustering of his own considerable resources. *Q.F.* 2.3.4.

80. Suetonius, *Jul.* 24. Cf. *Fam.* 1.7.10. *Q.F.* 2.5(4).2–3. The intensified optimate attacks on Pompey and Caesar in early 56 were helped by the heightened activity of Clodius, now back in office, and were, no doubt, further encouraged by Crassus's evident break with Pompey.

adding to the problems of the treasury by reducing revenues, and was aggravating the food shortage by disrupting grain production in one of Italy's most fertile regions. It was an angry, clamorous attack very much in line with the aggressive stance of the *optimates* in all their dealings with Pompey and Caesar in 56, and is most plausibly seen as a continuation of the revitalized optimate opposition to them both.[81]

Cicero's involvement in the debate is the only factor connecting Pompey with it, but Cicero's alleged role in the affair is even more difficult to reconcile with the overall evidence than Pompey's, as is the general political posture attributed to him in this period. Cicero himself has contributed to the distortion of his position. In a long letter written to Lentulus Spinther in 54, he explains and defends his political life before Luca and attempts to show that, after his restoration, he resumed his old position as a leading defender of republicanism and, despite a lack of optimate support and his indebtedness to Pompey, adhered to his old policies for as long as was feasible. He cites in proof of his claim his attack on Vatinius and the illegalities of 59 delivered in the presence of Pompey during the trial of Sestius, and his proposal in the senatorial debate on the Campanian land on April 5. These actions he presents as an onslaught on the citadel of the coalition and says the Senate's decree caused a considerable stir, upsetting not only Caesar but Pompey also.[82]

The letter is an elaborate *apologia* by a masterful pleader, written after Cicero had effectively withdrawn from political life and designed to show that he had done so only after gallant efforts and after he failed to win due support from a spiteful and self-centered *nobilitas*. It naturally seeks to shape the facts to suit the case being argued, and it makes the most of any act of Cicero following his exile that could be seen as a blow for the *respublica* and against the triumvirate. It has had an undue influence and has been allowed to cloud the more reliable evidence of contemporary letters to Atticus and Quintus. There has resulted a tendency to magnify considerably the political role and ambitions of Cicero in the period before Luca.

It must be emphasized, however, that not even in the letter to Lentulus does Cicero suggest that he had any grand design in early 56 to sunder the

81. *Q.F.* 2.5.1.
82. *Fam.* 1.9, esp. sections 6–9.

coalition by having Pompey appear to withdraw support from Caesar, nor does he claim the dominant role in the debate on April 5 that is commonly ascribed to him. When all the evidence is taken into account, it is clear his part was modest in the extreme. He did not initiate the debate, nor is there any reason to believe that when he spoke he took a particular line or made any substantive proposal about the issue. The available record strictly limits his participation to a procedural motion that a discussion, already under way, be postponed to a later occasion for consideration by a full Senate.[83]

That his involvement had little significance is strongly borne out by the fact that he made no mention of it whatever in a report of the proceedings written to his brother three days later. The *argumentum ex silentio* has particular cogency in this instance. Quintus was in Sardinia, serving as a *legatus* to Pompey. Cicero had the task—one which held high importance in the Roman scheme of things—of keeping him informed of all that was happening in Rome. That he should conceal from his brother an important initiative of his own, and one that Quintus would duly learn about in any case from the published proceedings of the Senate, defies explanation.

The political importance he attached in the letter to Lentulus to the attack on Vatinius is similarly unsupported in his contemporary report of the event to Quintus, which describes his conduct of the case as follows: "I satisfied to the fullest possible extent by my defense a man hard to please and achieved his fondest desire by demolishing at will to the applause of gods and men Vatinius, who was openly attacking him." There is no hint here of any ulterior motive or political design. In fact, a

---

83. *Q.F.* 2.6(5).1. Cicero on no occasion alludes to splitting the triumvirate. The idea of an undermining strategy is a totally modern creation. Cicero presents his opposition as directed against the coalition as a whole and likely to displease Pompey as well as Caesar. See *Fam.* 1.9.6–7, 10. *Att.* 4.5.2. There is no hint he saw a split or the hope of creating one. It is also worth noting Cicero does not claim to have originated the motion adopted on April 5. Generally he uses phrases such as "me auctore" or "sententiae princeps fui" when he was the originator of a senatorial decree. *Pis.* 35. *Balb.* 61. *Dom.* 10. In *Fam.* 1.9.8 he merely says "mihi est senatus assensus." In any event, his speech does not appear to have gone beyond advocating a full debate of the *Lex Campana*. Not long afterwards he was able to claim in the Senate he had never attacked Caesar's *acta* (Prov. cons. 44). There is no doubt that in general Cicero attempted to follow the optimate line in the Senate after his restoration and most likely took positions on occasion, as he claims, that did not please Pompey and Caesar. But the indications are he was a follower rather than a leader.

short time later Cicero indicates particular dissatisfaction with his political life and expresses a desire to retire from political activity altogether.[84]

The evidence of the speeches delivered at the trial is often adduced to support the claim of the letter to Lentulus. The *Pro Sestio* is sometimes presented as a denunciation of Caesarism and a plea for Ciceronianism, and the *In Vatinium* as a still more open attack on Caesar and the work of his consulship.[85]

The charge against Sestius intimately concerned Cicero himself in that it dealt with events connected with his exile and restoration. It gave him a welcome opportunity to have vindicated in a court of law the justice of forceful resistance to the lawlessness of Clodius, and to promote again his pet analysis of the events of 58 and 57, namely, that an unfortunate combination of circumstances had unleashed the villainous elements in the state, resulting in his banishment and the destruction of the *respublica* and of all that was good and desirable in Roman life. These anarchic forces had been checked through the bravery of men like Sestius. Such resistance to lawless violence was the only protection of *virtus* against *audacia*. It deserved acclaim, not punishment.[86]

The first part of the *Pro Sestio* concentrates on elaborating this defense, which was also a vindication of Cicero himself, linking the fortunes of the *respublica* to his own and turning his exile from a source of shame into a source of glory. The same themes had been developed in the speeches following his restoration and in the *De domo,* and there is no greater effort in the *Pro Sestio* to denounce Caesar and whatever he was thought to represent than in the earlier orations. The role of the triumvirs is, in fact, left vague and shadowy, and apologies are found for their failure to act. Clodius and the consuls of 58 are the primary villains, whose brand of politics must be repudiated by the acquittal of Sestius.

The latter part of the speech is largely taken up by a digression on the meaning of *optimates,* a term used disparagingly by the prosecution with an insinuation that Cicero and his kind were a dying breed that no longer commanded general support in a Senate and a society that seemed more inclined to favor Clodius. This touched a raw nerve, and stirred Cicero to restate with an eloquent intensity reminiscent of 63 the substance and enduring merits and appeal of the optimate ideal, and to reassert his

84. *Q.F.* 2.4.1; 2.5(4).3.
85. See Smith, *Cicero,* 172. Pocock, *In Vatinium,* 5ff.
86. See esp. *Sest.* 49ff., 90ff.

cherished contention that his restoration represented a new consensus in support of that ideal, and that those who had caused his exile were a passing aberration in Roman politics and now a spent force abhorred by the vast majority of citizens.

He responded to the insinuation of the prosecution that *optimates* were a set or clique of increasing irrelevance by declaring that the term designated all right-minded citizens of reasonable means and that the wish of such *boni et beati* was peace combined with the dignity guaranteed by the great traditions and resources of the *respublica*. The leaders of the *optimates* were those who fearlessly defended this peace with dignity against the ever-present threat from that small band of vicious politicians who, because they were criminals or mad revolutionaries, were always intent on destroying all that good men wanted to preserve. He went on to show that these defenders of republicanism were never more strongly supported by the public, which was now firmly united in the desire for peace, and he used the recent consensus in regard to his restoration, which he claimed had repeatedly shown itself at elections, at the *ludi,* and at public meetings, to prove his point.[87] It was mostly familiar stuff, a continuation of Cicero's sustained effort since his exile to portray himself as the great republican patriot who suffered for the state while it was dominated by evil forces now defeated. This was the predominant purpose behind the political statements of the *Pro Sestio.* It would have been easily recognizable by an audience familiar with Ciceronian rhetoric and would have evoked no great surprise or reaction.

The attack on Vatinius would hardly have caused surprise either. Vatinius was an important prosecution witness, a bitter enemy of Sestius, and in giving his testimony he had gone to great lengths to attack Cicero personally, taunting him with charges of political inconsistency and cowardice. The *In Vatinium* was therefore not merely an attempt to discredit a prosecution witness but to answer an abusive personal attack. Cicero liked to exact a heavy price from those who dared to engage him in exchanges of *vituperatio*, and Vatinius's tribunate and the illegalities surrounding it provided rich material for his satiric powers. He made the most of it. His duties as an advocate and his personal *dignitas* demanded that he should, and his contemporaries would have understood.[88]

---

87. See *Sest.* 96–143. Its importance as a political manifesto can be exaggerated. See W. K. Lacey, "Cicero, *Pro Sestio* 96–143," *CQ* n.s. 12 (1962), 67–71.

88. *Vat.* 5ff. *Sest.* 132. *Q.F.* 2.4.1 expresses clearly Cicero's satisfaction at having

The absence of any preplanned political design on Cicero's part is clearly indicated by the very important fact, seldom emphasized, that Cicero did not crossexamine Vatinius at all when the latter first testified, but merely made some derogatory remarks about him. Vatinius, incensed by Cicero's slurs, returned to court next day and gave further evidence during which he took the opportunity to deliver an angry tirade against Cicero. It was only then, in response to an attack upon himself, that Cicero used his right of *interrogatio* and made what Quintilian called an *actio,* or set speech, answering Vatinius in kind. The entire sequence of events argues against any idea of premeditated political strategems.[89]

Cicero does attempt in the letter to Lentulus to give political significance to his *interrogatio,* and implies he criticized Caesar, extolling Bibulus and indirectly blaming Caesar for his exile. But there is, significantly, no trace of such criticism in the extant speech. On the contrary, Cicero explicitly disclaims any intent to involve Caesar in Vatinius's wrongdoing and repeatedly seeks to separate him from any responsibility for Vatinius's actions. There was, of course, some criticism of Caesar, and indeed of Pompey too, implicit in any condemnation of Vatinius's tribunate, but that was also true of all of Cicero's many denunciations after his exile of various allies or benefactors of the coalition, such as Piso, Gabinius, and Clodius. In particular, his outspoken condemnation of the adoption of Clodius in the *De domo* and his challenge to its legality were a far more explicit rebuke of Caesar than anything in the *In Vatinium.*

Such indirect criticism, incidental to a justified attack on someone else, does not appear to have been a cause for offense at Rome. The tangled nature of Roman personal relationships and the recognition that the defense of oneself and one's friends and the avenging of injury were not only a right but a sacred duty made it unavoidable. Cicero did his best to minimize its extent in the *In Vatinium.* Little more could have been expected of him.[90]

---

demolished an enemy. That had been his concern. See U. Albini, "L'orazione contro Vatinio," *PP* 66 (1959), 172–84.

89. *Vat.* 1–4, 40–41. Pocock's commentary, 134ff. Quintilian, *Inst.* 5.7.6.

90. *Fam.* 1.9.8. For Cicero's efforts in the extant speech to separate Caesar from Vatinius, see *Vat.* 13, 15, 22, 29, 38–39. The right to defend one's *dignitas* and avenge injury was unquestioned by the Romans. Cicero strongly asserts it in *Sest.* 14. Even in the *De officiis* he defends the right to exact retribution for injury (*Off.* 1.20). Cf. *Att.* 4.18.1

But in the final analysis, the most compelling argument against attributing any bold political design or initiative to Cicero in the months before Luca is the persistent uncertainty and despondency, described earlier in this chapter, that characterized his political outlook in the entire period. His alienation from the conservative *boni,* building since 61, aggravated by suspicions of betrayal during his exile, was made complete by renewed signs of *invidia* from the *nobilitas* after his return and above all by their support of Clodius, whom he saw as the Republic's, as well as his own, most dangerous enemy. His personal estrangement from the *optimates* was combined with contempt for their statesmanship, which left him cut off from the only political group with which he had any ideological affinity. His friendship with Pompey, now strengthened by a deep sense of gratitude, made his position still more uncomfortable. He was linked to a man who faced unrelenting hostility from the Senate's *principes* and whose intentions he rarely fully knew and even more rarely fully approved. To crown it all, he faced real physical danger from Clodius, whose fortunes seemed firmly on the rise again. He did attempt, despite these unhappy circumstances, to adhere initially to his old policies and to support the conservative line in the Senate, but he was more follower than leader, and his growing alienation from his former allies, his fears for his safety, and the conflicting demands on his loyalties all led him by degrees toward a policy of inaction and withdrawal, the course he informed Quintus in March 56 he was increasingly disposed to follow.

The traditional reconstruction of the events that led to the Conference at Luca must also be questioned for a further reason, namely, the importance attributed to the issue of the Campanian land itself. It is clear that those attacking the *Lex Campana* were not demanding cancellation of the measure or challenging the legality of its passage, but seeking a suspension, temporary or permanent, of its implementation to avoid further erosion of the public revenues and further displacement of productive tenants.[91] The controversy did not therefore threaten those already settled, nor did it raise the larger issues of the legality of all the Julian laws of 59. It did have political ramifications in that any interference with any of his laws would represent an affront to Caesar's *dignitas* and would con-

---

and Caesar's appeal to his army to defend the *existimatio* and *dignitas* of their commander as he prepared to invade Italy in 49. Caesar, *BC* 1.8.

91. See Cary, *CQ* 17 (1923), 106. Brunt, *Manpower,* 316ff. M. A. Levi, *Atene e Roma* 3 (1922), 239–52. Meyer, *Caesars Monarchie,* 64ff., 136.

stitute a political defeat damaging to his general position. It might also create difficulties for him by removing a valuable source of land in Italy for his Gallic veterans. He undoubtedly did not, therefore, want the attack on the bill to succeed, but the issue did not critically threaten his interests and was not the most urgent of his concerns in the spring of 56.[92]

But whatever the importance of the debate on the Campanian land, its timing alone removes it as a reason for the meeting between Pompey and Caesar at Luca, though it may have contributed to the urgency of their discussions and to the form of the agreements reached. The issue had been moribund since December 57 and there had been no indication it was likely to surface again. When it was resurrected on April 5, Caesar was at Ravenna, normally a five- or six-day journey from Rome. Pompey left the capital on April 11, destined for Sardinia but intending, he told Cicero, to take ship from a northerly port, Pisa or Labro. The arrangement to meet Caesar must have been made before he left the city, and his unusual and circuitous route to Sardinia was most likely a consequence of that arrangement. The conference had therefore been planned long before Caesar had any chance to react to the debate on April 5, and probably before the debate even took place.[93]

The political maneuvers associated with Pompey and Cicero and the Campanian land are not necessary to explain the Conference at Luca. There were many reasons for the meeting and for fresh agreements. The coalition was no longer controlling the course of political events in Rome in early 56. Its members had less unity of purpose after 59 and were less actively cooperating in dictating political decisions. Its impact diminished further with the emergence of the rift between Pompey and Crassus, which made it seem the alliance was crumbling and encouraged enemies of both Pompey and Caesar to step up their opposition. The conservative *boni,* aided by the collaboration of some of their leaders

92. *Fam.* 1.9.10. Caesar's displeasure at the attacks on the *Lex Campana* need not be doubted.

93. News of the debate on April 5 could not have reached Caesar in time for him to get a message to Pompey before the latter left Rome on April 11. If one accepts the debate precipitated the conference, one must also accept that Caesar knew Pompey's travel plans precisely and was able to intercept him with a message on the road. One must also ignore the coincidence that Pompey was heading in the direction of Luca anyway, even though his destination should have taken him south. See T. Rice Holmes, *The Roman Republic,* vol. 2 (Oxford, 1923), 292ff.

with Clodius, were reasserting themselves with particular vigor in 56 and showing their determination to bring down their enemies.

Pompey's declining influence and difficult political circumstances in 56 have already been discussed. Caesar's position was, in many respects, even more precarious. He was losing control of the magistracies that he had worked hard and spent lavishly to maintain in the preceding years. Two of his staunchest supporters, P. Vatinius and C. Alfius Flavus, both tribunes of 59, had been defeated, to his considerable dismay, at the aedilician elections in January. One of his most outspoken critics, Cn. Domitius Calvinus, had been elected to the praetorship. More serious still, L. Domitius Ahenobarbus, brother-in-law of Cato and a rigid conservative, was a candidate for the consulship of 55 and considered certain to succeed. He was pledging to have Caesar recalled from Gaul and seemed likely to succeed in this also. Caesar had been granted Transalpine Gaul by senatorial decree. He could be removed from it by senatorial allocation of the province under the *Lex Sempronia* to one of the consuls of 55, a decision not subject to veto. Caesar, who had recently seen his best efforts to secure additional money and legates successfully blocked by his opponents, could not feel confident of being able to prevent such a move in the Senate. But a recall at this stage would frustrate his grandest ambitions and could threaten all his achievements. He needed more time to complete the subjugation of Gaul. A fresh revolt by the Veneti and other tribes of northern Gaul in the spring of 56 showed how much remained to be done. He had also, according to Strabo, already formed plans for an invasion of Britain. He had the most urgent need to insure an extension of his tenure of the Gallic provinces.[94]

It would seem that he began to take steps to buttress his position in early March when he was visited in Ravenna by Appius Claudius, who was soon to take over as governor of Sardinia. The behavior of Clodius and ways of securing his support for Caesar were no doubt central topics of that meeting. Crassus made a similar trip to Ravenna at the end of March or early April. It was most likely at this point that arrangements for a meeting with Pompey to work out new agreements and reactivate the alliance were set in train. But plans were also made to meet with large

---

94. *Vat.* 38. Suetonius, *Jul.* 24. Caesar, *BG* 3.7.ff.

numbers of other politicians and to build by generous bribes and promises the broadest possible support for the new alliance.[95]

But the meeting with Pompey was, of course, the crucial event, and it produced agreements designed to eliminate the immediate difficulties and to insure the continuing dominance and stability of the coalition by arrogation of unchallengeable power and its even distribution among the partners. The danger from Domitius Ahenobarbus was to be ended by having Pompey and Crassus gain election to the consulship for 55, and to boost their electoral campaign, Caesar was to send as many of his troops as possible to Rome on furlough. Once in office they were to implement laws granting Pompey the provinces of Spain and Crassus the province of Syria, both to hold their commands for a term of five years. Caesar's *imperium* was to be extended for a similar period. All three would now have powerful provincial commands, and collectively they would control the great bulk of the armed forces of the empire.[96]

The details of the new agreements were not immediately known, but it quickly became abundantly clear in Rome that the dynasts had regrouped and that a totally new power structure now prevailed. The debate on the Campanian land scheduled for May 15 did not take place. Soon afterwards the Senate, with few dissenters, granted Caesar what had been persistently denied him earlier in the year, ten legates and an additional grant from the treasury to pay the four new legions he had raised on his own authority. In early June, when the consular provinces for 55 came up for discussion in accordance with the *Lex Sempronia,* the efforts of Caesar's optimate enemies to have the Gallic provinces reallocated failed utterly.[97]

---

95. *Q.F.* 2.5(4).4. *Fam.* 1.9.9. Plutarch, *Caes.* 21; *Pomp.* 51. Appian, *BC* 2.17. Suetonius, *Jul.* 24. The extent to which the Conference at Luca was a single, formal gathering remains disputed, It most likely was not. What is certain is that Pompey and Caesar met there around the middle of April. Whether Crassus was present at that meeting or had already made his arrangments with Caesar at Ravenna must remain uncertain. Caesar's meetings with other politicians probably took place over a period, and were merely an expanded form of Caesar's regular contacts with senators during his winter sojourns in Cisalpine Gaul. See L. Hayne, "Who Went to Luca?" *CP* 69 (1974), 217–20. Ward, *AJAH* 5(1980), 48–63. J. F. Lazenby, "The Conference at Luca and the Gallic War," *Latomus* 18 (1959), 67–76. Gruen, *Historia* 18(1969),93.

96. See Gelzer, *Caesar,* 122–23. Rice Holmes, *Roman Republic,* 2:74.

97. *Fam.* 1.7.10. *Prov. cons.* 28. *Balb.* 61. Dio 39.25. *Q.F.* 2.7(6).2. The text of Cicero's reference to the debate on the *Ager Campanus* is disputed. See Shackleton Bailey, *Ad Quint.,*185.

Meantime, Pompey and Crassus were facing strong optimate opposition to their bid for the consulship, and their success was being particularly threatened by the hostility of the consul Marcellinus. They therefore decided to have the elections postponed to the beginning of 55, when Marcellinus would be out of office and the greatest number of Caesar's troops would be available to come to Rome. The tribune C. Cato, who, like many others, had offered his allegiance to the revived coalition, insured postponement by use of his veto. The elections finally took place in January 55. Domitius Ahenobarbus, urged on by Cato, persisted with his candidacy, but he provided the only opposition, and the presence of Caesar's troops and the free use of intimidation guaranteed success for Pompey and Crassus.[98] They then manipulated the praetorian elections to exclude Cato and secure the election of Vatinius.[99]

Their next step was to secure their provincial commands, and in time-honored fashion they had a friendly tribune, C. Trebonius, introduce the necessary legislation. There was fierce opposition, led by Cato and two tribunes, Aquillius Gallus and Ateius Capito. The bill was passed only after the obstructive efforts of the opposition had been suppressed by the crudest violence. Pompey and Crassus themselves introduced the bill to extend Caesar's command. It too required strong-arm tactics to secure passage. The politics of force had returned to Rome with a vengeance.[100]

Cicero Changes Course

The Conference at Luca had important consequences for Cicero's political life. Caesar, intent on gathering as many allies as possible and isolating his enemies, was no longer willing to tolerate any level of opposition from him. He complained at length to Pompey at Luca about Cicero's stance in the debate on April 5, and demanded full compliance with the pledges given when he consented to restoration. Pompey responded by sending his confidant, L. Vibullius Rufus, to tell Cicero not to commit himself in the upcoming debate on the Campanian land. As a result Cicero stayed away altogether from the Senate on May 15. When

98. Dio 39.27–31. Plutarch, *Pomp.* 51–52; *Crass.* 14–15; *Cat. min.* 41–42. Appian, *BC* 2.17–18. Velleius 2.46. Cf. *Att.* 4.8a.2.
99. *Q.F.* 2.8(7).3. Plutarch, *Pomp.* 52; *Cat. min.* 42. Dio 39.32. Livy, *Per.* 105.
100. Plutarch, *Pomp.* 52. *Crass.* 15. *Cat. min.* 43. Dio 39.33–36. Velleius 2.46.

Pompey arrived in Sardinia a few days after the meeting at Luca, he expressed himself in much stronger terms to Quintus, reminding him of the pledges made and warning that, if Cicero could not support Caesar, he must at least refrain from attacking any of his *acta*. Cicero received this message from Quintus when the latter returned to Rome toward the end of May. It forced him to review, as he had done in early 59, his entire political position and what response he should make to what was, in effect, a revival of the *dominatio* of Caesar's consulship. He had fewer options this time. Resistance was not feasible in view of the ultimatum to Quintus. He could, however, resort again to a policy of quiescence, which had been his preferred course in 59 and which would meet the demands of Caesar. But he did not take the less controversial middle road on this occasion, deciding instead to end his lifelong association with the optimate side and give active support to the coalition.[101]

It was a momentous decision for a man who was so concerned about *laus* and *gloria* and so genuinely proud of his record as a selflessly committed champion of traditional republicanism. It was certain to bring him censure and ridicule from the conservative *nobilitas;* it gave his enemies fresh material for their invectives, and it exposed him to charges of *inconstantia* even from friends. Yet the decision was taken with little apparent hesitation or soul searching, a measure of how much Cicero's political will and aspirations had changed since 63, or indeed since 59.[102]

The reasons governing his decision are apparent from contemporary letters to Atticus and Lentulus Spinther. His long-building disaffection from the conservative *nobilitas* on both a political and personal level was the predominant factor. He believed they bore the chief responsibility for all the evils that had befallen the *respublica* since 63. They had alienated the equestrian order and in the process had shattered the foundations of senatorial supremacy. They had failed to stand up to Clodius in 58, and, worst of all, had failed to capitalize on the opportunity to reestablish

101. *Fam.* 1.9.9–10. *Q.F.* 2.7.(6).2. In reporting his avoidance of further involvement in the debate on the Campanian land, Cicero uses the much-discussed phrase "in hac causa mihi aqua haeret." It appears to relate to situations where no progress is being made, where a blockage or obstacle has appeared and the water cannot run. Cf. *Off.* 3.117. For a recent discussion, see Hornblower, Seager, Treggiari in *LCM* 5 (1980), 107, 133–35, 187–88.

102. Cicero was aware charges of *inconstantia* would be made (*Fam.* 1.9.11), and they came in abundance. See *Fam.* 1.9.4, 17. *Planc.* 91–94. *Prov. cons.* 18, 24, 26, 47. Yet he made his decision with apparent ease. *Att.* 4.5.2–3.

senatorial control created by the new *consensus bonorum* that had emerged at the time of Cicero's restoration. Instead, driven by spite and hate, they had protected and encouraged the greatest enemy of the Republic and had alienated its greatest potential protectors. They had, in short, lost sight of the true *sensus bonorum* and could no longer be regarded as its chief exponents or defenders.

These harsh judgments were undoubtedly colored by Cicero's deep anger at the manner in which he had been personally treated by the optimate leadership, and it was private bitterness more than political disagreement that shaped his attitude toward his former allies in the mid-fifties and drove him from further association with them. He saw himself as a constant victim of their jealousy and spitefulness. They had betrayed him at the time of his exile and had shown their determination to keep his wings trimmed on his return. They greeted his efforts to restore and extend his properties with criticism of his upstart pretensions to the homes of *nobiles*. They coddled his enemy without regard to his dignity or safety, and even when he sided with them in political matters they showed, not gratitude, but open delight that his stand would damage his friendship with Pompey and make Caesar his enemy. He could retain no faith in such faithless allies, and he told Atticus in the middle of 56 he felt an absolute fool not to have long ago severed his connections with them.[103]

Fears for his safety also weighed heavily with him. The trauma of his exile was still vividly before his mind, and he was determined not to repeat the experience. He was afraid that anything less than positive support would not satisfy Pompey and Caesar and might invite reprisal. But a more compelling consideration was the prospect of lasting security that full friendship with the potentates would give him against future attacks from Clodius and his following. The latter was still a power and Cicero continued to fear him. In fact, he believed he was a special target of all *improbi* and in need of special protection against their hostility. His general nervousness is very apparent in the years after his exile, and even after he was assured of the protection of Pompey and Caesar, he continued to count his defenses and was still seeking to strengthen them as late as 54.[104]

---

103. *Fam.* 1.7.7,10; 1.8.4; 1.9.12–17, 20. *Att.* 4.5.2. *Prov. cons.* 47.
104. Clodius's escape from prosecution and election to the aedileship had heightened

Cicero was well aware that his support of the coalition was in conflict with his political beliefs and previous posture, and he was prepared to admit to Atticus that it was a less than honorable course. He even admitted to Lentulus that it meant some sacrifice of *dignitas* in the interests of *salus*. But he believed there were mitigating circumstances in his case that justified relaxing the normal demands of honor and consistency. Foremost among these were his bonds to Pompey, a longtime friend and now his great benefactor, for whom he felt the deepest gratitude and affection. There was also his concern for his brother, whom he had endangered once before, who had gone surety for him and could easily be put at risk again. Finally, he considered that he had labored and suffered to an extraordinary degree on behalf of the state and had earned an extraordinary right to take account of personal obligation and personal expediency.[105]

In terms of his public duty Cicero found no moral difficulty in lending his support to the coalition. He denied it was an abnegation of his political goals or belief, or was in any way at variance with the political principle he held supreme, namely, that political activity must always serve the safety and utility of the state or at least do them no harm. He argued that the ascendancy of Pompey and Caesar was not a *dominatio* of the *improbi*, but a primacy based on power that accrued from outstanding services to the state. It therefore derived from *virtus* and should be recognized and converted to the benefit of the *respublica*. Resistance was, he maintained, in any event futile, especially in view of the sterile and reckless policies of the coalition's main opponents. It was preferable to adapt to circumstances and trim one's sails to the wind, like a wise sailor altering course to preserve the ship but striving ultimately to reach the intended harbor.[106]

Much of this was specious rationalization directed at the general public and posterity and designed to embroider a policy that was basically dictated by private concerns. Cicero had fundamental objections to the aims and tactics of the dynasts. They had created the situation he most

---

Cicero's fears. *Q. F.* 2.2.2. *Fam.* 1.7.7, 10; 1.9.21. *Planc.* 91ff. shows *salus* was very much a factor in his decision. For his continuing fears for his safety, see *Q.F.* 2.15(14).2; 2.16(15).2; 3.4.2, 4; 3.6(8).1. *Att.* 4.15.4. *Fam.* 2.6.4.

105. *Att.* 4.5.1. *Fam.* 1.7.7; 1.9.10–12. *Planc.* 91–94. Cf. *Att.* 8.11d.7; 9.4.2; 11.9.1.
106. *Fam.* 1.9.21. *Planc.* 91–94. *Balb.* 60–61. Cf. *Att.* 8.11.1.

abhorred as a republican, where one group or individual held more power than the entire state and threatened the supremacy of the law. More distressing for Cicero personally, they had ended the free regulation of public policy by the Senate under the leadership of its most authoritative *principes,* and had deprived him of the life of high dignity and influence that he had anticipated as a prestigious consular. On the other hand, he had no fears that Pompey, or the coalition while Pompey was part of it, posed any threat to the survival of the *respublica,* and he believed the damage to republican institutions could be better contained by a policy of acquiescence than by resistance. In short, Cicero's view of Pompey and his partners and of the likely consequences of opposition to them allowed him to conclude that he could consult his self-interest and support them without harming the *respublica* or omitting an opportunity to help it. It was in this sense that he could claim his change of course was not a betrayal of his political principles.[107]

The first indication of Cicero's changed political posture came in late May or June, when he lent his support in the Senate to the proposals to grant Caesar the ten legates and money for the new legious. Soon afterwards he opposed the recall of Caesar in the senatorial debate on the consular provinces and strongly defended his new position as Caesar's friend and supporter. His speech, the *De provinciis consularibus,* is often considered to be the "palinode" he wrote about to Atticus in the middle of 56. In any event, it was a clear, public pronouncement of his transfer of support to the coalition. Cicero had no wish to conceal his *nova coniunctio,* as he termed it. He wanted his commitment to the dynasts to be seen as unequivocal and irrevocable, and he relished besides the thought of the anger and chagrin his open espousal of Caesar's cause would stir among the *optimates.*[108]

He quickly found, however, that there was little joy for him in his new political situation. His sense of satisfaction at having in some measure

107. See *Fam.* 7.3.5; 5.21.2. *Ad Brut.* 1.16.5. *Att.* 7.1.2–3. *Cluent.* 146. *Leg.* 3.1–3. See M. C. Mittelstadt, "Cicero's Political velificatio mutata, 54–51 B.C.: Compromise or Capitulation?" *PP* 40 (1985), 13–28.

108. *Att.* 4.5.1. *Prov. cons.* 28. *Balb.* 61. The identity of the palinode has been endlessly debated. See Shackleton Bailey, *Ad. Att.* 2.233ff. If a speech, it could be any of the several in support of Caesar that Cicero made after Luca. But it appears from the reference in *Att.* 4.5.1 to be a special composition, not something already a matter of public record. Some literary composition, in prose or verse, extolling Caesar's achievements seems the likeliest possibility.

repaid his noble colleagues for their malevolence and spite soon waned, and he was left with the realization that he had lost his independence and his capacity to accomplish anything in politics likely to benefit the state or enhance his *dignitas*. He was compelled to say what pleased others, not himself. Dissent he saw as vain and foolish while assent was slavish and devoid of any semblance of *gravitas*. He found his political choices particularly painful at a time when his influence as a prestigious consular should have been at its greatest.[109]

He found more painful still the obligations laid upon him by his new allies to defend their friends in court. The opposition to the triumvirate asserted itself vigorously after Luca, as it had done in 59, fighting back strongly at elections, and using the criminal courts to try to embarrass the dynasts and destroy their chief adherents.[110] There was a steady stream of prosecutions of prominent triumviral associates in the years following Luca, and Cicero was repeatedly pressed into service to lead the defense, as Pompey and Caesar determinedly marshalled all their resources to protect their friends. The first such case was the trial of L. Cornelius Balbus in the autumn of 56 on a charge of falsely laying claim to Roman citizenship. Balbus, a native of Gades in southern Spain, had received his citizenship from Pompey in reward for services during the Sertorian War and he had gone on to become a trusted friend of Caesar. He was also on good terms with Cicero who, on this occasion, happily and successfully undertook the defense and used the opportunity to berate the powerful men behind the prosecution, who, he alleged, were unjustly endangering an innocent man in pursuit of a quarrel with his prestigious friends.[111]

There were many other cases, however, that proved to be far less pleasing experiences for Cicero, as he found himself laboring to protect men whom he despised or who had even done him injury. He expressed his resentment to his reclusive friend M. Marius in the late summer of 55, complaining that he found no good in a life in which he had lost his freedom of choice and was compelled to defend those who did not deserve well of him at the request of those who did.[112]

109. *Att.* 4.6.1–2. *Q.F.* 2.14(13).5. *Fam.* 1.8.3–4; 7.1.4.
110. The success of enemies of the coalition at elections was impressive. Gruen has assembled the evidence. See *Last Generation,* 146ff.
111. For Cicero's friendship with Balbus, see *Balb.* 4, 58. For his criticism of optimate policies and methods, see *Balb.* 58–62.
112. *Fam.* 7.1.4. The main cases in 55 and the earlier part of 54 were those of L. Caninius Gallus, tribune in 56; T. Ampius Balbus, a tribune in 63; C. Messius, tribune in

Worse lay ahead. Vatinius was brought to trial in August 54 on a charge of *ambitus* in connection with the praetorian elections for 55. Caesar pressed Cicero with unusual urgency to undertake the defense. Cicero complied and won the case with an impressive eulogy of his former enemy. It seemed an abject turnabout to friends as well as enemies, and there was a barrage of criticism.[113] But a still more humiliating reversal was forced upon him before the end of 54. A. Gabinius, who had governed Syria since 57, returned to Rome in September 54. As Pompey's most distinguished and persistent supporter, he was a prime target of the enemies of the coalition. He had also exposed himself to attack by a corrupt and oppressive regime and by an unauthorized intervention in Egypt in 55, where he had ended the Ptolemy controversy by restoring the king to his throne. He was first charged with *maiestas* arising out of the unauthorized restoration of Ptolemy. Pompey, who was intent on protecting his friend and his own *dignitas,* pressed Cicero hard to become reconciled to Gabinius and lead his defense. But this time Cicero resisted. Next to Clodius, Gabinius and Piso were his most hated enemies, and he had missed no opportunity since his return from exile to pillory every aspect of their characters and actions. To appear for the defense in such circumstances would, he believed, earn him *sempiterna infamia.* He declared to Quintus there would be no reconciliation while he had any vestige of liberty left, and he showed he was in earnest by delivering a blistering attack on Gabinius on the latter's first appearance in the Senate. He even considered conducting the prosecution himself, but decided Pompey would not stand for that, and he finally settled for a middle course and testified against his enemy with dignity and restraint. He was fervently hoping for a conviction, but, to his dismay, Gabinius was narrowly acquitted, helped by the feebleness of the prosecution, but above all by Pompey's vigorous solicitations of a venal jury.[114]

57; M. Livius Drusus Clodianus. There is a full discussion in Gruen, *Last Generation,* 312ff. See J. W. Crawford, *M. Tullius Cicero: The Lost and Unpublished Orations* (Göttingen, 1984), 170–83.

113. *Q.F.* 2.16(15).3. *Fam.* 1.9.19; 5.9.1. *Schol. Bob.* 160, Stangl. For the criticism, see Ps. Sallust, *Inv. in Cic.* 7. *Fam.* 1.9.19. Quintilian, *Inst.* 11.1.73.

114. *Q.F.* 3.1.15, 24; 3.2.1; 3.3.2–3; 3.4.1–3; 3.5.5; 3.7(9).1, 3. *Att.* 4.18.1, 3; 4.19.1. Dio 39.55, 62. Cicero had recently attacked Gabinius at the trial of his friend, Plancius. *Planc.* 86–87. He had also delivered a famous invective against Caesar's father-in-law Piso in the Senate in 55. Piso published a rejoinder, to which Quintus wanted Cicero to respond, but he refused on grounds it would draw attention to Piso's composition, which otherwise no one would read. *Q.F.* 3.1.11.

But Gabinius's troubles were far from over. His conduct in Syria and allegations that he had received ten thousand talents for his restoration of Ptolemy gave abundant grounds for a charge of extortion. Three separate applications to prosecute had been lodged in early October well before the trial for treason took place. The result of that trial intensified rather than inhibited the movement against Gabinius, and it was thought likely he would not escape a second time. Pompey and Caesar redoubled their efforts. Pompey defended Gabinius before a *contio* and read a letter from Caesar pleading on his behalf. He also increased the pressure on Cicero and made clear that this time he would not be satisfied with a middle course. Cicero decided to capitulate, swallowing his pride and accepting the *infamia* entailed in such an egregious volte-face. The result of the case, however, may have eased the pain. Gabinius was condemned and went into exile.[115]

But despite the generally unsatisfactory and sometimes humiliating nature of his political life after Luca, Cicero had no second thoughts about his alliance with the triumvirs. Some strain did develop in his relationship with Pompey, especially in 54. He was bothered by the latter's reticence and duplicity and he feared his self-centered ambition and intolerance of opposition. He never forgot what had happened in 58 and he continued to feel that Pompey's constancy and loyalty were strictly bounded by self-interest. The indifference shown to his feelings and dignity in the matter of Gabinius's defense must also have rankled deeply.[116] On the other hand, Pompey's benefactions in 57, his opposition to Clodius, and his unfailing friendliness and courtesy offset many of these misgivings and resentments. There was no danger of a rupture, and the links became stronger again in November 54, when Cicero was appointed a legate of Pompey to take effect from January 1, 53.[117]

115. Dio 39.63. Val. Max. 4.2.4. *Rab. post.* 20, 32–33. The date of the trial is not specified. See A. W. Lintott, ''Cicero and Milo,'' *JRS* 64 (1974), 67ff. Gruen, *Last Generation,* 326ff. E. Fantham, ''The Trials of Gabinius in 54,'' *Historia* 24 (1975), 425–43.

116. *Q.F.* 2.12(11).1; 3.1.9; 3.4.2; 3.6(8).4. *Att.* 4.15.7. Cicero does not appear as a confidant of Pompey at this time. He heard, for instance, from Quintus that Pompey was going to appoint him as a *legatus.* Pompey had not discussed it with him. *Q.F.* 3.1.18. When Pompey's wife, Julia, died in late summer of 54, Cicero speaks of Caesar's grief and is highly sympathetic, but never alludes to any contact with Pompey about the bereavement. *Q.F.* 3.1.17, 25; 3.6(8).3.

117. *Att.* 4.19.2. Pompey's charm had an important effect on Cicero. *Att.* 4.9.1. *Fam.* 1.8.2; 1.9.11.

But whatever coolness may have arisen in Cicero's feelings towards Pompey in the years after Luca, it was more than outweighed by a burgeoning friendship with Caesar that became particularly marked in the course of 54. Caesar worked hard at this period to cultivate Cicero and win his full loyalty. He kept in frequent touch, reaffirming his friendship and regard in extravagant terms. He treated Cicero's protégés with special favor and made repeated promises to shower money and honors on Cicero himself. He dedicated to him his treatise *De analogia,* which he wrote during a crossing of the Alps on his way to rejoin his army in Gaul and prefaced with remarks highly flattering to the orator, extolling him as the originator and inventor of eloquence.[118] He extended the friendly overtures to Cicero's brother, appointing him to a legateship in early 54 and giving him favored treatment and important responsibilities. He was even careful in his dealings with Clodius to do nothing that might offend the Ciceros or encourage their archenemy in his vendetta against them.[119]

Cicero's volatile temperament and craving for recognition and acceptance responded effusively to Caesar's blandishments. He was captivated by the attention and unreserved friendliness of a man of Caesar's eminence and power. The relationship gave him the form of acceptance and the assured status within the Roman elite that the *boni* had so persistently denied him. By the middle of 54 he was alluding to himself as one of Caesar's closest *amici,* and he was acting as one of his chief agents in overseeing his elaborate plans to spend sixty million sesterces in extending the Forum and building a new marble enclosure for meetings of the assemblies in the Campus Martius. His praise of Caesar and protestations of friendship for him became ever more profuse as 54 progressed. He declared that Caesar stood next in his affections after his immediate family, their friendship the one consolation that he had in the midst of the Republic's woes. He frequently affirmed his determination to do all in his power to cement the ties between them, and he told Quintus that, like a traveler who had got a late start and wanted to make up lost ground, he was eager to make extra efforts in cultivating Caesar because of past differences and the lateness of his recognition of Caesar's worth.[120] Part

118. *Brut.* 223. Suetonius, *Jul.* 56. Pliny, *NH* 7.30. *Fam.* 7.5.2. *Q.F.* 2.14(13).1, 3; 3.1.9–10. 3.5.3–4. *Att.* 4.16.7; 4.15.10. *Fam.* 7.17.2.

119. *Q.F.* 2.11(10).4; 3.1.11. *Att.* 4.19.2.

120. *Q.F.* 2.12.(11).1; 2.14(13).1–2; 3.1.18; 3.5.3–4. *Att.* 4.16.8; 4.19.1.

of those efforts took the form of poetry commemorating Caesar's exploits, especially his invasion of Britain. Cicero sent Caesar a specimen of this enterprise in the middle of 54 and he had finished an epic, of which he felt quite proud, by December. He also sent Caesar other writings for his evaluation, the latter's literary interests and admiration for Cicero's talents further aiding the new friendship.[121]

But there were also more mundane reasons of plain self-interest behind Cicero's enthusiasm for closer relations with Caesar in this period. Both he and Quintus remained concerned about the family's safety. The feud with Clodius continued unabated after Luca, and there had been renewed clashes in the latter part of 56. An earthquake near Rome had brought an announcement from the *haruspices* that sacred sites were being treated as profane. Soon afterwards Clodius called a *contio* at which he argued that the response of the *haruspices* referred to the reoccupied site of Cicero's house. Cicero responded with the speech *De haruspicum responsis* in the Senate, in which he sought to turn the tables on Clodius by showing it was his behavior that was being referred to in the response. He also rehearsed again the evils perpetrated by Clodius throughout his career and the destructive consequences of the political divisions that were providing protection for this greatest enemy of the state. The confrontation was further embittered by yet another onslaught on Clodius by Cicero in the Senate in relation to the tax farmers of Syria, whose claims Clodius was attempting to resist.[122]

Around the same time Cicero attempted to remove from the Capitol tablets containing Clodius's bill of outlawry against himself. Clodius seized and returned them, but Cicero removed them a second time and took them to his house. The Senate then intervened, and Cato, recently back from Cyprus, undermined Cicero's position by insisting that Clodius's laws, however pernicious, were valid. The final outcome of this strange incident is not recorded, but it must be assumed Cicero emerged the loser. There are no details of further confrontations, but

121. *Q.F.* 2.16(15).5; 3.6(8).3; 3.7(9).6.

122. *Har. resp.* 1, 9, 11, 14, 20, 61–62. Dio 39.20. The date of the speech remains disputed. It was undoubtedly after Luca, since Clodius is presented as now a friend of Pompey (*Har. resp.* 51–52), but the reconciliation seems recent and suggests a date in the early summer of 56. See K. Kumaniecki, ''Ciceros Rede de haruspicum responsis,'' *Klio* 37 (1959), 135–52. J. O. Lenaghan, *A Commentary on Cicero's Oration de Haruspicum Responsis* (The Hague, 1969),22–37.

there are indications the conflict never flagged, and the Ciceros remained fearful, constantly anticipating trouble. The search for a *praesidium firmissimum* against such trouble was a primary consideration in the initial decision of both Cicero and Quintus to seek closer relations with Caesar.[123]

Money was also a factor. Both brothers remained in debt, and Cicero was extremely anxious that they should get rid of their liabilities. He was also anxious that they should have sufficient funds to enable them to live in the style they wanted. It was a style that he considered modest, but in this very period it was involving both him and Quintus in large outlays for the purchase of property and for building and refurbishing.[124] While it is clear from the letters that financial gain was never a primary reason for the Ciceros' cultivation of Caesar, it was nonetheless a definite subsidiary consideration. Caesar was well known for his generosity, and Gaul for the richness of the booty that it yielded. Cicero and Quintus had high hopes that close ties to Caesar and in particular Quintus's legateship would relieve their financial worries. There are signs their hopes were largely realized. Cicero repeatedly mentions Caesar's *liberalitas* to himself and Quintus, and it seems certain that it was at this time that he received the large loan of five hundred thousand sesterces from Caesar that he speaks about in 51, when he was most anxious to repay it.[125]

Political ambition may also have entered the reckoning. Cicero disclaims any such ambition in this period and makes light of the *honores* that Caesar was offering him. But he had been interested in the censorship after his restoration and he definitely retained interest in a priesthood. Throughout 54 Quintus kept urging him to work ambitiously, to keep on building *gratia* and *dignitas,* and to maintain a conciliatory stance in politics, offending no one. This was not simply concern for security; the language is reminiscent of the *Commentariolum petitionis* and denotes the concerns of the politician seeking to build friends and favor.[126] It has been suggested that Quintus was thinking of his own

123. Dio 39.21–22. Plutarch, *Cat. min.* 40. *Q.F.* 3.6(8).1. See n. 104 above.

124. *Q.F.* 2.5(4).1; 2.15(14).3. Quintus seems to have been more concerned about money than Cicero. He had extravagant tastes.

125. For expectations of wealth from Gaul, see *Fam.* 7.13.1; 7.16.3; 7.17.1. Caesar's *liberalitas* is frequently mentioned. See *Fam.* 1.9.12, 18, 21; *Fam.* 7.7.2; 7.17.2. For the loan from Caesar, see *Att.* 5.4.3; 5.5.2; 5.6.2; 5.9.2; 5.10.4; 7.3.11; 7.8.5.

126. *Att.* 4.2.6. *Fam.* 15.4.13. Cf. *Att.* 2.5.2. For Quintus's exhortations, see *Q.F.* 2.14(13).4; 2.16(15).1; 3.1.12; 3.5.3, 5.

ambitions and that he had plans to seek the consulship. But it seems doubtful that the mercurial Quintus, who had tired of his labor in Gaul as early as mid-54 and wanted to resign, and who had even less appetite for the demands of the Forum than for those of the battlefield, had set his sights so high. He never did seek the consulship, and there is not even a vague hint in Cicero's letters of any such eventuality. His exhortations in 54 relate directly to Cicero's own standing, and it seems most likely it was to Cicero he was looking for any further enhancement of the family's *dignitas*.[127] Cicero did in fact soon afterwards achieve a coveted new honor, when he was coopted into the College of Augurs in 53 to fill the vacancy created by the death of Crassus's son in Parthia. He had the direct backing of the coalition, Pompey acting as one of his nominators. The alliance with the triumvirs was yielding some definite benefits.[128]

But besides these various lures binding Cicero to Pompey and Caesar in the years after Luca, the attachment was also sustained by the absence of any palatable or feasible alternative. His relationship with the leading conservatives did not improve. He continued to find jealousy and perfidy in their behavior toward himself. When he became involved in an altercation with Crassus at the first trial of Gabinius, they openly showed their glee at the prospect of a breach in his friendship with the dynasts. Cato's defense of the validity of Clodius's laws was a more grievous blow, and a further painful reminder of the persistent optimate support for his enemy, often at his expense.[129]

He found other reasons for outrage in their public policies. The renewed ascendancy of the triumvirate after Luca he blamed largely on their stupidity and fickleness, and he saw further proof of their unreliability and ineptitude in their failure to give stronger support to the candidature of Domitius Ahenobarbus in 56. It was reminiscent of their treatment of himself and of Lentulus Spinther. In general, he could not overcome his anger at their spiteful, partisan brand of politics that had denied him his rightful place as a leading voice in the Senate, had fo-

127. *Q.F.* 2.15(14).2; 3.6(8).1. For Quintus's reluctance to engage in oratory, see *De or.* 2.3. See also T. P. Wiseman, "The Ambitions of Quintus Cicero," *JRS* 56 (1966), 108–15. W. C. McDermott, "Q. Cicero," *Historia* 20 (1971), 702–17.

128. *Brut.* 1. *Phil* 2.4. *Fam.* 8.3.1. Hortensius was the second nominator, only recently reconciled to Cicero, no doubt through the efforts of Atticus. See *Att.* 4.6.3.

129. *Fam.* 1.9.20. Plutarch, *Cat. min.* 40. He continued publicly to show his resentment at optimate support for Clodius. At the trial of Vatinius he declared he had the right to defend their enemy since they defended his. *Fam.* 1.9.19.

mented division, and strengthened the hand of his archenemy, all to the great detriment of the Republic. His bitterness ran deep, so much so that he could declare to Atticus in late 54 that he accepted with equanimity the decline of the Republic because of the distress the predominance of Pompey was causing certain *optimates*.[130]

He was further discouraged from any thoughts of resuming old affiliations and policies by the deteriorating state of politics, especially in 54 and 53. The consular elections for 53 brought a level of intrigue and corruption that shocked and outraged even the hardened political world of the late fifties. There were four candidates, two patricians, M. Aemilius Scaurus and M. Valerius Messala, and two plebeians, Cn. Domitius Calvinus and C. Memmius. Scaurus and Memmius had the backing of the coalition, but Memmius evidently believed this was not sufficient to insure his election, and he entered into a formal, written *coitio* with Calvinus and the consuls of 54, Appius Claudius and Domitius Ahenobarbus. The consuls agreed to support the election of Memmius and Calvinus, and they in turn pledged, if elected, to fabricate proof of a *lex curiata* and a decree of the Senate confirming the proconsular *imperium* of the outgoing consuls and the desired requisitions for their provinces. The pact, which was an open secret by July, led to a massive campaign of bribery that caused interest rates to soar from 4 to 8 percent. There was a public outcry, and several days of angry debate about the bribery in the Senate. The outcome was the postponement of the elections to September.[131]

But in September the affair took a dramatic new turn when Memmius, on the urging of Pompey, disclosed the details of the pact in the Senate.[132] The Senate responded by decreeing that a *tacitum iudicium* should investigate the behavior of each of the candidates, which appar-

130. *Fam.* 1.7.10. *Att.* 4.8a.2; 4.18.2.
131. *Att.* 4.15.7; 4.16.6; 4.17.2. *Q.F.* 2.15(14).4; 2.16(15), 2–3. See E. S. Gruen, "The Consular Elections for 53 B.C.," *Hommages à M. Renard,* vol. 2 (1969), 311–21. G. V. Summer, "The *coitio* of 54, or waiting for Caesar," *HSPh* 86(1982), 134–39.
132. *Att.* 4.17.2–3. *Q.F.* 3.1.16. Pompey's motives are uncertain. He may have felt the pact had backfired and that disclosure was the best way of cutting losses. If so, he showed poor judgment. The move ruined Memmius's chances and annoyed Caesar (*Att.* 4.17.3). It is conceivable Pompey was maneuvering to discredit the campaign sufficiently to insure no elections took place, clearing the way for a dictatorship in 53. There were soon rumors of a dictatorship, and Cicero had a suspicion Pompey wanted one. *Att.* 4.18.1. *Q.F.* 3.4.1; 3.6(8).4–6.

ently meant a sworn inquiry before a jury, but without a prosecutor. The bill to establish the *iudicium* was vetoed, however, and the Senate then declared the elections should go ahead. Cicero believed Calvinus and Messala, who had been foremost in bribing the electorate, would win. But there were further postponements. All four candidates were indicted *de ambitu* under the usual procedures soon after the failure of the proposal to hold a *tacitum iudicium,* and the elections continued to be postponed by use of *obnuntiatio.* [133] By late November it was clear the year would end without consuls, and there were rumors that proposals would be made to appoint Pompey dictator. The *boni* and some of the tribunes were strongly opposed to that idea and certain to resist it vigorously. The prospects for peace in the year ahead were very uncertain at the end of 54. [134]

But in the event no major crisis developed. Proposals to make Pompey dictator were brought forward by two tribunes, Coelius Vincianus and Lucilius Hirrus. Pompey yielded to the opposition, however, after an appeal from Cato to preserve the peace, and he renounced any interest in the position. The consular elections eventually went ahead in July and, as expected, Calvinus and Messala were the winners. But the electoral system had suffered enormous damage and would not easily recover. [135]

The electoral corruption was matched by corruption in the courts. The blatant determination of the opponents of the triumvirate to use the courts as an indirect means of attacking its members through endangering their friends inevitably politicized the judicial process and brought into play the full weaponry of pressures, promises, and straight payoffs. Cicero details the wholesale trafficking and venality. Murder continued to be frowned on, but in all else guilt and innocence were subordinate considerations. The administration of justice became capricious, unpredictable, destroying any confidence in the system. At the end of 54 the deterioration had reached the stage where a *iustitium* had to be declared. [136]

133. *Att.* 4.17.2–4. *Q.F.* 3.3.2. The candidates were anxious for postponement into 53 so that those elected could enter office at once and avoid prosecution. Memmius also wanted postponement until Caesar returned to Cisalpine Gaul. *Q.F.* 2.6(8).3.

134. *Q.F.* 2.14(13).5; 3.2.3; 3.3.2; 3.4.1; 3.6(8).4; 3.7(9).3. *Att.* 4.17.4–5; 4.18.3; 4.19.2. The tribunician elections for 53 were also disrupted by bribery and went ahead only because of special efforts by Cato. *Att.* 4.15.7. *Q.F.* 2.15(14).4.

135. *Fam.* 8.4.3. Plutarch, *Pomp.* 54. The trials kept being postponed, held up also by *supplicationes* at the end of 54 (*Q.F.*3.6[8].3). See Gruen, *Homages à Renard,* 320.

136. *Att.* 4.16.5; 4.15.4; 4.18.3; 4.19.2. *Q.F.* 3.1.15; 3.2.2; 3.3.3; 3.4.1; 3.5.4.

Cicero saw no grounds for hope in the course of political events in the years after Luca. He found increasing reason to believe the Republic was in decay beyond repair; it was senescent, its vitality gone, its institutions crumbling, disorder pervading everything.[137] His pessimism, combined with the awkwardness of his association with Pompey and Caesar, banished all thought of returning to an active role in search of remedies. He was intent instead on viewing it all with equanimity and on detaching himself from it, turning back to the things he found most congenial, his studies and his pleading. He increasingly sidestepped the major controversies, avoiding the Senate or holding his peace. He was strongly reinforced in this desire to assume a passive role by both Atticus and Quintus, the former by nature and long practice inclined toward caution and quietism, the latter preoccupied with concerns for the family's safety and popularity.[138]

As early as January 55 Cicero was beginning to devote more time to his studies. He first occupied himself with an epic on his exile and restoration, which he entitled *De temporibus suis*. It finally comprised three books, the first of which was finished by February 55. Quintus approved it, though Caesar, to whom Cicero sent the poem in 54, gave it an indifferent reception. The intent was clearly to immortalize in poetry the version of events relating to his exile that he had so carefully promoted in his speeches after his restoration. But the material was sensitive, and Cicero was anxious not to offend by omission any friends who had helped him, so he decided the work should not be published in his lifetime.[139]

A much more important work was the *De oratore,* which he had completed by the middle of November 55, after what he described as a long and concentrated effort. It set forth in three books the qualities and training of the ideal orator, whom Cicero equated with the ideal statesman, and it had as its main speakers his great patrons and oratorical idols,

---

137. *Att.* 4.18.2; 4.19.1. *Q.F.* 2.14(13).5; 3.7(9).1. *Fam.* 2.5.2. The pessimism was not intermittent, but persistent from 55 through 53.

138. *Fam.* 1.8.3; 7.1.5. *Att.* 4.8a.4; 4.10.1; 4.11.2; 4.13.1; 4.18.2. *Q.F.* 2.8(7).1; 2.14(13).4; 2.16(15).2; 3.5.4; 3.7(9).2. Only once does Cicero indicate he spoke out, and that was in connection with the Senate's handling of the bribery scandal. He expected Atticus to be annoyed. *Att.* 4.17.3.

139. *Q.F.* 2.8(7).1; 2.16(15).5; 3.1.24. *Fam.* 1.9.23. *Att.* 4.8a.3. It was at this time also that he tried to persuade L. Lucceius to write of his *res gestae* (*Fam.* 5.12). He was intent on making the most of the past and drew consolation from reflecting on past achievements. *Att.* 4.18.2. For Lucceius, see McDermott, *Hermes* 97 (1969), 233–46.

L. Crassus and M. Antonius.[140] By May of the following year he had embarked on an even more exacting enterprise, the *De republica,* originally designed to comprise nine books relating conversations lasting nine days about the ideal state and the ideal citizen. It was set in 129, with Scipio Aemilianus as the chief interlocutor. He found the writing heavy going, requiring large amounts of free time, and he was further slowed by frequent remodeling of the design. In late October, after completing two books, he was thinking of a totally different plan, with himself as the main speaker. In the end, however, he retained his original scheme, but settled for a three-day discussion in six books. The date of completion is not recorded, but the books were in circulation in early 51.[141] By then he was also writing the supplementary dialogue, *De legibus,* which dealt with the nature of law and justice and set forth the specific statutes that should govern the ideal state. This time he did assume the leading role himself. The work, of which most of the first three books survive, was most likely designed to have the same number of books as the *De republica.* It may never have been completed, however, and was almost certainly not published in Cicero's lifetime.[142]

The content of these important writings has been discussed earlier. They dealt with the great passions of Cicero's life, oratory and politics. They were obvious areas for his attention, as he sought to divert himself by study. But they also offered other benefits. They gave him the opportunity to combine his experience as a practicing orator and statesman with his knowledge of philosophy and abstract reasoning to produce a persuasive intellectual underpinning for his beliefs about the state, statesmanship, and political education. They further provided a new source of fame as literary monuments of a type not previously attempted in Latin with any success. But perhaps most important of all to Cicero, they were a means indirectly to vindicate and exalt his own brand of statesmanship and the form of government that he had so vigorously promoted and briefly reestablished as consul in 63.[143]

---

140. *Att.* 4.13.2; 4.17.5; 13.19.4. *Fam.* 1.9.23. Gelzer, *Cicero,* 187. G. Achard, "Pourquoi Cicero a-t-il écrit le *De Oratore?"* *Latomus* 46 (1987), 318–29. Kennedy, *Rhetoric,* 205ff.

141. *Q.F.* 2.13(12).1; 3.5.1–2. *Att.* 4.16.2; 5.12.2. *Fam.* 8.1.5.

142. *Fam.* 9.2.5. Rawson, *ANRW* 1.4 (1973), 335–55.

143. See *Att.* 4.18.2 and n. 139 above. The long established notion that Cicero developed in the *De republica* the idea of quasimonarchic *gubernator* must be totally

Alongside his increased literary activity, he maintained a busy schedule in the courts. His heavy workload was, in part at least, his own choice. Aside from the political cases forced upon him by Pompey and Caesar, he enjoyed pleading and made little effort to escape from it. He remained at the disposal of his political friends, always willing to meet the demands of *amicitia*.[144] But he was sought after, as he had always been, by a great variety of clients, and he largely continued, as he had always done, to accept a variety of cases. As a result, the pace of his life was often hectic, and he frequently complained that he never had a moment to spare when in Rome and that he was even forced at times to dictate his letters. In 54 he had so many cases he had to stay in Rome through an unusually hot summer and could not escape to the country until September. A month later he was complaining again that there was no day on which he was not defending someone. His time for writing was therefore mostly restricted to the periods he spent on his country estates.[145]

But there were rewards, and they were important to Cicero. Aside from the pleasure that he took in oratory, he was achieving high popularity, which was shown every day at the *salutatio* and in the enthusiastic way he was received in the Forum and the theater. He was greatly gratified by these signs of general public favor, which gave assurance of enduring *gratia* and *dignitas*.[146]

Cicero also helped fill the void created by political inaction by taking a greater interest in his properties and in his family. He found both were important sources of consolation and pleasure. His newly built house on the Palatine, which had the final finishing touches applied in October 54,

---

rejected. He was intent on idealizing the *respublica* in which he had been the *gubernator*. See *Att.* 4.18.2: "Recordor enim quam bella paulisper nobis gubernantibus civitas fuerit." He certainly would not have cast Pompey in the role of the ideal monarchic *rector* in the late fifties, when his opinion of him was at a low point. For a review of modern scholarship on this issue, see Schmidt, *ANRW* 1.4 (1973), 319–23.

144. He defended Plancius, who had treated him with such kindness during his exile, in the latter part of 54. The outcome is not recorded but was probably acquittal, since Cicero quickly published the speech. *Q.F.* 3.1.11. He successfully defended Scaurus around the same time on a charge of extortion. *Att.* 4.15.9; 4.16.6; 4.17.4–5. *Q.F.* 2.16(15).3; 3.1.11,16. He offered his services to all four consular candidates in 54 when they were indicted for bribery. *Att.* 4.17.5. *Q.F.* 3.3.2.

145. *Q.F.* 2.14(13).2; 2.16(15).1; 3.1.1; 3.3.1; 3.5.4. *Att.* 4.15.5; 4.16.1–2. *Fam.* 7.1.4.

146. *Att.* 4.15.6. *Q.F.* 2.15(14); 2.16(15).1.

delighted him. It was as comfortable as any of his villas and a haven of quiet.[147] His country homes pleased him equally. He had rebuilt the damaged villas at Tusculum and Formiae, and had recently acquired a new luxury villa at Cumae overlooking the sea, which complemented the villa at Pompeii on the other side of the Bay of Naples that he had owned since the late sixties. Cicero loved the scenic beauty, the comfort, the leisure, the opportunities for social and cultural diversions that the villas afforded, and he took particular advantage of their benefits in the years after Luca.[148]

The education of his son and nephew was another important interest for Cicero in this period. His son, born in 65, and his nephew, born in 67 or early 66, were both launched on their rhetorical studies by 54, and Cicero, not surprisingly, carefully supervised their program and progress. He was keeping an especially close eye on his nephew during Quintus's absence. The young Quintus was lively and talented. Except for his voracious appetite, Cicero had little fault to find with him and he kept him with him as much as possible. He frequently alludes to the *pueri* in his letters to Quintus in 54 and was clearly enjoying his closer involvement in their lives. In general his energies and interests were sharply focused by late 54 on his private affairs, which were providing an effective anodyne for his political despondency and frustration. He had come to terms with the political realities of the late fifties and had achieved relative contentment.[149]

The only political matter that seriously occupied him at the end of 54 was Milo's impending bid for the consulship of 52. *Pietas* demanded that Cicero show his gratitude for Milo's part in his restoration, and he was determined to fulfill his obligations to his benefactor and to work as hard for Milo's election as he had for his own. He had a further incentive in

147. *Att.* 4.18.2. *Fam.* 6.18.5. *Q.F.* 3.3.1.
148. *Q.F.* 2.5(4).1; 2.13(12).1; 3.7(9).2. *Att.* 4.10.1; 4.11.2. Cf. *Att.* 16.6.2; 16.3.4. *Fam.* 2.16.2. Cicero also had a townhouse at Antium that he loved. *Att.* 4.8.1–2. He was further involved at this time in supervising his brother's building operations, on the Palatine, on estates near Arpinum at Arcanum and Laterium. *Q.F.* 3.1.1, 4; 3.3.1; 3.7(9).7. He was also seeking collections of Greek and Latin books for him. (*Q.F.* 3.4.5; 3.5.6), and a suitable suburban property (*horti*). *Q.F.* 3.1.14, 23.
149. *Att.* 1.2.1; 1.10.5. *Q.F.* 3.1.7,14; 3.3.1, 4; 3.7(9).2, 9. Tullia was settled again after the death of her husband, Piso, in 57. In April 56 she was betrothed to Furius Crassipes of patrician family (*Q.F.* 2.6[5].2) and was married by 54 (*Fam.* 1.9.20). There is no mention of Terentia in the letters of this period.

that Clodius was a candidate for the praetorship, and Milo would be needed to hold him in check in that important office.[150]

Milo's prospects were reasonably good. He had some high connections through his marriage in late 55 to Sulla's daughter, Fausta. He had general support from the *boni,* including M. Cato, and had won over the *iuventus* and key electoral figures by his wide popularity and vigorous canvassing. He also stood well with the masses because of the magnificance of the shows he provided and his general liberality. Cicero alludes disapprovingly in late 54 to one of those shows in which Milo was proposing to spend one million sesterces. His munificence was ruining him financially, but it was improving his chances of election.[151]

Ranged against him were Q. Caecilius Metellus Scipio Nasica and P. Plautius Hypsaeus. The former was uninspiring, but had the benefits of *summa nobilitas* and the crucial backing of Pompey; the latter was Pompey's primary candidate, a former quaestor of the general and a longtime political agent. Both candidates also had the active support of Clodius, who was determined to keep Milo from the consulship at all costs.[152]

The campaign quickly assumed the pattern of the electoral contests of 54, but with greater violence as Clodius and Milo resumed their gang warfare. Cicero had one major confrontation with Clodius in the Senate over the issue of Milo's debts, and he delivered yet another stinging invective against all that Clodius had done and represented. But the contest was waged mainly in the streets between the rival gangs. The consuls were unable to maintain control, and the continual violent clashes made the holding of elections impossible. Another year began without consuls. Then on January 18, in a chance encounter between Milo and Clodius on the Appian Way, the latter was killed. His wife Fulvia and the tribunes opposed to Milo attempted to incite the populace by displaying the body and its wounds. The body was carried by a mob to

150. *Q.F.* 3.6(8).6; 3.7(9).2. Asconius 30, Clark. *Fam.* 2.6. shows the depth of Cicero's determination to get Milo elected. Cf. *Att.* 9.7.3. Cicero's loyalty and his need to repay *beneficia* were extraordinary. *Mil.* 100.

151. *Att.* 4.13.1. Asconius 28, Clark. *Fam.* 2.6.3. For Milo's games and general extravagance, see *Q.F.* 3.6(8).6; 3.7(9).2. *Mil.* 95. Pliny (*NH* 36.104) says Milo owed 70 million sesterces when he went into exile. According to *Schol. Bob.* 169, Stangl, Milo himself gave his debts in 53 as 6 million.

152. For Hypsaeus, see Asconius 35, Clark. *Fam.* 1.1.3. *Flacc.* 20. For Metellus, see *Brut.* 212. *Att.* 6.1.17.

the Forum and then to the Senate House, where it was set on fire. The building was burned to the ground.

Violence continued in the succeeding weeks and a succession of *interreges* failed to hold elections. Finally, the Senate passed the *consultum ultimum* calling on the *interrex*, tribunes, and Pompey to save the state, and authorizing Pompey to hold a levy throughout Italy. He quickly gathered a force and took control of the city. There was pressure to appoint him dictator to restore order, but the leaders of the *optimates* preferred to offer him a sole consulship, considering it a safer arrangement constitutionally, and, on a decree of the Senate moved by Bibulus with Cato's approval, Pompey was appointed sole consul by the *interrex* and entered office shortly before the beginning of March.[153]

Pompey immediately took measures to deal with the two great abuses of the preceding years, bribery and violence. New laws *de ambitu* and *de vi* were quickly passed with the full consent of the Senate. The bribery bill was a comprehensive statute designed to update and supplement existing legislation; it was also to be applied retroactively to bring within its ambit the egregious offenders of the recent past. The *lex de vi* had a more specific purpose, establishing a special *quaestio* to deal with those involved in the violence surrounding Clodius's death and its aftermath. The court was to operate under new, speedier procedures, and with a new system for selecting jurors that was designed to reduce the possibilities of bribery or intimidation. It was an extraordinary mechanism to deal with an extraordinary crisis, concerned to defuse the high feeling generated by Clodius's death and to deter further violence by dealing speedy justice to those responsible for Clodius's killing and other recent disorders.[154]

The man most vulnerable to charges under the new law was, of course, Milo, and he was quickly indicted by Clodius's nephews, assisted by Mark Antony, a quaestor in 52 and a longtime associate of Clodius.[155] Cicero led the defense, though he was being subjected to constant attacks and even threats of prosecution at inflammatory *contiones* being held by

153. Asconius 30–34, Clark. Dio 49. 46–50. Plutarch, *Pomp.* 54–55; *Cat. min.* 47–48; *Caes.* 28. Appian, *BC* 20–23. Velleius 2.47. See Rice Holmes, *Roman Republic,* 2:164–68. For Cicero's clash with Clodius in the Senate, see *Schol. Bob.* 169, Stangl. K. Kumaniecki, ''Ciceros Rede de aere alieno Milonis,'' *Klio* 59 (1977), 381–401.

154. Asconius 36, 44, Clark. *Mil.* 15. Appian, BC 2.23. Dio 40.51–52. Plutarch, *Cat. min.* 48. For a full discussion, see Gruen, *Last Generation,* 234–39.

155. *Mil.* 59. Asconius 34, 41, 54, Clark. For Antony's friendship with Clodius, see *Phil.* 2.48.

three tribunes opposed to Milo. He was also risking the disfavor of Pompey, who had made it clear he was seeking a conviction.[156]

The case came to trial in April. Clodius's partisans tried to intimidate the defense by noisy, threatening behavior. Pompey responded by posting troops in the Forum. This brought relative calm to the proceedings until the fifth and final day, when the main speeches for the prosecution and defense were delivered. On the urging of the tribune, Pacinus, an opponent of Milo, the shops were closed throughout the city on the final day and large crowds gathered to show their hostility to Milo. As soon as Cicero began to speak, the *Clodiani*, undeterred by the presence of the troops, began shouting and totally upset his composure. His performance as a result fell far below his usual standard. But it is unlikely his ineffectiveness had much impact on the outcome. Milo stood little chance of acquittal, given his record and the new determination to eliminate violence. His conviction was voted by a large majority, and he went into exile at Massilia.[157]

Many other prosecutions under Pompey's new legislation followed and helped make 52 another busy year in the courts for Cicero. M. Saufeius, who had commanded Milo's gang in the final encounter with Clodius, was prosecuted twice *de vi*, under Pompey's law and the earlier *Lex Plautia*. Cicero defended on both occasions and won two acquittals. He defended three other friends during 52, all prosecuted under Pompey's *lex de ambitu:* M. Scaurus, the consular candidate in 54, P. Sestius, the tribune of 57, and T. Fadius, who had been Cicero's quaestor in 63. Sestius was acquitted, but Scaurus and Fadius were both convicted.[158]

But the most remarkable aspect of Cicero's forensic activity in 52 was a prosecution—only the second of his entire career—that he launched at the end of the year against T. Munatius Plancus Bursa. Plancus had

---

156. *Mil.* 12. Asconius 37–38, Clark. Pompey had begun to distance himself from Milo as early as November 54 (*Q.F.* 3.6[8]6), concerned about his extremism and Milo's willingness to oppose him. His conviction in 52 was essential to Pompey's goal of stamping out violence. His fear of Milo in 52 and desire for a conviction are well documented. *Fam.* 3.10.10. Asconius 36, 38, 50–52, Clark. *Mil.* 64–68. Velleius, 2.47. *Schol. Bob.* 112, Stangl.

157. Asconius 39–42, Clark. *Mil.* 3. Plutarch, *Cic.* 35. Dio 40.53–54. Quintilian, *Inst.* 4.3.17. *Opt. gen. or.* 10. For a good discussion of the trial and Cicero's general relations with Milo, see Lintott, *JRS* 64 (1974), 62–78.

158. Asconius 55, Clark. *Off.* 1.138. Appian, *BC* 2.24. Quintilian, *Inst.* 4.1.69. *Att.* 13.49.1. *Fam.* 2.45.2; 5.18.1–2. For other prosecutions, see Gruen, *Last Generation,* 342ff.

previously been defended by Cicero, but as tribune in 52 he had taken a
foremost part in the tribunician agitation against Milo and was one of the
tribunes who had attacked Cicero and threatened him with prosecution.
The case came to trial in early 51, and, despite strenuous efforts by
Pompey to save him, Plancus was condemned. Cicero, who declared he
hated Plancus more than Clodius, was jubilant.[159]

The evidence for Cicero's personal feelings and view of events in 52 is
scantier than usual because there are no letters from the year to Atticus or
Quintus, but there is no reason to believe there was any significant
change in his life or attitudes. He maintained his high level of involvement in the courts, but otherwise held aloof from public life and remained
as despondent as ever about the condition of the *respublica*. Pompey's
sole consulship brought him no hope of better things. He had been
distinctly cool to the idea of such a transfer of power to Pompey in the
preceding years, and the latter's use of his new office did nothing to
relieve his misgivings. Pompey's administration by no means exemplified the impartial rule of law and selfless devotion to the common
good that Cicero demanded of the good statesman. Though he tackled the
state's immediate problems with firmness and efficiency in 52, Pompey
never scrupled to bend his own enactments to serve the interests of
himself and his friends. When his father-in-law, Metellus Scipio, was
indicted *de ambitu,* he first tried to influence the jury, and then resorted to
a more drastic expedient, appointing Scipio as his consular colleague,
which gave him immunity from prosecution. He intervened illegally in
the trial of Plancus in an effort to save his friend, and in other cases used
his influence to try to insure conviction. Cicero resented such self-serving displays of *potentia,* which confirmed his worst fears about the
dangers of unchecked power.[160]

Nor can he have been pleased by another development in 52 that forced
him once more to bend to pressure from Pompey and Caesar and act
against his better judgment. Early in the year, Pompey began preparations to introduce a bill to allow Caesar to stand for the consulship in
absentia. This would enable Caesar to retain his *imperium* until he entered the consulship and thus avoid the threat of prosecution. There was,

159. *Fam.* 7.2.3. *Att.* 6.1.10. Asconius 38, Clark. Dio 40.55. Plutarch, *Cat. min.* 48;
Cic. 25. Val. Max. 6.2.5
160. Dio 40.51, 53. Val. Max. 9.5.3. Plutarch, *Pomp.* 55; *Cat. min.* 48. *Fam.* 5.18.2.
The disrepute of Pompey's administration long survived. Tacitus, *Ann.* 3.28.

however, a risk of a veto from Caelius Rufus, a tribune in 52 and a vigorous opponent of Pompey. The latter called on Cicero to use his influence to dissuade Caelius from opposing the proposal, and Caesar summoned him to Ravenna to add his own personal pressure. Cicero was opposed to the bill and initially attempted to persuade Pompey to abandon it, but in the end he was forced again to do the bidding of his powerful allies. He obviously succeeded in converting Caelius, since the bill was passed with the support of all ten tribunes.[161]

Cicero did show greater independence in the courts in 52, where he was in frequent conflict with Pompey. This was perhaps not significant in cases where Cicero was defending friends, since he was exceptionally committed to meeting the obligations of *amicitia,* but it was significant in regard to his prosecution of Plancus, whom Pompey was unusually anxious to preserve. Cicero's tenacity in pursuing a Pompeian adherent to defend his honor and avenge an injury shows a degree of independence absent in 54, when he had backed away from prosecuting Gabinius and had ended up actually defending him. The death of Clodius may account for the change. This was an event that undoubtedly brought Cicero enormous satisfaction and relief, ridding him of an obsessive hatred and fear that had clouded his life for a decade.[162] There is no sign that the removal of the danger from Clodius inspired any wish to change his basic relationship with Pompey and Caesar, but it may well have given him the confidence to assert his right to defend at least his personal dignity, if not his political views.

In any event, the entire pattern of his life in the years after Luca was soon to undergo a radical change. Early in 51, as a result of another law of Pompey, he was assigned the governorship of Cilicia by the Senate in succession to Appius Claudius. He left Rome in early May to begin another new phase in his political life.

---

161. Suetonius, *Jul.* 26. Dio 40.51. Appian, *BC* 2.25. Caesar, *BC* 1.9, 32. *Att.* 7.1.4; 7.7.6; 8.3.3. *Fam.* 6.6.5. *Phil.* 2.24. The idea advanced by Lintott (*JRS* 64 [1974], 75ff; see also J. Geiger, *CP* 79 [1984], 38–43) that Pompey's sole consulship was welcome to Cicero and a realization of a dream of rapprochement between Pompey and *boni,* misreads Cicero's entire relationship with both Pompey and *boni* in the late fifties. His allusion to Pompey's regime in 52 in *Att.* 7.1.4 as "illo divino tertio consulatu" is, without question, ironic.

162. An indication of the importance of Clodius's death to Cicero can be seen in *Att.* 5.13.1, where he dates the letter by reference to it, although the event was already 599 days old! It marked a new era in his life.

5: CICERO,
THE PROVINCIAL
GOVERNOR

Cicero was appointed to Cilicia under the *Lex Pompeia de provinciis,* which was passed in 52 and prescribed that an interval of five years must elapse between the holding of a magistracy in Rome and a provincial command. It replaced the *Lex Sempronia* and was chiefly designed to discourage electoral corruption by insuring that extravagant spending on campaigns could not be quickly recouped in the provinces. It would also have the effect of reducing the motivation to engage in extortion.[1] Under the new procedure the Senate decided each year which provinces should receive new proconsuls and propraetors, and the new governors were then selected by lot from the pool of eligible consulars and praetorians. In

1. Dio 40.30; 46.50. Cf. *Fam.* 2.7.4; 15.9.2; 15.14.5. The law confirmed a decree of the Senate passed in 53. Dio.40.46, 56. See Willems, *Le Sénat,* 2:588. Caesar later claimed (*BC* 1.85) that the bill was aimed against him, giving greater control of provincial appointments to the oligarchy. But Caesar was, at this time, attempting to present all the decisions of the late fifties as part of a lengthy conspiracy against him. The new procedure would make immediate replacement of him easier on the expiry of his term in Gaul, but it also gave him a new means of preventing it in that decisions made under the new law were subject to veto, unlike decisions under the *Lex Sempronia.* The bill is more reasonably seen as a sensible and needed reform. See Balsdon, *JRS 29* (1939), 173–74. Gruen, *Last Generation,* 457ff. The terms of the law are discussed in detail by A. J. Marshall, "The *Lex Pompeia de provinciis* (52 B.C.) and Cicero's Imperium in 51–50 B.C.: Constitutional Aspects," *ANRW* 1.1 (1972), 887–921.

51 the designated consular provinces were Cilicia and Syria, and the two ex-consuls selected to govern them were Cicero and Bibulus.[2]

Cicero's View of Empire

Cicero's administration of Cilicia can be most satisfactorily examined against the background of his views about empire and its government. He has left no single, comprehensive discussion of these issues, but there is abundant evidence of his views to be found throughout his writings. As often, he emerges as a defender of the ancestral outlook and practice, the traditional views modified by a humanizing and rationalizing veneer drawn from philosophy.

His longest discussions of war and empire occur in association with analyses of the nature of justice in the *De republica* and *De legibus*. He reproduces the Platonic and Stoical idea that justice fundamentally meant giving to each his own, otherwise stated as giving to each his due. It required above all that no one should harm another unless provoked by injury. The qualification was important. Cicero saw the requiting of injury not only as a right but as a duty, necessary to deter future wrongs but also demanded by honor and duty.[3] Justice also required the prevention of injury to others to the extent possible, particularly in situations where there existed a specific obligation to protect those suffering the wrong. In this connection and in regard to all aspects of just behavior, Cicero emphasized that *fides,* by which he meant a firm and genuine fidelity to promises and agreements, was the great foundation on which justice rested.[4]

The principles governing just behavior between individuals Cicero believed should also apply to behavior between states, and his view of war and the conditions that justified it derived essentially from his gener-

---

2. The use of the lot is confirmed in Caesar, *BC* 1.6 and Plutarch, *Cic.* 36. It is apparent that only those who had not previously governed a province were eligible. *Fam.* 8.8.8; 2.15.4. The bill also prescribed a tenure of one year, measured from the date of entering the province. *Att.* 5.21.9; 6.6.3. These provisions indicate a desire by the Senate to exercise closer control over provincial government and to limit the political and financial benefit any individual could acquire from provincial commands. Marshall, *ANRW* 1.1 (1972), 890ff.

3. *Rep.* 3.18. *Off.* 1.15, 20, 33; 3.76. *Man.*6–7.

4. *Off.* 1.23, 28.

al concept of justice. He started from the premise that all use of violence was incompatible with the higher nature of man and justifiable only where diplomacy had failed. No war could be just, therefore, unless it was preceded by demands for satisfaction and by due warnings. In addition, there had to be adequate grounds for hostilities, and these included defense against attack, the avenging of injury, and the protection of friends and allies. But the ultimate goal of all warfare must be peace in a life free from injury. The chief concern of any state should be to create for its citizens a well-ordered society that made possible a secure and civilized way of life in conformity with the dignity and social instincts of human nature. Such a society could only be achieved when men's minds had been turned from brutish habits of war to gentler ways and to a love of peace and the arts of peace. Only in such conditions could justice and good faith, the chief bonds of a *respublica,* prevail.[5]

Cicero's eloquent affirmation of the benefits of peace and their importance to the realization of man's true aspirations and happiness did not prevent him, however, from approving many aspects of the militarism that dominated his own society. He freely acknowledged the Romans were preoccupied with glory and held forth military achievement as the best and noblest means to achieve it. Success in war was seen to confer the greatest benefit on the state, and military prowess was, in consequence, the most highly prized ability and bestowed the highest *dignitas.* Successful military commanders returned to glory and applause, to the highest honors the Senate could confer, to the esteem of the equestrian order, to the affection of the general public. Their fame was perpetuated in song and poetry, in monuments and commemorative festivals. Their subordinates shared their glory and popularity and could expect to reap ongoing benefits in their future careers. No civil achievement could similarly capture the people's imagination or similarly win their favor and acclaim.[6]

Cicero saw dangers in this exaltation of military heroism. It could lead

5. *Off.* 1.34–36, 39–40, 80. *Rep.* 2.26–27; 3.34–35. *Att.* 8.11.1. *De or.* 1.33.

6. *Man.*7. *Arch.*22–30. *Mur.*24,30. *Prov. cons.* 29–30. *Rab. post.* 42. *Pis.* 57–62. *Brut.* 256. *Off.* 1.74; 2.45. See P. A. Brunt, "*Laus Imperi*," *Imperialism in the Ancient World,* ed. P. D. A. Garnsey and C. R. Whittaker (Cambridge, 1987), 162ff. W. V. Harris, *War and Imperialism in Republican Rome* (Oxford, 1979), 9–40. H. Drexler, "*Gloria*," *Helicon* 2 (1962), 3–36. J. A. North, "The Development of Roman Imperialism," *JRS* 71 (1981), 1–9. M. G. Morgan, "*Imperium sine finibus*," *Essays in Honor of T. S. Brown* (Lawrence, Kan., 1980), 143–54.

to the pursuit of false glory in forms of military adventurism that were inspired solely by a lust for fame, and that could result in the squandering of the state's resources or the endangering of its security. The greater a man's military ability and courage the greater the risk of such a misdirection of excellence to the service of private ambition rather than the common good. He saw some need for a change of attitude, especially in his time, when the greatest tasks of leadership had shifted from the military to the civic arena.[7]

But on the whole he approved the spirit of the old morality and its pronounced militaristic leanings. It had sustained in the Roman character the love of true glory, the great guarantor of vitality and dedication in political leaders. The military virtue and discipline it nurtured had raised the name of Rome to greatness, and forced the world to obey her. It had tolerated no injury, and had brought safety to Rome's allies and protection to her merchants and to her citizens living abroad. It had moved the world toward a permanent peace and transformed the Mediterranean into a safe, enclosed harbor under Roman control.[8]

Cicero believed all this had been achieved without serious lapses into naked aggression or expansionism incompatible with justice. He found no difficulty in stretching his triad of just causes to provide valid grounds for all of Rome's major wars, though in the process he was often forced to ignore historical reality and strain principle to the point of distortion. He saw in fetial law, which required a demand for satisfaction, a waiting period, and a formal declaration of war before any hostile action was taken, proof of Rome's awareness of and commitment to the principles of just procedure in war, but he ignored the fact that the demands might be unwarranted, and that, in any event, fetial procedure had ceased to be used in any full sense by the time of Rome's greatest expansion.[9] He was prepared to accept the idea that those who threatened to attack or were likely to do so could be deemed enemies equally with those who had commenced hostilities. He was thus able to justify preemptive attacks by

7. *Off.* 1.74, 82–83. Cf. *Man.* 65. Crassus's invasion of Parthia gets specific mention as an unwarranted military escapade. *Fin.* 3.75.

8. *Rep.* 5.9. *Mil.* 97. *Arch.* 14, 29. *Mur.* 22. *Man.* 7–12. *Pis.* 58–59. *Prov. cons.* 31. *Tusc.* 1.1

9. *Off.* 1.36. *Rep.* 2.31; 3.35. See Harris, *War and Imperialism,* 166ff. W. Dahlheim, *Struktur und Entwicklung* (Munich, 1968), 171ff. H. Drexler, *"Justum Bellum,"* RhM 102 (1959), 97–140. J. W. Rich, *Declaring War in the Roman Republic* (Brussels, 1976), 56 ff. T. Wiedermann, *"Fetiales,"* CQ 36 (1986), 478–90.

a vague principle that any conflict that contributed to greater peace and security was morally acceptable. Cato made such an argument in advocating the destruction of Carthage, and it was the basis on which Cicero justified Pompey's conquests in the East and Caesar's in Gaul.[10]

Cicero was also prepared to stretch the right to avenge a wrong to provide justification for massive retaliation in response to trifling insults. He could accordingly present as a sign of strength and resolution such disproportionate reactions by Rome as the destruction of Corinth because of disrespect to an envoy.[11] His third just cause, the defense of allies, he also interpreted in regard to Roman actions in a highly elastic fashion, presenting it as the leading and laudable reason for Rome's great wars, but ignoring the historical fact that in many cases the connection with the alleged allies was slight or initiated after they had come under threat.[12]

Cicero further accepted that the primary goal of war could legitimately be glory or ascendancy rather than strictly defensive considerations, though the latter, obviously, would never be entirely absent. Such wars, like all others, had to have a just cause arising from some form of provocation, but they differed in that they could be avoided without serious danger or disadvantage to the state or its allies. In other words, glory could not justify acts of unprovoked aggression, but could legitimately determine the nature and extent of a state's response to injury.[13] Overall, Cicero shared the aggressive spirit that had consistently marked Roman international relations in the Republic, a spirit that brooked no threats or rivals, that aimed never to show weakness, and seldom omitted an opportunity to increase Rome's glory and influence. Cicero gave his clearest expression and approval of this outlook in the treatise in which he was most concerned to promote the cause of justice and peace, the *De officiis*, making clear that war must never be shunned when to do so might endanger liberty, incur disgrace, give the appearance of timidity,

---

10. *Font.* 12–15. *Prov. cons.*29–35. *Pis.* 81–82. *Off.* 2.18. H. Malcovati, *ORF*, 2d ed., fr. 195. Cicero also had no difficulty in accepting Caesar's invasion of Britain as a glorious event. *Q.F.* 2.16(15).4.

11. *Man.* 11. Elsewhere, however, he is more ambivalent about the justice of destroying Corinth. *Off.*1.35; 3.46.

12. *Man.* 6,14. *Rep.* 3.35. He includes among the wars fought on behalf of allies those with Antiochus, Philip, the Aetolian League, and Carthage. *Man.*14. Cf. Sallust, *Cat.*6.5. Caesar, *BG* 1.43.

13. *Off.*1.38. Wars *de imperio* he lists as those against the Latins, Sabines, Samnites, Hannibal, and Pyrrhus.

or otherwise damage the public good. In another section of the same work he seems to condone a still more aggressive and expansionist line, when he declares that a statesman must do his best in peace and war to increase the state's power, lands, and revenues.[14] Cicero's view of war shows a considerable tension between an attachment to his enlightened, theoretical concept of the nature of man and the principles of justice and a chauvinism that sought to make whatever seemed good for Rome seem good absolutely. He worked hard to resolve the tension, but did not entirely succeed.

The empire that arose from Rome's success in war and the manner of its government allowed less tortuous and conflicting forms of defense. Cicero accepted the conventional belief that, by the rules of war and right of victory, the lands of those conquered in a just war became the property of the conqueror.[15] The rights of the vanquished varied depending on the harm they had inflicted and the degree of barbarity and lawlessness they had exhibited. A savage enemy that had behaved with cruelty retained few rights, and the execution of the most guilty, the sale of other captives, and the plundering of property were legitimate forms of retribution. A more civilized foe had a right to more humane treatment. There should be no cruelty or indiscriminate plundering in such cases, and the mass of the population should be protected and treated with mercy and generosity. In particular, those who surrendered and placed themselves under the protection of a commander should be safeguarded.[16]

With regard to the government of subject peoples, it must, like all government, be based on justice and good faith. Force and fear were not a stable basis for empire. The system should draw strength from mutual benefit and from the trust and goodwill generated by a just and benevolent regime. The *ius imperi* justified certain demands, in particular the payment of taxes, which might be seen as the reward of victory, or as a return for benefits that provincials could not enjoy without Roman rule, namely, security against external threat and internal stability and order.[17]

Cicero believed Rome had created and organized her empire with due regard for all these principles. She had justly acquired her imperial

14. *Off.*1.80–82; 2.85. See E. S. Gruen, *The Hellenistic World and the Coming of Rome* (Berkeley, Calif., 1984), 1:274ff.
15. *Leg. agr.* 2.40, 50. *Verr.* 2.3.13. *Off.*1.21.
16. *Off.*1.33–35, 82. *Verr.*2.5.66, 127. *Am.*11.
17. *Off.*2.26–27. *Rep.*3.41. *Verr.*2.3.12; 2.4.20. *Man.*41. *Q.F.* 1.1.24, 33–35.

possessions and had dealt generously with the inhabitants. Cruel and intractable enemies had been destroyed when justice and security demanded it, but the bulk of Rome's victories had been marked by exceptional leniency and clemency, and her immediate neighbors had even been admitted to citizenship.[18]

The rule she established was equitable and designed to benefit her subjects. *Aequitas* and *fides* became its hallmarks and the greatest source of praise for those who governed the empire's provinces. The provincials were not treated as servile inferiors, but were referred to as *amici* and *socii,* and to the extent possible were allowed to manage their own affairs. The taxes imposed were often no more than those previously paid by provincials to their own governments, and were a fair payment for the provision of security and the preservation of a peaceful, stable society.[19] Finally, as a powerful earnest of her commitment to just government and the preservation of *fides,* Rome had established the extortion court as a bulwark for the provincials against exploitation, opening to them the same forms of legal redress available to Roman citizens.[20]

Cicero did not attempt to play down the benefits Rome received in return. Aside from the glory of ruling an empire and the added security an empire bestowed, there were important economic rewards. The provinces provided the great bulk of the funds needed by the treasury and freed the Romans from the burden of direct taxation. They supplied grain and other foods that became increasingly necessary to feed the growing population of Rome. They also provided opportunities for a variety of profitable business enterprises for Roman citizens.[21] Cicero's central point, however, was that Roman rule did not seek to be exploitative. It aimed to confer greater benefits than it extracted, to maintain harmony

18. *Off.*1.35; 2.26. *Am.* 11. *Verr.*2.2.4.

19. *Off.*2.26–27. *Verr.*2.3.14. *Q.F.*1.1.33–34. For the history and significance of the terms *amici* and *socii,* see Gruen, *The Hellenistic World,* 1:54–95. A. N. Sherwin-White, *Roman Foreign Policy in the East* (London, 1984), 58–70.

20. *In Caec.*11, 17, 27, 65. *Verr.*1.42; 2.3.218; 2.4.17; 2.5.126. Some scholars have argued the extortion court was established to protect senators, but this directly contradicts repeated statements of Cicero to the contrary. See E. S. Gruen, *Roman Politics and the Criminal Courts* (Cambridge, Mass., 1968), 13ff. W. S. Ferguson, "The *Lex Calpurnia* of 149 B.C.," *JRS* 11 (1921), 86–100. J. S. Richardson, "The Purpose of the *Lex Calpurnia de repetundis,*" *JRS* 77 (1987), 1–12.

21. The glory of empire is a frequent theme in Cicero. *Man.*12.53. *Verr.*2.2.2. *Off.*1.38. For the economic benefits, see *Verr.*2.2.5–6; 2.3.11, 127. *Man.*17,34. *Leg. agr.*2.50–51. *Fam.*15.1.5.

and stability by building goodwill and loyalty, to establish a system more akin to a *patrocinium* than an *imperium*.[22]

The benefits that Cicero maintained were intended and conferred by the manner of Roman rule enabled him to find further justification for Roman imperialism in the ideas of Greek philosophy. In the *De republica* he reproduces the Aristotelian argument that nature gives dominion to the best to the advantage of the weak, and that subjection is therefore just when the superior rules the inferior to the clear benefit of the latter. In less philosophical contexts, this law of nature appears as the will of the gods, directing a nation of superior piety and virtue to world dominion.[23]

Cicero was not, of course, unaware of the numerous and flagrant abuses endemic in Roman provincial administration. He fully understood and constantly decried them, as shall be seen later. But, as in the case of the evils besetting the government of Rome itself, he placed the blame on the moral degeneracy of political leaders, not on any fundamental flaws in the system. He remained convinced of the justice and wisdom of the basic ancentral objectives in regard to provincial administration and of the institutions devised to realize them, and, as so often, his hopes for change centered on people rather than structures.

Cicero's View of a Governor's Task

Cicero had expounded his ideas about the responsibilities of provincial governors and the qualities needed to discharge them in a long letter of advice to Quintus during the latter's governorship of Asia from 61 to 58. His other writings, and especially the letters from Cilicia, supplement the opinions expressed to his brother.[24] He believed that the general goal of provincial rulers must be the same as that of all who were entrusted with the power to govern, namely, the welfare of the governed. The rewards should also be the same, the glory that came from the display of *virtus* in

22. *Man*.41. *Off*.2.26–27.
23. *Rep*.3.37. Cf. Aristotle, *Politics* 1254A-B. J. Vogt, *Cicero's Glaube an Rom* (Stuttgart, 1935), 89–92. For the role of the gods, see *Man*.47. *Har. resp*.18–19. *Phil* 6.19.
24. *Q.F*. 1.1. It is written in a formal style, which suggests it was intended for a wider audience. See Shackleton Bailey, *Ad Quint.*, 147.

the public interest.[25] More specifically, Cicero saw the task of government in relation to the provinces as comprising three great responsibilities. First, a governor had a duty to protect provincials against exploitation and in particular against the burden of debt by himself refraining from illegal or inequitable practices and by insuring that others did the same. He had a further duty to administer justice with fairness and consistency, and, finally, he had the task of defending the province against internal or external threat.[26]

Cicero considered that, in the circumstances in which provincial rulers had to work, these were highly demanding responsibilities, requiring exceptional dedication and integrity. First of all, governors had to contend with societies in which corruption and inducements to corruption were often rampant. Cicero shared the racial prejudices of most of his countrymen, believing that the Romans were a morally superior race, whose moral values, institutions, and general way of life were unmatched by any other society. Even the Greeks, whom he freely acknowledged possessed unrivaled skills in all branches of learning and literature and had brought *humanitas* to the world, he considered morally flawed in his own day, a race that had become self-indulgent, irresponsible, untrustworthy, and deceitful, and had proved wholly unworthy of the great men of *vetus Graecia*.[27] The non-Greek peoples of Africa, Spain, and Gaul commanded even less respect from Cicero and his contemporaries. They were the *barbari,* unconstrained by any developed sense of right, or by religious scruple, their behavior marked by treachery, mendacity, and capriciousness.[28]

The problem of dealing with unprincipled natives Cicero saw compounded by the fact that many of the Roman citizens who chose to live in the provinces were equally unscrupulous and untrustworthy. As a result, governors were surrounded by men of dubious character, and had to stay

25. *Q.F.* 1.1.13, 24, 27, 31. *Att.*8.11.1.
26. *Q.F.* 1.1.7–13, 20–23, 25–26, 32–36.
27. *Q.F.* 1.1.6, 16, 27–28. Cf. *Verr.*2.2.7. *Cael.*40. *Flacc.* 9–12, 16–20, 23–24, 57, 61–66, 71. *De or.*1.47. *Fam.*16.4.2. J. P. V. D. Balsdon, *Romans and Aliens* (London, 1979), 30–54. N. Petrochilis, *Roman Attitudes to the Greeks* (Athens, 1974), passim. H. Guite, ''Cicero's Attitude Towards the Greeks,'' *Greece and Rome* 9 (1962), 142–59. For Cicero's view of the moral superiority of the Romans, see *Tusc.*1.1–3. *Rep.*5.1–2.
28. *Q.F.* 1.1.27. *Font.* 4, 30–31. *Prov. cons.*10. *Scaur.* 38, 40–45. See Balsdon, *Romans and Aliens,* 59–71.

constantly on guard against lies and sycophancy that could lead them to befriend and support individuals who were certain to bring them dishonor. Cicero warns Quintus at length of this pitfall and prescribes it as a cardinal rule that Roman residents and native provincials should be accepted as friends only after the most stringent testing.[29]

He saw far greater dangers, however, in the many direct inducements to corruption offered to governors, and in the many opportunities for exploitation of provincials afforded by the absolute nature of their power. There was a multitude of abuses endemic in provincial administration that he realized imposed extreme pressures on the integrity and self-restraint of even the most upright and best-intentioned politicians.[30] Many of the abuses were encouraged and facilitated by a general expectation that governors would use their power for personal gain, and by established practices that required communities to provide a variety of services, honors, and gifts to their Roman rulers.[31] Grain for the governor's needs and sometimes other basic commodities were supplied by the communities. Food, lodgings, and oftentimes entertainment and presents were provided for governors and their staff when traveling. The erection of statues and monuments, the building of shrines or temples in a governor's honor, the decoration in his name of existing temples, deputations to sing his praises in Rome—these were other common perquisites offered to most governors.[32] Some of these practices were approved by law, most hovered on the brink of the morally and legally acceptable, but all encouraged patterns of honoring and giving by provincials that gave Roman officials expectations of high rewards and led easily into increased demands and illegal exactions.[33]

Large payments of money were often extorted in place of the grain for the governor's needs. Hospitality on a lavish scale along with gifts of

29. *Q.F.* 1.1.15–18.
30. *Q.F.* 1.1.7–8. *Man.*40–41.
31. Quintus's self-restraint in Asia caused amazement. So did Cicero's in Cilicia. *Q.F.*1.1.7–8. *Att.*5.16.3; 5.20.6; 5.21.5.
32. For the requirement to supply grain for the governor's household, the so-called *frumentum cellae nomine*, see *Verr.*2.3.188. Food and lodgings for traveling Roman officials were also required by law. The *Lex Julia repetundarum* of 59 had attempted to define the obligations and limit abuses. *Att.*5.10.2; 5.16.3. Gruen, *Last Generation*, 240ff. Cicero considered the *dignitas imperi* demanded honored, hospitable treatment of traveling Roman officials. *Verr.*2.4.25. Cf. *Verr.*2.1.63ff.
33. *Q.F.*1.1.26, 31. *Verr.*2.2.137. *Fam.*3.7.2; 3.8.2–3; 3.10.6. *Att.*5.21.7.

money or art treasures or other valuables were demanded by traveling governors and their subordinates. Expensive commemorative buildings and statues, and deputations to Rome were often imposed, not offered.[34]

The system encouraged bribery of various forms and massive dimensions. Offers of money came not only from individuals seeking personal favors, but from communities anxious to divert or lighten unwelcome burdens or to secure a governor's goodwill in disputes with neighbors or Roman businessmen. The scale of this form of corruption can be seen from Cicero's statement that the people of Cyprus regularly paid governors 200 Attic talents, or 4.8 million sesterces, to avoid having troops billeted on the island.[35] The governor's absolute judicial authority extended the scope for bribery, and gave rise to frequent trafficking in verdicts. Spurious challenges to wills, particularly where large amounts of money were involved and large payments could be demanded in return for ratification of the terms of the will, were an especially common and profitable form of such trafficking, though, in Cicero's opinion, the most pernicious was the bringing of false accusations against wealthy individuals, who were then forced to pay large sums to secure acquittal.[36]

Every area of a governor's responsibilities offered opportunities for illegal gains. He was the ultimate arbiter of the amount of taxes to be paid by the communities of his province, and, especially in areas where the tithe system operated, he could readily manipulate the system for profit. He could enable the tax farmers to take more than they were owed by failing to provide proper legal protection against unfair exactions. Where compulsory purchases existed in addition to the tithe, he could refuse to pay the full amount for grain received, or indeed to pay anything at all. In Sicily Verres had required payment of cash bonuses in addition to the

34. Provincials were entitled to payment for the grain and for any other basic commodities they were forced to supply for a governor's household, but many farmers preferred themselves to pay money rather than take responsibility for supplying and delivering the grain. This became an acceptable practice, but it gave rapacious governors another pretext for the extortion of exorbitant sums. For this abuse, see *Verr.*2.1.95; 2.3.188ff. For the hardships caused by officials traveling in the provinces, see *Verr.*2.1.44–85. *Leg. agr.*1.8; 2.45. *Man.*38 ff. *Leg.*3.18. For the extraction of honors, see *Verr.*2.2.141 ff.

35. *Att.*5.21.7, 11. Cf. *Q.F.*1.1.8, 13. *Verr.*2.5.61–62, 64. *Font.*17. *Pis.*86. *Prov. cons.*4. *Sest.*94.

36. *Q.F.*1.1.25. Cf. *Verr.*2.2.19ff., 35–50, 53–61, 83–100. *Pis.*83, 87.

tithe. He had also adopted the strategem of refusing to approve the quality of the grain delivered and of extorting money in compensation.[37]

A governor's military powers might also be exploited as a source of personal gain. Promotions could be offered for sale. Military funds could be embezzled or loaned on interest. A military action could be initiated to widen the opportunities for profiteering. Even in relatively pacified provinces there were unsecured areas that gave some scope for military action to determined commanders. The primary incentive was often the glory of a triumph, but it was generally strengthened by the hope of profit.[38] A war could provide a pretext for special levies to provide food, armaments, and pay, and a resourceful governor could pocket much of the proceeds. It also made possible the collection of the so-called *aurum coronarium,* the money that was originally intended to pay the cost of a general's triumphal crown.[39] Booty and money from the sale of prisoners was another potential source of major gain, most of which could be diverted to the commander's coffers.[40]

There were still other means of enrichment for governors at the expense of the provincials. Money might be loaned to individuals or communities at exorbitant rates of interest. Communities struggling to meet the burdens imposed on them often had no choice but to borrow at whatever cost, and governors had all the resources necessary to enforce payment. The theft or open seizure of statues and other art objects from temples and public places was another common occurrence. Sometimes the treasures were appropriated under the guise of being borrowed to decorate the Forum for a famous occasion; the more brazen and rapacious governors scorned subterfuge and simply took them. The result in both cases was the same; the treasures ended up decorating luxurious town-houses and villas.[41]

37. *Verr.*2.3.25–35, 67–100, 165ff., 171ff.
38. *Man.*37. *Pis.*86. The searching out of wars for glory and profit is alluded to by Cicero in *Man.*65, *Pis.*57–62, *Off.*1.74.
39. For levies and abuses associated with them, see *Verr.*2.5.43, 60. *Font.*13. *Flacc.*27–33. *Pis.*87–92. *Prov.cons.*5. *Sest.*94. For the *aurum coronarium,* see *Pis.*90. *Leg. agr.* 1.12; 2.59. The *Lex Julia* forbade the collection of this money unless a triumph had been awarded.
40. Roman law in relation to the disposition of booty was extremely lax and gave wide scope for the personal enrichment of commanders and officers. See *Leg.agr* 2.59–60. I. Shatzman, ''The Roman General's Authority over Booty,'' *Historia* 21 (1972), 177–205.
41. *Verr.* 2.2.170ff. For a detailed discussion and sources, see Shatzman, *Sentorial*

Long before his service in Cilicia, Cicero was well aware from his experience in Sicily and involvement in extortion trials of these varied forms of malpractice open to provincial rulers, and it is not surprising that he lists *continentia* and its virtual synonyms *temperantia, abstinentia,* and *innocentia* as the foremost qualities required in a good governor. These were virtues that he considered vital in every sphere of public life, but he believed that in the provinces they meant the difference between an empire based on fear and a protectorate maintained by the beneficence of the ruler and the goodwill of the ruled.[42]

Cicero emphasized, however, that it was not sufficient for a governor to observe these virtues himself; he had a further duty to enforce similar standards of honesty on all who had authority or who sought to do business within his province. This meant exercising tight control over the activities of every member of his staff, from his *legati* and quaestor to the lowest member of his entourage. It also meant stamping out corruption among local officials.[43] But most of all it meant regulating the activities of the *publicani,* who held the public contracts for the collection of the direct and indirect taxes. For Cicero, this was a governor's most delicate problem, requiring great skills in persuasion and diplomacy. His long friendship with the public companies and his continuing belief in the importance of their support for the survival of republicanism left him opposed to any policy of direct confrontation with them. On the other hand, he was well aware of the unscrupulous rapacity of the tax farmers and acknowledged that, if given free rein, they would bring total ruin on the provinces. He advocated, as often, a middle course, designed to encourage flexibility and equanimity among provincials in their dealings with the *publicani* and to keep the latter from imposing undue hardship by offering them a sympathetic hearing and minor concessions.[44]

The control of injustice and corruption could also involve difficult

---

Wealth, 75–79. For the plundering of art treasures, see *Verr.* 2.1.45–61, 2.4 passim. *Man.*40. *Sest.*94. *Prov. cons.*6–7. *Dom.*111.

42. *Q.F.*1.1.7, 18, 32. *Man.*40–41. *Verr.*1.34. *Att.*5.20.6; 5.21.5. *Off.*2.26–27.

43. *Q.F.*1.1.10–14. Cf. *Off.*1.23. Justice demanded not only refraining from wrong-doing oneself, but restraining others. For a governor's entourage, the so-called *cohors praetoria,* see Th. Mommsen, "Die Gardetruppen der römischen Republik und der Kaiserzeit," *Hermes* 14 (1879), 25ff. For local corruption and its control, see *Q.F.*1.1.25. *Att.*6.2.5. *Verr.*2.2.138.

44. *Q.F.*1.1.7, 32–35. Cf. *Att.*6.1.16; 6.2.5. See Badian, *Publicans and Sinners,* 79ff.

clashes with other business interests, and sometimes with Roman politicians who were seeking in some way to exploit the provincials. Governors were frequently pressured to use their power to enforce payment of debts of doubtful legality, most of them the result of moneylending at illegal rules of interest. The lenders were often Roman politicians acting through agents. The assistance sought was generally a requisitioning letter instructing the debtor to pay under threat of penalty, but sometimes more extreme expedients were demanded, including the conferring of a prefecture on the creditor or his agent and the provision of troops to compel payment.[45]

Another form of exploitation that Cicero thoroughly disapproved and believed honest governors had a duty to suppress was the practice of imposing a special levy to help pay the cost of aedilician entertainments at the *ludi.* Aediles pressed their friends in provincial commands to impose this so-called *vectigal aedilicium,* which could amount to as much as two hundred thousand sesterces on each occasion. They also often sought the loan of works of art to enhance the setting for the celebrations and a supply of wild animals to provide spectacular beast fights. There was no legal justification for imposing such burdens on the provincials, but refusal could strain the bonds of *amicitia.*[46]

The other main areas of a governor's responsibility, the administration of justice and the defense of the province, Cicero considered similarly challenging, with special complexities peculiar to provincial administration. As a judicial officer a governor stood supreme, unchecked by colleagues, by any right of veto or protest, or by the restraining power of Senate or people. The absoluteness of his authority imposed a special need to show a level of fairness and consistency that would remove even the suspicion of partiality. It also demanded courtesy and gentleness to temper power with humanity and lessen the anxiety and resentment generated by uncontrolled authority.[47]

The military aspects of a governor's duties varied considerably depending on the region, but even in the most tranquil provinces there was a need for vigilance to maintain internal harmony and to protect the public against brigandage and other forms of violent crime. In the more unset-

45. *Q.F.*1.2.8, 10. *Att.*5.21.7, 10; 6.1.6; 6.2.8–10.
46. *Q.F.*1.1.26. Cf.*Verr.*2.4.6, 126. *Dom.*111. *Att.*6.1.21. *Fam.* 8.2.2; 8.6.5; 8.9.3; 2.11.2.
47. *Q.F.* 1.1.20–23.

tled and more vulnerable frontier provinces, the military demands on governors were heavy and the risks were high. Cicero considered military command in any circumstances the most worrisome aspect of statesmanship, in that success was generally determined more by fortune than by skill, but in the provinces he saw the hazards magnified by special difficulties, such as the treacherous nature of the enemy, and the danger of defection by the allies and of mutiny by the soldiers. These were factors that he had often seen bring woe to even the wisest of Roman leaders and that made him view provincial commands in troubled areas as especially daunting assignments.[48]

Cicero's Administration of Cilicia

His appointment came as an unwelcome surprise to Cicero, and he immediately began a determined petitioning of friends, which he continued throughout his governorship, to insure there would be no prorogation of his command.[49] Provincial government held no appeal for him. His one experience of it in Sicily in 75 had convinced him that, aside from military exploits, provincial administration offered small hope of glory or of any form of political reward. He had, accordingly, declined the opportunity to govern provinces after his praetorship and consulship. His talents made the activities of Senate and Forum his natural metier and, in addition, the life and limelight of the capital admirably suited his temperament and interests. His love of the cut and thrust of senatorial debates and judicial contests, his insatiable interest in every minute particular of Roman political life, his desire to be with his family, his delight in the amenities provided by his houses and villas and in the social round and intellectual interchange that he experienced in the capital and on his country estates—all these bound him firmly to Rome and Italy, and made life and service abroad seem trivial, uninspiring, and inglorious.[50]

48. *Q.F.* 1.1.4–5, 25. Cf. *Att.* 6.1.14.
49. *Fam.* 3.2.1; 15.12.2. For his efforts to prevent prorogation, see *Att.* 5.1.1; 5.2.3; 5.9.2; 5.11.1, 5; 5.13.3; 5.17.5; 5.18.1; 5.20.7. *Fam.* 2.7.4; 2.8.3; 2.10.4; 3.8.9; 15.9.2; 15.12.2; 15.13.3; 15.14.5.
50. *Planc.*64–66. Putarch, *Cic.*6. *Fam.* 2.11.1; 2.12.2. *Att.*5.15.1. Cicero claimed he gave up his provinces in 63 to avoid being beholden to anyone (*Leg. agr.*1.25. *Cat.*4.23), but that was mere rhetoric. Cf. *Fam.* 15.4.13. Refusal of provinces was not unheard of (*Mur.*42. *Fam.* 8.10.3. Balsdon, *JRS* 29 [1939],63), but the benefits of a governorship could be substantial (*Cat.*4.23. *Mur.*42) and failure to avail of the opportunities was considered unusual. *Att.* 5.2.3; *Fam.* 2.12.2; 15.4.13.

Cicero left Rome around May 1, heading for Brundisium, which he reached on May 22. Early in June he sailed for Actium, arriving June 14. He then went by land to Athens, where he lingered from June 24 to July 6. He greatly enjoyed the city and his reception, and had the opportunity to renew contact with the schools of philosophy. He found philosophic thought in a state of disorder, however, the only bright spot represented by his host Aristus, brother of Antiochus and his successor as head of the Fifth Academy. From Athens he sailed to Delos in atrocious weather, and then to Ephesus, where he arrived July 22. After three days rest he proceeded to Tralles, and finally entered his province at Laodicea on July 31. He dated the beginning of his year as governor from that date.[51]

Cilicia in this period was a large province extending from the Amanus range on the border of Syria along the southern coast of Asia Minor, and including Pamphylia and Lycia. Inland it comprised the areas of Pisidia, Isauria, and Lycaonia. Attached to it also was the island of Cyprus and three administrative districts or dioceses, Laodicea, Apamea, and Synnada, that were normally part of the province of Asia. It was generally a consular province and had considerable military importance, made greater at this time because of the threat of a Parthian invasion in the wake of Crassus's defeat at Carrhae in June 53.[52]

Despite his definite distaste for the task ahead of him, Cicero took it seriously and was determined that it should redound to his credit. His principal goals as he began his tenure were essentially those he had urged on Quintus almost a decade earlier, namely, the pursuit of glory through an exemplary administration dedicated to the welfare of the province and the empire. His mission provided many opportunities for the display of *virtus*, and he was intent on using them all to win praise and admiration at home and abroad. He had a model in his patron Scaevola, whose upright and austere regime in Asia in the nineties had secured him lasting fame, and a potent source of encouragement in Atticus, who continually urged him to conduct a rule of the highest rectitude.[53]

51. *Att.* 5.1.15. See O. E. Schmidt, *Der Briefwechsel des M. T. Cicero* (Leipzig, 1893),74–82. L. W. Hunter, "Cicero's Journey to His Province of Cilicia in 51 B.C.," *JRS* 3 (1913), 73–97. Shackleton Bailey, *Ad Att.*,3:313.

52. See Magie, *Roman Rule,* 1.383ff. R. Syme, "Observations on the Province of Cilicia," *Anatolian Studies Presented to W. H. Buckler* (Manchester, 1939), 299–332.

53. *Att.* 5.9.1; 5.10.2; 5.13.1; 5.20.6; 5.21.5, 7; 6.1.8; 6.3.3. *Fam.* 2.12.3. For his use of Scaevola as a model, see *Att.* 5.17.5; 6.1.15.

Cicero wished, above all, to establish honesty and self-restraint as hallmarks of his administration, and to win particular renown for these virtues in an area of government where they were notoriously lacking. He aimed not merely to stay within the law in the demands he made and the benefits he accepted, but to impose no unnecessary expense and to accept no gifts or honors that entailed significant costs. He was determined that his staff should observe the same rules, and he applied them from the beginning of his journey through the provinces, traveling through Greece and Asia without cost to anyone and without demanding even the services and hospitality prescribed by the *Lex Julia*. His staff cooperated fully, impressed by his example and anxious to protect his reputation.[54]

On reaching Cilicia he found a province drained dry by the excesses of Appius Claudius and his subordinates. He was besieged by aggrieved provincials protesting their inability to pay the special taxes made necessary by Appius's exactions and bewailing the many outrages of the latter's regime. There were complaints also about the costs of a building in Appius's honor and of deputations he was expecting to be sent to Rome. The depressed state of the province gave Cicero a further reason to persist in his policy of *abstinentia*, and a further opportunity to highlight the exceptional integrity of his rule through contrast with the unbridled rapacity of his predecessor.[55]

He proceeded to reassure and conciliate the communities wherever he went and continued to insure that no expense ensued for anyone from his presence. In many places he refused even the offer of a roof and billeted his men in tents. He showed similar restraint in regard to honors and offers of money. He refused statues, temples, and any form of honor other than cost-free verbal tributes. He similarly refused offers of payments for the relief of unpopular burdens, such as the billeting of troops. Even the military action in which he became involved he conducted without cost or inconvenience to the subject communities. Such unexpected forbearance and benevolence brought quick relief to the financially oppressed communities and a resurgence of hope and goodwill.[56]

54. *Att.* 5.10.2; 5.11.5; 5.14.2. *Modestia, moderatio, abstinentia, continentia, integritas* dot the letters in descriptions of the conduct of himself and staff. *Att.* 5.9.1; 5.15.2; 5.16.3; 5.17.2; 5.20.6; 6.2.4. For the cooperation of his staff, see *Att.* 5.10.2; 5.11.5; 5.14.2; 5.17.2. Later he had some complaints, and he felt at the end their restraint was only a veneer. *Att.* 5.21.5; 7.1.5–6; 7.3.8.
55. *Att.* 5.16.2; 6.1.2. *Fam.* 3.7.2–3; 3.8.3–5; 3.10.6.
56. *Att.* 5.16.3; 5.21.7. *Fam.* 15.4.10.

Cicero worked equally hard to shield the provincials from exploitation by others. He carefully investigated the conduct of local officials, going back over the entire previous decade, and he forced restitution wherever he found evidence of peculation. He abolished oppressive, emergency taxes imposed by Appius or by local governments to meet special expenses. He also attempted to limit abuse of the practice of sending deputations to Rome by inserting in his edict a requirement that all such deputations have his express approval and by reiterating that sums allocated for this purpose must not exceed the amount prescribed in the *Lex Cornelia.*[57]

He also managed, to his great delight, to deal satisfactorily with the delicate problem of the *publicani,* retaining their goodwill while making sure they did no injury to anyone. He was helped by the fact that agreements between the companies and the communities about the amount of tax to be paid had been concluded without incident before his arrival in the province. His disciplined regime and general efforts to improve the financial position of the communities helped also in that it enabled the provincials to pay the tax farmers on time and even to eliminate arrears. A policy of blandishment and conciliation further improved relations. Cicero was careful to make his edict as acceptable as possible, and he agreed to add to it, at the request of a delegation of *publicani,* a recently devised section designed to reduce the expenditures of the communities. This would help insure they had sufficient funds to pay their debts to the public companies. In general, Cicero humored and honored the *publicani* in every way possible and succeeded as a result in winning their consent to a crucial reform that established more equitable procedures for dealing with the pervasive and contentious problem of indebtedness. Cicero prescribed that if debts were paid within a certain period, the rate of interest would be 12 percent, as stated in his edict. If the debts were not paid within the appointed time, the rate of interest would be whatever was specified in the agreement. Previous governors had felt compelled to allow the *publicani* to charge the highly usurious rates to which provincial borrowers frequently had to agree. Cicero's compromise exacted a major concession from the companies and was a considerable advance in checking one of the most oppressive abuses in provincial life.[58]

---

57. *Att.* 6.1.2; 6.2.5. *Fam.* 3.8.4–5; 3.10.6; 15.4.2. Plutarch, *Cic.*36.4.
58. *Att.* 5.13.1; 5.14.1; 6.1.16; 6.2.5; 6.3.3; *Fam.* 2.13.4. See Badian, *Publicans*

Cicero encountered greater difficulty in his efforts to control injustice when he had to deal with pressure from friends or their associates or from powerful politicians for unjustifiable favors or assistance. On the whole he was successful in resisting requests injurious to the provincials, and after the first six months of his administration he was able to report to Atticus the amazement of certain communities that they had not even received a compulsory guest or a single letter of requisition. More extreme abuses such as the granting of prefectures to facilitate the collection of debts he ended altogether.[59] But he did experience a number of situations where the pressures were unusually strong and where his resolve was severely tested. He came into conflict with Appius Claudius on a number of issues. The latter reacted angrily and with all the hauteur of a patrician dealing with a parvenu when Cicero attempted to keep within legal limits the costs of laudatory deputations to Rome, and to investigate special taxes that had been levied on the people of Appia to pay for a building in Appius's honor. Cicero saw no merit in Appius's complaints and he defended his actions with spirit and occasional touches of acerbity, but he was most anxious to avoid alienating such a powerful figure, and in the end he did make concessions to his predecessor and generally tried to play down the depredations of his regime.[60]

He was also placed in a difficult position by his close friend M. Caelius Rufus, who was aedile-elect in 51 and was planning to provide spectacular entertainments at the aedilician games in the following year. He wanted Cicero to impose a special levy to pay for the spectacles and also to oversee the hunting and shipping of panthers for the beast fights. Cicero totally rejected the request for money, and felt most reluctant to burden any community with the task of finding and transporting panthers, but in the end he made a gesture towards accommodating his friend

---

and Sinners, 113ff. For Cicero's care to make his edict acceptable to the *publicani,* see *Att.* 6.1.15. *Fam.* 3.8.4.

59. *Att.* 5.21.7, 10; 6.1.4, 6. He was quite willing to grant prefectures to friends of his friends, provided they were not businessmen, but he was adamant in refusing such powers to those doing business in the province, even when they were friends of people like Pompey and Atticus. *Att.*6.1.4, 6.

60. *Fam.* 3.6–10. *Att.* 6.1.2; 6.2.10; 6.6.1. *Fam.* 2.13.2. See Magie, *Roman Rule,* 393ff. Cicero's position was complicated by the fact that Pompey was now an *adfinis* of Appius and had reconciled Cicero to the latter in 54. *Fam.*1.9.19; 3.10.8. Quintilian, *Inst.* 9.3.41.

and ordered a hunt. He warned Caelius, however, that the panthers were scarce and that he should not expect much.[61]

But Cicero's most difficult dilemma arose in regard to a debt owed to M. Brutus by the people of Salamis, a town in Cyprus. Cicero was initially unaware that Brutus was the creditor and thought the debt was owed to a friend of Brutus named Scaptius. The latter had been granted a prefecture and some squadrons of cavalry by Appius to enforce payment by the Salaminians, and he had used the troops in a most oppressive way, going so far as to imprison the Salaminian senate in their meeting house, which led to the death of five senators. A delegation from the town had met Cicero at Ephesus to seek his help, and as soon as he reached his province he ordered the troops withdrawn from Cyprus. Scaptius later visited Cicero in camp and, since Brutus had warmly recommended him, Cicero gave him a sympathetic hearing and promised to see to it that the debt was paid. He refused, however, to give him a prefecture. Around the end of 51 he met Scaptius and the Salaminians at Tarsus and ordered the latter to pay the debt. They agreed, but Scaptius demanded interest at 48 percent, as specified in the agreement. Cicero insisted, however, that he was entitled only to the 12 percent prescribed by law and confirmed by Cicero's edict. The sum owed was fixed accordingly, and amounted to 106 talents or about 2.5 million sesterces. The Salaminians wanted to settle immediately, but Scaptius, hoping that under a future governor he might yet exact the 48 percent, asked Cicero to leave the debt open. Cicero considered the request outrageous, but he granted the concession out of friendship for Brutus.

Later Scaptius came to Cicero with a letter from Brutus indicating the latter was himself the lender and requesting a prefecture for Scaptius. Soon afterwards the pressure mounted further, when Atticus, the great abettor and encomiast of Cicero's virtuous rule, urged him to accede to Brutus's request. Cicero was clearly shaken by his friend's unexpected turnabout, but he refused to yield, believing any further concessions would mean betrayal of the principles of statesmanship he had recently

61. *Att.* 5.21.5; 6.1.21. *Fam.* 2.11.2; 8.2.2; 8.4.5; 8.6.5; 8.9.3. M. Octavius, a colleague of Caelius, was also seeking panthers. *Att.* 5.21.5. Cf. Plutarch, *Cic.* 36.5. Caelius also sought help for a friend in collecting a debt and an exemption from taxes for certain lands bought by another friend. *Fam.* 8.2.2; 8.4.5; 8.9.3–4.

expounded in the *De republica*. Scaptius never got his cavalry. Cicero was a practical man who believed in reasonable compromise to meet the requirements of *amicitia* and political expediency, but he showed admirable firmness in abiding by his principles in the Salaminian affair and in resisting in general any form of injustice that he considered incompatible with his cherished goal of maintaining an honest and honorable administration in Cilicia.[62]

His concern with honesty and in particular with personal clean-handedness persisted to the very end of his tenure. As he prepared to leave office he decided to return a million sesterces left over from his expense allowance to the treasury, despite the protests of his staff, who thought, no doubt on the basis of a well-established practice, that it should be divided among them. He was equally scrupulous in dealing with the booty from his military operations. The general booty was distributed among the soldiers in the normal way. The money from the sale of captives went to the state, and Cicero was insistent that no one would touch it until it was delivered to the city quaestors. His own share of the booty came to four hundred thousand sesterces, and that too he intended to have officially supervised and entered in the records of his quaestor, like all moneys allocated to him.[63]

But Cicero's objectives in Cilicia extended beyond the stemming of corruption and exploitation. He wanted all aspects of his government to

---

62. *Att.* 5.21.10–13; 6.1.5–8; 6.2.7–9; 6.3.5. Brutus was also owed money by Ariobarzanes, king of Cappadocia, and he pressed Cicero to help him collect that debt also. Cicero did all he could by urging the king to pay when he met him and by constant petitioning in letters. He had less compunction about using his influence in matters that did not involve the people or resources of his own province. *Att.* 5.18.4; 6.1.3; 6.2.7; 6.3.5. Badian, *Roman Imperialism*, 84ff. Magie, *Roman Rule*, 394ff. R. O. Jolliffe, *Phases of Corruption in Roman Administration* (Menasha, Wis., 1919), 100ff. H. M. Cotton, "The Role of Cicero's Letters of Recommendation; *Iustitia versus Gratia*," *Hermes* 114 (1986), 443–60.

63. *Att.* 5.20.5; 7.1.6. *Fam.* 2.17.4. The precise meaning of the last passage is disputed, but the interpretation given here seems demanded by the Latin. See Shackleton Bailey, *Ad. Fam.* 1.459–60. Magie, *Roman Rule*, 393–94. E. Fallu, "Les rationes du proconsul Cicéron," *ANRW* 1.3 (1973),209–38. Cicero did manage to accumulate for himself, *legibus salvis*, 2.2. million sesterces (*Fam.* 5.20.9.). This figure no doubt included his share of the booty. The rest may have been left over from his *vasarium*, equipment money, which was distinct from the expense allowance and exempt from the normal accounting procedures. *Att.* 11.1.2; 11.2.3. Mommsen, *Staatsrecht*, 1:296. He might also have saved money from sources such as the *frumentum cellae nomine*. See n. 15 above.

be a source of admiration and praise and gratitude, a fitting, living demonstration of the precepts set forth in the *De republica*. When a serious famine arose in the Asian districts of his province in early 50, he saw it as another opportunity to show his benevolence and skill, and everywhere he went he used his influence and powers of persuasion to induce the provincials and Roman citizens who had hoarded grain to make it available to the public.[64] He gave particular attention to the administration of justice, an area to which he attached special importance. He spent almost his entire first month in the province holding assizes in the main centers as he traveled to join his army at Iconium. At the end of the campaigning season in December he spent a further two weeks attending to judicial business at Tarsus before heading back for Laodicea on January 5. From mid-February to mid-May, when he had to depart once more for his army at Tarsus, he held continuous sittings at Laodicea for all the districts north of the Taurus. Altogether, he devoted almost half his period in Cilicia to judicial matters, a surprisingly large proportion in view of the heavy demands made on his time by the military situation.[65]

Cicero modeled his administration of justice to a large extent on that of Scaevola, and included in his edict many of the latter's key provisions. In particular he followed Scaevola's practice of allowing the provincials to use their own laws and courts to settle disputes between themselves. The arrangement was warmly welcomed by the provincials, who saw it as a restoration of self-government. In his own handling of cases he was careful to observe all the precepts he had stressed in his letter to Quintus. His rulings were expert and strict, but fair and tempered with clemency. Above all, he gave reassurance to the people and won their gratitude by his affability and accessibility. No one had to work through his chamberlain; he made himself available to all, getting up before dawn, as busily meeting people as if he were a candidate. He further carried the entire burden of jurisdiction himself, delegating judicial responsibility only in the case of Cyprus, which he had no opportunity to visit. At the end he was well satisfied with his management of judicial affairs. He had applied the principles he believed in and had set a pattern that surprised

64. *Att.* 5.21.8. Cf. *Att.* 6.3.3.
65. For Cicero's movements during his first month in Cilicia, see *Att.* 5.20.1–2. *Fam.* 15.4.2. L. W. Hunter, "Cicero's Journey to His Province of Cilicia in 51 B.C.," *JRS* 3 (1913), 73–97. A. J. Marshall, "Governors on the Move," *Phoenix* 20 (1966), 231–46.

and delighted the natives, and that far exceeded the standards of his predecessors.[66]

His other main area of responsibility, the defense of the province, he also handled with distinction, achieving considerable success with limited resources. Cilicia was threatened with a Parthian invasion in 51, which gave added importance to the military side of Cicero's duties. He had no great relish or aptitude for military command, and he made sure to take with him legates of proven military ability. His team of legates comprised his brother Quintus, C. Pomptinus, M. Anneius, and L. Tullius. Quintus had achieved considerable experience and distinction during his service with Caesar in Gaul. Pomptinus had been a praetor in 63 and had assisted in the arrest of the Allobrogian envoys. He had subsequently governed Transalpine Gaul from 62 to 59, and had suppressed a rebellion of the Allobroges. He had been awarded a *supplicatio* in 59 and had celebrated a triumph in 54.[67] M. Anneius was also an experienced soldier whose military skills were highly admired by Cicero. Less is known about L. Tullius, who was a friend of Atticus and had been recommended by another friend of Cicero, Q. Titinius, but at least three of the four legates were experienced commanders capable of conducting large-scale military operations.[68]

Cicero had greater worries in relation to the strength and preparedness of his forces in Cilicia. Even before he left Rome he was concerned that Cilicia was inadequately equipped to deal with a major invasion. The Senate as a whole shared his view, but a proposal to recruit reinforcements in Italy was blocked by the consul, Sulpicius Rufus, presumably because of the general unpopularity of such conscriptions.[69] When he reached Cilicia he found the situation was even worse than he had feared.

---

66. *Att.* 5.21.5–6; 6.1.15; 6.2.4–5; 6.3.3. Cicero's edict was shorter than usual, with two main sections. The first dealt with matters specific to provincial government, covering the financial affairs of the communities, debt, interest, and bonds, and everything concerned with the *publicani*. The second dealt with procedures governing common, everyday matters relating to inheritances and property transactions. All other issues Cicero simply declared he would deal with in accordance with the provisions of the *edicta urbana*. See A. J. Marshall, "The Structure of Cicero's Edict," *AJP* 85 (1964), 185–91.

67. *Cat.* 3.5-6, 14. *Prov. cons.*32. *Vat.*30. *Schol. Bob.*149–50, Stangl. *Pis.*58. *Att.* 4.18.4. *Q.F.*3.4.6. Dio 39.65.

68. For Anneius, see *Att.* 5.4.2. *Fam.* 13.55.2; 13.57.1; 15.4.2,8. For Tullius, see *Att.* 5.4.2; 5.11.4; 5.14.2; 5.21.5. *Fam.* 15.4.8.

69. *Fam.* 3.3.1; 15.1.4. The unpopularity of such levies had been shown very clearly in 55. See Dio 39.39. Brunt, *Manpower*, 410.

He had only two skeletal legions, and they had serious problems of morale and discipline. There had been a near mutiny because of the failure of Appius to pay the troops on time, and part of the army was scattered without proper leadership. Cicero assembled the legions at Iconium and, acting on a decree of the Senate, he strengthened them with a strong band of reenlisted veterans and with a corps of cavalry and a force of voluntary auxiliaries from the free allies. He himself arrived at Iconium on August 24.[70]

On August 28 he received word that the Parthians had invaded Syria, and he proceeded at once to Cybistra in southern Cappadocia so as to protect that kingdom as well as the border of Cilicia. He had been given a special commission by the Senate to protect Ariobarzanes, king of Cappadocia, which no doubt entitled him to enter the kingdom. While he was at Cybistra he learned of plots against Ariobarzanes, and he took measures to end them and to strengthen the king's authority and control. He also instituted a levy of Roman citizens in the province and wrote to the Senate urgently requesting reinforcements and emphasizing there were not enough trustworthy men among the Roman citizens in the province or enough strength or goodwill among the free allies to provide the help he needed.[71]

After he had spent five days at Cybistra, Cicero learned that the Parthians were threatening Antioch and Cilicia proper rather than Cappadocia, and that a large force of their cavalry had crossed into Cilicia but had been routed by his own cavalry, which he had earlier sent ahead to the border region. Cicero decided he could now safely leave Cappadocia, and he marched immediately toward the Amanus range dividing Syria from Cilicia. He arrived there around October 11 to discover the Parthians had been defeated in an encounter with C. Cassius, the proquaestor in Syria, and had retreated from Antioch. He then decided to undertake a campaign to subdue the inhabitants of the Amanus mountains, whom he described as perpetual enemies of Rome. He won a major victory on

70. *Att.* 5.14.1; 5.15.1. *Fam.* 3.6.5; 15.4.2–3. The free allies comprised free communities, especially in Pisidia and Lycia (*Att.* 6.5.3), and client kings, notably Deiotarus, king of Galatia, and Tarcondimotus, who ruled in the Amanus mountains. *Fam.* 15.1.2,6; 15.4.5.

71. *Att.* 5.18.1–2; 5.20.2–3. *Fam.* 15.1.2–6; 15.2; 15.4.4–6. The weakness of Cicero's forces and the failure to reinforce him even in the face of a serious threat show the Roman tendency to maintain minimum standing forces in the provinces and the many difficulties in the way of any quick reinforcement when a crisis arose. *Fam.* 8.10.1–3.

October 13 and was greeted with the title *imperator* by his troops. After a five-day campaign subduing and laying waste the area, he marched against Pindenissum, a nearby mountain stronghold held by Free Cilicians, who had never been subdued by anyone. He laid siege to the town, which held out for fifty seven days, but which was finally stormed on December 17. The town was totally destroyed and the captives sold. After taking hostages from the neighboring and equally truculent tribe of the Tebarani, Cicero sent his army into winter quarters in unsettled areas under the command of Quintus. He remained himself at Tarsus until January 5, and then returned to Laodicea.[72]

Cicero's drive against the tribes of the Amanus and the town of Pindenissum was, no doubt, inspired in part by a desire for the coveted honors of *supplicatio* and triumph that could be won from the Senate in the late Republic for relatively modest victories over foreign foes. It was the kind of small, relatively safe war that was eagerly sought by many governors and precisely the scale of operation that Caelius had a short time earlier told Cicero he was hoping would develop in Cilicia. On the other hand, the campaign should not be dismissed as a mere self-seeking exercise in laurel hunting. Cicero had not sought or planned any such operation. He had come to the Amanus to confront a potentially dangerous invasion. When he found the external threat had temporarily receded, he used an army that had been mustered and readied for war to secure the border area and to destroy a well-equipped and strongly fortified mountain settlement that had shown itself ready to welcome the enemies of Rome. In the dangerous situation facing eastern Cilicia in 51, the destruction of Pindenissum had definite military significance and ready justification.[73]

Cicero did not see the fall of Pindenissum, however, as his only achievement in regard to the defense and security of Cilicia. He also emphasized his success in stabilizing the political situation in neighboring Cappadocia and confirming the rule of a staunch friend and ally of Rome. He further claimed that his restrained and benevolent regime had

72. *Fam*. 2.10.2–3; 15.4.4–10. *Att*. 5.20.1, 3–5; 5.21.7. Plutarch, *Cic*.36.4.

73. *Fam*. 2.10.2; 8.5.1. For triumph hunting and the proliferation of such honors in Cicero's day, see *Pis*.56–63. *Fam*. 15.4.14; 15.6.2. M. Wistrand, *Cicero Imperator* (Göteborg, 1979), 26ff. There was a general need for greater Roman control of the eastern border of Cilicia. Cicero speaks of dangerous levels of brigandage in the area (*Att*.6.4.1). His campaign was a significant step toward asserting such control.

done more than any legions could to strengthen and maintain the security of his province by restoring to loyalty the provincials themselves, some of whom had actually revolted at the approach of the Parthians, and all of whom he had found either totally disaffected or wavering in their allegiance in anticipation of a revolution.[74]

Cicero's military worries did not end with the campaign of 51. A fresh invasion by the Parthians was expected in the summer of 50. Cicero, who planned to rejoin his army at the beginning of June, feared what the last two months of his tenure might bring, and feared even more the possibility of prorogation. It was widely believed Pompey would be sent to take charge of the war, and Pompey himself had told Cicero he expected the command, but that still left the possibility that Cicero would be asked to remain until Pompey arrived. Even if he were not, he foresaw a difficulty in finding a suitable person to leave in charge. His quaestor, Mescinius Rufus, he considered irresponsible. Quintus was the senior *legatus,* but Cicero was reluctant to place him in such a dangerous position and was not at all sure he would agree, in any event, to accept the position.[75]

The situation became increasingly worrisome for Cicero as June progressed. The Parthians duly invaded Syria and a major war erupted there. Cicero kept his army as close as possible to the enemy, but to his relief Bibulus did not ask for his help. He continued to worry, however, about his own departure and the problem of finding a suitable deputy to take command. Then in early July the Parthians withdrew and the crisis was over. There was no prorogation of Cicero's command, and he felt able to leave his new quaestor, C. Coelius Caldus, in charge. He left his province by ship from Tarsus, presumably on July 30, the day his term of office officially ended.[76]

74. *Fam.* 15.1.3; 15.4.14.
75. *Att.* 5.21.2; 6.1.3, 14; 6.2.6; 6.3.1.
76. *Att.* 6.4.1; 6.5.3; 6.6.3–4. *Fam.* 2.15.4; 3.12.4; 13.57.1. Cicero's eagerness to leave his province and his willingness to entrust it to an inexperienced quaestor have often been unfairly critisized. Under the terms of the *Lex Pompeia* he was bound to leave his province one year after he had entered it, unless his command had been expressly prorogued. *Att.* 5.21.9; 6.3.1; 6.6.3. He had behaved responsibly in holding his army in readiness to help Bibulus in the middle of 50, and he was prepared, if circumstances demanded it, to stay without senatorial authorization or appoint Quintus to command (*Att.*6.6.3). Once the crisis was over, he followed proper procedure, departing on time and transferring command to his quaestor in the absence of an available *legatus* who outranked him. Pomptinus had already gone home and Quintus was unwilling to stay. Anneius and Tullius were only of quaestorian rank. *Fam.* 2.15.4. See Marshall, *ANRW*

He was well satisfied with his accomplishments. He believed he had faithfully adhered to his strict standards of integrity, had placed the communities on a sound financial footing, had satisfied the *publicani* without complaint from the provincials, had insulted no one, had administered justice with offense to very few, and had achieved military success deserving of a triumph. His achievement represented an important step for him in his drive for restoration to a position of high honor after the injury of exile.[77]

Historians have not always judged his performance so generously. His willingness to bend law and principle to placate the special interests and the grandees of the Roman nobility has exposed him to charges of weakness and hyprocisy. Other criticisms have centered on his preoccupation with personal glory and on the detached, self-centered nature of his probity, which showed little real concern for the permanent plight of the provincials or for the critical flaws that made possible the multitude of abuses he had had to fight so hard to contain or repress. This indifference and the general narrowness of his objectives have made him seem to many callously egotistic, and deficient in genuine moral idealism or altruism.

Some of these criticisms have little validity, and all need careful qualification. Cicero's willingness, when major issues of justice were at stake, to place the rights of lowly provincials above the strong claims on his support imposed by the conventions of *amicitia* was admirable and exceptional. Minor concessions to the powerful interests, accepted without complaint by the provincials themselves, should not disguise that fact. The shallowness of his motivation and his general indifference to the problems in provincial administration are less commendable, but become more understandable when considered in the light of Cicero's general moral and social beliefs and the values of his age.

Personal glory was the great motivating force in Roman public life, the ambition to achieve it regarded as a cardinal virtue. Cicero laid it before others as the noblest aspiration of the *bonus civis;* for him it was an

---

1.1 (1972), 889ff. A. N. Payne, "Cicero's Proconsulate," Ph.D. diss., Cornell University, 1969, 46ff. L. A. Thompson, "Cicero's Succession-Problem in Cilicia," *AJP* 86 (1965), 375–86.

77. *Att.* 6.3.3. *Fam.* 2.12.3; 2.13.4. Cf. *Att.* 6.6.4, where he speaks of his rebirth, and *Att.* 3.20.1.

entirely praiseworthy and sufficient motivation for a statesman.[78] His lack of any deep concern about general conditions in the provinces had several reasons. As noted earlier, he believed the existing system of provincial administration was essentially sound. He had no vision of a better structure and, beyond wishing for better governors, he had little to offer by way of reform.[79] The provinces were, besides, remote from his political interests, and his generally low opinion of provincials reinforced his disinterest in their affairs. In general, Cicero was not fired with any enthusiasm for the betterment of the downtrodden. His sense of social justice was blunted by his aristocratic commitment to a social order sustained by vast inequalities in the conditions of life of its various classes. He had never come to appreciate or sympathize with the hardships and injustices of the lower classes even in Rome and Italy. It is therefore hardly surprising that he was not preoccupied with the removal of all inequity and deprivation in the provinces.

78. See chapter 1 above and *Sest.* 138–39.
79. Cicero proposed only one reform in relation to the provinces in his entire career, the abolition of *liberae legationes* to relieve the burdens created by Roman officials traveling in the provinces. *Leg.* 3.18.

6: CIVIL WAR
AND DICTATORSHIP

Cicero's journey home from Cilicia took almost four months. He had traveled by way of Rhodes, which he was anxious to show to his son and nephew.[1] He was delayed there for an extra twenty days because of bad weather and problems with his ship. His next stop was Ephesus, from which he sailed for Athens on October 1, reaching the Piraeus on October 14. From there he headed for Corcyra, with stops at Patrae, Leucas, and Actium, arriving at the port of Cassiope on November 16. More bad weather delayed the crossing to Italy until November 22. He finally reached the Italian coast at Hydrus on the 23rd, and proceeded the following day to Brundisium, where Terentia arrived just in time to meet him.[2]

A Troubled Homecoming

He had many things on his mind, including a number of personal worries. He had been forced to leave behind at Patrae his trusted and beloved secretary and freedman, Tiro, who had fallen seriously ill. Tiro had most likely been born a slave in Cicero's household, but his exceptional abilities had quickly earned him special attention from Cicero, who

1. *Att.* 6.7.2. *Fam.* 2–17.1. The *pueri*, Marcus and Quintus, had accompanied Cicero to Cilicia. They had spent the campaigning season at the court of Deiotarus in Galatia, and had then joined Cicero at Laodicea, where they resumed their studies under Dionysius, Atticus's learned freedman. *Att.* 4.15.1; 5.18.4; 6.1.12.
2. *Fam.* 16.9, 1–2. *Att.* 6.8.4; 6.9.1; 7.2.1.

had taken personal charge of his education.[3] He served primarily as a secretary, taking dictation in his own system of shorthand, supervising copyists, cataloguing books, and assisting Cicero generally in his research and writing.[4] But he also played a wider role in Cicero's life, acting as his adviser and helping in every aspect of his activities, domestic and public. Cicero found him indispensable, and he was captivated by his brilliance and loyalty and upstanding character.[5] He gave him his freedom in April 53 and treated him with extraordinary kindness and affection. He was deeply distressed by his illness in 50 and was willing to go to any trouble or expense to get him well again.[6]

Other aspects of his domestic affairs were also causing Cicero unease. He had recently become seriously concerned that a freedman of Terentia, Philotimus, was cheating him. He wrote about the matter to Atticus in enigmatic Greek on two occasions. He does not indicate that Terentia was involved, but the mysterious manner in which he writes about it makes clear it was a delicate issue with wider implications than a freedman's honesty, and it fits a pattern of ongoing difficulty with Terentia about financial matters.[7]

Quintus was a further worry. His marriage to Pomponia, Atticus's sister, was threatening to disintegrate. Pomponia was rude and shrewish, Quintus hot-tempered and generally unpredictable. The relationship had always been stormy, but by the middle of 50 a divorce was looming. Cicero was very anxious to preserve the marriage and especially concerned that nothing should arise to damage his friendship with Atticus. He encouraged the young Quintus to work for a reconciliation, and a truce did emerge, but the whole situation and Quintus's generally erratic temperament remained a source of anxiety for Cicero.[8]

3. *Fam.* 16.3.1. Gellius 6.3.8; 13.9. See Treggiari, *Freedmen*, 259ff., for a discussion of his birthdate; also Shackleton Bailey, *Ad Att.* 3.231.

4. *Q.F.* 3.1.19. *Att.* 13.25.3. *Fam.* 16.10.2; 16.20; 16.22.1.

5. *Fam.* 16.4.3–4; 16.14.1–2. *Att.*6.7.2; 7.5.2. Tiro also enjoyed the affection of Quintus. *Fam.* 16.8; 16.16. W. C. McDermott ("M. Cicero and M. Tiro," *Historia* 21 [1972], 259–86) goes so far as to speculate that Tiro was Cicero's eldest son, an extreme view, but indicative of the striking affection Cicero showed for his freedman.

6. *Fam.* 16.4.2. There is some uncertainty as to whether the manumission took place in 54 or 53, but Shackleton Bailey's arguments (*Ad fam.* 1.344) seem to point conclusively to 53. Cicero's distress at Tiro's illness is vividly represented in *Fam.* 16.1–9.

7. *Att.* 6.4.3; 6.5.1–2; 6.7.1; 7.1.9. See Treggiari, *Freedmen*, 263ff.

8. *Att.* 5.1.3; 6.2.1–2; 6.3.8; 6.7.1. For Quintus's difficult temperament, see *Q.F.* 1.1.37–40. *Att.* 6.6.4. The young Quintus was also difficult to handle, talented but

Tullia had also added a complication to his life. She had been divorced from Crassipes in early 51, and, shortly before Cicero left Cilicia, had become engaged to P. Cornelius Dolabella, a patrician of dubious character whom Cicero had twice defended on capital charges. The possibility of such a match had been raised by Caelius as early as February 50, when Dolabella's wife had divorced him, but Cicero had shown no enthusiasm for the idea, and he was surprised when he got news of the engagement in early August.[9] He was by no means unwilling to approve the marriage, despite reservations about Dollabella's past and general character, but its timing brought him particular embarrassment in that Dolabella had earlier in 50 twice prosecuted Appius Claudius, whom Cicero was straining every effort to conciliate. The first prosecution, on a charge of treason, had come to trial around the beginning of April, the second, on a charge of bribery, a couple of months later. Appius, backed strongly by Pompey and defended by Brutus and Hortensius, gained easy acquittal on both occasions.[10] Cicero, anxious to have Appius's friendship and pressed to do all he could to assist him by Pompey, Brutus, and Atticus, wrote him letters of warm sympathy and support during the course of the proceedings, with sundry derogatory remarks about the prosecutor. He then found himself, as he wrote Appius his congratulations after learning the outcome of the second trial, suddenly about to become the prosecutor's father-in-law. He used his considerable placatory skills to limit any damage, assuring Appius that his goodwill toward him was undiminished and would be more evident than ever in the future. It was a troublesome development, however, in his relations with a *nobilis* of exceptional influence and varied connections at a time when he was seeking to rally support from every political quarter to help him gain the honor most coveted by provincial commanders, a triumph.[11]

---

mercurial, in need of a tight rein. *Att.* 5.20.9; 6.2.2; 6.9.3. Cicero's own son, by contrast, was sluggish, in need of a spur. *Att.* 6.1.12.

9. *Att.* 5.4.1; 6.1.10; 6.6.1; 7.3.12. *Fam.* 2.15.2; 3.10.5; 8.6.2; 8.13.1. See J. H. Collins, "Tullia's Engagement and Marriage to Dolabella," *CJ* 47 (1951), 164–68.

10. *Fam.* 3.10.1,5; 3.11.1–3; 3.12.1; 8.6.1. *Att.* 6.1.2; 6.2.10. *Brut.* 230, 324. It is not explicitly stated that Hortensius defended at the first trial, but the strongest possible team of defenders was doubtless rallied for both trials. See Sumner, *Orators,* 122ff.

11. *Att.* 6.1.2; 6.2.10; 6.6.1. *Fam.* 3.12.2–4. Appius's influence and Cicero's desire to have his friendship are most clearly indicated in *Fam.* 2.13.2. Cicero, of course, was also anxious to please Brutus and, above all, Pompey, who seems to have been very close to Appius at this time (*Fam.* 3.10.10), and who had worked hard to reconcile Cicero to him. Quintilian, *Inst.* 9.3.41.

Cicero was most anxious to achieve the fullest public recognition of his military achievements in Cilicia, his natural love of acclaim intensified by a desire to pile up distinctions that would bury any trace of disgrace lingering from his exile.[12] At the end of his campaign in 51 he had sent an official dispatch to the Senate recounting his victories, and had followed it with personal letters to all but two of the entire body of senators requesting support for a *supplicatio,* the honor customarily given as a preliminary to the award of a triumph. His dispatch was delayed by bad weather and arrived during the Senate's April recess, but it finally came up for discussion when meetings resumed around the middle of May.[13] It had been favorably received and a *supplicatio* was voted, though not without difficulties. Lucilius Hirrus, a bitter enemy of Cicero, threatened to obstruct the proceedings and had been dissuaded only by the urgent intervention of Caelius. A more serious threat had come from the tribune Scribonius Curio, who, though well disposed to Cicero, was opposed to *supplicationes* because they deprived him of comitial days needed for his legislation. He had, accordingly, indicated he would use his veto. He had finally relented after the consuls agreed to a compromise proposed by Caelius that the *supplicatio* would not be celebrated in that year. Signs of the old oligarchic *invidia* had also reappeared. Cato, despite a long, supplicating letter from Cicero detailing his successes and his reasons for wanting the honor, had refused to lend his support, and other leading *optimates,* such as Domitius Ahenobarbus and Metellus Scipio, while voting for the proposal, did not want to see it passed and had hoped that Curio would block it by his veto.[14]

12. *Att.* 6.3.3; 6.6.4. *Fam.* 15.4.13. He realized his longing for laurels was not entirely compatible with his higher ideals, and he occasionally tries to play down his eagerness, but the disguise is thin. *Att.* 6.3.3; 7.3.2. *Fam.* 15.4.13.

13. *Fam.* 2.7.3; 3.9.4. *Att.* 5.20.7; 6.1.9. There seems no reason to think, as does Shackleton Bailey (*Ad. fam.* 1.419), that Cicero's dispatch arrived, contrary to Cicero's expectation (*Fam.* 3.9.4), ahead of the April recess. See Wistrand, *Cicero Imperator,* 41ff. W. K. Lacey, "The Tribunate of Curio," *Historia* 10(1961), 318–29. The senators omitted by Cicero were Lucilius Hirrus, a noted opponent, and Crassipes, his son-in-law. *Att.* 7.1.8. For Hirrus, see *Q.F.* 3.6.4. *Fam.* 2.9.1–2; 2.15.1; 8.2.2; 8.9.1.

14. *Fam.* 8.11; 15.5. *Att.* 7.1.7. The duration of the *supplicatio* is not recorded, which suggests it was brief. Cato spoke in praise of Cicero's administration but refused to recommend a *supplicatio.* His faithful disciple, Favonius, sided with him, as did Hirrus. There were no other dissenters. Cato's stance, which Cicero initially found acceptable (*Fam.* 15.6. *Att.* 7.1.7), may have been based in part on an objection in principle to such honors for minor successes, but, in view of his later support of a lengthy *supplicatio* for

But despite these difficulties and signs of disfavor, Cicero was delighted when he got word of the Senate's decision from Caelius at the
beginning of August, and he was confident the triumph could now be
secured. His friends in Rome were also optimistic, and Caesar, who
wrote to congratulate him on the *supplicatio,* promised his full support.
Pompey did likewise in a conversation with Atticus.[15]

The matter took on greater urgency for Cicero about the time he
reached Italy, when he learned that Bibulus, whose achievements he
considered far less significant than his own, had been voted, with the full
support of Cato, a *supplicatio* equal in duration to the record length of
twenty days, and was actively seeking a triumph. Cicero resented the
extraordinary honor done to Bibulus and was outraged by Cato's unequal
treatment of himself, but above all he was disturbed by the prospect that
Bibulus would be awarded a triumph and he would not. He felt that would
be a mark of dishonor, and he was determined to do all in his power to
prevent it happening.[16]

But Cicero's greatest worry by far as he returned home was the highly
volatile political situation that seemed ever more likely to erupt into civil
war. Even before he left for Cilicia there were signs of impending trouble
in connection with Caesar's command in Gaul and the right accorded him
in 52 to stand for the consulship in absentia. There was a further less
serious source of contention relating to the establishment by Caesar of a
Roman colony at Novum Comum in Cisalpine Gaul, an action apparently
authorized by the *Lex Vatinia.*[17]

The main author of the rising tensions was one of the consuls of 51, M.
Claudius Marcellus, a confirmed enemy of Caesar, who was determined
to use his office to undermine the latter's position. He made clear his

---

Bibulus, a touch of *malevolentia* may also have been at work. There can be little doubt
that the other *optimates* who secretly wished for the motion's defeat were motivated by
their customary resentment of honors for Cicero.

15. *Fam.* 2.15. *Att.* 7.1.7; 7.2.5,7. Caesar's support for Cicero was also shown by the
fact that his agent Balbus worked actively to insure the *supplicatio* was passed. *Fam.*
8.11.2.

16. *Att.* 7.2.6–7; 7.3.5. Caesar had fueled Cicero's anger against Cato by gloating
over the latter's breach of *amicitia. Att.*7.1.7; 7.2.7. A further, though undoubtedly
subordinate, reason for seeking a triumph had occurred to Cicero as he headed home.
While awaiting the Senate's decision he would have to remain outside the city and might
thus avoid having to take a stand in the dispute that was looming over Caesar's command.
Att. 7.1.5.

17. Suetonius, *Jul.*28. Strabo 5.1.6.

intention to seek Caesar's immediate recall on grounds that the war in Gaul was over and that the victorious army should be disbanded. He also challenged Caesar's right to stand for the consulship in absentia, contending the privilege given him by the Law of the Ten Tribunes had been set aside by a subsequent law of Pompey, the *Lex de iure magistratuum*.[18] His first formal action, however, concerned the colony at Novum Comum. In April he introduced a resolution in the Senate declaring that Caesar's colonists did not have valid Roman citizenship. The motion was accepted but vetoed. It was nonetheless a major affront to Caesar and generated rumors and fears throughout Italy. Marcellus went further in June when he had a citizen of Novum Comum flogged to dramatize his repudiation of Caesar's grant of citizenship. It was a controversial, provocative action condemned by Cicero as disgraceful treatment of a man who at the very least had Latin rights.[19]

It was September before Marcellus succeeded in having his proposal to recall Caesar debated in the Senate. This time he met with little support. His colleague, Sulpicius Rufus, who was deeply anxious to avoid any heightening of tensions and, besides, considered the proposal unjustified, since Caesar's term had not yet expired, expressed opposi-

---

18. Suetonius, *Jul.* 28. Dio 40.56. *Fam.* 8.1.2. *Att.* 8.3.3. Among the provisions of the *lex de iure magistratuum* was a reaffirmation of the existing requirement that candidates must submit their names in person. After the bill had been passed, Pompey had a codicil added to the official text specifically exempting Caesar. The legal validity of the codicil was, of course, disputable. Pompey's purposes have been much debated. The bill was a wide ranging one and fits in with Pompey's general efforts to check abuses and clarify the law with regard to elections and the general rights of magistrates. It doubtless reaffirmed many existing regulations, among them the requirement to make the *professio* in person. It seems far-fetched in the extreme to suppose such a comprehensive law was designed to damage Caesar's position or reverse a privilege so recently given. Since the clause relating to *professio* in person was tralatician, it was probably considered to have no effect on Caesar's *privilegium*. There seems to have been no objection from any side during passage of the bill. The issue was raised subsequently, and Pompey then attempted to remove any ambiguity. His method still left grounds for dispute, but nowhere is there plausible evidence he was seeking by some devious means to deprive Caesar of the privilege he had recently worked so hard to secure him in the Law of the Ten Tribunes. Besides, the issue never surfaced again. The dispute between Caesar and his opponents centered on the date on which he should relinquish his provinces. There is no evidence of any continuing challenge to the ongoing validity of the Law of the Ten Tribunes.

19. *Att.* 5.2.3; 5.11.2. Plutarch, *Caes.*29.2. Appian, *BC* 2.26. From Cicero's account it seems there was a question as to whether the man was an ex-magistrate, which would have given him the right to citizenship in any event. Even if he were not, Cicero implies his position as a Transpadane and possessor of Latin rights should have exempted him from such a form of punishment. See W. W. How, *Cicero: Select Letters, 2:*244.

tion.[20] Pompey was also opposed to any action at that particular time. He wanted the matter deferred to March 1, 50, when he considered it could be settled without injustice to Caesar, and in line with his wishes his father-in-law, Metellus Scipio, put forward a proposal that the question of the Gallic provinces should be brought before the Senate on that date and considered separately from all other issues. Marcellus's motion was lost and Scipio's eventually adopted on the last day of September, ending senatorial action on the Gallic provinces for 51.[21]

The dispute was just beginning, however. It was becoming apparent that Caesar would relinquish his command only if he were first allowed to stand for the consulship in absentia. His case and the reasoning behind it were clear enough. Under the terms of the *Lex Licinia Pompeia* of 55, the Gallic provinces could not be reassigned before March 1, 50.[22] Under the

20. Suetonius, *Jul.* 29. *Fam.* 4.3.1. Dio 40.59. Livy, *Per.* 108.

21. *Att.* 8.3.3. *Fam.* 8.8.4–5; 8.9.5. Hirtius, *BG*, 8.53. Marcellus's motion apparently specified March 1 as the terminal date for Caesar's command (*Att.* 8.3.3). This must be taken to mean March 1, 51. It is quite clear Marcellus wanted Caesar replaced in 51. Suetonius (*Jul.* 28) says Marcellus was proposing to have Caesar succeeded *ante tempus*. Hirtius (*BG* 8.53) is less clear, stating that Marcellus was bringing the question before the Senate *ante tempus*, but there would have been little point in Marcellus's arguments about the Gallic wars being over, and his proposal would hardly have aroused such strong opposition, if he were not seeking to move forward the terminal date of Caesar's tenure. The exact date on which his motion was considered is not stated. There were clearly several meetings dealing with the question between Sept. 2 and 29. See *Fam.* 8.8.4: "saepe re dilata et graviter acta." Three other resolutions were carried in the Senate on Sept. 29 but vetoed (*Fam.* 8.8.6–8). The first declared that anyone obstructing the proposed debate would be deemed to be acting against the public interest. The second made provision for the Senate to consider the discharge of those of Caesar's troops who had served their full term or were otherwise eligible for release. The third sought to insure the Gallic provinces would be up for allocation, prescribing that the eight existing praetorian provinces together with Cilicia should be reassigned to eligible *praetorii*. That left only one consular province available, namely, Syria, which meant the other consular province to be assigned would have to be one or both of the Gauls.

22. *Fam.* 8.8.9. Pompey's insistence that the Gallic provinces could be reassigned after March 1, 50, but not before, and his obvious care to avoid contravening the letter of the law in regard to Caesar's rights must surely be accepted to mean that March 1, 50, was clearly understood, and most likely specified in the *Lex Licinia Pompeia*, as the date after which a successor to Caesar could be designated. That there was a *legis dies*, and that it fell in 50 is also indicated by *Att.* 7.7.6 and 7.9.4. March 1 was probably the standard time at which the consular provinces were allocated under the *Lex Sempronia*. The entire question of the legal terminus of Caesar's command has become one of the most celebrated controversies in Roman republican history. The analysis given here agrees in general with that of P. J. Cuff, "The Terminal Date of Caesar's Gallic Command," *Historia* 7 (1958), 445–71. For other detailed discussions, see Th. Mommsen, *Die*

Lex Sempronia, which was then operating, that meant these provinces, certain to remain consular, would be allocated to one or both of the consuls of 49, who would not normally take possession of them until early 48. When Caesar was given the right in 52 to stand for the consulship in absentia, the expectation must have been that he would still be in command in Gaul in 49, and what he was being conceded in the common understanding was the right to stand in absence in that year, the precise time when he would be eligible under the *Lex Cornelia* to seek a further consulship. But the *Lex Pompeia de provinciis* radically altered the legal circumstances and made possible his replacement immediately after March 1, 50. If the terms of that law were rigidly applied to him, the privilege given him in 52 would be totally nullified. Caesar refused to accept that a right given him by the people could be thus set aside and he saw the efforts to do so as a clear violation of the intention of the Law of the Ten Tribunes and a thwarting of the public will. He considered that his safety and dignity required that he resist such legal legerdemain and he was determined not to yield.[23]

His optimate foes, on the other hand, saw an opportunity to reduce their enemy to the status of a *privatus,* with all the risks that that entailed for him, by bringing the Gallic provinces within the scope of the *Lex Pompeia* and applying its terms to achieve the earliest possible transfer of command.[24] More important, Pompey was prepared to adopt the same position, allowing Caesar the least that the letter of the prevailing law

---

Rechtsfrage zwischen Caesar und dem Senat (Breslau, 1857). F. E. Adcock, "The Legal Term of Caesar's Governorship in Gaul," *CQ* 26 (1932), 14–26. C. E. Stevens, "The Terminal Date of Caesar's Command," *AJP* 59 (1938), 169–208. J. P. V. D. Balsdon, "Consular Provinces under the Late Republic," *JRS* 29 (1939), 167–83. G. R. Elton, "The Terminal Date of Caesar's Gallic Proconsulate," *JRS* 36 (1946), 18–42. R. Sealey, "*Habe rationem meam,*" *CM* 18 (1957), 75–101. S. Jameson, "The Intended Date of Caesar's Return from Gaul," *Latomus* 29 (1970), 638–60. Gruen, *Last Generation,* 460–90. D. Stockton, "*Quis iustius induit arma,*" *Historia* 24 (1975), 222–59.

23. Caelius states what he believed were Caesar's intentions in *Fam.* 8.8.9. That the Law of the Ten Tribunes implied Caesar's right to retain his command until he could stand for the consulship is explicitly stated by Cicero in *Att.* 7.7.6: "Cum id datum est, illud una datum est." Caesar's concern about his safety if he returned to Rome as a *privatus* is clearly attested. *Fam.* 8.14.2. Suetonius, *Jul.* 30. Caesar was, of course, also determined to protect his dignity and his rights as he saw them. Caesar, *BC* 1.9.

24. The dispute in the final analysis was therefore concerned with intentions and understandings at the time the *Lex Licinia Pompeia* and the Law of the Ten Tribunes were passed, and whether the subsequent *Lex Pompeia de provinciis* should be allowed to set aside the clear intent of the earlier laws.

required, but conceding nothing to the spirit of earlier laws and understandings. He moved with his usual caution and was slow to reveal his
true intentions, but there are consistent signs that by early 51 he was
edging away from his association with Caesar and was no longer committed to defending his interests. He had emerged from the consulship in 52
in a greatly strengthened position that left him little incentive to remain as
Caesar's ally. He had been given a position of high trust by action of the
oligarchy itself and had achieved a primacy as an instrument of the Senate
and as a restorer of the organs of republican government that was more
akin to his true ambitions than the dynastic position afforded by the
alliance. He had also secured an extension of his Spanish command,
which upset the equality carefully worked out in the agreement at Luca
and gave him an important advantage over his ally.[25] The mutual need
and balance of power that had sustained the alliance were gone. Pompey
was now in an independently powerful position that was in some respects
superior to Caesar's and, while he sought no confrontation with his
former ally, at least not in 51, he had no reason any longer to promote the
cause of the man who was his greatest rival, and he had considerable
reason, based on inclination and plain self-interest, to side with the
Senate in any conflict with him.

The first firm evidence of Pompey's changed posture comes from
Cicero's references to conversations he had with him over three days at
Tarentum prior to his departure for Cilicia. Cicero emerged from the
meetings convinced that Pompey was a loyal republican ready to take any
measures necessary to preserve the integrity of the constitution. Pompey
was prone to humor Cicero, and the latter was susceptible to his blandishments and assurances, but his enthusiastic response to the meeting at
Tarentum and absolute confidence in Pompey's commitment to the Republic represent a radical change from his uncertain and often disapprov-
ing attitude toward the general in the preceding years, and must reflect a
strong and calculated effort by Pompey to convey a new direction and
new objectives.[26]

25. The importance of the extension of Pompey's Spanish command in 52 is seldom
sufficiently emphasized. It became the critical factor in the dispute with Caesar in the
latter part of 50, as the whole Gallic controversy resolved itself into a power struggle
between the two potentates.

26. *Att.* 5.5.2; 5.6.1; 5.7. *Fam.* 2.8.2. Cicero's trust in Pompey grew steadily during
51 and 50. *Att.* 6.2.10; 6.3.4. *Fam.* 2.13.2; 3.10.2.

His actions and statements later in 51 bore out the sentiments he had expressed to Cicero and clearly indicated that his association with Caesar was at an end. In late July he declared his intention to take back a legion he had lent to Caesar in 53, and he signaled his general position in regard to the Gallic provinces with a statement that everyone had a duty to obey the Senate. During the September debates he made clearer still precisely where he stood: he did not want Caesar elected consul while in command of his provinces and army, and he favored his recall immediately after March 1, starkly revealing the conflict between his view of what was legal and justified and Caesar's.[27] He further worked to have his views adopted as senatorial policy. Scipio incorporated his wishes in the proposal to have the process of recall initiated with all expeditiousness after March 1, and that was essentially the course approved by the Senate in its decree of November 29. Among those who oversaw the drafting of that decree were Scipio himself and another noted Pompeian partisan, Lucilius Hirrus.[28] Pompey had now plainly shown his hand, and there resulted a general belief that he was at odds with Caesar. There was also an upsurge of confidence that he would defend the *respublica* against any threat, which was reflected in a general concern in the Senate to insure he remained in Italy.[29]

The political atmosphere in Rome was relatively calm during late 51 and early 50. There was as yet no sense of unavoidable upheaval. Caelius saw nothing but torpor and lethargy all around him. The political scene was enlivened in February when the talented but volatile tribune Scribonius Curio, who had earlier been a vehement opponent of Caesar, suddenly switched sides and began speaking on Caesar's behalf. Caelius ascribed the change to anger at the refusal of the pontiffs to insert an intercalary month, which Curio needed to provide him with additional

27. *Fam.* 8.4.4; 8.8.4, 9; 8.9.5. The text of the last passage is corrupt, but the meaning is clear.

28. *Fam.* 8.8.5; 8.9.5. Caesar's feelings about the decree can be deduced from the reaction of his agent Balbus, who remonstrated with Scipio after the latter first made his proposal. Among others who were present at the drafting of the decree were some noted foes of Caesar, Domitius Ahenobarbus and Scribonius Curio.

29. *Fam.* 8.8.9. Caelius reported to Cicero that people believed "Pompeio cum Caesare esse negotium." Some have argued that *negotium* means "deal" (Balsdon, *JRS* 29 [1939], 176), but Shackleton Bailey (*Ad Fam.* 1.407) has put paid to that controversy. The concern to keep Pompey in Italy is mentioned by Cicero as early as September 51. *Att.* 5.18.1. Cf. *Att.* 5.11.3; 5.21.3. *Fam.* 3.8.10; 8.10.2.

comitial days for an ambitious program of social legislation.[30] But whatever the reason, his switch of allegiance was a critical development,
providing Caesar with an able tribunician ally capable of sustained
obstruction of any senatorial decision regarding the Gallic provinces.
Curio duly used his veto to block senatorial action on March 1, and gave
every indication he would continue to do so indefinitely. The Senate and
Pompey attempted a compromise, offering to allow Caesar to retain his
command until the Ides of November. The date probably represented
roughly the end of the campaigning season, and would allow Caesar a
considerable additional period to finalize the pacification and settlement
of Gaul. It still did not give him, however, what he primarily sought and
believed he had been granted by the sovereign wish of the people, namely, the right to retain his provinces until he could exercise his privilege to
stand for the consulship in absentia. Curio rejected the offer and stepped
up the political temperature with a series of abusive attacks on Pompey.
The stalemate continued.[31]

Around mid-year Pompey fell seriously ill at Naples and was unable
for a time fully to control developments in Rome. In his absence the
Senate rejected overwhelmingly a proposal by M. Marcellus to begin

---

30. *Fam.* 8.6.4–5. The switch did not surprise Cicero, well aware of Curio's volatility. *Fam.* 2.7.2; 2.13.3. *Brut.* 280ff. There was an ancient tradition that Curio was
bribed to change sides (Dio 40.60. Appian, *BC* 2.26. Plutarch, *Pomp.* 58.1; *Caes.* 29.2.
Suetonius, *Jul.* 29.1. Val. Max. 9.1.6), but it deserves little credence. See Lacey,
Historia 10 (1961), 318–19.

31. *Att.* 6.2.6. *Fam.* 8.11.3. In late May an attempt was made to weaken Caesar
militarily by a senatorial decree requisitioning one legion from Pompey and one from
Caesar for the Parthian war. Pompey contributed the legion earlier lent to Caesar. The
latter accordingly lost two legions, brought to Italy by a young officer, Appius Claudius,
and kept there. *Fam.* 2.17.5. *Att.* 7.13.2; 7.15.3; 7.20.1. Plutarch, *Pomp.* 57; *Caes.* 29.
Hirtius, *BG* 8.54–55. Dio 40.65.2. Appian, *BC* 2.29. The offer to extend Caesar's tenure
to the Ides of November raises the question as to why he did not stand for the consulship in
50. Caelius earlier had thought he might do so (*Fam.* 8.9.9) and clearly the Law of the
Ten Tribunes did not preclude him exercising his privilege in 50. His work in Gaul was
further drawing to a close and nothing in the situation there demanded that he should try to
stay on into 49. The only apparent explanation is that he was denied the opportunity to
stand in 50, or believed he would be, because he was not yet eligible under the *Lex
Cornelia*, which required a ten-year interval between consulships. Dispensations from
that requirement were not unprecedented, but given the rigidly legalistic manner in which
he was being treated by his optimate enemies and Pompey, Caesar had little reason to
expect any such dispensation in 50. It is possible, of course, that he felt unprepared to
contest the elections in 50 or felt he should insist on the precise arrangements envisaged at
the time the Law of the Ten Tribunes was passed.

negotiations with the tribunes, a euphemistic formula that meant putting pressure on Curio to compel him to lift his veto. Caelius had earlier told Cicero he believed any such move would bring a violent response from Caesar. The Senate was not willing to risk provoking such a reaction and, according to Caelius, had in fact come around to the view that Caesar's demands should be met and that he should be allowed to retain his command and stand for the consulship in absentia.[32] Pompey, however, was wholly opposed to any such concession, increasingly determined that Caesar should not be elected consul unless he first surrendered his army and provinces. The dispute was now plainly a power struggle between the two potentates: Pompey determined to maintain the advantage his third consulship had given him and to do all the strict application of the law would allow to limit Caesar's power; Caesar determined to safeguard his own ascendancy and dignity by insisting on what he saw as his indisputable right.[33]

The controversy became even more clearly a contest between the dynasts, when, in late July or early August, Caesar offered to give up his army if Pompey did likewise. The offer had a specious reasonableness, but was demanding unequal concessions and came to nothing. It would have cost Pompey the crucial advantage he had achieved by having his Spanish command extended in 52. He could hardly have been expected to surrender that. Civil war was now beginning to seem more likely. Both leaders seemed intent on confrontation, and there was talk that Caesar was already moving legions into northern Italy.[34]

Cicero began to be seriously worried about the situation around the time he began his journey home. His anxiety increased further when he reached Ephesus and received pessimistic reports from Atticus and others indicating war was imminent.[35] His own sympathies and opinions about the merits of the contending sides were unambiguous. From early 51 he was convinced that Pompey was at heart a loyal adherent of re-

32. *Fam.* 8.11.3; 8.13.2. Cicero expressed worries about Pompey's health in *Att.* 6.3.4. His recovery was greeted with exuberant rejoicing in Italy. *Att.* 8.16.1; 9.5.3. Plutarch, *Pomp.* 57. Dio 41.6. Velleius 2.48.2.

33. *Fam.* 8.14.2. Cf. *Att.* 7.3.4.

34. *Fam.* 8.14.2. *Att.* 6.9.5; 7.1.1. Hirtius, *BG* 8.52. Dio 40.62. Appian, *BC* 2.27–28. Appian states that Pompey wrote to the Senate during his illness offering to give up his *imperium.* Curio saw the offer as a ruse to get Caesar relieved of his command while Pompey merely made promises. No other source mentions such an offer by Pompey.

35. *Fam.* 2.15.3. *Att.* 6.8.2; 6.9.5; 7.1.1.

publicanism and was, indeed, the Republic's chief remaining hope and bulwark. He also felt personally close to Pompey at this time and in duty bound to support him for reasons of friendship and gratitude as well as politics. Pompey would, moreover, receive the backing of those committed to the Republic in any contest with Caesar; his side would be the side of the *boni* in the broadest sense, the side that Cicero's political beliefs and record demanded he support.[36]

Caesar and his cause had no countervailing appeal or claim on his allegiance. Despite the genuine friendship he had developed with him in 54, Cicero never came to trust Caesar's political instincts and intentions. He continued to see him as an *audacissimus* who stood ready to subvert the constitution and endanger the public good for personal ends, and whose backing came from the forces of disorder and discontent that Cicero considered the greatest enemies of himself and the Republic. His claims in regard to the Gallic provinces he found wholly unjustified, a further impudent attempt to exact a special privilege and build personal power in defiance of the Senate and in violation of the constitution. It was a cause as disreputable as Caesar's aims and following.[37]

Cicero's clear-cut view of the opposing personalities and issues did not relieve him, however, of worrisome indecision about his own immediate course of action. If it came to war, the choice would be clear, since he had decided he would prefer defeat with Pompey to victory with Caesar. The stand he should take, however, in the ongoing debates and negotiations was far less obvious to him. His friendship with Caesar made him reluctant to stand openly against him while the chance of a settlement remained. He had carefully cultivated the proconsul in the preceding years and had won a favored place among his friends. Caesar was continuing to extend the hand of friendship. He had recently helped secure passage of Cicero's *supplicatio* and had pledged fully to support the granting of the triumph that Cicero so badly wanted. The thought of having to cast aside this valued friendship the first time his opinion was sought made Cicero almost wish he were back in his province again.[38]

36. See n. 26 above, and *Att.* 7.3.5; 7.6.2; 7.7.7.
37. *Att.* 7.3.3–5; 7.6.2; 7.7.7; 7.9.4.
38. *Att.* 7.1.2–7; 7.2.7; 7.3.11. *Fam.* 8.11.2 recounts the efforts of Caesar's agent Balbus to secure passage of Cicero's *supplicatio*. Cicero also still owed money to Caesar and was not yet in a position to pay it. *Att.* 7.3.11; 7.8.5.

He faced a further and more serious dilemma in that he sharply disagreed with the hardline and belligerent position being adopted by Pompey and the leading *boni*. He was convinced that in a civil war the Republic was bound to lose regardless of who emerged the victor, a conviction he had acquired from his patron Q. Scaevola and from his own experience in the eighties. A military solution to disputes between powerful men meant military supremacy for the winner, and such power won in war he believed would inevitably be used to impose the victor's will and most likely to exact vengeance through proscriptions and confiscations. The result would be an end to true constitutional government and the birth of bitterness and division, seeds of future conflict and oppression.[39]

He had a further objection to precipitating war with Caesar in that he considered he was now too powerful to oppose after a decade of concessions that had steadily built his strength. Cicero saw Caesar as a most formidable foe in 50, commanding eleven legions and unlimited cavalry, and supported by the Transpadani, the *iuventus*, the *publicani*, the urban *plebs*, and the sizeable body of citizens comprising the disgraced, the disaffected, and the impoverished. The level of both his military and political strength precluded any assurance of a republican victory.[40]

Cicero therefore wanted above all else to preserve peace, and he accordingly favored a policy of conciliation toward Caesar. His hope was that the latter would give up his army in return for an assurance of election to the consulship. He saw this as a reasonable solution and thought it should be attractive to Caesar. If he refused such an offer, however, Cicero was prepared, in preference to forcing a military confrontation, to concede his more extreme demand to have his candidature admitted while he retained his army. He considered the demand disgraceful, but saw this concession as merely another in a lengthy series, and no worse than many that had been made earlier when Caesar's power could have been far more easily challenged. He further felt, unlike Pompey and Caesar's optimate foes, that the Law of the Ten Tribunes lent some justification to Caesar's claims; the right given to the proconsul to stand

39. *Fam.* 2.15.3; 2.16.3; 4.9.3; 4.14.2; 6.4.4; 6.21.1; 9.6.3; 12.8.2. *Att.* 7.5.4; 7.7.7; 8.11d.6. *Marc.* 14. *Phil.* 2.24. Cf. *Off.* 2.27ff. Mitchell, *Ascending Years,* 86ff.
40. *Att.* 7.3.4–5; 7.4.3; 7.5.5; 7.6.2; 7.7.5–6. *Fam.* 5.21.2; 7.3.5. Cicero's view of Caesar's strength was shared by Caelius. *Fam.* 8.14.3.

in absence implied the right to stay at his post until he could submit his candidature.[41]

Cicero became clearer about the course he should pursue in the evolving crisis as he proceeded at a leisurely pace toward the capital in December. He decided he could no longer take account of Caesar's friendship and benefactions; his commitment to the preservation of the Republic precluded such personal considerations. He retained his reservations about Pompey's policies, but his side was manifestly the better, the side of the *boni,* and he did not feel he could honorably disassociate himself publicly from it. But he was resolved to press his own convictions in private and urge Pompey to peace, the only course that he believed could serve the true interests of the Republic.[42]

The prospects for peace, however, were fading fast. Though the great bulk of the senatorial and equestrian orders continued strongly to favor a peaceful settlement, Pompey, the consuls, and leading *optimates* such as Cato, Scipio, and Domitius Ahenobarbus were taking an increasingly intransigent line.[43] At the beginning of December the consul C. Marcellus again raised the question of Caesar's recall in the Senate and secured approval for the appointment of a successor. Curio responded by reviving the earlier proposal that Pompey and Caesar should both resign their commands, and that too was approved, and with only twenty-two senators dissenting. Marcellus then attempted to force the issue by using rumors that Caesar was about to invade Italy as justification for authorizing Pompey to mobilize troops to defend the state. Pompey accepted the commission and proceeded to Campania to conduct a levy and take command of two Caesarian legions that had been requisitioned six months earlier by the Senate for possible use against the Parthians.[44] The move was widely disapproved among senators and *equites* and had the effect of virtually eliminating any possibility that Caesar would relinquish control of his own army.[45]

---

41. *Att.* 7.3.5; 7.5.4; 7.6.2; 7.7.6; 7.9.2–3. Cf. *Phil.* 2.24. *Att.* 9.11a.2. *Fam.* 6.6.5.

42. *Att.* 7.3.3–5; 7.6.2; 7.7.5–7.

43. The general desire for peace is stressed by Cicero in *Att.* 7.3.5; 7.5.4; 7.7.5. For the attitude of the hard-line *optimates, see Fam.* 6.21.1; 16.11.2; 16.12.2. Caesar, *BC* 1.1–4. Plutarch, *Caes.* 29; *Pomp.* 59.

44. Appian, *BC* 2.30–31. Plutarch, *Pomp.* 58–59; *Caes.* 30. For the two legions sent back by Caesar for service against the Parthians, see n. 31 above.

45. *Att.* 7.5.4. Pompey admitted to Cicero that these military preparations would lessen the chances of Caesar giving up his province. *Att.* 7.8.4. Cf. Caesar, *BC* 1.2.

Pompey was by now convinced that war was inevitable and preferable to a peace that involved any form of concession to Caesar. He believed the latter was now implacably his enemy, a threat to the constitution, and could no longer safely be allowed to enter the consulship even if he first gave up his command. An abusive speech by Mark Antony, one of Caesar's allies among the new tribunes, delivered at a *contio* on December 21 and containing open threats of armed force, confirmed his fears and strengthened his determination to keep Caesar and his minions from power. He was further inclined toward war by a strong confidence that he could withstand any military threat from Caesar. Cicero met him twice in the course of his journey to Rome, at Capua on December 10 and at Formiae on December 25, and reported to Atticus a growing belligerence in his attitude that showed no desire for peace and seemed actually to betoken fear of it.[46]

Pompey's militancy was shared by Caesar's optimate foes and left little room for compromise. A proposal mooted by Caesar's friends that he be allowed to hold Cisalpine Gaul and Illyricum with two legions until he assumed the consulship was rejected.[47] A dispatch from Caesar delivered to the Senate on January 1, 49, restating his claims and proposing once more that all commanders give up their armies, was not referred for discussion by the consuls, who instead stampeded the Senate into approving a resolution put forward by Scipio that Caesar should disband his army by a certain date and that failure to do so would constitute an act against the state. The decree was vetoed by the tribunes Mark Antony and Q. Cassius, but marked the beginning of a final, concerted drive by Caesar's enemies to break his power.[48]

It was at this stage that Cicero at last reached Rome, approaching the city on January 4, but remaining outside the *pomerium* so as to retain his *imperium* and his chance of a triumph.[49] He received an elaborate welcome, and there were immediate demands in the Senate that he be awarded a triumph. The consul L. Lentulus promised to bring a motion as soon as he had dealt with the immediate crisis. But Cicero was more concerned for the moment with the rapidly growing threat of all-out civil

---

46. *Att.* 7.4.2; 7.8.4–5.
47. Appian, *BC* 2.32. Suetonius, *Jul.* 29.2. Plutarch, *Caes.* 31. Velleius 2.49. See Rice Holmes, *Roman Republic,* 2:331ff.
48. Caesar, *BC* 1.1–7. Appian, *BC* 2.32–33. Dio 41.1–3. Plutarch, *Caes.* 30; *Ant.* 5.
49. *Att.* 7.5.3; 7.7.3. *Fam.* 16.11.2.

war. Though he had been keenly aware of the gravity of the situation since his meetings with Pompey, he was surprised and dismayed by the mood of militancy and intransigence he encountered among the leading *boni* on his arrival at the city. He saw in it a quality of unreason and frenzy that made war a virtual certainty, and it quickly brought a reversal of his earlier resolution to stand with the *boni* whatever course they followed. He immediately devoted all his energies to counteracting the eagerness to fight, hammering home the evils of civil war, urging Pompey to a peaceful settlement, and searching for compromises to break the deadlock. He suggested Pompey go to Spain, which would remove Caesar's fear of an armed antagonist and leave him no reason for armed intervention. He advocated acceptance of Caesar's candidature *in absentia* on grounds that it was a privilege granted by the people. He also put forward a modified version of a compromise earlier proposed by Caesar's friends, to the effect that Caesar be allowed to hold Illyricum with one legion until he entered the consulship.[50]

Cicero believed he could have persuaded Pompey to make concessions if the optimate leadership had not been bent on war. But their obduracy defeated him, and during the days following his return the attacks on Caesar and on the tribunes supporting him continued unabated in the Senate. Finally, on January 7 the ultimate decree was passed, calling on the consuls, praetors, tribunes, and all proconsuls who were near the city to take measures to protect the state from harm. Levies followed throughout Italy. The tribunes Antony and Cassius fled to Caesar. When the latter, who was at Ravenna, heard what had happened, he led the thirteenth legion, the only part of his army wintering with him, across the Rubicon into Italy and seized Ariminum. The civil war had begun.[51]

Caesar pushed quickly southward from Ariminum, and within days he had taken control of Arretium in Etruria and of the coastal towns of Pisaurum, Fanum, and Ancona.[52] When news of the invasion reached Rome on January 17, Pompey at once decided to abandon the capital, and

50. *Fam.* 4.1.1; 6.6.4–5; 6.21.1; 8.17.1; 16.11.2; 16.12.2. *Att.* 8.11d.7; 9.11a.2. Plutarch, *Pomp.* 59; *Caes.* 31. Cicero urged his policy of peace publicly in the Senate as well as in private. *Att.* 9.11a.2; 15.3.1.

51. *Fam.* 6.6.6; 16.11.2. Caesar, *BC* 1.1–7. Appian, *BC* 2.33. Plutarch, *Pomp.* 60; *Caes.* 31–32. Dio 41.1–3. The date was January 10 or 11. See Gelzer, *Caesar,* 192.

52. Caesar, *BC* 1.11. *Fam.* 16.12.2. See T. P. Hillman, "Strategic Reality and the Movements of Caesar, January 49 B.C.," *Historia* 37 (1988), 248–52.

he ordered magistrates and senators to accompany him to Campania, where he intended to concentrate his recruiting efforts and to assemble the two so-called Appian legions earlier requisitioned from Caesar during the height of the Parthian threat.[53] Pompey's decision dismayed and outraged many of the *optimates*, but he had been caught unprepared by Caesar's unexpected offensive, and he had little choice but to avoid a direct encounter until he could muster stronger forces.[54] He also evidently hoped that Picenum, where he had posted several of his most trusted adherents and where his family had long predominated, could be held, and that Caesar, if he advanced as far as Rome, could be cut off from his main forces in Gaul.[55]

Pompey's unfavorable military situation also prompted him to renew negotiations, seeking either to buy time or to secure a genuine settlement. He sent conciliatory messages to Caesar by two different emissaries, L. Caesar, a relative of the proconsul and son of one of his *legati,* and L. Roscius, a praetor. Caesar sent them back with the response that he was willing to give up his army and provinces and to stand in person for the consulship in free elections, provided Pompey went to Spain and his troops and all the armed forces in Italy were disbanded. He sought a meeting with Pompey to ratify a settlement.[56]

The proposals offered major new concessions. Caesar was no longer insisting on the right to stand for the consulship in absentia, nor was he demanding that Pompey give up his *imperium,* but merely his army in Italy. The new terms were, in fact, fully acceptable to Pompey and his optimate allies, who, chastened by recent events, were now willing to contemplate a second consulship for Caesar. In their distrust of the

53. *Att.* 7.11.3; 7.12.2; 8.3.3; 9.10.2. Caesar, *BC* 1.14. Dio 41.6–9. Appian, *BC* 2.36–37. Plutarch, *Pomp.* 60–61; *Caes.* 33. For the Appian legions, see n. 31 above.
54. Dio 41.5–6. Appian, *BC* 2.37. Plutarch, *Pomp.* 60. Caesar, *BC* 1.30. *Att.* 7.11.3; 7.13.2; 7.15.3.
55. *Att.* 7.8.5; 7.9.2; 7.23.1. *Fam.* 16.12.4. In late January Pompey was still planning, as soon as he had gathered sufficient forces, to march to Picenum. *Att.* 7.16.2. He had some of his closest adherents already posted in or near the region. He had sent Vibullius Rufus to try to secure the loyalty of the Picenes, and his kinsman, Lucilius Hirrus, was holding Camerinum with six cohorts. Lentulus Spinther commanded ten cohorts at Asculum. Attius Varus, a former praetor, was holding Auximum and actively recruiting throughout Picenum. *Att.* 7.13a.3; 8.11a.1. Caesar, *BC* 1.12, 15.
56. *Att.* 7.13a.2; 7.14.1. *Fam.* 16.12.3. Caesar, *BC* 1.8–9. Dio 41.5. The role of L. Caesar and L. Roscius has been examined in detail by Shackleton Bailey, *JRS* 50 (1960), 88ff. See K. von Fritz, *TAPA* 72 (1941), 125ff.

proconsul, however, they insisted that, before any of his stipulations
could be met, he must first evacuate Italy, disband his army, and provide
sureties of his good faith. Caesar would accept no such precondition, and
he continued his advance southward, gaining control of the vital area of
Picenum in the early days of February.[57]

Pompey, whose confidence had been boosted by the defection of one
of Caesar's ablest *legati,* T. Labienus, who arrived in Campania on
January 22 reporting serious weakness in Caesar's army, remained hope-
ful to the end of January that he could raise sufficient forces to defend
Italy.[58] But difficulties with recruiting and doubts about the loyalty of the
Appian legions together with the reverses in Picenum changed his mood
and strategy.[59] In the first weeks of February he abandoned all hope of
assembling an army capable of confronting Caesar's forces and further
concluded that none of the areas of Italy still under his control could form
a defensible base from which to launch a counteroffensive. He therefore
decided Italy had to be evacuated. He first planned to dispatch one of the
consuls with the new levies from Campania to secure Sicily, and to send
with him the new procounsul of Transalpine Gaul, Domitius Ahenobarbus, who had established himself at Corfinium with twelve cohorts. All
remaining forces were to assemble at Brundisium for removal to
Dyrrachium.[60]

But Domitius, who had been reinforced at Corfinium by nineteen

57. *Att.*7.14.1; 7.21.2. *Fam.* 16.12.3. Caesar, *BC* 1.10–11, 15. The distrust of
Caesar was very deep. *Att.* 7.15.3.

58. *Att.* 7.12.5; 7.13.1; 7.13a.3; 7.15.3; 7.16.2. *Fam.* 16.12.4. Dio 41.4. Plutarch,
Caes. 34. See R. Syme, "The Allegiance of Labienus," *JRS* 28 (1938), 113–25.

59. For the difficulties with recruiting, see *Att.* 7.13.2; 7.14.2; 7.21.1; 7.23.3;
8.12a.3; 8.12d.1. For Pompey's doubts about the Appian legions, see *Att.* 8.12a.2–3;
8.12c.4; 8.12d.1.

60. *Att.* 8.12a.3; 8.12c,1–3. The date at which Pompey decided to abandon Italy and
the reasons for his decision have been widely debated. The idea had been in the air as
early as December 50 (*Fam.* 2.16.3) and Cicero had heard discussions among leading
principes of a plan to collect vast eastern armaments and blockade Italy (*Att.* 9.9.2. Cf.
Att. 8.11.2; 9.10.6). From the beginning of the war he considered the evacuation of Italy a
real possibility (*Att.* 7.10; 7.12.2; 7.17.1; 7.20.2; 7.21.2; 7.22.1; 8.1.2; 8.3.1; 9.10.4).
But Pompey had never discussed such a strategy with him and it was only after the
reverses in Picenum that he saw it a likely eventuality (*Att.* 7.21.2). The indications are it
was merely a contingency plan until the first half of February. See A. Burns, "Pompey's
Strategy and Domitius' Stand at Corfinium," *Historia* 15 (1966), 74–95. K. von Fritz,
"Pompey's Policy before and after the Outbreak of the Civil War of 49 B.C.," *TAPA* 73
(1942), 145–80. D. R. Shackleton Bailey, "Exspectatio Corfiniensis," *JRS* 46 (1956),
57–64. O. E. Schmidt, *Der Briefwechsel des M. Tullius Cicero von seinem Proconsulat
in Cilicen bis zu Caesars Ermordung* (Leipzig, 1893), 95ff.

cohorts retreating from Picenum under the command of Pompey's henchmen Vibullius and Hirrus, was determined to remain and confront
Caesar, if the latter lingered in his area. His main reason, well appreciated by Pompey, was his obligation to protect the estates of his client
army from pillage by Caesar's troops. Pompey badly needed the reinforcement Domitius's army, and especially the nineteen loyal Picene
cohorts, would give him, and Domitius's refusal to move south forced
him to abandon the Sicilian plan and gather all available forces together at
Brundisium. He gave no thought to going north to support Domitius,
considering his army untrustworthy and inadequate for such an enterprise.[61] Domitius, as Pompey had forecast, was hemmed in by Caesar
and, after a week's siege, was forced to surrender on February 21.
Caesar, whose public standing had suffered as a result of his invasion of
Italy, was anxious to appear magnanimous and conciliatory, and he
prevented any plundering and released Domitius and all the other prisoners of senatorial or equestrian rank. His clemency and general restraint
had a major impact on public opinion and won him wide support in the
municipalities and rural areas of Italy.[62]

Caesar proceeded directly after the fall of Corfinium to Apulia and on
to Brundisium, which he reached on March 9. He still had some hope of a
reconciliation with Pompey, and he made several attempts to arrange a
conference. But Pompey's present position was too weak to allow him
much hope of a favorable or honorable settlement, and he used the
absence of the consuls, who had already taken part of his army to Dyrrachium, as an excuse for not negotiating. As soon as ships became
available he began preparations to evacuate Brundisium, and on March
17 he crossed to Dyrrachium.[63] Caesar did not have sufficient ships to
pursue him, and he was anxious, in any case, to gain control of the
Spanish provinces before departing for the East. He therefore decided to
go to Spain, but first he stopped at Rome, hoping to repair further his
public image and to broaden his support among the senatorial order. At a
meeting of the Senate on April 1, called by the tribunes M. Antony and

61. *Att.* 8.11a; 8.12a.1–3; 8.12b.2; 8.12c.2; 8.12d.1–1. Cf. Dio 41.11.

62. For the effect of the invasion on Caesar's popularity, see *Att.* 7.11.4; 7.13.3. For
Caesar's actions and policy at Corfinium and its effects, see Caesar, *BC* 1.16–23. *Att.*
8.9a.1; 8.12d.1; 8.13.2; 8.14.1; 8.16.2; 9.7c.1; 9.13.4; 9.15.3; 9.16.2. Plutarch, *Caes.*
34. Appian, *BC* 2.38.

63. Caesar, *BC* 1,24–28. *Att.* 9.13a; 9.14; 9.15a. Plutarch, *Pomp.* 62. Dio
41.12.

Q. Cassius, he defended all his actions at length and recounted his efforts for peace, ending with a proposal that senatorial delegations should be sent to Pompey to discuss a settlement. The proposal was passed, but no envoys could be found. Caesar's purposes in visiting Rome were, in general, unfulfilled. He was opposed at every turn by the tribune L. Metellus, and he had a damaging public confrontation with him when he tried to remove funds from the sacred treasury in the Temple of Saturn. He left Rome for Gaul after only a few days, deeply chagrined by his experience and so uncertain of the public mood that he decided against holding a *contio* that he planned for the eve of his departure.[64]

Cicero's Cruelest Political Dilemma

The outbreak of war and the events of the early months of 49 left Cicero on the brink of despair, floundering in an agony of indecision as he vainly struggled to find a political course that would meet the demands of honor and duty without unduly endangering himself and his family. His position as a proconsul brought him immediate complications. The Senate's ultimate decree of January 7 included proconsuls in the neighborhood of Rome among those it charged to protect the state from harm.[65] Cicero therefore found himself in a foremost position, and he was thrust even further to the fore in the ensuing arrangements for the defense of Italy by being assigned control of the important region of Capua. The commission did not please him. He was being given no army or money, without which he did not believe Capua could be defended. Moreover, the appointment would give him an involvement and prominence in the republican military effort that he was most anxious at this stage to avoid. He therefore declined the post and settled instead for a quiet but insignificant assignment supervising the northern coastline of Campania.[66] He treated the position as a sinecure, and based himself at

64. Caesar, *BC* 1.32–33. *Att.* 10.4.8–9; 10.9a.1. Dio 41.15–17. Appian, *BC* 2.41. Plutarch, *Caes.* 35. Velleius 2.50.1. Lucan 3.143.

65. *Fam.* 16.11.2. Caesar, *BC* 1.5.

66. *Fam.* 16.11.4; 16.12.5. *Att.* 7.11.5; 7.17.4; 8.3.4–5; 8.11d.5; 8.12.2; 9.11a.2. Capua was a vital Pompeian stronghold. See Caesar, *BC* 1.14. *Att.* 7.14.2; 7.23.3; 8.2.3. Pompey was still anxious to defend it as late as Feb. 17. *Att.* 8.6.2; 8.11d.3.

Cicero's command in 49 has been the subject of much discussion. His phrase, "Nos Capuam sumpsimus" in a letter to Tiro on Jan. 12 (*Fam.* 16.11.3) has caused most of the difficulty, leading some scholars to argue that he accepted the position but later resigned

his Formian villa, in effect standing aloof from the war while he tried to decide what his future course should be.[67]

It proved a protracted and harrowing exercise, as he found himself paralyzed and tormented by shifting emotions and conflicting pressures. From one standpoint it seemed clear to him that honor and duty demanded he should commit himself fully and openly to Pompey. His cause was the *causa reipublicae,* and was supported by all the most illustrious *boni.*[68] Pompey was, besides, his friend and benefactor; Cicero was deeply conscious of his personal obligations to him and was determined not to be found ungrateful.[69]

Caesar, by contrast, evoked only his anger and contempt. He saw no merit in the man or his cause. His invasion of Italy he considered the ultimate act of criminality and frenzy, the final consequence of the reckless lust for power that had inflicted ten years of political turmoil on the state. He had no hope that such a man, devoid of any sense of right, would behave moderately. He believed his life and character, political record, and entourage of desperadoes guaranteed that his victory would be followed by slaughter and pillage and all the evils normally attendant on the domination of an *improbus,* namely, confiscation of property, cancellation of debts, recall of exiles, and elevation of the disreputable to high office. Rome would experience a tyranny on the model of Phalaris or Pisistratus.[70]

Cicero could not envisage remaining in Rome under such a regime. To stand aloof would be dangerous, to cooperate dishonorable. He thought

---

it, others that he accepted it and retained it, though reluctantly. Shackleton Bailey (*Ad Att.* 4.438ff.) has done much to clear the fog, and it is essentially his conclusion that is represented here. The statement to Tiro was most likely made immediately after the arrangements for the defense of Italy were put forward and before Cicero made his final decision. See Schmidt, *Briefwechsel,* 116ff. J. D. Duff, "Cicero's Commission and Movements at the Beginning of the Civil War," *JP* 33 (1914), 154ff. Wistrand, *Cicero Imperator,* 65ff., 206ff.

67. *Att.* 7.17.4; 8.3.5; 9.11a.2. His only active involvement consisted of two brief trips to Capua, once in response to a request from Pompey to go there to help with the levy (*Att.* 7.14.2; 7.15.2; 8.11b.2), once in response to a summons from the consuls (*Att.* 7.18.1; 7.20.1; 7.21.1). He seems to have done little on either trip.

68. *Att.* 7.12.3; 7.20.2; 7.26.3; 8.1.3; 8.3.2; 8.14.2.

69. *Att.* 9.1.4; 9.2a.2; 9.5.3; 9.7.3–4; 9.9.2; 9.10.2; 9.11a.3; 9.12.1–4; 9.13.3; 9.19.2; 10.7.1. See P. A. Brunt, "Cicero's *officium* in the Civil War," *JRS* 76 (1986), 12–32.

70. *Att.* 7.11.1; 7.12.2; 7.13.1; 7.14.1; 7.15.3; 7.17.2; 7.18.2; 7.20.2; 7.22.1; 8.9a.2; 8.16.2; 9.2a.2; 9.7.5; 9.9.4; 10.4.2; 10.8.2; 10.10.5; 10.12a.3; 10.14.1, 3.

of respected Romans who had chosen to coexist with Cinna, and he rehearsed philosophical arguments in favor of quiet acceptance of despotism, but he concluded that his own high achievements in defense of republicanism and his writings on statesmanship made it especially incumbent on him never to seem lacking in devotion to the Republic or subvervient to those against whom the Senate once armed him for the protection of the state.[71]

But Cicero found all his efforts at such principled analyses of his predicament confounded by a host of practical and personal considerations. He had the gravest misgivings about the war itself and about Pompey's leadership and the overall strength of the republican forces. His aversion to civil war was in no way lessened by its onset. He abhorred what was happening and the consequences he believed would inevitably follow: the parricidal devastation of Italy, the anger and bitterness, the proscriptions and confiscations, the diminished liberty, whoever won. He was convinced any terms of peace were preferable, even if it meant Caesar securing a position of power. The *potentia* of a *togatus* was more tolerable than the victory of an *armatus*. Pompey and the optimate leadership had made the wrong choice.[72]

His anger and dismay at the failure of his efforts for peace were magnified by the abandonment of Rome and by what he saw as the total unpreparedness of Pompey for the war he had refused to avoid. The flight from Rome left Cicero shaken and bewildered. He equated the city with the fatherland, and viewed Pompey's withdrawal, which left the capital without Senate or magistrates, laws or courts, and a prey to arson and pillage, as a virtual dissolution of the Republic and an act of deep dishonor that their ancestors had refused to contemplate even in the face of the Gallic hordes. He also considered it an act of inexplicable folly, handing over to Caesar the public and private wealth of the city and depriving republican coffers of desperately needed funds.[73] The private consequences for leading *boni* reinforced his sense of outrage. They were forced from their homes, which were left exposed to plundering at the

71. *Att.* 7.20.2; 7.22.2; 8.2.4; 8.3.2–6; 8.7.2; 8.9a.1; 8.14.2; 9.2a.1; 9.4.2; 9.5.2; 10.8.8.
72. *Att.* 7.13.1; 7.14.3; 8.11.4; 8.11d.6; 9.6.7; 9.7.1; 9.9.2; 9.10.2; 10.4.3; 10.14.1. *Fam.* 4.9.3; 4.14.2; 6.1.6; 6.4.4; 9.6.3; 12.18.2. Cf. *Fam.* 15.15.1.
73. *Att.* 7.10; 7.11.3; 7.12.5; 7.13.1; 7.15.3; 7.21.1; 8.2.2–3; 8.3.3. *Fam.* 4.1.2.

hands of the Caesarians, and made virtual refugees, wandering with their wives and children and living in need, misery, and shame.[74]

The weeks following intensified his exasperation and anxiety. He found nothing but panic and confusion among the republican leadership and saw the usual apathy paralyzing the *boni* as a whole. There were no men and no money. Pompey had failed to recruit the forces he had been kept at Rome to prepare. The levies, conducted halfheartedly under ineffective direction by the consuls, were producing little or no results. The only available forces were the two Appian legions, and they could not be fully trusted.[75]

Pompey's behavior continued to baffle and infuriate him. The once great general seemed to have no plan, to be uninformed about his own strength and the enemy's, and to lack the courage and drive to mobilize support and prosecute a war against an opponent as crafty and dynamic as Caesar. The republicans were adrift at sea without a rudder, at the mercy of the storm.

Cicero remained personally attached to Pompey and retained his sense of obligation to him, but his faith in his leadership was gone. Pompey neither sought nor heeded his advice in this period and did not trouble to inform him of his intentions, all of which undoubtedly contributed to Cicero's disaffection, but the harshness of his judgments of the general in the first weeks of the war shows a disillusionment deeper than wounded pride or pique. Pompey's political life in the entire previous decade now seemed to him a sorry tale of misjudgment and error. Successful in bad causes, he had failed in the best, adding further to the catalogue of mistakes of the fifties and confirming his general lack of political acumen. The art of good statesmanship had eluded him, and Cicero no longer believed he could save the Republic and no longer saw him as a man to follow.[76]

There were also purely personal factors deterring Cicero from committing himself to the republican side. His former ties to Caesar were a

74. *Att.* 8.2.3. Cicero exaggerated. He himself was comfortably established at Formiae. But the emotional outburst illustrates the depth of his feelings.

75. *Att.* 7.12.2; 7.14.1; 7.15.3; 7.20.1–2; 7.21.1; 8.3.4.

76. *Att.* 7.13.1–2; 7.21.1–2; 7.22.1; 7.25; 8.1.2–3; 8.2.2–4; 8.3.3–4; 8.7.1–2; 8.8.1; 8.9a.1; 8.11.1–2; 9.5.2; 9.10.2. *Fam.* 4.7.2. For Cicero's pique at rejection of his advice and the failure to consult him, see *Att.* 7.12.3; 7.21.3; 8.3.3; 8.11d.5; 9.10.2.

complication. The latter expected their earlier friendship to count for
something, and from an early stage he began to press Cicero to stay
neutral. Cicero felt a refusal would bring retribution, and might especially endanger Quintus, on whose friendship Caesar had particular
claims.[77] Cicero also had many friends and connections on Caesar's side,
all of them intent on keeping him from casting his lot with their enemies.
His son-in-law, Dolabella, was a stalwart and favored Caesarian. He kept
in close touch with Cicero in the early stages of the war and was used by
Caesar as a subtle means of influencing the orator. So was Trebatius, the
protégé whom Cicero had sent into service with Caesar in Gaul and who
became a firm Caesarian while remaining on intimate terms with Cicero.
Caelius, who, long before the war started, was advising Cicero to pick
the side most likely to win, was another Caesarian voice opposing open
backing of Pompey.[78]

The safety and welfare of himself and his family also counted heavily
with Cicero during this crisis. He was still haunted by the memory of his
exile, the bitter fruit of his earlier courageous defense of the *causa
reipublicae*. He was in no mood to risk a repetition of that experience. He
felt that he and his family had suffered enough in the public interest, and
that he had earned the right to consult his safety and avoid stirring anew
the special hatred the *improbi* felt for him, just when it was finally being
laid to rest.[79]

While there was a hope of peace and the war was centered in Italy,
Cicero felt reasonably justified in remaining at Formiae and maintaining
the position he had assumed after the flight from Rome. He believed no
one could reasonably blame him for refusing to make an enemy of Caesar
while Pompey was offering him a triumph and a second consulship.
Later, when hopes for peace had faded and Pompey decided to abandon
Campania and consolidate his forces in Luceria, he was able to argue that
he had no safe way of making the trip from Formiae to join him.[80] But his
dilemma deepened once the evacuation of Italy and an all-out war became more certain. Remaining in Italy after Pompey's departure would

77. *Att.* 7.21.3; 7.23.3; 8.2.1; 8.3.5; 8.11.5; 9.1.4.
78. *Att.* 7.17.3; 7.21.2–3; 7.23.3; 9.13a.1; 9.16.3; 10.4.11. 10.9a. *Fam.* 8.15. Cf.
Fam. 9.9.1.
79. *Att.* 7.13.3; 7.19; 7.26.2; 8.3.4–5; 8.11d.7; 8.12.2, 5; 9.1.3; 9.6.4, 7; 9.4.2;
10.8.5; 11.9.1.
80. *Att.* 8.11d.7; 8.12.2–3; 9.2a.2.

represent an explicit refusal to support the republican cause and, worse still, would make it difficult to avoid some level of association with Caesar's side. He would incur Pompey's displeasure and charges of ingratitude and would be exposed to angry denunciation by the *boni,* who were already highly critical of his posture.[81]

On the other hand, the direction the war was taking made him more reluctant than ever to participate in it or to link himself to Pompey and his optimate associates. Pompey's failure to help Domitius at Corfinium and his decision to leave Italy he considered despicable and saw as alarming signs of the resurrection of a sinister design he had once heard discussed: to stir a massive war throughout the empire and blockade Italy from the East. He foresaw a good cause being horribly perverted, armadas being assembled to starve the fatherland into submission, and Pompey coming in anger, like Sulla, to wreck devastation and exact a terrible vengeance. His fears were reinforced by reports from the republican camp of threats of reprisals and promises of largesse.[82] The domination of Caesar, which he still thought likely anyhow, seemed a lesser evil than such a war. Caesar was, after all, a mortal man, and could be removed by various means. It was more important to preserve intact the Roman state and people. Patriotism was no longer summoning Cicero to join the republican side.[83]

The thought of leaving Italy in winter, hampered by lictors, and of giving up his family and his beloved villas at a time of life when his age inclined him to retirement and the comforts of domestic life was an added deterrent. He was also subjected to growing pressure to remain from his Caesarian friends and from Caesar himself. Atticus, influenced by Caesar's moderation, added his powerful voice to those urging him to avoid, or at least postpone, any commitment.[84]

81. *Att.* 7.20.2; 8.3.2; 8.11.3; 8.14.2; 9.2a.1–3. For the criticism of his behavior by the *boni,* see *Att.* 8.11d.7–8; 8.16.1–2; 9.2a.3; 9.7.6.

82. *Att.* 8.7.1; 8.8.1; 8.9a.1; 8.11.2; 8.16.1; 9.4.2; 9.6.7; 9.7.3–4; 9.9.2; 9.10.2, 6; 9.11.3–4; 10.4.3; 10.7.1. *Fam.* 4.7.2; 4.9.2; 4.14.2.

83. *Att.* 9.10.3; 9.13.4.

84. *Att.* 7.20.2; 7.23.3; 8.3.5; 9.5.1; 9.10.3. For the increased attention and the complications of traveling with his laurel-wreathed *fasces* and lictors, see *Att.* 7.10; 7.12.4; 7.20.2; 8.1.3; 8.3.5; 9.1.3. He remained reluctant, however, to discharge them and abandon hope of a triumph, despite occasional remarks to the contrary. *Att.* 9.7.5. For the continuing pressure he received from Caesarians and Caesar, see *Att.* 8.15a; 9.6a; 9.7a; 9.7b; 9.11.2; 9.11a; 9.16.2; 10.9a. Atticus's views, almost as variable as Cicero's, are summarized in *Att.* 9.10.4–10.

Cicero began to edge closer to a definite decision in early March. His personal regard for Pompey kept surfacing, as did his sense of obligation to him and fear of the charge of ingratitude. Reports of mounting criticism from the *boni* were also having an impact. News of the evacuation from Brundisium affected him strongly and made him feel dishonored by his absence from Pompey's side and from the ranks of the *boni*. [85] But it was the thought of being near the indigent riffraff that comprised the bulk of Caesar's entourage and of witnessing their subversion of the constitution that most powerfully persuaded him he could not stay in Italy. [86] A meeting with Caesar at Arpinum on March 28 greatly intensified his feelings of loathing for those around Caesar and confirmed his worst fears that Caesar would demand his participation in public affairs. The latter's concern to assemble as impressive a gathering of senators as possible at Rome for a meeting that he hoped would provide greater respectability and legitimacy for himself and his cause made him especially anxious to secure the attendance and, if possible, the support of a consular of Cicero's status. He had already attempted to create a public impression that Cicero was sympathetic and willing to cooperate by circulating a friendly and somewhat flattering letter that Cicero had recently sent him, offering his help, though strictly in the service of peace. He now pressed him hard to attend the meeting of the Senate scheduled for April 1. But Cicero declared he would attend only if allowed to speak his mind about the war and express his sympathy for Pompey's position. Caesar would permit no such thing, and he departed issuing veiled warnings and leaving Cicero in no doubt about his displeasure. He also left him feeling highly pleased that he had honorably stood his ground and certain that he must now leave Italy as soon as possible. [87]

away from any contact with the Caesarians. But wearying indecision still plagued him. He was resolved to get out of sight of Caesar and his minions, but, while certain whom to flee, he still had no one he could happily follow. His opinion of Pompey remained harsh as ever. He considered him more moderate and moral than Caesar, but a warlord very much in the same mold, intent on power, concerned more with personal

85. *Att.* 8.14.2; 8.16.1–2; 9.1.4; 9.2a.2–3; 9.5.3; 9.6.4; 9.7.3–4; 9.9.2; 9.10.2; 9.12.1–4; 9.13.3; 9.19.2; 10.7.1; 11.12.1. Cf. *Fam.* 6.6.6; 9.5.2.
86. *Att.* 7.22.1; 9.2a.2; 9.7.5; 9.9.4; 9.18.2; 9.19.1; 10.8.3, 8.
87. *Att.* 8.9.1; 9.15.2; 9.18.

gain than the public good, and preparing a war of a kind certain to bring calamity on the state.[88] Cicero could not yet bring himself to join such a war, and by early April he was seeking a neutral haven, away from both camps. His first choice was Greece, but later he began to think of Malta. He received encouragement from Curio, who had recently been appointed to the command of Sicily, and who visited him at Cumae in mid-April. Curio thought Caesar would approve Cicero's plan and he offered to help him make his journey through Sicily.[89]

But he was still troubled by doubts about the propriety of his entire course, and he remained generally discontented, yearning for a role that would remove the ingloriousness and risk of blame inherent in a policy of neutrality. He continued to grasp at the hope that he might yet be asked to act as peacemaker, and he began to form plans, with encouragement from Atticus, for some unspecified grand gesture that he refers to as "illud Caelianum" and that he hoped would crucially affect the war.[90] But his most immediate concern was to get out of Italy, and his plans for that met a new obstacle in early May, when Mark Antony, whom Caesar had left in charge of Italy, refused him permission to leave. Cicero continued his preparations, however, determined to go by stealth or by force, if necessary.[91] He managed to leave unhindered, but not until early June, by

88. *Att.* 9.9.2; 9.10.2; 10.4.3–4; 10.7.1. *Fam.* 4.9.2.

89. *Att.* 10.1.2; 10.4.8–10; 10.7.1; 10.9.1.

90. *Att.* 9.11.2; 9.11a.3; 10.1.2; 10.1a; 10.8.5; 10.10.3; 10.12.2; 10.12a.1, 3; 10.14.3; 10.15.2; 10.16.4. Cicero makes various references in early May to hopes he had of doing something notable (*Att.* 10.10.3; 10.12.2; 10.12a.2), and then suddenly he begins to speak of a more particular design, something he describes as "illud Caelianum" (10.12a.3; 10.15.2). The precise nature of these grand gestures cannot be determined, but it seems certain that all of them, including the Caelian plan, were designed somehow to advance the cause of peace. Atticus is unlikely to have encouraged a military adventure, and any such move would be totally at odds with Cicero's outlook and inclinations at this point. In the end the Caelian scheme came to nothing, and even at the time Cicero claimed it was maturing (*Att.* 10.15.2), he was willing to abandon it if offered what he saw as a more important assignment, the role of peacemaker. The likelihood is the plan involved no more than some dramatic public proclamation or rally for peace at a venue abroad, and that it, and the other grand gestures referred to by Cicero, were no more that the wishful thinking of a deeply frustrated, discontented mind striving to satisfy the urge to achieve something significant. For discussions of the plan, see Shackleton Bailey, *Ad Att.* 4.461– 69. Tenney Frank, *CP* 14 (1919), 287–89. Schmidt, *Briefwechsel,* 178.

91. *Att.* 10.8.10; 10.10.2–3; 10.11.4; 10.12.1; 10.12a.2. In the course of his efforts to allay suspicion about his intentions he made a trip to Pompeii on May 12, and was informed on his arrival that the centurions of the three cohorts in the town wanted to meet him and place their troops in his hands (*Att.* 10.16.4). He left before daybreak next day to avoid any entanglement. He would not be drawn into any rash military ventures.

which time he had again changed his thinking and decided to join Pompey. Duty and honor seemed in the end to require it. His family also felt it was the right course. In addition, he had come to believe that, despite Caesar's military superiority, his tyrannical nature and the degeneracy and incompetence of so many of his followers would bring his speedy collapse.[92] He sailed from Caieta on June 7, taking with him the boys and Quintus.[93]

Cicero's prolonged and sometimes helpless wavering in 49 has brought him little credit from historians, but it was more a product of his earlier political experiences and difficult political position than of weakness or indecision. His youth had been marred by civil war between potentates, and he had never forgotten the awful private and public consequences of such conflicts. The memory of his exile was an additional powerful disincentive to any further prominent involvements in civil disputes. But his greatest difficulty derived from the shifts in his political relationships and general political posture that had taken place in the fifties. His aversion to the optimate *principes* and their policies, which had been building through the previous decade, remained strong as ever, and Pompey's emergence as the leader of their cause only added to his misgivings. He lacked entirely the factional zealotry driving the republican leadership toward war, and he found himself more than ever politically alone in 49, with no party to which he could give his unreserved support. His personal ties to both protagonists, product of a long association with Pompey and of the anomalous alliance with the triumvirate forced on him in 56 by his sense of isolation and insecurity, further complicated his position, leaving him no choice fully compatible with the claims of friendship and the public good. He was very much a displaced

92. *Fam.* 6.6.6; 7.3.1; 8.17.1; 9.5.2; 14.7.2. *Att.* 10.8.6–8; 11.9.1–2; 11.12.1. Cf. *Att.* 9.6.4. Cicero was especially influenced by Tullia, to whom he seems to have been very close at this time. She was concerned about his reputation and anxious that he should do what duty demanded. *Att.* 9.6.4; 10.8.9. She gave birth prematurely to a son in the midst of Cicero's preparations to leave on May 19. *Att.* 10.18.1.

93. *Fam.* 14.7.2. Cicero had always intended to take the boys with him (*Att.* 10.11.4). Marcus had recently received the *toga virilis* (*Att.* 9.17.1; 9.19.1), and Cicero was at this time highly satisfied with him (*Att.* 10.9.2; 10.11.3). The young Quintus was another story. He had seriously upset his father and Cicero by writing to Caesar and making a trip to Rome in April. The Ciceros initially feared he had told Caesar they were hostile to him and planning to leave Italy. The truth, not related in detail, proved to be less serious, but the incident left Cicero worried about the boy's character and determined to impose strict discipline. *Att.* 10.4.5–6; 10.6.2; 10.7.3; 10.11.3; 10.12.3; 10.15.4.

figure who retained a strong yearning to maintain his record of honorable service to the Republic, but saw no acceptable means of doing so.

Cicero was no more contented after joining Pompey and his army. He found no comfort in anything he saw. Pompey's forces were meagre and showed no appetite for war. The leaders, aside from Pompey and a few others, had their minds set on plunder and vengeance, and he shuddered to think of what they would do in victory. Even the wealthiest were now sunk deeply in debt, and Pompey himself was so short of funds that Cicero felt obliged to make him a large loan from the 2.2 million sesterces that had accrued to him from his proconsulate and that he had deposited with the *publicani* at Ephesus.[94]

Cicero's reception in the camp did nothing to relieve his gloom at what he found there. Cato told him he could have better served his friends and country by remaining neutral in Italy. When he attempted once again to persuade Pompey to think of peace he was rebuffed in the strongest terms, and his warnings against any decisive engagement with Caesar were also lukewarmly received, and eventually ignored. He was, besides, offered no position of responsibility, and he saw no opportunity to accomplish anything worthy of his rank and record. He remained a figure out of place and he gave vent to his disgruntlement by exercising his sardonic wit on everyone and everything around him, a practice that did nothing to improve his standing with his colleagues.[95]

Domestic worries added to his despondency. He lacked detailed knowledge of his financial affairs and by now totally distrusted his chief manager, Terentia's freedman Philotimus. He also had continuing suspicions that Terentia was cheating him. The result was that he feared he might be insolvent and that his credit would be damaged.[96] His most pressing worry was to find the money to pay the second installment of Tullia's dowry, which was coming due in July 48. The matter was complicated by the fact that by early 48 it was clear the marriage would not last much longer, and the question therefore arose whether a divorce should take place before payment of a large sum that it might be difficult

94. *Fam.* 7.3.2. Cf. *Fam.* 4.7.2. *Att.* 11.1.2; 11.2.3; 11.3.3; 11.6.2, 6; 11.13.4. Cf. *Fam.* 5.20.9.

95. Plutarch, *Cic.* 38. *Phil.* 2.37–39. *Fam.* 7.3.2. *Att.* 11.4. Cicero continued to believe Caesar's forces were superior, a view also held by Caelius. See *Fam.* 8.17.2.

96. *Att.* 11.1; 11.2. For his earlier suspicions of Philotimus, see *Att.* 6.4.3; 6.5.1–2, and n. 7 above.

to recover later. Cicero was prepared to leave the decision to Atticus and Tullia, but he was full of regret that he had not made better provision for his daughter, and worries about her added greatly to his misery.[97]

By early January 48 Caesar had managed to move seven legions across the Adriatic, and he took up position north of Apollonia on the southern bank of the river Apsus. Pompey established his camp on the other side. At the end of March, Antony succeeded in landing a further four legions at Lissus north of Dyrrachium, and Pompey failed to prevent Caesar linking forces with him. New positions were then established, with Caesar just south of Dyrrachium and Pompey south of him at Petra. Caesar attempted to surround him with a line of fortifications, but suffered a serious reverse in an attack by Pompey that forced him to retreat to Apollonia. From there he moved to Thessaly followed by Pompey, who was buoyed by his success and eager to finish his opponent. The decisive confrontation took place at Pharsalus on August 9. Pompey's army was routed, and the main surviving force of about twenty four thousand men was forced to surrender. Pompey himself fled the battlefield when he saw defeat was inevitable, and eventually decided to seek help in Egypt, where he was murdered on his arrival.[98]

Cicero, who had fallen ill in June, had remained behind in Dyrrachium, where Cato commanded a garrison of eighteen cohorts and three hundred ships anchored at Corcyra. When news of the defeat at Pharsalus arrived, Cato asked Cicero to take command as the senior surviving consular. But Cicero was totally opposed to continuing the war and he declined the command, determined to return to Italy. His decision almost cost him his life at the hands of Pompey's elder son, from whom he had to be rescued by Cato. He then left the camp and went to Patrae, and from there sailed to Italy, arriving in Brundisium about the middle of October.[99]

---

97. *Att.* 11.2.2; 11.3.1; 11.4a; 11.4.1. *Fam.* 14.6. Dolabella was notoriously unfaithful (*Att.* 11.23.3), but the divorce did not take place until late in 46. *Att.* 12.8.

98. Caesar, *BC* 3.6–104. Plutarch, *Pomp.* 64–79; *Caes.* 37–47. Appian, *BC* 2.49–85. Dio 41.44–42.4. Velleius 2.51–53. A good account of the military events of 48 is provided by J. Leach, *Pompey the Great* (London), 1978, 186–209. Cicero's response to Pompey's death was surprisingly unemotional. He wrote to Atticus (11.6.5): "Non possum eius casum non dolere: hominem enim integrum et castum et gravem cognovi:" The news was softened by the fact that he had anticipated it. He was also becoming inured to tragic developments.

99. Plutarch, *Cic.* 39; *Cat. min.* 55. *Att.* 11.5.4.

His decision to end his involvement in the war was taken without hesitation or reservation. He believed he had met the demands of honor and duty in a war he had disapproved from the start as unlikely to be won by the republicans and certain, whoever won, to do serious harm to the state. To prolong such a war once all hope of victory had gone he considered an insane compounding of earlier republican misjudgments that could only bring further useless deaths of citizens and a crueler outcome to the war with greater resultant damage to the Republic. The attitudes he had found in Pompey's camp were a further deterrent to continuing any association with the republicans, as was the prospect of increasing dependence by them on barbarian kings and auxiliaries, an expedient Cicero found degrading and impossible to stomach. He was left with two choices: to go into exile or to return to Italy to make his peace with Caesar. He chose the latter, influenced heavily by personal considerations, but also by the hope that he might have some influence in moving Caesar to use his victory well and that there might persist some semblance of a Republic, however impaired and enfeebled.[100]

But Caesar's decision to follow Pompey to Egypt and his long entanglement, lasting until June 47, in Egyptian affairs, upset all Cicero's calculations.[101] The republicans got an unexpected respite, enabling them to gather ten legions in Africa, which were reinforced by four legions and fifteen thousand cavalry supplied by Juba, king of Numidia. Disturbances in Rome precipitated by Dolabella's radical proposals as tribune to abolish debts, unrest in Spain and threats of mutiny among the legions in Italy, and a general swing of Italian public opinion against the Caesarians brightened republican prospects further and made an invasion of Italy a distinct possibility in the first half of 47. A long war was now in prospect, and its result was no longer a foregone conclusion.[102]

These developments brought Cicero another period of intense anxiety and depression that lasted until Caesar's return to Italy in September 47. He immediately regretted that he had not gone to some quiet retreat and stayed out of Italy, where he found himself in a position both humiliating

100. *Att.* 11.6.2; 11.7.3. *Fam.* 4.7.2; 4.9.3; 7.3.3; 9.5.2; 15.15.1–3. For his aversion to the idea of using barbarian auxiliaries to fight Roman citizens, see *Att.* 11.6.2; 11.7.3. *Fam.* 7.7.3; 9.6.3.

101. *Att.* 11.16.2. *Fam.* 15.15.2.

102. Plutarch, *Cat. min.* 55–57. Appian, *BC* 2.87. *Bell.Afr.*1. Dio 42.29. *Att.* 11.10.2; 11.11.1; 11.12.3; 11.15.1; 11.18.1; 11.25.3.

and precarious. He was initially threatened with disbarment from the country by Antony, acting on an order from Caesar that all republicans should be barred from Italy except those whose cases he had himself reviewed. Antony relented when Cicero pleaded that he had returned on word from Dolabella that Caesar wished him to do so, and he issued an edict exempting Cicero and another prominent Pompeian, D. Laelius, from Caesar's order. Cicero was embarrassed by the public nature of the concession, which brought him unwanted attention and which he felt tied him to Italy and foreclosed his option of retiring to a quiet haven abroad.[103]

The concession also did little to relieve his anxieties about his safety. He hoped for little from Antony and was so distrustful of the Caesarians generally that he did not dare move from Brundisium for fear of attack. Worst of all, he received no indication of a pardon from Caesar and was afraid the latter's mind was being turned against him by his enemies among the Caesarians.[104]

The rise in the fortunes of the republicans greatly increased his concern for his safety and his general depression about his situation. He believed that other *boni* who had abandoned the republican cause after Pharsalus but had not returned to Italy would now flock to Africa or at least stay uncommitted in some free location. He had no such options, no means to blunt the anger of republicans against him; his desertion of their cause was conspicuous, and certain to bring him retribution from them if they invaded Italy or eventually won the war. He found it a painful irony that his safety now required him to wish for the defeat of the cause he had always wanted to triumph. At his most depressed, he saw himself uniquely afflicted and dishonored, an outcast from both camps, made to fear both sides, the only one who had blundered into such a hopeless predicament.[105]

His domestic woes continued to grow, compounding his misery. He had quarreled with Quintus at Patrae for reasons nowhere specified, but it

103. *Att.* 11.6.2; 11.7.2–4; 11.9.1.
104. *Att.* 11.6.2; 11.7.5; 11.8.1; 11.9.1; 11.14.2; 11.16.3; 11.17a.2; 11.18.2. He might have left Brundisium and safely traveled to Rome, if he had been willing to dismiss his lictors. But he refused to do so, perhaps still clinging to the hope of a triumph, perhaps simply wishing to preserve as much *dignitas* as possible. Cf. *Att.* 11.6.2–3; 11.7.1. There is no reason to believe Cicero was compelled to remain in Brundisium by order of Caesar or his deputies. See Wistrand, *Imperator*, 167ff.
105. *Att.* 11.7.3; 11.12.3; 11.13.1; 11.14.1; 11.15.1–2; 11.16.2; 11.24.1.

was a bitter break, which Quintus exacerbated by abusing his brother to all and sundry and by sending his son to Caesar to insure the blame for the decision to join Pompey rested on Cicero.[106] Tullia's marital problems were still unresolved, and she was also being plagued by ill-health. She joined Cicero at Brundisium in June, but her evident unhappiness made her presence more a burden than a comfort. Her divorce from Dolabella had been postponed and the second installment of the dowry had been paid in the middle of 48 to avoid a rupture with a powerful Caesarian in the uncertain political situation then prevailing. Dolabella's notorious womanizing had continued, and he had further outraged and embarrassed Cicero by the radicalism of his tribunate. But he remained influential and Cicero remained persuaded throughout 47, despite occasional wavering in moments of anger and frustration, that he must swallow his pride in this, as in so many things, and postpone the divorce still further.[107]

But it was Tullia's financial circumstances and fears for her future financial security that troubled him most of all. She had an income from certain properties that Cicero had settled on her, but it was inadequate to meet her expenses and she was apparently receiving no support from Dolabella at this time. Cicero blamed himself for her predicament and, to his great frustration, found himself utterly unable to help. The second installment of the dowry had used up all the ready cash he could lay his hands on, and he was himself in dire straits for money after his return to Italy. He got Atticus to help him provide for Tullia's immediate needs, but was unable to find a more permanent solution to her problems. He attempted to raise funds by the sale of property, but soon discovered that the general political uncertainty and fears of confiscations made it impossible to sell fixed assets and difficult to sell anything.[108] Nor was any help forthcoming from Terentia. She was intent on safeguarding her own resources, and her dealings with him in 47 left Cicero more convinced than ever of her avaricious nature and of her readiness to cheat him at every opportunity. He also suspected that a will she had recently made

106. *Att.* 11.5.4; 11.6.7; 11.7.7; 11.8.2; 11.9.2; 11.10.1; 11.11.2; 11.12.1–3; 11.13.2; 11.15.2; 11.16.4–5; 11.21.1; 11.22.1; 11.23.2. For a good, if speculative, analysis of the quarrel, see Shackleton Bailey, *Cicero*, 179–85.

107. *Att.* 11.3.1; 11.6.4; 11.12.4; 11.14.2; 11.15.3; 11.17.1; 11.23.3; 11.24.1; 11.25.3. *Fam.* 14.9; 14.13.

108. *Att.* 11.2.2; 11.4.1; 11.7.6; 11.17.1; 11.17a.1; 11.23.3; 11.24.2; 11.25.3. *Fam.* 14.6; 14.11; 14.15.

did not make adequate provision for the children, adding to his anxiety about Tullia's future. As he looked ahead and considered the likelihood of wholesale destruction and confiscation of property after the war, his only hope was that he could hide away moveable assets such as plate, draperies, or furniture as some protection for Tullia against total impoverishment.[109]

Cicero's general anxiety about his own and his family's future was allayed somewhat when he got news on July 8 that a friendly letter from Caesar was being brought to him by Philotimus. The letter arrived on August 12 and not only restored Cicero to his usual position in the state but recognized his status as *imperator* and proconsul.[110] Cicero was naturally relieved, but his rejoicing was tempered by continuing fears of a republican victory and what that would entail for him, and by doubts about the reliability of Caesar's pledges and his own capacity to coexist with a regime that he detested. But Caesar's letter did at least spell an end to the hated sojourn at Brundisium. Cicero thought of leaving immediately, but when it became clear that Caesar would soon be returning from Greece to Italy he decided to stay on to greet him. Caesar landed at Tarentum near the end of September, and Cicero went to meet him as he traveled north toward Brundisium. Caesar greeted him warmly and walked alone with him for a considerable distance. The meeting marked the beginning of another complicated stage in Cicero's variable relationship with Caesar.[111]

Life Without Liberty

Caesar's stay in Italy was brief. The African situation called for quick action and, after settling the most pressing problems at Rome relating to debt, unrest among his veterans, and the magistrates for 47 and 46, he left the capital for Africa in early December.[112] A full-scale encounter with

109. *Att*.11.16.5; 11.21.1; 11.22.2; 11.23.1; 11.24.2–3; 11.25.3. Terentia had made some form of contribution to Tullia in the middle of 58 (*Fam.* 14.6), but Cicero clearly did not believe that she would continue providing support. Cf. *Att.* 11.24.3. See S. Dixon, *Antichthon* 18 (1984), 88ff.; *The Roman Mother* (London, 1988), 55ff.

110. *Att.* 11.23.2. *Fam.* 14.23; 14.24. *Lig.* 7. *Deiot.*38. See Wistrand, *Imperator*, 193ff.

111. *Att.* 11.20.1.; 11.21.3; 11.22.2. Plutarch, *Cic.* 39.

112. *Off.* 2.84. Dio 42.51–55; 43.1. Suetonius, *Jul.* 38, 70. Plutarch, *Caes.* 51. Appian, *BC* 2.93–94. The problem of debt was particularly acute, aggravated by the war, which had created a general shortage of money and disrupted all financial transactions

the republican forces took place at Thapsus in April 46 and resulted in a decisive victory for Caesar. Utica, the last significant republican stronghold, where Cato commanded, surrendered soon afterwards. Cato committed suicide rather than place himself at Caesar's mercy, a characteristic decision that helped establish him as a great republican martyr and powerful symbol of republican ideals.[113]

Caesar was back in Rome by the end of July. He was showered with honors and new powers by the Senate. He was voted a forty-day thanksgiving and seventy-two lictors to accompany him in the celebration of his triumphs. He was to give the signal at the games in the Circus. His name was to be inscribed on the Capitoline Temple in place of that of Catulus, and inside the Temple a triumphal chariot and his statue mounted on the globe were to be erected with an inscription describing him as a demigod. He was to have the office of dictator for ten years and of *praefectus morum* for three, together with the right to designate all magistrates and to sit with the consuls in the Senate and to give his opinion first.

Caesar combined his acceptance of these honors and powers, which confirmed his autocratic position, with a determined bid to reconcile opponents, promoting former Pompeians to important positions and giving pardons even to such diehard enemies as M. Marcellus, the consul of 51.[114] He also immediately began the task of rebuilding and reforming,

---

(*Att.* 7.18.4; 9.9.4; 10.11.2; 11.24.2). Many of Caesar's supporters had expected he would favor a cancellation of debts. But during a brief stay in Rome in December 49 following the Spanish campaign he had made clear that he had no intention of despoiling the wealthier classes, when he issued an edict as dictator that gave only modest relief to debtors, allowing interest payments made to be deducted from the principal up to a quarter of its value (Caes. *BC* 3.1. Suetonius, *Jul.* 42. Dio 41.37. Appian *BC* 2.48). The problem remained and continued to stir unrest, and early in 48 Caelius Rufus, who was now praetor and thoroughly disillusioned with the Caesarians, took up the issue and proposed cancelling debts and remitting one year's rent. Disturbances led to his suspension from office and to passage of the *consultum ultimum*. Caelius then attempted to organize a revolt in Italy where he was joined by Milo, but the uprising was quickly suppressed and both Caelius and Milo were killed (*Fam.* 8.17. Caesar, *BC* 3.20–22. Dio 42.22–25. Velleius 2.68). The issue had surfaced again in 47 when the tribune Dolabella once more proposed cancellation of debts and remission of rents. Disturbances again led to passage of the *consultum ultimum* and Antony brought troops into the Forum to quell agitators in a bloody operation that left 800 citizens dead (Dio 42.32–33. Livy, *Per.* 113. Plutarch, *Ant.* 9. Cf. *Att.* 11.23.2). Caesar on his return sought to defuse the unrest by imposing a rent reduction for the current year, but once again he refused to make any radical concessions to the debtors. Cf. Suetonius, *Jul.* 38. Dio 42.33.

113. Dio 43.7–10. Plutarch, *Cat. min.* 58–72. *Bell.Afr.* 80.88. Cf. *Att.* 12.4.2.

114. Dio 43.14–15. The most notable Pompeians promoted were Marcus Brutus, who

assembling a wide-ranging program of political and social legislation. His most immediate need, as in the case of so many successful commanders before him, was to provide for his veterans. He did not intend, however, to settle them, as had Sulla, in closed colonies, but to distribute them in many parts of Italy on public or specially purchased land. Overseas colonies also formed part of the settlement plan. It seems certain there were some confiscations to help supply the needed land, but the overall evidence indicates Caesar was careful in this, as in other respects, not to alienate the well-to-do by any extensive assault on private property. He began the process of settlement immediately, but it proved lengthy, and was still in progress at the time of his death.[115]

On other fronts he banned all *collegia,* source of so much political turmoil in the past. He simplified the jury system by restricting its members to senators and *equites.* He increased the penalties for major crimes. He limited the tenure of provincial governors to one year for propraetors and two years for proconsuls.

In the social and economic area he tightened the administration of the corn dole, reducing the number of recipients from 320,000 to 150,000. To make this easier to achieve he planned to settle large numbers of the Roman proletariat in citizen colonies overseas. On the other hand, he sought to increase the more productive and skilled elements of the population of Rome and Italy by offering citizenship to doctors and teachers from abroad and by restricting the length of time citizens between the ages of twenty and forty, who were resident in Italy, could spend out of the country. He was also concerned to increase the birthrate, chiefly, one must assume, among the more productive classes, and he offered rewards to those with large families. To reduce the danger of slave revolts, and presumably also to increase employment for poorer citizens, he prescribed that at least one-third of the herdsmen on every estate must be freemen. A sumptuary law sought to curb the extravagance of the wealthy, a vain aspiration of many statesmen of the first century B.C. Finally, his most enduring reform, undertaken in his capacity as *pontifex*

---

was appointed to govern Cisalpine Gaul, and C. Cassius, who was appointed a *legatus* (Fam. 6.6.10). For Marcellus, see *Fam.* 4.4.3–4; 4.8; 4.9; 6.6.10. *Marc.* passim.

115. Dio 42.55. Suetonius, *Jul.* 38. Appian, *BC* 2.94. The evidence for Caesar's settlement of his veterans is scanty and unsatisfactory, and there is no definite evidence that he enacted any agrarian law in this period. See Yavetz, *Caesar and His Public Image,* 137–43, Brunt, *Italian Manpower,* 319–26. Gelzer, *Caesar,* 283–84.

maximus, was his introduction, as from January 1, 45, of a solar year of 365 days, with the intercalation of an extra day every four years. The transition was achieved by the insertion of sixty-seven days between November and December in 46. Overall, it was a miscellaneous program that addressed particular problems while skirting the crucial constitutional issues. It revealed no pronounced revolutionary or ideological purpose, directed more by practicality and the political needs and realities of the day. No radically new social or economic order was being signaled.[116]

Caesar's plans were interrupted toward the end of 46 by a new crisis in Spain, where Pompey's sons had managed to assemble an army of thirteen legions. In November he left Rome once more for the final reckoning with the Pompeians. In March 45, at the battle of Munda, the civil war came at last to a close in a fiercely fought encounter that broke the strength of the Pompeians and brought the death of their most talented leader, Labienus. Soon afterwards, Pompey's oldest son was killed in flight.[117]

More honors and powers for Caesar followed the victory. A thanksgiving of fifty days was decreed. The title of *liberator* was added to that of *imperator,* and the latter was now made a hereditary name. He was given the right to wear triumphal garb on public occasions and a laurel wreath at all times. His statue was to be carried with those of the gods in the procession to the Circus, and statues of him were also to be placed in the Temple of Quirinus and on the Capitol among those of the kings of Rome and Lucius Brutus. A ten-year consulship was added to the ten-year dictatorship.[118]

Caesar, who returned to the capital in early October, continued his efforts to establish harmony and goodwill by offering pardons and full restoration of rights to all his opponents, but the naked despotism that was emerging with the steady accumulation of his honors and powers was building a resentment among the aristocracy that no clemency or gener-

---

116. Dio 43.21, 25–26. Suetonius, *Jul.* 40, 42. Plutarch, *Caes.* 59. See Yavetz, *Caesar and His Public Image,* 58–184. Caesar also had major plans for urban development and for road building and drainage schemes in Italy. *Att.* 13.20.1. Pliny, *NH* 4.10. Suetonius, *Jul.* 44.

117. Dio 43.28–40. *Bell. Hisp.* passim. Plutarch, *Caes.* 56. Suetonius, *Jul.* 35. Appian, *BC* 2.103.

118. Dio 43.42–45. Suetonius, *Jul.* 45. Appian, *BC* 2.106. Cf. *Att.* 13.44.1. *Deiot.* 33.

osity could ever appease.[119] Moreover, Caesar's handling of power and his general behavior often added further provocation. His dealings with the Senate and senators gave particular offense. He framed laws and senatorial decrees often with perfunctory consultation of the Senate or with no consultation at all. He was strangely tactless in his general relations with senators, showing scant regard for their *dignitas* and making little effort to disguise the primacy of his position and the absoluteness of his authority.[120] He also gradually expanded the Senate until its numbers eventually reached nine hundred, a development offensive to the old nobility, who were further outraged by the inclusion among the new members of many *indigni,* including centurions, sons of freedmen, and even a number of Gauls.[121]

Caesar's handling of elections also brought him unpopularity. He had rejected the right given him to designate all magistrates, but in practice he fully controlled the electoral process and used his authority with a certain arbitrariness. In 45 he held the consulship without a colleague until his return from Spain, when he abdicated to make way for two leading adherents, Fabius Maximus and C. Trebonius. Such appointment of *consules suffecti* was resented, but worse was to follow. When Fabius died suddenly on the last day of December, Caesar had another of his henchmen, C. Caninius, elevated to the consulship for the remaining hours of the year.[122] The electoral system was further undermined in 44

119. Caesar spent time on his estate at Labici, southeast of Rome, in September (Suetonius, *Jul.*83) before entering Rome in early October (Velleius 2.56.3). Cf. Dio 43.50. Suetonius, *Jul.*75. Appian, *BC* 2.107.

120. *Fam.* 9.15.4. *Att.* 14.1.2; 14.2.3. *Fam.* 6.14.2. Plutarch, *Caes.* 60. Dio 43.27; 44.8. Suetonius, *Jul.* 77–78.

121. Dio 43.47. Suetonius, *Jul.* 72,76,80. Cf. *Fam.* 6.18.1. *Div.* 2. 23. *Phil.* 11.12; 13.27. Gellius, *NA* 15.4.3. Syme, *Roman Revolution,* 78–96. Caesar's relations with the Senate had always been acrimonious, and had worsened during the civil war. *Att.* 10.4.9. He would have caused further offense by a plan to demolish the Curia, rebuilt by Faustus Sulla, and to replace it with a Curia Julia (Dio 44.5). Caesar's purpose in expanding the Senate was not simply to pack it with low-born henchmen slavishly loyal to himself. The bulk of the new appointees came from the propertied classes of Italy and would provide a more broadly based ruling class likely both to provide more talent and to curb the control of the old conservative *nobilitas.*

122. Dio 43.46–47. Suetonius, *Jul.* 41, 80. *Fam.* 7.30. *Att.* 12.8. *Phil.* 2.80. There is some evidence that Caesar was authorized by a *Lex Antonia* in late 45 (proposed by the tribune L. Antonius, brother of Mark Antony) to nominate with binding effect half the candidates in all elections except the counsulship, but this is doubted by Yavetz (*Caesar and His Public Image,* 130ff.).

when Caesar was authorized, in association with his command of a new military expedition against Parthia, to select, before his planned departure on March 18, the magistrates for the following two years, the expected duration of his absence.[123]

Signs of an unrelenting drift toward a total and lasting despotism increased in late 45 and early 44. Ever more extravagant honors were heaped on Caesar by a totally subservient Senate. He was given the title *pater patriae* and his birthday was declared a public holiday. His statues were to be placed in all the temples of Rome and on the Rostra in the Forum. Quintilis, the month of his birth, was renamed Julius. He was awarded the *sacrosanctitas* enjoyed by tribunes and a gilded chair, golden wreath, and the all-purple garb of the ancient Roman kings. His dictatorship and prefecture of morals were made perpetual. An oath to protect his life was introduced for all senators.[124] Other decrees came close to declaring him a god and affording him divine worship. His statue in the procession to the Circus was to have a *pulvinar* like other deities; he was to have a temple in association with Clementia, and Antony was appointed as his *flamen*. He may also have been accorded the title of Divus Julius.[125]

A series of incidents in early 44 gave further grounds for suspicions that he was moving the state toward kingship. In January, as he returned to the city from the Latin Festival, he was greeted with the title *rex* by some of those who met him. Soon afterwards his statue on the Rostra was crowned with a diadem. When two tribunes ordered its removal, he took offense and ended up insisting they be deposed from office and expelled from the Senate. At the feast of the Lupercalia on February 15 he appeared on the Rostra wearing for the first time the full ceremonial garb of

123. Dio 43.51. *Att.*14.6.2. Appian, *BC* 2.128, 138. Suetonius, *Jul.* 76. Cicero's statement that Caesar's appointments were for two years in advance must be taken to mean the arrangements did not extend beyond 42. Other actions of Caesar likely to stir resentment were his expansion of the number of praetors to sixteen and of quaestors to 40, and his appointment of governors without casting lots (Dio 43.47, 49). He gave further offense to many in the latter half of 46 when Cleopatra appeared in Rome and he lodged her in his gardens across the Tiber, and set up a statue of her in the Temple of Venus Genetrix. *Att.* 14.8.1; 15.15.2. Dio 43.27; 51.22. Appian, *BC* 2.102.

124. Dio 44.4–5. Suetonius, *Jul.* 76. Appian, *BC* 2.106. For the oath, see Taylor, *Party Politics,*174–75. P. Herman, "Der römische Kaisereid," *Hypomnemata* 20 (1986), 66–78.

125. Dio 44.6. *Phil.* 2.110–11. See L. R. Taylor, *The Divinity of the Roman Emperor* (Middletown, Conn., 1931), 58–71. A. S. Weinstock, *Divus Julius* (Oxford, 1971).

the kings. When the Luperci arrived in the Forum, their leader Antony went up to Caesar and placed a diadem on his head. Caesar refused the diadem and had an entry made in the Fasti to record publicly his rejection of royalty, but by now many of his leading associates as well as inveterate republicans were convinced he was intent, if not on a grandiose monarchy, at least on a permanent dictatorship. The notion remained abhorrent to great numbers of politicians of all factions, and a conspiracy to assassinate him, before his departure for Parthia, was formed, led by two of his prominent protégés, M. Brutus and C. Cassius. The deed was done on March 15 at a meeting of the Senate in the hall of Pompey's theater. A new era of civil upheaval and uncertainty had opened.[126]

Cicero had no involvement in the conspiracy, and very little in any aspect of public affairs during Caesar's autocracy. The years under Caesar were the least active politically of his entire career. He had returned to Rome from Brundisium clear in his mind that, if Caesar restored some form of republic, he would participate in it. If not, he would stand aloof from public life, a virtual exile in his own country, but at least able to enjoy his family and possessions.[127]

He found little to encourage him on his arrival in Rome. All was misery in the city. The Forum was silent, and all his talents, now at their zenith, had been rendered redundant. Many of his friends, both personal

126. Appian, *BC* 2.108. Suetonius, *Jul.* 79. Dio 44.9–11. Plutarch, *Caes.* 61. *Phil.* 2.85–87; 3.12; 5.38; 13.17, 31, 41. *Div.* 1.119. Val. Max. 1.6.13. According to Dio (43.43), Caesar also began to wear high red shoes associated with the Alban kings. The controversy surrounding Caesar's plans for the government of Rome continues and can never be fully resolved. There are useful discussions in Meyer, *Caesars Monarchie*, 460ff. E. Rawson, "Caesar's Heritage: Hellenistic Kings and Their Roman Equals," *JRS* 65 (1975), 148–59. Syme, *Roman Revolution*, 53ff.; *JRS* 1944, 99ff. A. Alföldi, *Studien über Caesar's Monarchie* (Lund, 1953). Weinstock, *Divus Julius* (Oxford, 1971). J. H. Collins, "Caesar and the Corruption of Power," *Historia* 4 (1955), 445–65. The main theories are examined in detail by Yavetz, *Caesar and His Public Image*, 14–57. The evidence is clouded by the fact that wild gossip and malicious rumors appear to have been rife in the period immediately preceding his assassination, e.g., Suetonius, *Jul.* 52, 79.3. Dio 44.7.3. For the plot itself, see N. Horsfall, "The Ides of March: Some New Problems," *Greece and Rome* 21 (1974), 191–99. J. Hubaux, "La mort de Jules César," *L'académie royale de Belgique* 13 (1957), 76–87. H. Strasburger, *Caesar im Urteil seiner Zeitgenossen* (Darmstadt, 1968), passim.

127. *Fam.* 7.3.3–4. Cf. *Fam.* 4.7.4; 4.8.2; 9.2.5. Cicero most likely spent a considerable period at his Tusculan villa before proceeding to Rome (*Fam.* 14.20). He also finally dismissed his lictors, satisfied, it would seem to resign his *imperium* once he had met with Caesar and received from him the respect due to a proconsul. *Lig.* 7.

and political, were dead or in exile. Other friends he found alienated, and he continued to suffer resentment from republicans generally because of his stance in the war. The conflict looming in Africa offered no hope of better things. The Pompeians were as extreme as the Caesarians, and certain to take vengeance on himself, if they emerged victorious. On no grounds was there a likelihood of a return to an acceptable form of republic.[128]

Domestic troubles added to his woes. His marriage, under severe strains in recent years, finally collapsed. His longstanding suspicions that Terentia and her agents were defrauding him had caused growing estrangement, and Terentia's generally unsympathetic attitude during his stay in Brundisium and, above all, her niggardly treatment of Tullia had greatly intensified his disaffection. On his return he found his worst fears confirmed and, probably early in 46, he divorced Terentia after more than thirty years of marriage.[129]

Faced with a variety of unhappy circumstances, Cicero quickly took refuge in his studies. He was resolved, unless some unexpected opportunity arose to help build a republic, to take no part in public life, and to devote himself instead, in the manner of the most learned men of old, to serving the state through writing and study, especially in the areas of law and ethics. Cicero was beginning to turn his mind to philosophy by early 46, and it seems likely that it was about this time that he began to conceive a plan to produce a comprehensive body of philosophical writing in Latin.[130] The main impetus for the enterprise undoubtedly came

128. *Brut.* 6–8. *Fam.* 5.21.1; 7.3.6; 9.1.1; 9.2.2, 4; 9.5.2; 9.6.3. Cf. *Off.* 2.2. *Fam.* 4.13.2; 7.33.1.

129. *Fam.* 4.14.3. Cf. *Att.* 12.11. Schmidt, *Briefwechsel,* 268. Cicero speaks of plots and treachery, but may be using colorful language to describe Terentia's financial machinations. Shackleton Bailey (*Cicero,* 201ff.) believes Cicero's accusations may refer to more sinister behavior on Terentia's part.

130. *Fam.* 5.21.2; 7.3.4; 9.1.2; 9.2.5; 9.3.2; 9.6.4–5. *Att.* 12.3.1. His intention to investigate and write about philosophical subjects is explicitly stated in *Fam.* 9.2.5, which dates from April 46, and the depth of his interest in philosophy in 46 is strongly evident in *Fam.* 9.6.4–5; 4.3.4, and 4.4.4. In the last two passages he tells Sulpicius he has turned to philosophy because there is no longer any scope for the exercise of oratory and he states that his passion for the subject becomes daily more intense, partly because of his advancing age, but also because there is nothing else that can relieve the distress the evils around him cause. *Fam.* 11.27.5 indicates Cicero was contemplating and being urged to write philosophy even before Caesar's return from Africa in mid-46.

from his need to fill the vacuum created by the lack of an acceptable role in public affairs.[131] Close contact in this period with the highly learned M. Varro, who was in political circumstances similar to Cicero's own, also whetted his appetite for philosophical study.[132]

But he had other reasons as well for turning to the writing of philosophy, which he later spelled out himself in the introductions to individual works. He strongly believed in the value of philosophy as a moral teacher and means to a richer, happier life, but saw it as a neglected subject in Roman education, part of the reason being that it could not be studied in Latin. There were philosophical Latin writings, but they dealt mainly with Epicureanism, and Cicero dismissed them as of no account, because they were so badly written that they commanded few readers and deserved even fewer. He was convinced, however, that if philosophy were presented in Latin in an eloquent style, it would be widely read, even by those who were expert in Greek. He felt, besides, that it would be a glorious achievement to end Roman dependence on the Greeks for philosophical literature and to snatch from the declining Greek world the fame in matters of philosophy it had so long exclusively commanded.[133]

Cicero was therefore seeking to make philosophy more accessible and more attractive to Romans and to bring honor to himself and to the state by a Latin contribution to philosophic discussion that would challenge the predominance of the Greeks. He considered himself uniquely well equipped to achieve these ends, because, as in the case of his political works, he could bring to the writing of philosophy a high level of expertise and a great range of literary skills. He repeatedly emphasized the breadth of his experience in the subject. He had eagerly pursued it from his earliest youth, and even during the busiest periods of his political life he had continued to study it and had cultivated the closest friendships with leading philosophers, including Diodotus, Philo, Antiochus, and Posidonius. He had, besides, applied it in his daily affairs, using it as

131. See references in preceding note; also *Fam.* 6.12.5; 9.26.1. *Acad.* 1.11. *Tusc.* 2.1; 5. 5. *ND* 1.7. *Div.* 2.6–7. *Off.* 2.2; 3.4.

132. *Fam.* 9.1–7. Cicero also give credit to Brutus (*Tusc.* 5.121. Cf.*Brut.*11) and to C. Matius (Fam.11.27.5). Brutus was himself involved in writing philosophy and had produced at least one ethical treatise, *De virtute* (*Tusc.*5.1. *Brut.*11). See G. L. Hendrickson, *AJP* 60 (1939), 401–13;

133. *Acad.*1.10–11; 2.6. *Fin.* 1.2–10. *Tusc.* 1.1–6; 2.5–6; 3.6; 4.6; 5.5. *Div.* 2.1–5. *Sen.*2. *Off.* 1.1, 4; 2.5–6; 3.5. *ND* 1.7–8.

inspiration for his oratory and as a guide for both his public and private life.[134]

He did not claim, however, a leading place among philosophers, as he did among orators, nor was he seeking to explore new ideas or forms of argument. His aim was more modest: to reproduce in Latin, in a distinguished and vivid style, the main tenets of the schools of Greek philosophy. In regard to content, therefore, he was claiming no great originality, though he was careful to emphasize that he was not merely translating the Greek sources but arranging and interpreting the material according to his own judgment.

But in regard to style he was claiming a great deal more—unsurpassed skills in language that could make philosophy intelligible and enjoyable.[135] The form he favored, as in his earlier political and rhetorical works, was the dialogue, with the interlocutors presenting their views in a continuous argument in the manner of the dialogues of Aristotle. In developing discussion of a topic he tended to follow the practice of arguing on both sides of the subject, the technique associated with the New Academy, to which he professed allegiance. Each exposition of a particular point of view was followed by the objections that could be lodged against it, often with no attempt being made to arrive at definitive conclusions. The method fitted well with Cicero's broad purpose of providing a comprehensive treatment of all the doctrines of all the schools.[136] Only in the *De officiis,* dealing with practical ethics, his last

134. *Acad.* 1.11. *Fin.* 1.6, 16. *Tusc.* 1.6; 5.5. *ND* 1.6–7. *Brut.* 306–09, 315. *Off.* 2.4. *Fam.* 4.4.4; 13.1.2.

135. *Off.* 1.2,6. *Fin.* 1.6–7. The comprehensive scope of the project is indicated in *Fin.* 1.12; *ND.* 1.9. *Div.* 2.4. In *Att.* 12.52.3 Cicero made an allusion to some writings of his, saying: ''ἀπόγραφα sunt, minore labore fiunt; verba tantum adfero, quibus abundo.'' The statement is often taken to mean Cicero saw his philosophical writings as mere transcriptions, casually composed, supplying words for the ideas of others. Such a conclusion runs counter to the extensive evidence for Cicero's intense interest in philosophy in this period and for the importance he attached to his philosophical writings. Moreover, the passage on which it is based has textual difficulties that make it impossible to determine to what writings Cicero is referring. The passage has little value as an indicator of Cicero's perception of his philosophical works.

136. For Cicero's philosophical writings and their character, see A. E. Douglas, ''Cicero the Philosopher,'' in *Cicero,* ed. T. A. Dorey (London, 1964), 135–70. W. Süss, *Cicero: Eine Einführung in seine philosophischen Schriften* (Wiesbaden, 1966). H. A. K. Hunt, *The Humanism of Cicero* (Melbourne, 1954). M. L. Clarke, *The Roman Mind* (London, 1956). O Gigon, ''Cicero und Die griechische Philosophie,'' *ANRW* 1.4 (1973),

and perhaps greatest philosophical work, completed in late 44, did he fully abandon both the dialogue form and the sceptical method, and set forth in dogmatic fashion his views about right and wrong conduct. There were clear reasons for the change. This was the area of philosophy about which he had the strongest personal views. It was also the area where he felt the Romans had nothing to learn from the Greeks and where he tried hardest to make an original contribution.[137]

Cicero's plans for the writing of philosophy appear to have evolved gradually. His other great and, to him, complementary literary interest, oratory, continued to occupy him as well, and initially took precedence in 46.[138] Much of his creative energy in the first year after his return was devoted to the production of two additional major works on oratory, the *Brutus* and the *Orator*. The former was a history of Roman oratory, presented as a conversation between Cicero himself and Brutus and Atticus. The internal evidence indicates it was written in late 47 and early 46.[139] Cicero believed that oratory at Rome had a remarkable history, rising to heights that rivaled the greatest achievements of the Greeks. He also believed that he himself represented the pinnacle of Roman oratorical prowess.[140] It is easy therefore to understand his desire to relate a story of Roman success in which he saw himself as a key figure. He had a further motivation in that a lively controversy concerning oratorical styles had recently arisen in Rome with implications for his own reputation. A number of younger orators, including a highly talented speaker, C. Licinius Calvus, had started a movement to promote the frugal, elegantly simple style associated with Lysias. They styled themselves At-

---

226–61.

137. *Tusc.* 1.1. Though the *De officiis* was based on a work of the Stoic Panaetius, Cicero declared that he intended to use his source to the extent and in the manner that suited his purpose (*Off.*1.6), and he blends in his own experiences and a host of Roman *exempla* to produce a highly personal treatment.

138. Cicero did produce one minor philosophical work in early 46, the *Pardoxa Stoicorum*. The date is fixed by the fact that Cato, mentioned in the introduction, was still alive. The work was a light-hearted exercise, more concerned with rhetoric than philosophy, to show how abstruse Stoical doctrines could be made intelligible and acceptable by the skills of rhetoric. Cicero may also have been continuing his work on the *De legibus*. See *Fam.* 9.2.5.

139. There appears to be a clear reference to it in the prologue to the *Paradoxa*, indicating it was already written. For a full discussion, see Douglas, *Brutus* (Oxford, 1966), ix–x.

140. *De or.* 1.14–15. *Tusc.* 1.5. *Brut.*6. For his estimate of his own achievement in oratory, see *Off.* 1.2. *Tusc.* 1.3. *Brut.* 317–24.

ticists and vigorously attacked the more copiose and elaborate mode of oratory for which Cicero was especially famous and which they pejoratively labeled Asianist. The *Brutus* contains a robust response, and is laced with polemical barbs directed at the naiveté and ignorance of the so-called *Attici*.[141]

The *Orator*, which took the form of a letter to Brutus and was completed by about September 46, contained a further and more specific response to the views of the *Attici*. But its purpose, as in the case of the *Brutus*, went far beyond polemic or self-justification. It was an exhaustive discussion of styles, a work, as he states himself, on which he had concentrated all his critical powers with respect to speech in an attempt to define the ideal form of oratory. It was an important sequel to the *De oratore* on the aspect of rhetorical theory that he believed mattered most.[142]

In the midst of all these literary activities Cicero remained ready, if there was any movement toward the restoration of the Republic, to resume an active part in public life. His expectations had been low, however, from the start and they changed little as the year 46 progressed. He considered the Republic shattered almost beyond repair. Everything was changed utterly. Even the courts were not functioning. Caesar's power was absolute, the power of the sword, and he was predictably using it to control and shape events according to his own wishes. The forms of republican government had become a sham, with decrees of the Senate being forged at Caesar's whim without any involvement by those

---

141. Quintilian, *Inst.* 12.10.10–15. *Fam.* 15.21.4. *Tusc.* 2.3. *Brut.* 51,67 ff., 280–85, 325–30. The importance of the Atticist movement can be exaggerated. See Douglas, *CQ* 5 (1955), 241–47. It is doubtful that Cicero was seeking to make a political statement or had any special political aim in the Brutus. He never suggests that any of his theoretical writings of this period had any such purpose, and he was being especially careful to avoid giving any political offense in 46. He never disguised, of course, nor does he in the *Brutus*, his grief at the lack of a true republic and his desire to see a stable republic restored.

142. *Att.*12.6a.1. *Fam.* 6.18.4; 12.17.2; 15.20.1. Cicero also produced about the same time a preface to a planned translation of speeches of Demosthenes and Aeschines. It was entitled *De optimo genere oratorum* and dealt again with the best form of oratory, with polemical allusions to the *Attici*. The *De partitione oratoria*, a technical summary of the precepts of rhetoric, presented as a question-and-answer session between himself and his son, may also date from this period. Cicero may have been encouraged to write extensively on oratory by the fact that, around the middle of 46, he began to conduct a kind of school of rhetoric for some of his younger friends among the Caesarians. *Fam.* 9.18.1–3.

whose names appeared as draftees and supporters. Cicero could see no political role for himself in such circumstances. He had been pushed from the stern of the ship of state and had scarcely been left a place in the bilge.[143]

He continued therefore to participate in public life to the least possible extent. He felt he should stay in the city while Caesar was there to avoid giving offense, and he did attend the Senate, but he decided that his presence should be purely passive and that he would take no part in the debates.[144] He did finally break this resolution, but in special circumstances, when Caesar, in a dramatic meeting of the Senate in September, agreed to a plea by the entire body of senators for the recall of his archenemy, M. Marcellus, the consul of 51. When Cicero, who was deeply moved by Caesar's generosity and saw the proceedings as the first piece of state business conducted with dignity since the outbreak of the civil war, was asked for his opinion, he responded with an emotional speech extolling Caesar's clemency. He also built in an urgent appeal for a broad program of reconstruction to heal the ravages of the civil war and restore a peaceful *respublica*.

The speech was a spontaneous and flattering tribute to Caesar on an occasion when Cicero considered he had acted with extraordinary magnanimity. Beyond that, it had no special significance. In its references to Caesar's task of reconstruction, it spoke in generalities about repairing damage and reestablishing the *respublica* and stabilizing the city. These were predictable platitudes, not a blueprint for the future government of Rome. They made no attempt to address the specific problems present in 46 or the specific remedies needed to resolve them.[145]

Nor did the speech herald any significant shift in Cicero's posture or expectations. In reporting the event to Servius Sulpicius, he made clear he intended to continue to keep his distance from politics and to concentrate on his studies. It was not long afterwards that he made some of his bitterest complaints against Caesar to his friend Papirius Paetus and

143. *Fam.* 4.3.4; 4.4.2; 4.9.2; 4.13.2–3; 6.22.1; 7.28.3; 9.15.3–4; 9.16.3; 9.17.1; 9.20.3. That the courts were not functioning is clear from *Fam.* 9.18.1. Cf. *Marc.* 23. *Brut.* 6.
144. His consuming interest remained his studies. *Fam.* 4.3.4; 4.4.4; 7.28.2; 7.33.2. 9.20.3; 9.26.1, 4.
145. *Fam.* 4.4.3–4. *Marc.* 1, 23, 27, 29. Cicero did attempt to write Caesar a detailed letter of advice in 45, but he found it a most difficult task, and it never got beyond Caesar's *familiares*.

declared his intention of getting out of Rome the moment Caesar left for Spain.[146]

But, though he was intent on remaining as detached as possible from political affairs, he was equally determined not to give any grounds for offense to Caesar or his associates. He was ready to accept the inevitable, consoled by the recollection of his achievements and by the knowledge that he had foreseen the outcome of the civil war and had done his best to avert a resort to arms. Old doctrines of compromise and of accommodation to circumstances that could not be changed, mooted in less extreme circumstances in the fifties, reappeared. He argued it was folly to oppose or antagonize *potentes*. Refusal to obey necessity was more a mark of *superbia* than of *magnitudo animi*. The philosophers of old had shown it was possible to live with dignity under a tyrant, accepting without approving, keeping silent when freedom of speech was denied. He was resolved to follow their example.[147]

On the one occasion in 46 when he was drawn into a politically sensitive situation, he handled it with supreme tact. In October, the Pompeian Q. Ligarius was charged in his absence with treason. The trial took place before Caesar in the Forum. Cicero had no choice but to appear on behalf of a friend and a Pompeian, whose recall he had already been actively seeking. Caesar was not sympathetic to Ligarius, but Cicero delivered a speech of such measured deference and gracious eloquence that he was moved to tears and to a verdict of acquittal.[148]

Only in one matter did he risk offending Caesar and his partisans in 46, when he reluctantly undertook, on the urging of Brutus and Atticus, to write a eulogy of Cato. He considered it a problem for an Archimedes to

---

146. *Fam.* 4.4.; 9.15.4–5. Cf. *Fam.* 9.26.1, from about October, where he describes his condition as *servitus*. He also reports about the same time that his attendance in the Senate is infrequent (*Fam.* 13.77.1). He does write in optimistic terms in this period to Servilius Isauricus and Q. Cornificius (*Fam.* 13.68; 12.17), but both were Caesarians, and Cicero was likely to speak of Caesar to them in the most positive terms possible. Another letter from the same time (*Fam.* 6.10.4), to a Pompeian exile Trebianus, is also optimistic, and does suggest Cicero may have briefly felt that Caesar's exceptional clemency betokened a broader moderation. In any event, any such feeling was short-lived.

147. *Fam.* 4.3.1; 4.9.2,4; 4.14.2; 5.21.2; 6.4.4; 7.3.2–4; 9.6.2; 9.16.3, 5–6.

148. *Fam.* 6.13; 6.14. *Att.* 13.19.2; 13.20.2–4. The speech, quickly published and widely circulated, delighted Caesar's friends, but did not please republicans.

find a way of doing justice to Cato without enraging the Caesarians. In the end he was pleased with what he produced, and the indications are he put the chief emphasis on Cato's exceptional *virtus* and celebrated *gravitas* and *constantia* rather than on his political policies and actions. Caesar commended the style, and seemingly took no offense at the content. He did, however, write a rejoinder in 45, as did Hirtius, but both works, while seeking to defame Cato and discredit the image portrayed by Cicero, were generous in praise of Cicero himself.[149]

Cicero was prepared to extend his policy of accommodation to personal friendship with the Caesarians. He had a long association with several of Caesar's intimates, such as L. Cornelius Balbus, whom he had defended in 56, the *eques* C. Oppius, Balbus's close collaborator, and another old client, C. Curtius Postumus.[150] He had been on close terms since his youth with another of Caesar's adherents, C. Matius, with whom he shared many intellectual interests.[151] But his friendships with Caesarians strengthened and widened considerably in 46. Caesar's younger associates were drawn to him because of their interest in oratory, most notably A. Hirtius, praetor in 46 and a notorious bon vivant with varied literary interests. Dolabella, who remained married to Tullia until late 46, also had literary leanings and kept on excellent terms with his father-in-law in this period. Both he and Hirtius were frequent visitors to Cicero's home in 46, and by mid-year Cicero had begun to give regular declamations for their instruction. Cicero found the new activity not only enjoyable but a means, in the absence of any opportunity for pleading in the courts, of preserving his skills and his physical fitness. His pupils reciprocated, especially Hirtius, by entertaining him regularly and elaborately. He found himself involved in a busy social round; he was a popular and respected figure with more callers at the *salutatio* than ever,

149. *Att.* 12.4.2; 12.5.2; 12.40.1; 12.41.4; 12.44.1; 12.45.2; 13.46.2. *Fam.* 6.7.4. *Topica* 94. *Orator* 35. Cicero returned Caesar's compliments by praising his *Anti-Cato* (*Att.* 13.50.1; 13.51.1). Brutus also wrote a *Cato* (*Att.* 12.21.1; 13.46.2), as did Fabius Gallus (*Fam.* 7.24.2). For other references to the literature in praise or blame of Cato, see Suetonius, *Jul.* 56. Plutarch, *Cic.* 39; *Caes.* 3; *Cat. min.* 11, 36, 52. H. Drexler, "Parerga Caesariana," *Hermes* 70 (1935), 203–34.

150. For his continuing association with these longtime friends, see *Fam.* 6.8.1; 6.12.2; 9.6.2; 9.17.1; 9.19.1. Curtius Postumus has been identified with reasonable certainty with C. Rabirius Postumus, defended by Cicero in 54. See H. Dessau, *Hermes* 46 (1911), 613–20.

151. *Fam.* 7.15.2; 11.27; 11.28.

Caesarians prominent among them as well as *boni*. It is clear he took considerable pleasure in his favored position among Caesar's friends, which he defended as sensible protection for his interests, but also as a means of helping Pompeian exiles and of exercising a generally beneficial influence on Caesar's regime.[152]

With Caesar himself he was also on friendly terms in 46. This was due in part to a strong wish on both sides for good relations, but also to the fact that Cicero found much to admire in Caesar's overall behavior. He was deeply affected by Caesar's generous treatment of his enemies, culminating in his pardon of Marcellus. It was a magnanimous departure from the normal pattern of events following victory in civil war that he believed would not have been matched by the Pompeians, had they been victorious. Caesar was showing qualities of justice and responsibility that surprised and impressed Cicero. It would seem he was also pleased with much of Caesar's legislation, though he does not discuss it in detail. But he does acknowledge that Caesar could claim among his civilian achievements that he had enacted many outstanding laws, and many of them dealt with issues that Cicero himself had urged Caesar to confront in the *Pro Marcello*.[153]

It is also noteworthy that Cicero at this stage took a highly tolerant view of Caesar's political behavior and did not blame him for the condition of political affairs. He had always predicted that autocracy would follow a civil war between potentates. It was in the nature of things that those who won power by the sword would use it as they saw fit. The Pompeians would have behaved no differently. He also felt that Caesar was not a free agent, but was compelled to respond to the wishes of his partisans and the demands of circumstances. He was experiencing his own brand of bondage, facing an uncertain future and uncertain how to deal with it. Cicero was prepared to give him time to work toward some settled form of law-based political order.[154]

152. *Att.* 12.2.2. *Fam.* 4.13.6; 6.6.13; 6.12.2; 6.13.2; 6.14.3; 7.28.2; 7.33.1–2; 9.6.2. 9.16.2, 4, 7; 9.18.1–3; 9.20.2; 9.26. Another of his literary protégés was C. Cassius Longinus (*Fam.* 7.33.2). He was also very friendly at this time with C. Vibius Pansa, recently appointed to govern Cisalpine Gaul. *Fam.* 6.12.2; 15.17.1.

153. *Fam.* 4.13.2; 6.6.5, 8; 6.10.2–5; 6.13.2–3; 9.16.3; 12.17.1. *Phil.* 1.18; 2.109. Cf. *Marc.* 23.

154. *Fam.* 4.4.2,5; 4.9.2; 7.28.3; 9.6.2–3; 9.17.2; 12.18.2. Cicero's tolerant attitude toward Caesar can also be seen in the fact that he accepted without fuss his son's decision to go to Spain with Caesar. *Att.* 12.7.1.

Cicero's posture of resigned detachment from public affairs, combined with a conciliatory and friendly relationship with Caesar and his associates, continued through most of 46. There are occasional glimpses in the letters, however, of an abhorrence of the notion of an absolute ruler that could not be repressed by philosophic calm or friendships or social diversions. He had fought all his life to preserve the greatest bulwark of liberty, the supremacy of law, the one impersonal master acceptable to a free people. It was now gone and he sharply felt the consequences, the fundamental indignity of subservience to the will of another and the despairing feeling of facing a future that held no guarantees and was as capricious as the whim of the man in power.

He was also unable, despite his plunge into his various literary projects, to fill the void created by the lack of any meaningful political involvement. The adjustment needed was too vast. He was wedded to the political life by his talents, inclinations, and long practice, and by the fame and influence he had earned in it and longed to retain. His restless energy could find no other fully satisfying outlet. He felt he had outlived his success, to his great unhappiness.[155]

His restiveness and dejection at the state of public affairs increased markedly in late 46 and early 45. The mood of detachment and tolerance gradually faded and was replaced by feelings of vexation and resentment. The dependence on Caesar's will and the requirement to play courtier soon proved repugnant. There was no *dignitas* left, no opportunity to speak one's views or seek their implementation. It was *servitus,* and humiliating to endure it.[156]

The war in Spain made matters worse. Caesar's absence brought the suspension of any semblance of normal government. Only tribunes and plebeian aediles were elected for 45 before Caesar's departure, and when Lepidus, the consul of 46 and *magister equitum,* finally held consular elections, it was only to have Caesar made consul for 45 without a colleague. Public business, as Cicero saw it, was mainly in the hands of

155. *Fam.* 4.6.2; 4.13.2–3; 5.16.4; 7.28.3; 9.16.3; 9.20.3. *Brut.* 7–9. *Att.* 12.21.5. Some of the evidence comes from letters to exiles in which Cicero tended to exaggerate the miseries of life at Rome, but his difficulties in coping with life under Caesar were undoubtedly genuine.

156. *Fam.* 4.14.1; 9.15.3–4; 9.26.1; 15.18.1. In *Fam.* 6.14.2 from late 46 Cicero tells Ligarius of the annoyance and humiliation he had to endure in trying to get to see Caesar. Cf. *Att.* 14.1.2; 14.2.3.

Caesar's intimates, Balbus and Oppius. [157] The war itself brought another period of anxious uncertainty. The outcome was very much in doubt, but, in Cicero's opinion, certain, whoever won, to worsen further the pitiable condition of the state. A victory for Pompey's son, which Cicero especially dreaded, would bring wholesale slaughter, a victory for Caesar a still more entrenched autocracy. [158]

Cicero's growing despondency about political affairs was overshadowed in early 45 by an overwhelming personal tragedy. Tullia, who gave birth to a son in January, died about a month later at the Tusculan villa. [159] Cicero was inconsolable. After a period of grieving at Atticus's house in Rome, he fled on March 6 to the solitude of his retreat at Astura, on the coast of Latium, south of Antium. He worked hard to contain his grief and to cope with his memories of a daughter to whom he had always been exceptionally attached and on whom he had come to depend heavily for comfort and companionship. He found little peace, however, in the early months and sought distraction by total immersion in writing, with little pause day or night. He began composing a *Consolatio* to himself and by mid-March was working on his first major ethical composition, the *De finibus boni et mali*. He also had his first version of his work on epistemology, the *Academica,* in hand. [160]

He sought further comfort in the idea of a commemorative shrine, which, he says, he found recommended in some of the authors he was reading. It was an extravagant notion, seeking the apotheosis of Tullia in a consecrated temple, but he became obsessed with it in the months following her death, and saw it as a an almost sacred duty, a statement and glorification of her worth that he felt he owed her. He kept pressing a reluctant Atticus to help him find a suitable site, preferably a suburban

157. Suetonius, *Jul.* 76. Dio 43.28, 48. Eight *praefecti urbi* were appointed to do the work of the praetors and urban quaestors. For the power of Balbus and Oppius, see *Fam.*6.8.1; 6.18.1. Certain actions of Caesar, such as his handling of the elections and appointment of *indigni* to the Senate, were beginning to evoke caustic comments from Cicero. Caesar's period of grace was coming to an end. *Fam.* 6.18.1. *Att.* 12.8.

158. *Fam.* 6.1.6; 6.3.3; 6.4.1. Cf. *Fam.* 15.19.4.

159. Tullia had been recently divorced from Dolabella. *Fam.* 6.18.5. See Schmidt, *Briefwechsel,* 276ff.

160. *Att.* 12.13–21. Cicero had earlier written the *Hortensius,* a protreptic dialogue that argued the value of the study of philosophy. Cf. *Div.* 2.1. Augustine, *Conf.* 3.4.7; 8.7.17. According to Pliny the Elder (*Nat. hist.* 31.6) Cicero wrote the *Academica* at Puteoli. If so, it must have been written in the autumn of 46, the *Hortensius* even earlier. The *Academica* was clearly not finished, however, until May 45. *Att.* 12.44.4.

property that might contain the shrine and also serve as a residence for Cicero's old age. The idea fades from the correspondence around mid-year, as his grief diminished, and it never materialized.[161]

Cicero moved from Astura at the end of March and spent April at Atticus's farm near Ficulea. He then returned to Astura and stayed until mid-May, when he had sufficiently mastered his grief to go back to Tusculum, where Tullia had died. His writing, which he found an effective distraction, continued at a frenetic pace. The first version of the *Academica* was completed by May 13. The first book of the *De finibus* was being copied in Rome by the end of the month. In June the *Academica* was recast into four books, a grander work but more concise. The *Tusculan Disputations,* a series of rhetorical discussions setting forth in a popular form stoical doctrines relating to control of the passions and to the sufficiency of virtue for happiness, followed, and by August the first of the theological works, *De natura deorum,* was under way. He was also engaged on a number of smaller projects around mid-year, a letter of advice to Caesar, a dialogue that he calls "A Political Conference in the Manner of Dicaearchus," and a *laudatio* of Cato's sister.[162]

Cicero revealed again his emotional temperament in his response to the death of Tullia. His prolonged mourning in seclusion was unseemly by Roman standards of self-discipline and decorum, and he was heavily criticized for it, even by his friends. But, as he himself responded, in a spirited defense of his handling of calamity, he had not surrendered to grief and he had not been paralyzed by it. Instead it had acted as a spur to his creative energies, and he had fully exploited his mood and solitude to produce the voluminous writings of 45, much of which might otherwise never have emerged.[163]

Tullia's death left Cicero generally dispirited, but with a particular distaste for any form of political involvement. Atticus pressed him to return to Rome and to the Forum, but he no longer felt able to cope with

161. *Att.* 12.12.1; 12.18.1. 12.19.1; 12.20.2; 12.21.2; 12.22.3; 12.23.3; 12.25; 12.29.2; 12.31.2; 12.35; 12.36.1; 12.37.2; 12.37a; 12.38a.2; 12.41.4; 12.42.1; 12.43.3; 12.47; 12.52.2; 13.1.2; 13.29.2. Shackleton Bailey (*Ad.Att.* 5.404–13) has discussed the matter of the shrine in great detail.

162. *Att.* 12. 35–13.38. *Att.* 12.44.3 records completion of the first version of the *Academica* in two books. For *De finibus,* see *Att.* 13.32.3; *De natura deorum, Att.* 13.38.1; 13.39.2; letter of advice, *Att.* 12.81.2; "Political Conference," *Att.* 13.30.2; the *laudatio* for Cato's sister, *Att.* 13.37.3.

163. *Att.* 12.21.5; 12.28.2; 12.38a.1; 12.40.2. *Fam.* 5.15.1.

the conditions of political life under Caesar. Tullia had been his great comfort and source of encouragement. Now that she was gone he realized, and was at last prepared to admit, that his public life was at an end and had been for some time. There were no courts, no real Senate, all the *membra* of the *respublica* had been shattered or enfeebled. His friends were dead or had become aloof, and the Forum was full of men he detested. He had lost the fruits of his success, all his distinctions were gone, and when he should have been at the peak of his glory he felt ashamed even to be alive. He wanted to stay out of Rome where there was no joy for him in his home and where the times, the people, the ambiance of Forum and Senate House filled him with loathing. He was now feeling the full impact of the *mutatio omnium rerum* that Caesar's dictatorship represented.[164]

In May he was prevailed upon by Atticus to attempt one political undertaking, a letter of advice to Caesar. He found it well-nigh impossible to think of anything that would do credit to himself and would be acceptable to Caesar, but he finally completed a draft that he sent to Atticus, who passed it for comment to Balbus and Oppius. They criticized it liberally and wanted so many changes that Cicero, considerably chagrined, abandoned the effort, convinced he could be successful neither in speaking his mind nor in pleasing Caesar. There are only fleeting references to the letter's content, but it would appear that in one part of it Cicero, while applauding Caesar's planned expedition against Parthia, urged him, no doubt in the manner of the *Pro Marcello,* first to restore tranquillity and stability to the city by a permanent constitutional settlement. Cicero, and no doubt many others, badly wanted an end to the uncertainty and to the improvisations in government that had marked the preceding years. He longed for some form of *status reipublicae;* if it could not be *bonus,* it could at least be *certus.*[165]

Cicero was bruised by the failure of his letter of advice. It brought home to him the impossibility of an acceptable association with a man of

---

164. *Att.* 12.21.5; 12.23.1; 12.28.2. *Fam.* 4.6.2; 5.13.3; 5.15.2–4. Cicero's attitude was certainly colored by his general despondency, but provides a graphic illustration of what Caesar's dictatorship meant to the conservative *nobilitas.* Cf. similarly dispirited sentiments from Servius Sulpicius Rufus in *Fam.* 4.5.2–3.

165. *Att.* 12.51.2; 12.52.2; 13.26.2; 13.27.1; 13.28.2; 13.31.3. For Cicero's concern to see a definite political settlement, see *Fam.* 6.21.2; 9.8.2. For a surviving example of a letter of advice to Caesar from this period, see Sallust's *First Letter* to Caesar.

Caesar's power. He could not tolerate the indignity of the dissembling and flattery inherent in the counseling of an autocrat. He preferred to remain at least half-free, which could only be achieved by silence and seclusion.

The events of the remainder of 45 dashed any remaining hope he had of a satisfactory political settlement and convinced him that Caesar, his dominance further reinforced by the victory in Spain, had no interest in the political reconstruction advocated in the *Pro Marcello* and in the letter of advice, and was intent on *regnum* in the sense of absolute power that would be exercised without the constraint of law at the discretion of the holder. Cicero was particularly dismayed by the honors showered on Caesar after Munda, especially by the association of the dictator with the gods, and the carrying of Caesar's statue in the procession to the Circus for the Ludi Victoriae at the end of July so affronted him that he abandoned a new letter to Caesar that he had undertaken to write at the insistence of Brutus. He saw such efforts to establish Caesar as more than mortal as a particularly sinister sign of the intemperateness and *superbia* that he associated with absolute monarchs. Amid such happenings he scoffed at the credulity of Brutus, who expressed the belief that Caesar, whom he visited in late July, was a *bonus civis*. Cicero considered *rex* a more apt description, and the word appears in the correspondence in reference to Caesar in late August.[166]

Further disappointments and provocations followed during the last months of 45. Caesar, though he reached northern Italy in July, repeatedly postponed his return to Rome and, in the end, did not enter the city until the beginning of October. The delay belied the earlier declared interest in political reform and was a further blow to Cicero's hopes for a permanent constitutional settlement. There followed a series of events that continually added to Cicero's outrage: extravagant celebrations, elections to the consulship for the last few months of 45 of handpicked henchmen, preparations for the Parthian campaign that brought new violations of republican traditions with the designation of magistrates for several years ahead. The crowning affront came on the last day of 45, when Caninius was elected consul for the remaining hours of the year.[167]

166. *Att.* 13.27.1; 13.28.3; 13.31.3; 13.37.2; 13.40.1; 13.44.1. Caesar's statue in the Temple of Quirinus also evoked scathing comment. *Att.* 12.45.2; 12.48.1; 13.28.3. For his attitude to such honors, see *Phil.* 1.13; 2.111.

167. For Caesar's postponements of his return, see *Att.* 13.21a.3; 13.45.1; 13.46.1. Suetonius, *Jul.* 83. Velleius 2.56.3. For his interest in a political settlement, see *Att.* 13.7;

Cicero fumed, but kept to his policy of silent detachment. He maintained his friendship with the younger Caesarians, and they continued to seek his company and to treat him with the greatest deference.[168] He attended the Senate when requested and did nothing to give offense. He resisted continuing pressure from Atticus and Brutus to compose something in Caesar's honor, but he did write to the dictator in August praising his *Anti-Cato*. The praise clearly related to matters of style, and Cicero insisted to Atticus that it was genuinely meant. The only other contact recorded was a visit by Caesar to Cicero's villa at Puteoli in December. Cicero found the occasion intimidating, but in the end it proved a reasonably enjoyable encounter full of talk of matters philological. Significantly, there was no discussion of politics. On that level a chasm had opened that both realized could not be bridged.[169]

Cicero was, in general, discontented and unhappy in this period. He had, to some extent, come to terms with Tullia's death, but there was little in either his private or public circumstances to give him any joy in life. He had tried marriage once more at the end of 46, but it lasted only a short time. His new wife, Publilia, was rich and well connected, but very young, and the relationship never blossomed. Cicero divorced her around the middle of 45.[170] His son Marcus, who never fully pleased him, he had sent to Athens in the spring of 45 to continue his education. He had never completely repaired the rupture with Quintus, and there is no evidence of any closeness or of much contact between them at this time. The young Quintus continued to worry both his father and uncle. Impetuous and erratic, he ended up having to join Caesar's Parthian expedition in the hope of finding funds to pay his debts.[171] The only

---

13.31.3. Cicero describes some of Caesar's proposed celebrations as *regia* (*Fam.* 6.19.2). For his feelings about the appointment of magistrates, see *Fam.* 7.30.1–2. *Att.* 14.6.2; 14.9.2. Near the end of 45 Cicero defended Deiotarus, king of Galatia, who was accused of plotting Caesar's death during the latter's visit to his kingdom in 45. The trial was held in Caesar's house, another circumstance that brought home to Cicero the changed order of things. He made clear his discomfiture at pleading under such conditions. The speech also reveals that many considered Caesar a tyrant at this point and that there was open resentment of his position. *Deiot.* 5–6, 33.

168. *Fam.* 7.24.1. *Att.* 13.49.
169. *Att.* 13.42.3; 13.47a.1; 13.50.1; 13.51.1; 13.52.
170. *Fam.* 4.14.3. *Att.* 12.32.1; 13.34; 13.47a.2. Quintilian, *Inst.* 6.3.75. Plutarch, *Cic.* 42. Dio 46.18.3.
171. For Marcus, see *Att.* 12.32.2; 13.1.1. For the young Quintus, see *Att.* 12.5.1; 12.38.2; 13.9.1; 13.42.1.

bright spot in Cicero's domestic affairs in 45 was a large legacy he inherited from a rich businessman named Cluvius, but on the whole his private circumstances provided no compensation for the collapse of his public life. His one consolation remained his studies, and he clung to them, continuing his scheme to treat in Latin all the major subjects of philosophy.[172]

Few letters survive from the early months of 44, but subsequent references make clear that Cicero's attitudes and reactions changed little from those of the previous year. Caesar's evident wish for ever greater dominance and the new divine-like honors voted in 44 further fueled his resentment and confirmed his worst fears of Caesar's intentions. Rome was in the grip of a tyranny; Caesar was a king and liberty was dead. Cicero was not stirred, however, to any action. His policy of passive acceptance prevailed. But when the assassination happened, he acclaimed it as a heroic act, the just killing of a vile and hated tyrant.[173] There was a venom in his reaction that showed the depth of his political discontent in 44 and his utter abomination of the despotism Caesar had created. Now there was a hope again of a return to a free republic, and it was a joyful prospect.

172. *Att.* 13.45. 2–3; 13.46.3; 14.10.3. Following completion of the *De natura deorum*, Cicero had begun work on the *De divinatione*, the first book of which was largely written before Caesar's death. He also wrote the *Cato maior* in late 45 or early 44. *Div.* 2.3–4.

173. *Phil.* 2.85–87, 110–11, 116; 5.49. *Fam.* 6.15; 11.27.8; 12.1.1. *Att.* 14.4.2; 14.6.2; 14.9.2; 14.13.2.

7: THE LAST STAND FOR REPUBLICANISM

The conspirators do not appear to have taken any precautions to insure a peaceful return to republican government following Caesar's death. Mark Antony, Caesar's colleague in the consulship in 44, was left free to react as he saw fit. M. Lepidus, the *magister equitum*, who commanded the only troops in the neighborhood of Rome, was similarly left out of the conspirators' calculations. It can only be concluded they had assumed the deed would be generally welcomed not only by the aristocracy but by the mass of the people, foreclosing any danger of a hostile response from Caesar's friends.[1]

The Rise of Antony

The conspirators had gravely miscalculated, as they quickly learned. When Brutus and Cassius held a *contio* in the Forum on the afternoon of the 15th to extol their actions and rally support, they were greeted with

1. Appian, *BC* 2.119–20. The period after Caesar's death has been extensively studied. See T. Rice Holmes, *The Architect of the Roman Empire*, vol. 1 (Oxford, 1928). Syme, *Roman Revolution*, 97–186. H. Frisch, *Cicero's Fight for the Republic*, trans. N. Halslund (Copenhagen, 1946). Yavetz, *Caesar and His Public Image*, 190–213. E. G. Huzar, *Mark Antony* (Minneapolis, 1978). H. Bengston, *Marcus Antonius: Triumvir und Herrscher des Orients* (Munich, 1977). A. Alföldi, *Caesar in 44 v. Chr.*, vol. 1 (Bonn, 1985).

cold silence. They then attempted to persuade Cicero at a meeting on the Capitol on the same day to approach Antony and seek his cooperation. But Cicero responded that Antony would agree to anything, while he feared for his safety, and he argued instead that Brutus and Cassius as praetors should immediately summon the Senate to the Capitol, get approval for what had happened, and assume the leadership of the state. The conspirators, however, failed to grasp the need to consolidate their position immediately and persisted in their decision to negotiate with Antony. The latter meanwhile, on the night of March 15, got possession of all of Caesar's private funds and papers. The same night Lepidus brought his troops into the Forum. He was eager for vengeance, as was Balbus, but Hirtius argued for conciliation, and Antony sided with him. The consul summoned the Senate to meet on March 17 in the Temple of Tellus on the Esquiline, not far from his own home.[2]

On March 16 or 17 Brutus held another *contio,* this time on the Capitol. His speech was a model of elegance and a flawless example of the austere so-called Attic style, but, in Cicero's view, it had no fire or persuasive vehemence. It certainly had no impact, and the tide of public opinion continued to swing against the conspirators.[3]

Troops surrounded the Temple of Tellus on March 17, an ominous sight for supporters of the conspiracy. The conspirators themselves did not think it safe to leave the Capitol. Antony took a moderate line, however, urging unity and conciliation and proposing that Caesar's *acta,* many of which were already in effect, be ratified and that the conspirators be pardoned but not praised. It seemed a reasonable, if not entirely logical, compromise, and was passed without demurral. Cicero, who felt he had to attend the Senate, spoke in the debate, sounding the theme of amnesty and reconciliation. He would have preferred an outcome more favorable to the conspirators, but he considered that, on the whole, Antony had behaved responsibly and that the compromise agreed was the best achievable. At the same meeting, Dolabella, who had been desig-

2. Nicolaus of Damascus, friend of Augustus and Herod the Great, wrote a life of Augustus, of which excerpts survive. The work has tendentious features, but is a useful source for the period immediately after Caesar's death. See also Appian, *BC* 2.119–22, 125. Dio 44.21–22. Plutarch, *Brut.* 18. *Phil.* 2.89.

3. *Att.* 15.1a.2. Appian (*BC* 2.137) links the *contio* on the Capitol to the meeting of the Senate on March 17. Cf. Dio 44.34.

nated by Caesar to assume the consulship after his own departure for Parthia, was confirmed as Antony's colleague.[4]

The decisions of the Senate were announced to the people on the same day at a crowded *contio,* where they were enthusiastically received. The conspirators were invited to come down from the Capitol, and Antony and Lepidus sent them their sons as pledges of their safety. Brutus dined that evening with Lepidus, Cassius with Antony.[5] But the new spirit of harmony was quickly shattered in the following days when Caesar's will was opened and it was learned he had donated his suburban property for public use and had left each citizen three hundred sesterces. Opinion began to swing once more against the conspirators. Their position worsened dramatically following Caesar's public funeral, which the Senate had approved as part of the process of compromise and conciliation, and which most likely took place on March 20. Antony delivered the oration. Cicero later accused him of deliberately inflaming the people, and no doubt his *laudatio* had the elements of extravagance and *miseratio* characteristic of the genre. In any event, the occasion generated a wave of emotion and indignation that culminated in rioting and attacks on the homes of the conspirators. They could no longer safely appear in public, and before mid-April Brutus and Cassius quietly left the city for the friendlier environment of the towns of Italy.[6]

Antony's position was growing stronger, but he continued to move carefully and to maintain a policy of conciliation. Cicero found much to praise in his administration in the period after Caesar's funeral. He refers to many outstanding measures, which he leaves unspecified, but which included a proposal, enthusiastically passed by the Senate, to abolish totally from the constitution the office of dictator. Antony also took tough action in the first half of April against radicals seeking divine honors for

4. Appian, *BC* 2.126–36. Dio 44.22–33. Plutarch, *Brut.* 19; *Ant.* 14; *Cic.* 42. Velleius 2.58. *Phil.* 1.1, 31. *Att.* 14.14.2. *Fam.* 12.1.2.

5. *Phil.* 1.32 makes clear the *contio* was held on the same day as the meeting of the Senate, contrary to Appian, *BC* 2.142. Cf. Dio 44.34.

6. For Caesar's will, see Appian, *BC* 2.143. Dio 44.35. Plutarch, *Caes.* 68. Suetonius, *Jul.* 84. For the funeral oration, see Seutonius, *Jul.* 84. Appian, *BC* 2.143–46. Plutarch, *Ant.* 14. Dio 44.35–49. *Phil.* 2.91. *Att.* 14.10.1. G. Kennedy, "Antony's Speech at Caesar's Funeral," *QJS* 54 (1958), 99–108. Cicero's evidence leaves little doubt that Antony delivered an emotional address. Brutus and Cassius left Rome between April 10 and 15. *Att.* 14.6.1; 14.7.1.

Caesar and retribution from his assassins. He had a demagogue named Amatius, who claimed to be the grandson of Marius and who set up an altar for the worship of Caesar in the Forum, summarily executed, and he used troops to suppress other disturbances by Caesarian extremists. He also had amicable discussions with Brutus and Cassius in early April, and had a motion passed exempting Brutus from the law which prescribed that urban praetors should not be absent from the city for more than ten days. Before restoring Sex.Clodius, a henchman of Cicero's archenemy, P. Clodius, from exile in late April, he sought Cicero's consent. It seemed to many that the *respublica* had been restored.[7]

Antony's behavior became less moderate during the following months as he moved resolutely to fortify his position over the longer term. He began to take advantage of the Senate's blanket ratification of Caesar's *acta* to spread patronage where he could, with grants of citizenship, concessions to client kings, privileges for provincial communities, the recall of at least one exile. He took possession of a special fund of seven hundred million sesterces placed in the Temple of Ops by Caesar, possibly for use in the Parthian campaign.[8]

But, most ominous of all, he went to Campania at the end of April to oversee land distribution for Caesar's veterans, but also to rally them in support of himself and of Caesar's *acta*. When he returned to Rome in the latter half of May, he was accompanied by large numbers of veterans, and from that point onwards many republicans, including Cicero, considered the rule of force had returned to Rome and that they could not safely appear in the city.[9]

Antony's next move was to secure a provincial command that would give him control of a strong army and a stategically important part of the empire. He went directly to the people, and, in the first days of June, had a tribunician law enacted, which gave him, in place of his previously assigned province of Macedonia, the provinces of Gallia Cisalpina and Gallia Comata with four legions, the troops to come from the army stationed in Macedonia. His command was to extend for five years, a privilege also accorded to his colleague Dolabella, who had been allotted

7. *Phil.* 1. 2–5, 32; 2.31, 91–92, 115. *Att.* 14.6.1; 14.8.1; 14.13.6; 14.13a; 14.13b. Appian, *BC* 3.3.

8. *Att.* 14.10.1; 14.12.1; 14.14.2, 5. *Fam.* 12.1.1. *Phil.* 1.17, 24; 2.93–98, 100. Appian, *BC* 3.5. Dio 44.53. Plutarch, *Ant.* 15.

9. *Att.* 14.21.2; 14.22.2; 15.5.3; 15.11.1. *Phil.* 2.100–108.

the province of Syria. Two other laws enacted around the same time further increased Antony's control and capacity for patronage: a new agarian law to be administered by a board of seven headed by Antony's brother Lucius, and a bill authorizing the consuls to examine and pronounce upon Caesar's *acta*. Soon afterwards, on June 5, he sought to neutralize the conspirators by having the Senate assign Brutus and Cassius a special commission to oversee the grain supply in Asia and Sicily respectively.[10]

Antony seemed by early June to have built powerful defenses against enemies and rivals, and to be headed for an extended period of ascendancy. But he soon had to contend with an unexpected competitor in Caesar's grandnephew and adopted son and heir, C. Octavius, commonly known as Octavian after his adoption and assumption of the name C. Julius Caesar Octavianus. He was now nineteen years old, and had been studying at Apollonia while waiting to join the Parthian expedition when he heard of Caesar's death. He had crossed at once to Italy, but he was in no hurry to go to Rome and went first to visit his stepfather, L. Philippus, in Campania and to meet prominent Caesarians. He also met Cicero, who was staying at the time at his villa in Puteoli, next door to Philippus.[11]

Octavian arrived in Rome in early May and at once began to exploit his position as Caesar's adopted son to build popularity and influence. He declared his acceptance of the adoption and inheritance and pledged to pay the legacies. He asked Antony for the money he had taken from Caesar's house, and, when Antony disdainfully refused to return it, raised funds by any means he could and used them not only to pay Caesar's gifts to the people but to provide lavish games at the end of July in honor of Caesar's victories and of Venus Genetrix, the ancestress of the Julian *gens*. During the games he attempted to display, to the applause of people and veterans, Caesar's golden chair, which the Senate had voted should be carried into the theater along with those of the gods, but he was prevented by Antony. But his effort to promote Caesar as a god got a powerful boost when, in the course of the games, a comet appeared which the crowd accepted as Caesar's star and a sign of his

10. *Att.* 14.14.4; 15.11.4; 15.19.2; 16.16c.3; *Phil.* 2.109; 5.7–8, 20–21. Dio 45.9.
11. *Att.* 14.16.1; 14.10.3; 14.11.2; 14.12.2. Plutarch, *Ant.* 16. Appian, *BC* 3.9–12. Dio 45.1–4, Velleius 2.61. Seutonius, *Jul.* 83. See A. Alföldi, *Oktavians Aufstieg zur Macht* (Bonn, 1976).

divinity. Octavian reacted by setting up a statue of Caesar in the temple of Venus with a star above its head. Caesar's heir was fast emerging as a potent rival to Antony, threatening his primacy among Caesarian leaders.[12]

Antony appears to have responded to the threat by seeking a new rapprochement with the conspirators and with republican elements in the Senate. At a *contio* he spoke in terms that Cicero found sufficiently encouraging to make him reconsider his plans to go on a trip to Greece. Soon afterwards Brutus and Cassius issued a new edict, most likely in response to Antony's conciliatory speech, in which they offered to resign their offices in the interests of harmony and freedom. A *frequens senatus* was scheduled for August 1. Brutus and Cassius wrote to former consuls and praetors asking them to attend. There were high hopes that Antony was ready to make concessions that would bring agreement and make possible the return of the conspirators to Rome.

Caesar's veterans now took a hand. Alarmed by the dissension between Antony and Octavian and by its likely consequences for Caesarian interests, they demanded a reconciliation. The peacemaking took place at a formal, public ceremony on the Capitol. Antony was forced away from his flirtation with the republicans, and quickly revealed his change of heart in a public edict and in a private letter in which he abusively rejected the overtures Brutus and Cassius had made in their recent proclamation. The meeting of the Senate on August 1 proved anticlimactic. L. Calpurnius Piso, the consul of 58, made a speech favorable to the conspirators in which he proposed some form of compromise, but he found no support from his thoroughly cowed colleagues, and his proposal came to nothing.[13]

Antony had now firmly abandoned any thought of alliance with the republican and moderate elements in the Senate. His hopes of maintaining his dominance and of countering Octavian lay with the *plebs* and the soldiers, the great mainsprings of Caesar's power. He continued throughout August to woo these two constituencies, promulgating laws to add to juries a third panel comprised of centurions and to give the right of appeal to the people to those convicted of treason and political violence. He was

12. *Att.* 14.20.5; 15.2.3; 15.13.2. Nic. Dam. 28. Appian, *BC* 3.12–24, 28. Plutarch, *Ant.* 16. Cf. Dio 44.6; 45.5–7.

13. *Att.* 16.7.1. *Phil.* 1. 8–10. *Fam.* 11.3.1. Nic. Dam. 29. Appian, *BC* 3.29. Dio 45.8. Plutarch, *Ant.* 16.

also determined to show himself a loyal Caesarian, committed to honoring Caesar's memory, and he indicated his intention to propose in the Senate on September 1 a proposal to add a day in honor of Caesar to all festivals of thanksgiving to the gods. This proposal was to create the circumstances that drew Cicero back into politics and into a relentless, all-out conflict with Antony.[14]

The Birth of the Philippics

Cicero had stayed away from Rome from the beginning of April to the end of August. His initial jubilation at Caesar's murder had soon given way to feelings of helplessness and frustration. He had failed to persuade the conspirators on March 15 of the need to rally at once senatorial and public support and take precautions against any counterstroke by the Caesarians, and by Antony in particular. He had then felt compelled to approve the compromise of March 17, in order to appease the Caesarians and especially the veterans, but he accepted with great reluctance the ratification of Caesar's *acta,* which he saw as a continuation of one of the most hateful aspects of his tyranny. The funeral and the demonstrations that followed it had dashed any remaining hope he had that the Caesarians could be dislodged from power. The tyrant was gone but not the tyranny. The conspirators had failed to complete their task, and Cicero believed the opportunity to do so was now gone. By the beginning of April he felt he could do no good in Rome, and he left the city to be away from sights and happenings that he found were more than he could endure.[15]

His gloom and pessimism persisted throughout April, as he did the round of his country estates. He saw the Caesarians securely in control. Caesarian magistrates were in place and would be for at least two years to come. Caesar's minions controlled the armies, and the veterans were close by in Italy. He could see no developments favorable to republicanism in these circumstances.[16] He had always loathed and distrusted the rank and file of Caesar's followers, but he expected little better from those most prominent within Caesarian ranks in 44. Above

14. *Phil.* 1.13, 19–23; 5. 12–16; 13.3, 37.
15. *Att.* 14.4.2; 14.6.2; 14.9.2; 14.10.1; 14.14.2. *Fam.* 12.1–2. *Phil.* 1.1. Plutarch, *Cic.* 42. Dio 44.23–33. See D. W. Knight, "Cicero's Political Acumen after Caesar's Death," *Latomus* 27 (1968), 157–64.
16. *Att.* 14.5.2; 14.6.2; 14.9.2; 14.12.2.

all, he despised and distrusted Antony. There had never been any real friendship between them and many points of difference. Throughout his career Antony had been linked to men that Cicero hated or disapproved of politically. He had been an associate of Clodius in the early fifties, had served with Gabinius in Syria from 57 to 55, and afterwards with Caesar in Gaul. His behavior as tribune had aggravated tensions at the end of 50 and, in Cicero's opinion, contributed to the outbreak of war. The profligacy of his style of living and the flamboyance of his excesses were also deeply offensive to Cicero, representative of the most disturbing features of the moral decadence that he so often deplored in the younger generation of politicians. Personal animosity was added in 49, when Antony clumsily tried to force Cicero to stay neutral and remain in Italy. There was further friction in 48 after Cicero's arrival in Brundisium, when Antony initially sought to bar him from Italy. The gulf between them widened again, when Antony purchased Pompey's confiscated property, a battening on civil war, as Cicero saw it, that placed Antony among the most contemptible of the Caesarians. Cicero found his early behavior after Caesar's death more moderate than he had expected, and he felt the threat from him was lessened by his addiction to his pleasures, but as the weeks passed that opinion changed and he began to see him as a dangerous, determined aspirant to Caesar's throne.[17]

But Cicero's fears of the Caesarian side extended well beyond Antony. Even long-term friends of his own among the Caesarian leaders he viewed with suspicion and believed unlikely to support the republican cause. He was in close contact with many of them during April, notably Balbus, Pansa, and Hirtius. Balbus he found evasive and disingenuous, and he believed he was secretly eager for war and likely to support Antony. More surprising, he had no greater faith in Pansa, or in the easygoing bon vivant Hirtius, despite a continuing close association with them and assurance from them that they wanted peace and the welfare of the Republic.[18] Caesar's friends in general, even moderate men, like the

17. *Att.* 7.8.5; 10.10.1–5; 10.12.1; 10.13.1; 10.15.2–3; 10.16.5; 11.7.2; 12.18a. 1; 12.20.1. Cicero bitterly resented Antony's recall of Clodius's henchman Sextus Clodius. It almost made him wish Caesar were back. *Att.* 14.13.6; 14.13a; 14.13b; 15.4.3. The *Second Philippic* contains the most detailed account of Cicero's complaints against Antony, but it must be read as an invective and weighed against the more reliable evidence of the letters.

18. *Att.* 14.12.2; 14.19.2; 14.20.4; 14.21.2; 14.22.1; 15.1.2–3; 15.3.2; 15.5.2; 15.6.1–4; 15.8.1; 15.22. The addiction of Pansa and Hirtius to the good life further

equestrian C. Matius, who were not politically active, Cicero found full of anger and eager for vengeance. Moreover, he believed they were afraid of peace and convinced that only through another war and another purge of republicans could their safety and status be guaranteed and Caesar's *acta* safeguarded.[19]

A peaceful and stable revival of republicanism therefore seemed remote to Cicero in the weeks after Caesar's death. So did the chance of a republican victory, if it came to war. He found rejoicing in many quarters at Caesar's death, but the *boni,* as usual, were slow to stir themselves, and the republican cause was left with few active supporters or resources and with its leaders virtual prisoners in their homes. D. Brutus commanded an army of two legions as governor of Cisalpine Gaul and the rebel Sextus Pompey had assembled six legions in Spain, but, while Cicero put some faith especially in the forces of Decimus, he saw no chance of the republican side amassing a sufficient following to win in war.[20]

Any hope Cicero retained of a return to a *respublica* he pinned on Brutus, peacefully exercising his influence in Rome. Cicero had a sometimes uneasy relationship with Brutus, but his admiration for his character and ability is unquestionable, and as a statesman he placed him high above any of his peers. Son of M. Junius Brutus, the tribune of 83, who was later put to death by Pompey during the revolt of Lepidus in 77, and of Servilia, the stepsister of Cato and Caesar's lover, Brutus had a checkered political heritage, but the dominant influence in his life was undoubtedly Cato, whose republican ideals and stern brand of Stoicism he firmly embraced. Like his uncle, he sided with Pompey in 49, but after Pharsalus he decided to abandon the war. He was pardoned and favored by Caesar and governed Cisalpine Gaul in 46 before becoming praetor in 44. He remained a committed republican, however, and once he lost hope that Caesar would heed the wishes of the *boni* and restore a republic, he quickly turned against his benefactor and plotted his murder.[21]

---

undermined Cicero's confidence in them. *Att.* 16.1.4.

19. *Fam.* 11.27; 11.28. *Att.* 14.22.1.

20. For the apathy of the *boni,* see *Att.* 14.6.2; 14.14.2. For his view at this stage about the outcome of a civil war, see *Att.* 14.13.2; 14.20.3. A letter of Decimus Brutus probably written in late March (Shackleton Bailey, *Ad. Fam.* 2.464), indicates the military weakness of the republican side in the first months after Caesar's death.

21. *Att.* 14.20.3. See M. L. Clarke, *The Noblest Roman: Marcus Brutus and His*

Brutus was a prestigious, rising political figure in the late fifties and in the forties. He was well connected and highly talented, and known and respected for his integrity and independence of mind and strict adherence to principle. He had a stern but forceful personality, blunt and resolute. Caesar had said of him that it was a problem to know what he wanted, but whatever he wanted he really wanted. He also had broad intellectual interests and was a skilled orator, favoring a plain, direct elegance that suited his character.[22] Cicero, urged by Atticus, had begun to develop a friendship with him in the late fifties. Though he sometimes found his blunt directness and forbidding manner—which were vastly different from his own more volatile but good-humored and good-natured personality—difficult to take, he greatly admired his talent and moral qualities, and he considered him, as he did Cato, an outstanding example of Roman *virtus*. He also admired him for his learning and literary skills. Brutus, though he held widely differing views about style, felt similarly about Cicero's intellectual talents, a mutual appreciation that proved an important bond, reflected in the number of Cicero's works undertaken on Brutus's urging and dedicated to him. The assassination of Caesar raised Brutus to heroic stature in Cicero's eyes. He now looked to him as the one man who could complete the task, and his fondest wish was to see him in a leading position in a firmly established republic.[23]

It needs to be emphasized that Cicero did not aspire to a commanding role for himself in efforts to restore the Republic after Caesar's death. He considered himself too old for such a burden; it was a young man's task. He had had his time and had done his bit. His life under Caesar had led him to decide that he was content with his past achievements, and he had found that a measure of *otium* had many attractions for a man of his years and interests. He longed, of course, as he had since 63, for the position of a prestigious consular, shaping public policy and counseling those charged to implement it. But that was far different from grasping the helm in stormy political waters. He had no relish left for that, as he freely confessed to Atticus, and as his quick departure from Rome in early April

Reputation (London, 1981). E. Wistrand, *The Policy of Brutus the Tyrannicide* (Göteborg, 1981).

22. *Att.* 14.1.2. For Brutus's learning and oratory, see Quintilian, *Inst.* 10.1.123; 12.10.11. Tacitus, *Dial.* 21, 25. *Att.* 14.20.3; 15.1a.2.

23. *Att.* 6.1.3; 12.36.2; 13.4.2; 13.11.1; 13.23.1; 13.35–36. 13.38.1; 13.39.2; 14.15.2; 14.17a.5; 14.19.1; 14.20.3,5. Cf. *Orator* 34.

illustrated. Soon, as his pessimism deepened, he began thinking of getting out of Italy altogether and of visiting Marcus in Athens. His only concern was not to seem to be abandoning the state at a crucial time. Apart from that he was eager to be gone. There was no role that he was seeking; he had no strategy to save the Republic, and no advice to offer the conspirators.[24]

He had a brief spell of optimism at the beginning of May, when Dolabella took strong action against demonstrators who were assembling at the altar erected by Amatius in the Forum and were offering sacrifices to Caesar. Dolabella arrested and summarily executed the demonstrators at the end of April and leveled the altar. Cicero was euphoric and wrote Dolabella an extravagant letter of praise. He thought better things might be on the way, and he decided to postpone his departure. He also wanted to see how Antony would behave at an important meeting of the Senate on June 1, at which proposals about the provinces would be discussed.[25]

But within a week his optimism had faded. Antony's trip to Compania and rallying of veterans convinced him the consul was set on domination. War now seemed to him inevitable, provoked by Antony, or by an invasion by Sextus Pompey, or by resistance from Decimus Brutus to Antony's takeover of Cisalpine Gaul. It was a grim prospect that made Cicero almost regret the Ides. This time there could be no neutrality. The Caesarians would treat all who had rejoiced at Caesar's death as enemies. But Cicero was determined that, whatever happened, there would be no fighting for him. He would prefer to die a thousand times than go near a military camp at his age.[26]

Towards the end of May he received warnings from Hirtius and Varro that it would not be safe for him to attend the Senate on June 1. Atticus had apparently been urging him to attend and to plead for peace as he had done in 49 in the Temple of Apollo. But Cicero considered that the case and circumstances were different this time around. The state was already being oppressed, there was a threat of violence, and Antony was unlikely

24. *Att.* 14.13.2; 14.19.1; 14.21.3–4; 14.22.2; 15.1.5; 15.5.1; 15.9.2; 15.10; 15.11.3. Marcus had gone to study in Athens in early 45 and Cicero was most anxious to visit him to make sure he was applying himself to his studies. *Att.* 12.8; 12.24.1; 12.27.2; 12.32.2; 13.1.1; 14.7.2; 14.11.2; 14.13.4; 14.16.3; 15.15.4; 15.16.1; 15.17.1; 16.3.2.

25. *Att.* 14.14.4–6; 14.15.1; 14.16.2; 14.17a; 14.19.4–5; 14.18.1; 14.20.4. *Phil.* 1.5.

26. *Att.* 14.13.2; 14.17.2; 14.18.4; 14.19.1; 14.21.4; 14.22.2; 15.4.1.

to be moved by pleas or arguments. He decided to stay away and to delay his trip abroad no longer. He asked Dolabella for a *legatio* so he could travel with official status. It was promptly granted on June 3.

He thought that, before he left, he should see Brutus, who had been vainly pestering him for advice, and around the end of the first week in June he attended a conference at Antium, at which Cassius and Brutus's mother, Servilia, and wife, Porcia, were also present. He argued that Brutus could not safely go to Rome and he urged him and Cassius to accept the corn commission in the interests of their safety. He came away utterly disconsolate. He found no plan, no reasoned strategy. The ship was in fragments. He could not wait to get away.[27]

His departure in the end, however, was unhurried, as his characteristic reluctance to leave Italy showed itself once more. He finally set out from Tusculum on June 30, heading for Pompeii, the port from which he planned to sail. He was avoiding Brundisium, because the legions Antony had withdrawn from Macedonia were due to land there. He intended to be back by January 1.

He was leaving in a most unhappy frame of mind. He had lost confidence in Brutus, who now seemed totally helpless, and he was now inclined to blame him for the collapse of republican hopes. War seemed inevitable, and he believed Antony was intent on a massacre of republicans. He felt certain he would be returning to an even worse situation than he was leaving. He continued at times to wonder if he should be going at all. He was still worried that he would be criticized for turning his back on the state at a critical time. He dreaded the journey, and hated the thought of leaving his beloved country estates. But he was anxious to insure Marcus was getting the most out of his stay in Athens, and it is evident that he also wanted to await developments in Italy at a safe distance and to keep his options open in the event of war.

His departure from Italy was further delayed when the possibility arose that he might sail with Brutus, who by now had also decided to leave the country. But Brutus dallied, still hoping for a favorable development, and Cicero finally sailed without him on July 17. By August 1 he had reached Syracuse, which he left the following day for the crossing to

---

27. *Att.* 14.22.2; 15.5.2; 15.6.1–4; 15.8.1; 15.11. His writing continued. By early July he was preparing to send Atticus a work entitled *De gloria*. *Att.* 15.27.2; 16.3.1; 16.16.4. *Off.* 2.31.

Greece. But contrary winds forced him back to Leucopetra. A second attempt to make the crossing on August 6 also failed. While he was waiting at Leucopetra for a change of weather, he got news of Antony's conciliatory moves in late July and of the edict of Brutus and Cassius. He also heard that he was being criticized for his absence. He decided at once to abandon his journey and return to Rome. Letters from Atticus and a meeting with Brutus on August 17 further convinced him that he could not honorably leave Italy at this time. It would be seen as an act of despair and a desertion of the Republic.[28]

Cicero was not returning to Rome, however, with any intention of taking a leading role in politics, though Brutus was urging him to do so. Brutus had been delighted by Piso's speech on August 1, and obviously wanted senior consulars to take a lead and put pressure on Antony. But Cicero saw no point. Piso had stepped to the fore, but had received no support and had achieved nothing. Cicero was not about to repeat such an exercise in futility. When the Senate was next faced with a controversial proposal from Antony on September 1, he accordingly attempted to escape involvement and stayed away, pleading fatigue after his journey. Antony, clearly anxious to assert himself as Caesar's champion by forcing agreement from all elements of the Senate to an extravagant honor for the dead dictator, reacted angrily and publicly threatened Cicero. The following day, when Antony happened to be absent, Cicero did appear, and he defended himself in the speech that became known as the *First Philippic*. He received support from another consular, P. Servilius Isauricus, consul of 48, a follower of Cato in the fifties who had later joined Caesar.[29]

Cicero's speech praised Antony's early actions after Caesar's death and complained of later developments, especially the misuse of Caesar's papers, the proposed laws relating to juries and to appeals in cases of treason and political violence, and the intimidation of the Senate and magistrates and people. It ended with a long appeal to both consuls to think of true glory and avoid the example of Caesar. It was critical but conciliatory, and carefully avoided any form of personal attack. Cicero

28. *Att.* 15.18; 15.19.1; 15.20.2–3; 15.22; 15.25; 15.29.1; 16.3.4; 16.4.4; 16.5.3; 16.6.1–2; 16.7. *Phil.* 1.6–10. While sailing south, Cicero had written a further rhetorical work, the *Topica*, an elucidation of a work of Aristotle on the discovery of arguments. *Fam.* 7.19. *Top.*5.

29. *Att.* 16.7.5–7. *Fam.* 12.2.1. *Phil.* 1.12, 14. Plutarch, *Cic.* 43.

used the occasion to present himself, alongside Piso, as a vigorous and outspoken champion of the *respublica,* but his speech was above all a response to intemperate strictures from Antony, a necessary defense of *dignitas,* and a justification of Cicero's conduct since the Ides of March. Moderate in tone, its substance predictable, it heralded no change in Cicero's posture of previous months.

Antony, desperately concerned to contain Octavian's rising influence and maintain control of Caesar's soldiers and supporters, could not tolerate any resurgence of republican voices, and he answered Cicero's speech with a blistering invective in the Senate on September 19, in which he derided and belittled the orator's entire political life and presented him as a baneful influence that had prompted Pompey to break with Caesar and the conspirators to murder him. Over the following month he repeated his attacks, as he continued his campaign to woo Caesar's following by honoring his memory and condemning his assassins. He had a statue of Caesar set up on the Rostra with the inscription "parenti optime merito." On October 2 he spoke at a *contio* at which he portrayed the conspirators as traitors and again alleged Cicero was their mentor. He also warned that, while he lived, such men would not be allowed a place in the state.[30]

Cicero's response was a prudent silence. He had satisfied the demands of honor with the *First Philippic,* and he considered further confrontation with Antony both dangerous and pointless. He saw no hope of mounting an effective political challenge to the consul. The Senate as a whole he considered paralyzed by inertia and servility and woefully short of capable leaders. Of the few surviving consulars for whom he had any regard, L. Cotta, consul of 65, was too dispirited to play a prominent part, L. Caesar, consul of 64, was ill, and Servius Sulpicius, consul of 51, was abroad. Piso, Servilius and himself stood alone, and could not even enter the Senate without the gravest risk to their lives.

But in any event, Cicero saw little benefit in senatorial opposition in the face of Antony's open use of force. Everything was controlled by weapons; the *respublica* was an armed camp. Such force could only be met with force, and the republicans had not the means to provide it. Cicero therefore kept his peace, avoiding the Senate and contenting

30. *Fam.* 10.1.1; 12.2.2; 12.3; 12.23.3; 12.25.4. *Phil.* 2.3–8, 11–30, 37–42. *Phil.*5.19–20.

himself with writing a vitriolic response to Antony's attacks in the form of an imaginary speech in the Senate. The speech, the *Second Philippic*, product of Cicero's mature oratorical skills, became his most famous invective, and was completed and on its way to Atticus for comment by October 25. It was intended for publication, however, only in the event of a return to a free Republic.[31]

Cicero left Rome in the second week of October for a further round of his villas and further writing. He was now embarked on the last of his major philosophical works, the *De officiis*, a treatise on practical ethics that he addressed to Marcus.[32] But before long his quiet was disturbed by new developments that presented him with another agonizing political dilemma. The rivalry between Antony and Octavian suddenly came to a head. Open dissension flared in early October, when Antony accused Octavian of attempting to have him killed. Octavian denied it and the public believed him, but Cicero and the *boni* believed Antony and were delighted. Soon afterwards, on October 9, Antony left Rome to take command of the Macedonian legions assembled at Brundisium. Octavian moved quickly to prevent him gaining an unchallengeable military superiority. He sent agents to Brundisium to stir mutiny among Antony's troops, and went himself to Campania where, by offering five hundred denarii to anyone who would enlist, he raised an army of three thousand men from among Caesar's veterans. Antony managed for the moment to maintain the loyalty of the three legions that had arrived from Macedonia, and he sent them northwards to Ariminum. Octavian marched to Rome and entered the city with his troops on November 10, where he

---

31. *Fam.*10.2.1; 12.2; 12.3.1–2; 12.23.3–4. *Att.*15.13.1–2; 15.13a.2–3; 16.11.1.

32. *Att.* 15.13a.2; 16.11.4. Cicero's interest in his studies and writing never flagged throughout 44. Following completion of the *Cato maior*, which was dedicated to Atticus (*Att.* 14.21.3. *Div.*2.3), he produced the *De gloria* and *Topica* around the middle of 44. The *De fato*, a dialogue between Cicero and Hirtius examining the problems of free will and determinism, was also written about the same time (*Div.* 2.3). Soon afterwards came the *Laelius* or *De amicitia*, with Laelius expounding his views on friendship (*Att.* 16.13a.2. *Off.* 2.31). Cicero was also planning a discussion of Caesar's assassination in the form of a Heraclidean dialogue (*Att.* 15.4.3; 15.13.1) and was polishing off the secret history, which he refers to as *Anecdota*, a polemical account of the events of his time, which was posthumously published under the title *De consiliis suis* (*Att.* 14.17.6; 14.11.3. Büchner, *RE* 7a.1268). Cicero was further considering writing a major work of history and was being strongly urged by Atticus to do so. He believed the Romans had achieved nothing of distinction in the area of history, and he was eager to remedy that deficiency. *Att.* 16.13a.2. *Leg.* 1.5–6. *De or.* 2.51–55.

attacked Antony at a *contio* and offered to oppose him in the interest of the state. But the *boni* did not rally and his soldiers showed no enthusiasm for such a contest, and he was forced to leave the city for a more secure base at Arretium, unready as yet for a trial of force with Antony. The latter reached Rome around mid-November with a select contingent of troops. He immediately launched a campaign of propaganda against Octavian, but the defection of two of the Macedonian legions, the Fourth and the Martian, to the latter in late November caused him to leave the city hurriedly on the 28th to prevent further disintegration of his forces. He could not trust what was left of his army to fight Octavian, so he headed directly for Cisalpine Gaul, which he proceeded to claim as his province. But Decimus Brutus, establishing himself at Mutina, refused to hand over the command. Antony promptly besieged Mutina, and a new civil war had begun.[33]

Cicero learned details of Octavian's plans to raise troops and oppose Antony from Octavian himself in a letter that reached him on November 1. Octavian was also seeking a secret meeting with Cicero and wanted his advice as to whether he should march to Rome or hold Capua or go to the Macedonian legions marching northwards to Ariminum. Cicero was surprised and clearly excited by the new situation, but he also felt in a terrible quandary. He had deeply conflicting feelings about Octavian. He had met him in the latter part of April when he came to stay at Philippus's villa in Puteoli. Octavian had sought to woo him from the start, and Cicero was impressed by the deferential treatment and general friendliness. He also quickly came to admire his obvious talent and courage, and was pleased to find that, outwardly at least, he was well disposed toward the conspirators. But at the same time he doubted that he could ever become a *bonus civis*. He was too young, too steeped in a Caesarian heritage, surrounded by too many Caesarian zealots, too intent on glorifying his adoptive father's name and achievements to warrant much confidence that he would truly befriend the conspirators and defend the Republic.[34]

But despite these misgivings, Cicero retained a hope that Octavian would create trouble for Antony that might weaken the latter's position,

33. *Fam.* 12.23.2; 16.8.1–2; 16.15.3. *Phil.* 3.15, 19–27; 13.19–20. Appian, *BC* 3. 39–46. Dio 45. 12–14.

34. *Att.* 14.5.3; 14.10.3; 14.11.2; 14.12.2; 14.21.4; 15.2.3; 15.12.2; 16.8.1–2.

and he favored efforts by the republicans to encourage Octavian and widen the distance between him and the consul. Now, beyond all expectation, the two men were on the brink of armed conflict. A new situation had been created that Cicero believed offered a new opportunity to republicans. Octavian seemed in a strong position. He had impressive energy, a sizeable army, and surprising support in the *municipia*. He was also likely to get the backing of D. Brutus, and he was actively seeking to win over the Senate. Cicero remained unsure of his ultimate objectives, and feared that if he gained much power it would not go well for the republicans, but he remained the best hope of toppling Antony, whose despotic intentions were plain, and whose victory would prove intolerable.[35]

But Cicero did not want to be the person leading republican interests in the new evolving crisis and in negotiations between Octavian and the senate. That was Brutus's task, and Cicero wished he were in Italy to undertake it. For the moment he advised Octavian to go to Rome to seek the support of *plebs* and *boni,* but he was most reluctant to come out into the open himself. Age, weariness with politics, the safety and comfort of his country estates, his continuing literary interests, his uncertainty about Octavian, and the outcome of the approaching conflict all deterred him from assuming an onerous and dangerous burden of leadership.

For a month he vacillated in a typical welter of indecision. Octavian pressed him relentlessly with daily letters and clever appeals to his vanity to come to the fore and save the state a second time. Cicero compared his dilemma to that of the Greeks challenged to single combat by Hector; he felt afraid to accept, ashamed to refuse. He was concerned, as always, not to seem to fail the Republic, but the risks were great, and he was determined not to be hurried into precipitate action. Octavian's performance in Rome and especially his speech at the *contio,* in which he had expressed aspirations to follow in Caesar's footsteps, increased his caution. He resolved to bide his time until the Senate met under the new consuls on January 1, by which time he hoped to have better evidence of Octavian's attitude toward republicans.[36]

In the event he came to Rome on December 9, ready to work to secure

---

35. *Att.* 15.12.2; 16.8.2; 16.9; 16.11.6; 16.14.1. See A. Bellen, "Cicero und der Aufstieg Oktavians," *Gymnasium* 92 (1985), 161–89.

36. *Att.* 16.8.2: "O Brute, ubi es?" Cf. *Att.* 16.9; 16.11.6; 16.15.3.

the defeat of Antony. The defection of the two Macedonian legions to Octavian no doubt convinced him Antony could be successfully resisted and helped end his indecision about his involvement. His immediate concern now was to insure that Octavian would have help from Decimus Brutus, and he sent urgent messages to the latter around mid-December appealing to him to resist Antony's takeover of Cisalpine Gaul, and to act, if necessary, without waiting for senatorial authorization. Brutus did refuse, on his own initiative, to surrender the province and declared his decision in an edict that reached Rome shortly before December 20. The new tribunes had meantime summoned a meeting of the Senate for December 20 to provide protection for the new consuls on January 1. Brutus's edict was added to the agenda. Cicero attended, now fully certain of his course, and he aggressively took the lead in rallying the Senate against Antony and in support of the actions of Octavian and Decimus Brutus.[37]

His speech, the *Third Philippic,* displays all the power and energy of Ciceronian oratory at its best, portraying Antony as a debauched oppressor, who had forfeited by his violence and illegalities all his rights as consul and was crowning his wrongdoing with an invasion of a province of the Roman people. He extolled the opportunity to rid the state of his vile domination that had been offered by the bravery of the young Caesar and Decimus Brutus, and he proposed that their actions should be commended and that all governors should be asked to retain control of their provinces until further notice. The motion was passed by the Senate with only one protesting voice, and the same day, at a *contio* called by the tribunes, Cicero repeated his arguments to the people in the *Fourth Philippic.*

Cicero had taken an uncompromising stand, advocating a truceless war to eliminate Antony and his partisans, and he had won a significant victory in persuading the Senate to take a crucial step toward legitimizing the position of Octavian and Decimus Brutus. Over the following months he continued to pursue his hardline policy with unwavering firmness and dynamic energy, and he emerged as the dominant force in the Senate, crucially affecting the direction of public policy and steadily moving the state toward all-out war with Antony. It was his finest hour since 63. In a Senate freed at last from threats of force, there was scope once again for

37. *Fam.* 10.5; 11.5.1; 11.6; 11.7; 12.22.1–3.

Cicero's masterly skills in deliberative oratory, and he had few rivals in a body led in 43 by undistinguished consuls and ineffective or indecisive consulars. He was the preeminent *princeps,* foremost in prestige and in the skills that mattered in free debate. It was the role he had yearned for all his life, and it inspired him and brought back the resolute leadership, backed by the power of eloquence, that had marked his consulship. He was also pursuing, as in 63, a cause to which he was totally committed, in circumstances where, to him, the interests of the Republic were plain, as was the action needed to secure them.

The vigor and determination of his stand against Antony have not always won him, however, the approval of modern historians. The rhetoric of the *Philippics* can easily be represented as dangerous warmongering, fanatical in the intensity of its hostility toward Antony, and lawless in its support of illegal arms. Syme, the most trenchant of recent critics of Cicero's stand against Antony, found the nature of his opposition so foreign to his character that he saw it as the fanaticism of a senior statesman made desperate by the memory of past humiliations.[38]

There are serious distortions and simplifications in such views. Cicero's campaign for armed suppression of Antony was not, to his mind, inconsistent with his well-known advocacy of peace in the preceding decade. He was unalterably opposed to civil war between potentates or political factions, since the result was inevitably bitterness and retribution and the supremacy of an individual or group with a consequent diminution of the general liberty. He saw the fight against Antony as essentially different, a fight by the *respublica* against a small group intent on destroying it and achieving personal domination. The rhetorical catchwords are those of 63 and the *Pro Sestio.* Antony and his partisans belonged in the category of Catiline and his followers, part of the body of *perditi* and *egentes* constantly threatening the ancestral institutions. They represented no irresistible power or political view or element that had to be accommodated in the interests of survival or future harmony. They were simply enemies and criminals, subverters of all that good citizens wanted to preserve, their eradication essential to lasting peace and stability.

Some of this was cant and rhetorical embellishment to rally the wavering and fainthearted, but it is essentially the view of the conflict with

38. Syme, *Roman Revolution,* 140–48.

Antony that Cicero repeatedly belabors in the letters to Brutus as well as in the *Philippics,* and it is certain he believed Antony and his followers represented the worst and most dangerous brand of *improbi,* their aims power and domination, their methods violence and oppression. He believed too that they could be isolated as the enemies of all political elements, and that their suppression could revive real hopes of a stable Republic. It was therefore for him, in its essential features, the struggle of 63 repeated, calling for a similarly aggressive and uncompromising stand.[39]

Cicero had also learned lessons from the events of the fifties. He believed that fatal concessions had then been made to Caesar that had enabled him to build his strength to the point where he could no longer safely be opposed. A policy of appeasement toward Antony held similar dangers and would only sow the seeds of future conflict on a greater scale. He was convinced there should be no trucking with men of Antony's stamp; a policy of coexistence with *improbi* could be justified only when resistance was reckless or futile.[40]

But there were other factors that lent unusual intensity to the fervor and intransigence of Cicero's campaign in 43. He was advocating a controversial policy of war against a proconsul lawfully appointed by act of the people. In the process he was proposing to legitimize the position of Octavian and Decimus Brutus who, by any strict interpretation, were acting outside the law, and he was seeking support for his policies in a Senate in which he could expect to find few, if any, allies of energy and influence. There no longer existed a strong *factio* of *principes* ready to close ranks in the face of a threat to their ascendancy and to the survival of the traditional order. The Caesarian-Pompeian divide persisted and hampered any such unity of purpose among the Senate's leadership. The anger and distrust of republicans that Cicero had found in 44 even among moderate Caesarians such as the consuls Pansa and Hirtius had not suddenly disappeared, and while most Caesarians had no wish to live under Antony's domination, they had equally no wish to be the instruments of the rise to power of Caesar's assassins and their supporters.

On the republican side there were too few *principes* of note remaining

---

39. *Phil.* 3.29, 34–36; 4.15; 5.32; 7.3, 9; 8.8, 13–16; 12.13–14; 13.1, 3, 6–7. *Ad Brut.* 1.2a.2; 1.15.4–5, 10; 2.5.1, 5. *Fam.* 10.6.1, 3; 10.27.1.
40. *Att.* 7.3.4–5; 7.5.5; 7.6.2. *Ad Brut.* 1.2a.2.

to offset the ambivalence of Caesarians and insure consistent and clear-cut decisions. Of the consulars who had backed Pompey and the republican cause in 49, only two survived, Cicero himself and Servius Sulpicius Rufus.[41] There were twelve other consulars present in Rome in early 43, but there was not one among them that Cicero regarded as likely to provide him with consistent and effective support. Many, such as L. Cotta, consul of 65, L. Caesar, consul of 64, C. Antonius, consul of 63, Domitius Calvinus and Valerius Messala, consuls of 53, were ill, inactive, or discredited.[42] Of the others, L. Marcius Philippus, consul of 56, and C. Claudius Marcellus, consul of 50, both kinsmen of Octavian and cautious men of no outstanding merits, were sitting on the sidelines; L. Aemilius Paullus, consul of 50, elder brother of M. Lepidus, had sold out to Caesar in 50 and offered little promise as a republican stalwart.[43] Piso and Servilius, who had both spoken out against Antony in 44, were men of distinction and courage, but Cicero could hardly put his full faith in either. Piso had been his bitter enemy and was a Caesarian of long standing, and Servilius, though a staunch follower of Cato in the fifties, had defected to Caesar in the civil war.[44] The two remaining consulars, C. Caninius Rebilus, the notorious half-day consul of 45, and Q. Fufius Calenus, consul of 47, were committed Caesarians, the latter an open and aggressive supporter of Antony.[45] The consuls themselves, though opposed to Antony, by no means shared Cicero's fervent republicanism and, in any event, lacked the drive and influence to provide strong leadership.[46]

The lower ranks of the Senate were similarly lacking in leaders of distinction and firm republican sentiment. Those who should have formed the influential nucleus of a new optimate grouping, the praetors Brutus and Cassius and their supporters, were absent in the East. Other adherents of republicanism were with Sextus Pompey in Spain. The bulk of the rank and file of the Senate consisted of Caesar's new appointees, men for whom Cicero had considerable respect, but who could not easily

41. *Phil.* 13.28–29.
42. *Fam.* 12.2.2–3.
43. *Att.* 14.11.2; 15.12.2; 16.14.2. *Fam.* 12.2.2. Plutarch, *Cic.* 44.
44. *Fam.* 10.12.4; 12.2.1. *Ad Brut.* 2.2.3. *Phil.* 12.18.
45. For Caninius, see *Fam.* 7.30.1. For Calenus, *Att.* 15.4.1. *Phil.* 8.9–19; 12.3, 18. For Cicero's overall view of the consulars, *Fam.* 10.28.3; 12.4.2; 12.5.2. *Phil.* 8.22.
46. *Ad Brut.* 2.1.1; 1.3a.1; 1.10.1.

be converted into a united and resolute party of republicanism. There was in general a lack of direction and cohesion in the Senate, which was aggravated by distrust and divided loyalties and by inertia at the top, creating the most unfavorable possible conditions for agreement and firm decisions. Delay or ambivalence in strategy or purpose might easily bring total paralysis. Cicero needed quick and determined action to build and sustain momentum against Antony. It was an uphill struggle that demanded all the forcefulness and vehemence his rhetorical powers could command.[47]

Strong leadership and prompt action from the Senate were also required to sustain the morale of the Italian *municipia* and of the veterans opposing Antony, and, even more important, to hold the loyalty of crucial commanders in the western provinces. Gallia Comata was governed by L. Munatius Plancus, a longtime Caesarian who had served as a *legatus* of Caesar in Gaul and in the civil war. Cicero tried hard in a series of letters in late 44 and early 43 to attach him to the republican side, but Plancus was a cautious man with a reputation as a timeserver, and he could not be counted on to support a cause that showed any sign of floundering.[48] Even less likely to risk anything for the Republic was M. Lepidus, governor of Gallia Narbonensis and Nearer Spain, described by Decimus Brutus as the most fickle of men. He was also the Caesarian leader with the closest ties to Antony.[49] Another loyal Caesarian, C. Asinuis Pollio, governed Farther Spain. Though he professed loyalty to the Senate, he remained distrusted by republicans.[50] These three men commanded twelve legions among them. Their support was obviously of crucial importance to the republican cause. The best hope of winning it lay in a quick defeat of Antony.

Cicero's relentless campaign for all-out war in 43 was therefore based on his perception of the nature of the crisis and of the strategy necessary to bring a republican victory. It needs no theories of fanatical hatred or frustrated ambition to explain it. He found himself thrust, considerably against his wishes, amid the dearth of capable republican *principes,* into

47. For Cicero's awareness of the need for speed and decisiveness, see *Ad Brut.* 2.1.1. *Phil.* 5.25; 6.2, 7.

48. *Fam.* 10.1–10.

49. *Fam.* 10.31.4; 11.9.1. *Ad Brut.* 2.2.1; 1.10.2. The traditional view of Lepidus as a fickle lightweight has been challenged by R. D. Weigel, *AC* 14 (1974), 67–73.

50. *Fam.* 10.31; 11.9.1.

leading a fight against men who, he believed, could not be accommodated without endangering the Republic but who could be defeated, if a
hesitant and divided Senate could be rallied to unite and assert its traditional authority.

Cicero had shown before that, in such situations, he could be ruthless
and uncompromising and willing to bend or overstep the law if circumstances required it. He was a pragmatist, not a legalist, governed by the
fundamental principle that the welfare of the state, which for him meant
the preservation of traditional republicanism, was the highest law and
that those who threatened by unlawful force the existing order had placed
themselves outside the law and could be dealt with by any means, legal or
extralegal, that was necessary to defeat them. In this he was consistent
throughout his political career, his attitude toward Antony in line with his
reaction to the forceful suppression of the violent dissidents of his earliest
years, Saturninus and Sulpicius.[51]

Cicero's drive to launch a full-scale war against Antony began in
earnest at the meeting of the Senate under the new consuls on January 1.
Pansa, who presided, called first on his father-in-law, Calenus, who
proposed that an embassy be sent to negotiate with Antony. Cicero
vigorously opposed the motion in the *Fifth Philippic,* reviewing Antony's misdeeds and arguing the need for speedy and drastic action. He
proposed passage of the *consultum ultimum,* the declaration of a state of
emergency and a full-scale levying of troops. He also proposed honors
for Decimus Brutus and for Lepidus, who had recently concluded a peace
with Sextus Pompey, and for Octavian he proposed *imperium pro
praetore* and membership of the Senate and the right to seek office as if he
had held the quaestorship in 44. The debate extended over four days and
brought approval of the proposal to send an embassy but also of Cicero's
motions in regard to Brutus, Lepidus, and Octavian. At the debate's
conclusion Cicero once more carried his campaign to the people. Brought
before a *contio* by a tribune, he deplored the sending of the embassy to
Antony, forecast its failure, and pledged his commitment to continue the
fight for freedom.[52]

Soon afterwards the Senate decreed that one or both consuls should

---

51. See Mitchell, *Ascending Years,* 66–67.
52. Appian, *BC* 3.50ff. Dio 45.17. *Ad Brut.*1.15.7. *Res gestae* 1. Velleius 2.61.
Plutarch, *Cic.* 45; *Ant.* 17. Suetonius, *Aug.* 10. Tacitus, *Ann.* 1.10.

proceed to the war at Mutina. Hirtius was assigned by lot to go, and Pansa was commissioned to levy troops throughout Italy. Toward the end of January Cicero delivered another major speech, the *Seventh Philippic,* in the Senate in response to propagandist talk that Antony was making offers of peace and should be conciliated. He argued that peace with Antony would be disgraceful, dangerous, and indeed impossible after all that had happened. He professed his own dedication to peace, but maintained that, in this instance, peace could be attained only through war. It was a stirring call to arms, showing clearly that the embassy had dampened enthusiasm for the war and had given Antony's sympathizers the chance to assail Cicero's hardline policy. The consensus Cicero was attempting to create was fragile, needing all the orator's rhetorical fervor to keep it intact.[53]

At the beginning of February the embassy, which had consisted of the senior consulars L. Piso, L. Philippus, and Servius Sulpicius, returned. Sulpicius had died even before the envoys reached Antony, and the mission had proved a failure, returning with counterdemands from Antony that would merely have the effect of strengthening his position. Cicero proposed that war should now be formally declared, but the irresolution of the Senate continued to show itself and a state of emergency was declared in preference to war. Cicero was determined, however, to keep pressing his case, and the following day he sounded again, in the *Eighth Philippic,* the need for all-out resistance to Antony, decrying the faintheartedness of the Senate's leadership and attacking, in particular, the stand of Antony's chief partisan, Fufius Calenus. A debate on the honors to be paid to Sulpicius Rufus gave him another opportunity, which he fully exploited in the *Ninth Philippic,* to denounce the man who had created the crisis that had led to Sulpicius's death and who had repudiated the mission Sulpicius had given his life to serve.[54]

Soon afterwards a dispatch from M. Brutus, detailing developments in the East, arrived in Rome. Brutus, who had left Italy in late August 44, had quickly established control over most of Macedonia and Illyricum, greatly aided by the support of his kinsman, Q. Hortensius, governor of Macedonia, and by the defection of the legions of P. Vatinius, governor of Illyricum. He had further consolidated his position in January 43,

53. *Phil.* 7. 11–13. *Fam.* 11.8.2; 12.24.2. Dio 46.29.
54. *Fam.* 10.28.3; 12.4.1. *Phil.* 9.1. Appian, *BC* 3. 62–63. Dio. 29–31.

when he had easily defeated the forces of C. Antonius, who had landed at Dyrrachium to claim the governorship of Macedonia. Antonius was forced to retreat southward and take refuge in Apollonia.

Pansa immediately summoned the Senate to consider the dispatch from Brutus. Calenus, who was again called on first by his father-in-law, argued that Brutus should be required to give up his army since he had no legal right to it and since any such command for him would be an affront to Caesar's veterans. Cicero responded in the *Tenth Philippic,* again berating Calenus for his support of Antony, and urging that Brutus's actions be commended and that he be confirmed in his command and instructed to defend the provinces of Macedonia, Illyricum, and Greece. The Senate was persuaded, and Cicero's proposals were carried.[55]

At this point Cicero was well pleased with the results of his efforts and with the general movement of events. He gave his view of the situation in February in a letter to Cassius. Brutus's success was an unexpected boost to republican fortunes in the East. The position in Cisalpine Gaul also gave grounds for optimism. There was a hope that Decimus Brutus would be able to break out of Mutina. Hirtius was holding Claterna, just south of Antony's stronghold of Bononia. Octavian was close by at Forum Cornelium with a loyal army. Pansa had a large force at Rome raised in the Italian levy. Almost all of Cisalpine Gaul, including the Transpadani, was enthusiastically supporting the republican cause. The Senate, despite the inertia and disloyalty of the consulars, was most resolute, and there was remarkable unanimity in Rome and Italy.[56]

Cicero's optimism was soon dampened, however, when news arrived at the end of February that Dolabella, while traveling through Asia on his way to assume the governorship of Syria, had captured, tortured, and killed C. Trebonius, the governor of Asia and one of Caesar's assassins. This left Dolabella in effective control of two crucial eastern provinces. The Senate reacted strongly and unanimously and, on the motion of Calenus, declared Dolabella a public enemy. No such consensus emerged, however, when the discussion turned on the following day to the question of who should have command of the war against him. Rivalry and ambition hampered agreement. Calenus proposed that Asia

55. Plutarch, *Brut.* 24. Appian, *BC* 3.63. Dio 47.20–21. Horace, *Ep.* 2.2.43–49. Velleius 2.69.
56. *Fam.* 12.5.

and Syria be allotted to the consuls. L. Caesar proposed an extraordinary command for P. Servilius. Cicero, risking offense to the consuls and their friends, opposed both motions in the *Eleventh Philippic,* and argued that Cassius, believed to be already active in Syria, should be made governor of that province and given command of all the forces in the area for the prosecution of the war against Dolabella. Pansa reacted angrily to Cicero's speech, and his opposition insured the defeat of Cicero's motion. Calenus's proposal carried the day. Cicero, convinced the appointment of Cassius was demanded by the interests of the Republic, continued to push the matter and went before a *contio* to argue the case anew. Once again he was publicly opposed by Pansa and failed to achieve his purpose.[57]

Cicero's position was weakened by this bruising and unsuccessful trial of strength with Pansa, and it was perhaps no coincidence that around this same time a further attempt was made to renew negotiations with Antony. Calenus and Piso, both known to be in close contact with Antony, indicated he was ready to make concessions and heed the Senate. Pansa also began to argue for peace. The Senate was persuaded and voted to send another embassy, consisting of five consulars representing different shades of opinion and including Cicero, who reluctantly consented to the decision. It soon became evident, however, that there were no grounds for supposing that Antony had suffered any change of heart, and Pansa was forced by the backlash from republicans to reopen the issue in a fresh senatorial debate. Cicero attacked the earlier decision in the *Twelfth Philippic,* alleging that the Senate had been misled. He repeated his arguments against any form of negotiation with Antony and emphasized the particular inappropriateness of including himself in any negotiating mission.[58]

This time he won the day, and the embassy was not sent. But he was a long way from achieving the form of firm consensus he was seeking. The coalition of republicans, neutrals, and moderate Caesarians that had emerged was inherently fragile. Vacillation continued to abound and the risk of divisions and turnabouts remained high. The situation in the provinces and the attitude of governors also remained unpredictable. There was uncertainty at home and abroad with an interacting effect that heightened further the general level of instability.

57. *Fam.* 12.7.1; 12.14.4. *Ad Brut.* 2.4.2. *Phil.* 11.1, 5, 22. Cf. Appian, *BC* 3.26. Dio 47.29. Velleius 2.69.

58. *Phil.* 12.1–3, 6. Cf. Dio 46.32. For the date of the *Twelfth Philippic,* see Rice Holmes, *Architect,* 206–07.

These impediments to strong government became evident again on March 20, when letters arrived from Lepidus and Plancus, in which both urged the Senate to seek a peaceful solution. There was also circulating at the same time a letter from Antony to Hirtius and Octavian, decrying the divisions between Caesarians and the concessions made to the conspirators through Cicero's pleadings and calling for unity to avenge Caesar and prevent a resurgence of the Pompeians. Antony also claimed Lepidus and Plancus as his allies and counselors. He was attacking Cicero's strategy at its core, presenting the struggle in the narrowest of partisan terms and seeking, by appeal to the factional fears and hatreds of the preceding decade, to remove any possibility of a grand coalition against himself. The letters from Lepidus and Plancus showed his propagandist offensive might well succeed.

Cicero recognized the danger, and, when the Senate met to discuss the dispatches from Lepidus and Plancus, he exerted his own formidable propagandist powers in the *Thirteenth Philippic* to counter it. He rehearsed again the dangers of a false peace and reminded Lepidus, in a tone of undisguised rebuke, of his obligations to the Republic by virtue of the standing of his family and the many high distinctions the state had conferred upon himself. But, above all, he sought to refute utterly Antony's portrayal of the crisis as an ongoing struggle between Caesarians and Pompeians, dissecting his letter sentence by sentence to hammer home again his basic theme that this was a war against violent criminals with whom no peace was possible. He followed the speeches with private letters to Lepidus and Plancus, in which he bluntly attacked their proposals for peace and urged them to stand unequivocally with the Senate and the *boni*.[59]

Cicero succeeded, with help from Servilius, in persuading the Senate to reject the proposals from Lepidus and Plancus. The shaky coalition was still holding. Pansa was now on his way to the war. Antony attempted to intercept him before he could link up with Hirtius. The latter, anticipating such a possibility, sent the veteran Martian legion to reinforce Pansa. Antony attacked near Forum Gallorum on April 14. It was a fierce encounter between seasoned veterans, but Pansa's forces were outnumbered and were eventually forced to retreat and withdraw into their camp. Pansa himself was seriously wounded. Antony failed to

59. *Phil.* 13.22–48. *Fam.* 10.6; 10.27.

storm the camp and decided to retreat. But Hirtius had marched from his own camp with two legions, one of them the veteran Fourth, and he suddenly fell on Antony's tired troops as they withdrew towards Mutina. The result was a decisive victory for Hirtius and heavy losses for Antony, who escaped to his camp at Mutina with only a small remnant of the two legions he had led forth against Pansa.[60]

The first reports to reach Rome told of a victory for Antony and caused considerable panic. There were also rumors circulating that Cicero intended to seize power on April 21, a story fabricated, according to Cicero, by partisans of Antony who planned to use it as a pretext for the murder of himself and the rest of the Senate. But dispatches from the consuls and Octavian arrived on April 20 with the true story. There was wide rejoicing. Cicero was escorted by a huge throng from his house to the Capitol. He was being acclaimed again as the saviour of the state and was reliving the glory of the Nones. The next day in the Senate he delivered the last extant speech of his career, the *Fourteenth Phillipic,* which he began with a sobering reminder that the war was not over and with a plea that now at last Antony should be declared a public enemy. He went on to praise the consuls and Octavian, saluting all three as *imperatores* and proposing a thanksgiving of fifty days in the name of all of them. He also proposed rewards and honors for the soldiers, and especially commended the two veteran legions, the Fourth and the Martian. The Senate readily approved the honors for the commanders and soldiers, but traces of the old hesitancy lingered and it still refused to commit the state to all-out war with Antony.[61]

Even as the Senate was deliberating, a second battle was being fought at Mutina, which resulted in another defeat for Antony at the hands of Hirtius, ably supported on this occasion by Octavian, and aided by a sortie by D. Brutus from Mutina. Antony had to abandon the siege, and he fled westward toward Transalpine Gaul with a small force. His opponents had won decisively, though at heavy cost. Hirtius was killed in the course of the battle, and Pansa died the day after from wounds received in the earlier encounter.[62]

60. *Phil.* 13.50; 14.1, 36–38. *Fam.* 10.30. Appian, *BC* 3.66–70. Dio 46.37.

61. *Phil.* 14.10, 12, 14–16, 16–28. *Ad Brut.* 1.3.1–2. Dio 46.38.

62. *Ad Brut.* 1.3a; 1.4.1; 1.5.1. *Fam.* 10.33.4. Appian, *BC* 3.71. Dio 46.38. Suetonius, *Aug.* 10.4.

The Republic's Final Slide into Autocracy

News of the second victory had reached Rome by April 26. Now at last a majority in the Senate was willing to take the step long demanded by Cicero and declare Antony and his followers public enemies. Other measures followed to strengthen the military control of the republicans and insure a total republican victory. D. Brutus was assigned the task of pursuing Antony and was given command of the armies of the consuls and of the Fourth and Martian legions. Lepidus and Plancus were summoned to assist him. Cassius was given the command in the East earlier denied him, with orders to pursue the war against Dolabella. Brutus was also authorized to move against Dolabella if it seemed to him expedient to do so. The aid of Sextus Pompey was also enlisted, and he was given command of the fleets and of the maritime coasts. There were high hopes that the war would be quickly over and that the Republic could rest secure for a long time to come.[63]

The optimism was premature. The events at Mutina and the subsequent military arrangements had radically altered the conditions that had held together the fragile coalition of republicans, neutrals, Caesarians who feared Antony's domination, and rivals of Antony, such as Octavian, who needed the help of the Senate to contain or break Antony's power. The common enemy now seemed beaten or sufficiently weakened, and what was looming, especially in light of the Senate's new military assignments, was a strengthening ascendancy of Caesar's assassins and their republican allies, a prospect certain to worry most Caesarians and force reassessment of their positions by Caesar's heir and other powerful and ambitious Caesarians such as Lepidus.

Other actions of the Senate further undermined the coalition. In the distribution of honors following the victory, Decimus Brutus got the primary recognition and was awarded a triumph, while Octavian received the much less prestigious *ovatio,* and that only through the efforts of Cicero and to the great displeasure of the hardline republicans. The veterans were offended by the slight to Octavian, and their resentment was increased by another senatorial decision to exclude commanders from a commission of ten set up to oversee the allocation of lands and

63. *Ad Brut.* 1.3a; 1.5.1. *Fam.* 10.33.1; 11.19.1. Appian, *BC* 3.74. Dio 46.40. Velleius 2.73.

other awards to the soldiers who had remained loyal to the state. Cicero, who was himself a member of the commission, had sought the inclusion of Octavian and Decimus Brutus, but had failed to get his way in a Senate that had become more assured and more intent on keeping power to itself.[64]

The death of the consuls was another blow to the survival of any broad alliance against Antony. It removed two leading moderates, who had formed a crucial bridge between the less extreme Caesarian elements and the republicans. The vacant consulships were a further destabilizing factor, creating a serious void in civil government and reviving factional and personal rivalries among those aspiring to fill the vacancies.[65] But the most serious consequence of the death of the consuls was that it deprived the republican cause of two competent and loyal military commanders who were also acceptable to the veterans and led to their replacement by a man who could not unify the forces opposing Antony and follow up the victory at Mutina. The armies of Pansa and Hirtius and the Fourth and Martian legions refused to accept the authority of an assassin of Caesar. They turned instead to Octavian who, chagrined by recent senatorial slights and eager to exploit the opportunity to increase his military strength and cement an independent position of power, also refused to cooperate with Decimus Brutus and remained in his position in the neighborhood of Bononia. As a result, Brutus was slow in beginning his pursuit of Antony and was forced to rely entirely on his own forces, which had been greatly depleted and weakened by the siege of Mutina. Antony, reinforced by three legions recruited for him in Picenum by a trusted adherent, P. Ventidius, easily evaded him and crossed into Transalpine Gaul in the early part of May.[66]

There he faced his old ally M. Lepidus, who was in command of seven legions. Lepidus had repeatedly professed his loyalty to the Senate in the previous months, but he was a committed Caesarian, and he had much in common with Antony and little incentive to risk a military confrontation

64. *Ad Brut.* 1.15.8–9. *Fam.* 10.22.2; 11.14.1; 11.20.1, 3; 11.21.2, 5. Dio 46.41. Velleius 2.62. Appian, *BC* 3.74. There is some doubt as to whether the *ovatio* for Octavian was carried. See A. Keaveney and J. A. Madden, ''An *ovatio* for Octavian?'' *Phoenix* 37 (1983), 245–47.

65. For the destabilizing effect of the death of the consuls, see *Ad Brut.* 1.5.4; 1.10.1. *Fam.* 11.10.2.

66. *Fam.* 11.10.3–4; 11.13.1–3; 11.14.2; 11.20.4. For Ventidius, see *Fam.* 10.33.4; 10.34.1; 11.10.3. Appian, *BC* 3.66, 72, 80.

with him to aid the ascendancy of Caesar's assassins and their allies. His soldiers had a similar reluctance to fight a Caesarian commander and Caesarian comrades, and on May 29 there was a peaceful union of both armies. Antony had overcome the setback at Mutina and was again a major military threat.[67]

In Italy, meantime, Octavian was biding his time and awaiting developments. He kept his army of eight legions intact and refused to send any reinforcements to Decimus Brutus. He also began to make secret overtures to Antony and Lepidus.[68] Cicero still hoped he could keep him loyal to the Republic and he continued his efforts to conciliate and cajole him. A strain developed when an alleged *mot* of Cicero to the effect that the young Caesar should be praised, honored, and discarded was reported to Octavian in May, but it is doubtful if any word or act of Cicero was any longer having any effect on Octavian's behavior.[69] Military might had emerged again as the measure of political power and Octavian was laying his plans accordingly. His design was the consulship which, combined with his control of a loyal army, would provide him with a secure base from which to treat with his Caesarian rivals in the West. The proposal for a consulship was mooted in early June, but the idea of an extraordinary office of such importance for a man of Octavian's years and associations was utterly unacceptable to the Senate. Cicero wrote him urgent letters attempting to dissuade him from his purpose, but he was fast losing confidence that he could counteract the ambition of Octavian and the designs of his associates.[70]

By early June Cicero was losing hope generally that he could any longer effectively lead the republican cause in Italy. He felt his control of the Senate was largely gone. The victory at Mutina had robbed republicans of their resolution and sense of urgency. Complacency had taken hold and Cicero's harangues now seemed like phantom-fighting. On the other hand, the Caesarians had gradually become more aggressive and the absence of consular control, such as was earlier exercised by

67. *Fam.* 10.21.4; 10.23.2; 10.35; 12.8.1. *Ad Brut.* 1.10.2. Appian, *BC* 3.83–84. The Senate reacted by declaring Lepidus a public enemy. *Fam.* 12.10.1. *Ad Brut.* 1.12.1–2; 1.13.1.

68. *Fam.* 10.24.4–6; 11.20.4. Appian, *BC* 3.80–81.

69. *Ad Brut.* 1.4.3; 1.15.9; 1.16.1; 1.17.1. *Fam.* 11.20.1; 11.21.1. Velleius 2.62. Suetonius, *Aug.* 12.

70. *Ad Brut.* 1.10.3. *Fam.* 10.24.6.

Pansa, was giving them a freer hand. Cicero felt weak and weary, and he feared that, if Octavian abandoned the Republic, as had Lepidus, all could be lost.[71]

The only solution he saw was the return of Brutus with his army to assume the leadership of the Senate and the defense of Italy. He had always considered Brutus the natural choice to direct the republican effort in Rome and Italy. It was he who had removed the tyrant and had the best claim on the allegiance of all republicans. Cicero believed that he had, besides, the skills and prestige to rally wide support and to give the Senate the authoritative direction that it needed. Brutus had disappointed Cicero by failing to provide the energetic, aggressive leadership needed in the months after Caesar's death and by choosing in the end to abandon Italy. But he continued to regard him as the great hope of the Republic and, as republican fortunes worsened steadily in the months after the battle of Mutina, he saw him as the one leader who could reverse the downward trend. He believed his appearance in Italy with his army would bring all right-minded citizens flocking to his banner and would provide the unifying and steadying influence needed in the Senate. It would also deter Octavian from any rash initiatives in Italy and would strengthen the loyalty of the armies of Plancus and Decimus Brutus, the chief remaining bulwark of the Republic in the West.[72]

Cicero's reasoning was soundly based, and the Senate supported him and recalled Brutus and his army in early June. But Brutus did not respond, nor was he in any mood to take advice or direction from Cicero. Relations between the two had become severely strained by the middle of 43, as profound differences in their general outlook and approach to the war came to the fore. Brutus had yearned from the start for a peaceful solution. He had not anticipated the upheaval provided by Caesar's assassination, and he remained desperately anxious to minimize the discord and civil violence that resulted from it. He had sought to negotiate with Antony in the immediate aftermath of the Ides, and, when it became clear no satisfactory accommodation was achievable, he had left Italy to avoid the risk of a civil war. He had secured a military base in Macedonia but, by all indications, never with the intention of embarking on an all-out trial of strength with Antony. Negotiation and reconciliation remained

71. *Fam.* 11.14.1, 3; 12.25a.1. *Ad Brut.* 1.10.1, 3–4.
72. *Ad Brut.* 1.10.1, 4; 1.12.2; 2.1.3. *Fam.* 11.25.2; 12.8.1. Decimus was also urging the recall of Brutus. *Fam.* 11.14.2.

his goal, as was illustrated in March 43, when he forced the surrender
of L. Antonius but treated him with high honor, allowing him to retain
his lictors and insignia. Cicero protested, arguing that there was no
room for clemency in dealing with desperadoes who, if victorious,
would eradicate every trace of their opponents, and with whom no peace
was possible without imperiling liberty. But Brutus would not accept
Cicero's view of the war or his uncompromising call for the rapid and
total suppression of the Antonii and their followers by any means available. An unbending legalist, he would not arrogate to himself prerogatives that, in a functioning republic, he believed belonged to the
Senate and people, nor would he take any action that smacked of vengeance or was likely to deepen civil divisions. He preferred to take risks
on the side of peace and clemency than pursue a total and vengeful
victory.[73]

He was equally unwilling to buy allies of dubious loyalty to the Republic with honors or promises, and he strenuously objected to Cicero's
efforts, especially after the battle of Mutina, to woo Octavian, whom he
distrusted utterly and considered a greater threat to the Republic than
Antony. He was particularly outraged by a letter of Cicero to Octavian
that had been sent to him by Atticus and that seemed to him fawning,
humiliating, and likely to inflame Octavian's already dangerous inso-
lence and ambition. He wrote in angry terms to Cicero decrying his
subserviance to the heir of Caesar and asserting he would rather be dead
than live by favor of Octavian.[74]

Brutus's inflexible highmindedness, laudable in the abstract and reminiscent of the principled but obtuse rigidity of Cato that had often caused
Cicero frustration in the fifties, ignored the hard realities facing the
republican side in 43. Antony could never have been opposed in the first
place without the help of Octavian, nor could there be any final victory or
indeed any likelihood of a negotiated settlement without continuing help
from commanders in the West who were unlikely to give it unless lured
by the prospects of political honors and preferment and convinced by
resolute leadership in Rome and a credible republican military force in
Italy that there was a reasonable likelihood of a republican victory.

73. *Ad Brut.* 1.10.1. Cf. *Ad Brut.* 1.2.3; 1.2a.2; 1.3.3; 1.4.2–3; 1.15; 2.3.2; 2.4.5;
2.5.1, 3, 5.
74. *Ad Brut.* 1.4.3; 1.4a.2–3; 1.15.8–9; 1.16; 1.17. The authenticity of the last two
letters remains in question. See Shackleton Bailey, *Ad Brut.*, 10–12.

Cicero made these points to Brutus in defense of his past policy and present advice, and he continued to plead with him throughout June and July to return to Italy. But Brutus was not to be persuaded, and occupied himself instead in settling affairs in Thrace and Asia.[75] In Italy and the West, republican fortunes continued on the course that Cicero had feared. The Senate, suffering from the absence of consuls and from its internal divisions, remained ineffectual and even failed to raise the funds it needed to pay the costs of the war and the rewards promised to the soldiers. In Gaul, Plancus, governor of Gallia Comata, had remained loyal following the link-up of Antony and Lepidus, and had established himself at Cularo, where he was joined by Decimus Brutus about the middle of June. His position, however, was precarious. He had fourteen legions, including the army of Brutus, but of these only four were veteran, and he could not hope to hold out indefinitely with such forces against the combined armies of Antony and Lepidus. He urgently requested reinforcements during June and July, but no reinforcements were forthcoming, and finally, probably in late August after the balance had been further tilted in Antony's favor by the defection to him of Asinius Pollio, he decided to join his Caesarian colleagues. Decimus Brutus attempted to escape to the East but was captured by brigands and killed on the orders of Antony.[76]

Octavian, meantime, remained committed to his plan to secure the consulship. When the Senate proved recalcitrant, he predictably brought into play the politics of force. In late July he dispatched four hundred of his centurions and soldiers to the Senate to press the case for his election. It was a clear warning of his intent to apply whatever military pressure was necessary, but the Senate refused to bend and disdainfully dismissed the soldiers' demands. Octavian responded by leading his army on Rome. The Senate, encouraged by the arrival of two legions from Africa, attempted at first to organize resistance but, in a familiar pattern, the African legions deserted to Octavian and the resistance collapsed. Octavian was welcomed into the city by crowds from all classes, and on August 19 he was elected consul together with his cousin Q. Pedius.[77]

75. *Ad Brut.* 1.15; 1.18.1–2.

76. *Fam.* 10.8.6; 10.9; 10.11; 10.15; 10.17; 10.18; 10.21; 10.23; 10.24; 11.13a; 11.26. Appian, *BC* 3.97. Velleius 2.64. Dio 46.53. Val. Max. 5.7.6; 9.3.3.

77. Appian, *BC* 3.88–94. Dio 46.41–45. Suetonius, *Aug.* 26. Cicero's role in these events is hard to determine. His last extant letter (*Ad Brut.* 1.18) dates from July 27 and

About two months later he marched northwards to confront Antony and Lepidus, who had crossed into Cisalpine Gaul. He had already signaled that he wished to negotiate by having the decrees of outlawry against Antony and Lepidus revoked. The negotiations took place on an island in a river near Bononia and resulted in a pact which established the three commanders as triumvirs holding dictatorial powers for a period of five years. On November 27 the pact was voted into law by the tribune P. Titius. The Republic had finally breathed its last.[78]

Proscriptions on a grand scale followed, the lists agreed by the triumvirs before they left Bononia. It was as ruthless a purge as Cicero had predicted, and it revealed the naiveté of Brutus's hopes for reconciliation and negotiation. All four Ciceros were on the lists, a measure of how far the vengeance of Antony was reaching. Cicero had been in the country since Octavian's takeover of Rome in August. Octavian had given him permission to leave the city and he had gratefully fled to the comfort and seclusion of his villas. He was at Tusculum with his brother and nephew when he heard the news of the proscriptions. They decided to attempt to reach Brutus in Macedonia. Quintus turned back to get more resources for the journey and was captured and killed along with his son. Cicero headed for Caieta and embarked, but was forced to put ashore again because of bad weather. Distraught and torn by the indecision that always assailed him in such predicaments, he took refuge in his nearby villa, where he was overtaken by a group of soldiers, led by Herennius, a centurion, and Popillius, a military tribune, whom he had earlier defended in a criminal trial. His slaves wished to defend him, but he refused to offer any resistance and calmly offered his neck to his executioner Herennius. He had long before told Atticus he would never again leave

---

indicates his sadness that he no longer seems likely to be able to fulfill his pledge to the Senate to keep Octavian loyal. According to Appian (3.82), Dio (46.42), and Plutarch (*Cic*.45), Octavian succeeded in enlisting Cicero's help in his bid for the consulship by offering to make him his colleague, but this is so totally at variance with the evidence of Cicero's letters to Brutus that it must be rejected. There had been talk after Mutina of electing Cicero to the consulship, but it was only rumor (*Ad Brut.* 1.4a.4). Cicero appears to have stayed active to the end, but, after Octavian gained control of the city, he left to seek consolation in his Tusculan villa. Octavian excused him from attendance at Rome and a fragment of a letter, preserved by Nonius (p.436, 22–24), records his appreciation: "Quod mihi et Philippo vacationem das, bis gaudeo: nam et praeteritis ignoscis et concedis futura." These are the last surviving words from Cicero's pen.

78. Appian, *BC* 3.95–96; 4.2–4. Dio 46.54–55. Suetonius, *Aug.* 96. Plutarch, *Cic.* 46; *Ant.* 19.

Italy for a military camp, and an honorable death may have been at the end his fondest wish. He died on December 7, slightly less than a month before his sixty-fourth birthday.[79]

The manner of his death brought Cicero praise and sympathy from the writers of antiquity.[80] His life and character have evoked more varied reactions. He was not liked or admired by all his contemporaries and modern judgments have been similarly mixed. The reasons are not hard to find. Cicero was a complex man with glaring faults and limitations counterbalanced by extraordinary gifts and outstanding virtues. He was never an ideal example of the political *virtus* he so highly admired. He had a craving for praise and recognition that made him offensive to many and left him susceptible to flattery and manipulation and to a measure of self-delusion. He was not always a sound judge of his own standing and accomplishments. It should be stressed, however, that his penchant for self-acclaim was to a large extent fueled by a desire to vindicate himself in the eyes of a spiteful and begrudging *nobilitas* and to eradicate any stigma associated with his exile. His vanity never led him consciously to put his own aggrandizement before the public good, and never approached the ungoverned egotism and megalomania of the military potentates of the first century who proved ready to subvert the law and go to the extremes of violence and civil war to safeguard their power and dignity.

A more serious flaw was his volatile temperament and general emotional fragility that deprived him of the capacity for calm judgment and of the constancy and resolution that were such a central part of his concept of *virtus*. He was prone to swings of mood and emotional responses that complicated his political relationships and led to quick shifts of attitude toward people and issues. His emotional brittleness and volatility proved a particular handicap in the disintegrating political world of the fifties, when he had to confront a variety of pressures and a succession of personal setbacks and political disappointments, and when his response was often compromise, withdrawal, or fumbling indecision and inaction.

But, while Cicero lacked the stoical constancy of Cato and the single-minded toughness and raw courage of Caesar, he had a wealth of com-

---

79. Appian, *BC* 4.5–20. Dio 47.8. Plutarch, *Cic.* 47–49; *Ant.* 20. Livy, frag. 120. Velleius 2.66. Florus 2.16. Augustine, *Civ. Dei* 30. Orosius 6.18.11. Seneca, *Suas.* 6.17.
80. Velleius 2.66. Livy, frag. 120. Seneca, *Suas.* 6 and 7. Appian, *BC* 4.20. Plutarch, *Cic.* 49. Quintilian, *Inst.* 12.1.17. Pollio *apud* Seneca, *Suas.* 6.14–15.

pensating merits. He abounded in human warmth and sociability that made him a loyal and devoted friend and family man, and an amiable, witty, and conversable companion who reveled in conviviality and all forms of social interchange. He had intellectual gifts that were rare and admirable and that give him a unique place in the intellectual history of antiquity. Opinion may vary about the originality of his thought, but few will dispute the breadth of his knowledge or his high importance as a transmitter of ideas, or his brilliant mastery of language seen in the articulate clarity and cogency with which he gave expression to many enduring ideals of Western culture, especially in relation to liberty, civil rights, and humanistic education. He admired and exalted *humanitas* and exemplified it in its fullest sense.

His political virtues were also considerable. He had a driving ambition, energy, and initiative, which, combined with exceptional oratorical ability, enabled him to rise from obscurity to nobility and to remain a prestigious and potentially commanding figure even when force had largely displaced constitutional government. He was deeply patriotic, devoted to the *respublica* and its ideals and, though a pragmatist and political realist, he was never deflected from his republican goals or from his conviction that all political action must have as its ultimate aim the public good. He also adhered with rigid consistency to the standards of self-restraint and cleanhandedness that he prescribed for the good statesman, and his all-round moral integrity set him far apart from a great many of his contemporaries in the increasingly corrupt and amoral world of the late Republic.

He made no lasting impact, however, on the course of political events in his time, and his political views and judgments were often deeply flawed. His consulship brought him distinction and a measure of acclaim, but its successes proved ephemeral. He had not found a solution to the ills of the Republic, his political vision circumscribed by his conservative heritage and its elitist political and social ideas. Apart from his gallant effort in 43, his career after 63 had only fleeting moments of success and satisfaction, as he became increasingly isolated, a lonely figure alienated from his only natural political allies, the conservative nobility, and forced by his concern to preserve his safety and dignity into politically perilous friendships that hopelessly complicated his subsequent political choices. His troubles were partly a consequence of the turbulent nature of the times and of his peculiarly difficult circumstances as a new man who had no independent power base and felt shut out from the inner ranks of those who shared his political beliefs. But they were also a product of false expectations after the successes of his consulship, of misplaced confidence in Pompey, and of a paranoiac distrust of the *boni* that, perhaps more than aristocratic haughtiness and begrudgery, kept him from a secure and prominent place in the optimate leadership.

But Cicero's political limitations can be easily exaggerated. None of his contemporaries had any better understanding of the problems of the Republic or pointed to better solutions, and none had a loftier concept of statesmanship or worked harder to abide by it. None, certainly, had as many varied talents and interests or has left so deep an imprint on Western thought and culture.

BIBLIOGRAPHY

Adcock, F. E. "The Legal Term of Caesar's Governorship in Gaul." *CQ* 26 (1932), 14–26.

Albini, U. "L'orazione contro Vatinio." *PP* 66 (1959), 172–84.

Alexander, M. "Repetition of Prosecutions, and the Scope of Prosecutions, in the Standing Criminal Courts." *Classical Antiquity* 1 (1982), 141–66.

Alföldi, A. *Studien über Caesars Monarchie.* Lung, 1953.

———. *Oktavians Aufstieg sur Macht.* Bonn, 1976.

———. *Caesar in 44 v. Chr.* Vol. 1. Bonn, 1985.

Allen, W., Jr. "The Vettius Affair Once More." *TAPA* 81 (1950), 153–63.

———. "Caesar's *Regnum* (Suet. *Jul.* 9.2)." *TAPA* 84 (1953), 227–36.

Anderson, W. S. *Pompey, His friends and the Literature of the First Century B.C.* Berkeley, Calif., 1963.

Ardley, G. W. R. "Cicero on Philosophy and History." *Prudentia* 1 (1969), 28–41.

Arnim, H. von. *Leben und Werke de Dio von Prusa.* Berlin, 1898.

Arnold, E. V. *Roman Stoicism.* Cambridge, 1911.

Astbury, R. "Varro and Pompey." *CQ* 17 (1967), 403–07.

Austin, R. G. *M. Tulli Ciceronis Pro M. Caelio Oratio.* 3d ed. Oxford, 1960.

Badian, E. *Foreign Clientelae.* Oxford, 1958.

———. "M. Porcius Cato and the Annexation and Early Administration of Cyprus." *JRS* 55 (1965),110–21.

———. *Roman Imperialism in the Late Republic.* Oxford, 1968.

———. "Two Roman Non-Entities." *CQ* 19 (1969), 198–204.

———. *Publicans and Sinners.* Oxford, 1972.

————. "The Attempt to Try Caesar." *Polis and Imperium: Studies in Honor of E. T. Salmon.* Ed. J. A. S. Evans. Toronto, 1974, 145–66.

————. Manius Acilius Glabrio and the *audacissimi.*" *AJP* 96 (1975), 67–75.

————. "The *Auctor* of the *Lex Flavia.*" 55 (1977), 233–38.

Balsdon, J. P. V. D. "Consular Provinces under the Late Republic." *JRS* 29 (1939), 57–73, 167–83.

————. "Roman History 58–56 B.C. Three Ciceronian Problems." *JRS* 47 (1957), 15–20.

————. "Fabula Clodiana." *Historia* 15 (1966), 65–73.

————. *Romans and Aliens.* London, 1979.

Bellen, A. "Cicero und der Aufstieg Oktavians." *Gymnasium* 92 (1985), 161–89.

Bengston, H. *Marcus Antonius: Triumvir und Herrscher des Orients.* Munich, 1977.

Benner, H. *Die Politik des P. Clodius Pulcher.* Stuttgart, 1987.

Bernadete, S. "Cicero's De Legibus I. Its Plan and Intention." *AJP* 108 (1987), 295–309.

Bersanetti, G. M. "La tradizione antica e l'opinione degli storici moderni sul primo triumvirato." *Rev. Indo - Grec. - Ital. Filol.* 11 (1927), 1–20, 185–204; 12 (1928), 21–42.

Botsford, G. W. *The Roman Assemblies.* New York, 1968.

Broughton, T. R. S. "Metellus Celer's Gallic Province." *TAPA* 79 (1948), 73–76.

Brunt, P. A. "The *Equites* in the Late Republic." *Second International Conference on Economic History 1962 (1965),* 117–37.

————. "The Roman Mob." *Past and Present* 35 (1966), 3–27.

————. *Italian Manpower, 225 B.C.–A.D.14.* Oxford, 1971.

————. "Dio Chrysostom and Stoic Social Thought." *PCPS* 19 (1973), 26–33.

————. "Cicero and Historiography." *Miscellanea di studi classici in onore di E. Manni.* Rome, 1976, 311–40.

————. "*Laus Imperii.*" *Imperialism in the Ancient World.* Ed. P. D. A. Garnsey and C. R. Whittaker. Cambridge 1978, 159–91.

————. "Cicero's *Officium* in the Civil War." *JRS* 76 (1986), 12–32.

Bruwaene, M. van den. "Précisions sur la loi religieuse du de legibus II 19–22 de Cicéron." *Helikon* 1 (1961), 40–93.

Büchner, K. "Sinn und Entstehung von De Legibus." *Atti del Primo Congresso Internazionale di Studi Ciceroniani.* Rome, 1961, 81–90.

————. "Humanum und Humanitas in der römischen Welt." *Studium generale* 14 (1961), 636–46.

————. *Cicero: Bestand und Wandel seiner gestigen Welt.* Heidelberg, 1964.

Burns, A. "Pompey's Strategy and Domitius' Stand at Corfinium." *Historia* 15 (1966), 74–95.

Calboli, G. "La formazione oratoria di Cicerone." *Vichiana* 2 (1965), 3–30.

Cancelli, A. F. "Iuris consensu nella definizione ciceroniana di respublica." *RCCM* 14 (1972), 247–67.

Cary, M. "The Land Legislation of Julius Caesar's First Consulship." *JP* 35 (1920), 174–90.

―――. "Asinus Germanus." *CQ* 17 (1923), 103–07.

Cauer, F. *Ciceros politisches Denken.* Berlin, 1903.

Ciaceri, E. *Cicerone e i suoi tempi.* 2 vols. Milan, 1939–41.

Clarke, M. L. *The Roman Mind.* London, 1956.

―――. *The Noblest Roman: Marcus Brutus and His Reputation.* London, 1981.

Classen, C. J. "Cicero, the Laws and the Law-Courts." *Latomus* 37 (1978), 597–619.

Collins, J. H. "Tullia's Engagement and Marriage to Dolabella." *CJ* 47 (1951), 164–68.

―――. "Caesar and the Corruption of Power." *Historia* 4 (1955), 445–65.

Cotton, H. M. "The Role of Cicero's Letters of Recommendation; *Justitia versus Gratia.*" *Hermes* 114 (1986), 443–60.

Crawford, J. W. *M. Tullius Cicero: The Lost and Unpublished Orations.* Göttingen, 1984.

Cuff, P. J. "The Terminal Date of Caesar's Gallic Command." *Historia* 7 (1958), 445–71.

Dahlheim, W. *Struktur und Entwicklung.* Munich, 1968.

Defourny, P. "Histoire et eloquence." *LEC* 21 (1953), 156–66.

Dessau, H. "Gaius Rabirius Postumus." *Hermes* 46 (1911), 613–20.

Dixon, S. "Family Finances: Terentia and Tullia." *Antichthon* 18 (1984), 78–101.

―――. *The Roman Mother.* London, 1988.

Dorey, T. A. "Cicero, Pompey and the Pro Archia." *Orpheus* 2 (1955), 32–35.

Douglas, A. E. "M. Calidius and the Atticists." *CQ* 5 (1955), 241–47.

―――. "Cicero the Philosopher." *Cicero.* Ed. T. A. Dorey. London, 1964.

―――. *M. Tulli Ciceronis Brutus.* Oxford, 1966.

―――. "The Intellectual Background of Cicero's Rhetorica: A Study in Method." *ANRW* 1.3 (1973), 95–138.

Dreizehnter, A. "Pompeius als Städtegrunder." *Chiron* 5 (1975), 213–45.

Drexler, H. "Parerga Caesariana." *Hermes* 70 (1935), 203–34.

―――. "*Justum Bellum.*" *RhM* 102 (1959), 97–140.

―――. "*Gloria.*" Helicon 2 (1962), 3–36.

Duff, J. D. "Cicero's Commission and Movements at the Beginning of the Civil War." *JP* 33 (1914), 154–60.

Du Mesnil, A. *Cicero: De Legibus*. Leipzig, 1879.

Earl, D. C. *Sallust*. Amsterdam, 1966.

———. *The Moral and Political Tradition of Rome*. London, 1967.

Elton, G. R. The Terminal Date of Caesar's Gallic Proconsulate." *JRS* 36 (1946), 18–42.

Epstein, D. F. "Cicero's Personal Enemies on the Ides of March." *Latomus* 46 (1987), 556–70.

Ernout, A. "Les noms latins en *-TUS*." *Philologica classica* 1946, 225–28.

Ernout, A., and Meillet, E. *Dictionnaire étymologique de la langue latine*. Paris, 1951.

Evans, R. J. "The *Consulares* and *Praetorii* in the Roman Senate at the Beginning of Sulla's Dictatorship." *Athenaeum* 62 (1983), 521–28.

Fallu, E. "Les rationes du proconsul Cicéron–Un example de style administratif et d'interprétation historique dans la correspondence de Cicéron." *ANRW* 1.3 (1973), 209–38.

Fantham, E. "*Aequabilitas* in Cicero's Political Theory and the Greek Tradition of Proportional Justice." *CQ* 23 (1973), 285–90.

———. "The Trials of Gabinius in 54 B.C." *Historia* 24 (1975), 425–43.

Fedeli, P. "De Officiis di Cicerone." *ANRW* 1.4 (1973), 357–427.

Ferguson, J. *Moral Values in the Ancient World*. London, 1958.

Ferguson, W. S. "The *Lex Calpurnia* of 149 B.C." *JRS* 11 (1921), 86–100.

Finley, M. I. *The Ancient Economy*. London, 1973.

Flambard, J. M. "Clodius les colleges, la plebe et les esclaves. Recherches sur la politique populaire au milieu du iᵉʳ siècle." *MEFR* 89 (1977), 115–56.

Frank, T. "Caelianum illud, Cic. Ad Att. X.15.2." *CP* 14 (1919), 287–89.

Frisch, H. *Cicero's Fight for the Republic*. Trans. N. Halslund. Copenhagen, 1946.

Fritz, K.von, "The Mission of L. Caesar and L. Roscius in January 49 B.C." *TAPA* 72 (1941), 125–56.

———. "Pompey's Policy before and after the Outbreak of the Civil War of 49 B.C." *TAPA* 73 (1942), 145–80.

Fuhrmann, M. "Cum dignitate otium. Politisches Program und Staatstheorie bei Cicero." *Gymnasium* 67 (1960), 497–500.

Gabba, E. "Per un' interpretazione politica de *De Officiis*." *RAL* 34 (1979), 117–41.

Gardner, R., ed. and trans. Cicero's *Pro Sestio* and *In Vatinium*. Loeb Library. Cambridge, Mass., 1957.

Gelzer, M. "Die *Lex Vatinia de imperio Caesaris*." *Hermes* 63 (1928), 113–37.

———. *Pompeius*. Munich, 1949.

_____. *Caesar: Politician and Statesman.* Trans. P. Needham. Oxford, 1968.

_____. *M. Cicero. Ein biographischer Versuch.* Wiesbaden, 1969.

Gigon, O. "Cicero und die griechische Philosophie." *ANRW* 1.4 (1973), 226–61.

Gilson, E. "Eloquence et sagesse selon Cicéron." *Phoenix* 7 (1953), 1–19.

Goar, R. J. *Cicero and the State Religion.* Amsterdam, 1972.

Greenidge, A. H. J. "The Repeal of the Lex Aelia Fufia." *CR* (1893), 158–61.

_____. *The Legal Procedure of Cicero's Time.* Oxford, 1901.

Grube, G. M. A. *The Greek and Roman Critics.* London, 1965.

Gruen, E. S. "P. Clodius: Instrument or Independent Agent?" *Phoenix* 20 (1966), 120–30.

_____. "The Consular Elections for 53 B.C." *Hommages à M. Renard.* Vol. 2. Brussels, 1969, 311–21.

_____. "Some Criminal Trials of the Late Republic: Political and Prosopographical Problems." *Athenaeum* 49 (1971), 54–69.

_____. "The Trial of C. Antonius." *Latomus* 32 (1973), 301–10.

_____. *The Last Generation of the Roman Republic.* Berkeley, Calif., 1974.

_____. "Pompey, The Roman Aristocracy and the Conference at Luca." *Historia* 18 (1979), 71–108.

_____. *The Hellenistic World and the Coming of Rome.* 2 vols. Berkeley, Calif., 1984.

Guillemin, A. M. "Cicéron entre le génie grec et le mos maiorum." *REL* 33 (1955), 209.

Guite, H. "Cicero's Attitude towards the Greeks." *Greece and Rome* 9 (1962), 142–59.

Gwatkin, W. E., Jr. "Cicero *In Catilinam* 1.19–Catiline's Attempt to Place Himself in *Libera Custodia.*" *TAPA* 65 (1934), 271–81.

Hanslik, R. "Cicero und das erste Triumvirat." *RhM* 98 (1955), 324–34.

Harris, W. V. *War and Imperialism in Republican Rome.* Oxford, 1979.

Hardy, E. G. "The Catilinarian Conspiracy in Its Context: A Re-study of the Evidence." *JRS* 7 (1917), 153–228.

Hayne, L. "Who Went to Luca?" *CP* 69 (1974), 217–20.

Heitland, W. E. *The Roman Republic.* Vol. 3. Cambridge, 1909.

Hellegouarc'h, J. *Le vocabulaire latin des relations et des partis politiques sous la république.* Paris, 1963.

Hendrickson, G. L. "Brutus, *De Virtute.*" *AJP* 60 (1939), 401–13.

Hermann, P. "Der römische Kaisereid." *Hypomnemata* 20 (1968), 66–78.

Hillard, T. W. "P. Clodius Pulcher, 62–58 B.C.: 'Pompeii Adfinis et Sodalis'." *PBSR* 1 (1982), 34–44.

Hillman, T. P. "Strategic Reality and the Movements of Caesar, January 49 B.C." *Historia* 37 (1988), 248–52.

Holmes Rice, T. *The Roman Republic.* Vols. 1–3. Oxford, 1923.

————. *The Architect of the Roman Empire*. Vols. 1–2. Oxford, 1928–31.

Horsfall, N. "The Ides of March: Some New Problems." *Greece and Rome* 21 (1974), 191–99.

How, W. W., ed. *Cicero: Select Letters*. Vols. 1–2. Oxford, 1926.

————. "Cicero's Ideal in His *De Republica*," *JRS* 20 (1930), 24–42.

Hubaux, J. "La mort de Jules César." *L'académie royale de Belgique* 13 (1957), 76–87.

Hunt, H. A. K. *The Humanism of Cicero*. Melbourne, 1954.

Hunter, L. W. "Cicero's Journey to His Province of Cicilia in 51 B.C." *JRS* 3 (1913), 73–97.

Huzar, E. G. *Mark Antony*. Minneapolis, 1978.

Jameson, S. "The Intended Date of Caesar's Return from Gaul." *Latomus* 29 (1970), 638–60.

Jolliffe, R. O. *Phases of Corruption in Roman Administration*. Menasha, Wis., 1919.

Jones, A. H. M. *The Cities of the Eastern Roman Provinces*. 2d ed. Oxford, 1971.

————. *The Criminal Courts of the Roman Republic and Principate*. Oxford, 1972.

Keaveney, A., and Madden, J. A. "An *ovatio* for Octavian?" *Phoenix* 37 (1983), 245–47.

Kennedy, G. "Antony's Speech at Caesar's Funeral." *QJS* 54 (1958), 99–108.

————. *The Art of Rhetoric in the Roman World*. Princeton, 1972.

Kenter, L. P. *Cicero, De Legibus: A Commentary on Book I*. Amsterdam, 1972.

Keyes, C. W. "Original Elements in Cicero's Ideal Constitution." *AJP* 42 (1921), 309–23.

Knight, D. W. "The Political Acumen of Cicero after Caesar's Death." *Latomus* 27 (1968), 157–64.

Knoche, U. *Magnitido Animi*. Ph. Supplbd, 27, 3. Leipzig, 1935.

————. "Cicero, ein Mittler griechischer Kultur." *Hermes* 87 (1959), 57–74.

Kroll, W. "Studien über Ciceros Schrift De oratore." *RhM* 58 (1903), 552–97.

Kuklica, P. "Ciceros Begriff *Virtus* und dessen Interpretation." *GLO* 7–8 (1975–76), 3–23.

Kumaniecki, K. "Ciceros Rede de haruspicum responsis." *Klio* 37 (1959), 135–52.

————. "Ciceros Rede de aere alieno Milonis." *Klio* 59 (1977), 381–401.

Labowski, L. *Die Ethik des Panaitios*. Leipzig, 1934.

Lacey, W. K. "The Tribunate of Curio." *Historia* 10 (1961), 318–29.

————. "Cicero, *Pro Sestio* 96–143." *CQ* n.s. 12 (1962), 67–71.

————. "Cicero and Clodius." *Antichthon* 8 (1974), 85–92.

Lazenby, J. F. "The Conference at Luca and the Gallic War." *Latomus* 18 (1959), 67–76.

Leach, J. *Pompey the Great*. London, 1978.

Lengle, J. "Pietas." *Römische Wertbegriffe*. Darmstadt, 1967, 229–73.

Lepore, E. *Il principe ciceroniano e gli ideali politici della tarda reppublica*. Naples, 1954.

Levi, M. A. "Una pagina di storia agraria romana." *Atene e Roma* 3 (1922), 239–52.

Linderski, J. "Ciceros Rede *Pro Caelio* und die Ambitus und Vereingesetzgebung der ausgehenden Republik." *Hermes* 89 (1961), 106–19.

———. "Constitutional Aspects of the Consular Elections in 59 B.C." *Historia* 14 (1965), 423–42.

———. "Der Senat und die Vereine." *Gesellschaft und Recht in griechisch - römischen Altertum* (1968), 94–132.

———. "The Libri Reconditi." *HSCP* 89 (1985), 207–34.

Lintott, A. W. *Violence in Republican Rome*. Oxford, 1968.

———. "P. Clodius Pulcher—*Felix Catilina?*" *Greece and Rome* 14 (1969), 157–69.

———. "Cicero and Milo." *JRS* 64 (1974), 62–78.

Liscu, M. O. *Etude sur la langue de la philosophie morale chez Cicéron*. Paris, 1930.

Luck, G. "Etymologie et usage du mot *sapientia* chez les Latins, notamment chez Cicéron." *ABG* 60 (1964), 203–15.

Luibhéid, C. "The Luca Conference." *CP* 65 (1970), 88–94.

McDermott, W. C. "*Vettius ille, ille noster index*." *TAPA* 80 (1949), 351–67.

———. "De Lucceis." *Hermes* 97 (1969), 233–46.

———. "Q. Cicero." *Historia* 20 (1971), 702–17.

———. "Curio *Pater* and Cicero." *AJP* 93 (1972), 381–411.

———. "M. Cicero and M. Tiro." *Historia* 21 (1972), 259–86.

McDonald, W. "Clodius and the *Lex Aelia Fufia*." *JRS* 19 (1929), 164–79.

Magie, D. *Roman Rule in Asia Minor*. 2 vols. Princeton, 1950.

Malcovati, H. *Oratorum Romanorum Fragmenta Liberae Reipublicae*. 2d edition. Turin, 1955.

Marsh, F. B. "The Policy of Clodius." *CQ* 21 (1927), 30–35.

Marshall, A. J. "The Structure of Cicero's Edict." *AJP* 85 (1964), 185–91.

———. "Governors on the Move." *Phoenix* 20 (1966), 231–46.

———. "The *Lex Pompeia de provinciis* (52 B.C.) and Cicero's *Imperium* in 51–50 B.C.: Constitutional Aspects." *ANRW* 1.1 (1972), 887–921.

Marshall, B. "Pompeius' Temple of Hercules." *Antichthon* 8 (1974), 80–84.

Martin, P. "Cicéron Princeps." *Latomus* 39 (1980), 850–78.

Meador, P. H. "Rhetoric and Humanism in Cicero." *Phil and Rhet.* 3 (1970), 1–12.

Meier, Ch. "Zur Chronologie und Politik in Caesars ersten Konsulat." *Historia* 10 (1961), 68–98.

_____. "Pompeius' Ruckkehr aus dem Mithridatischen Kriege und die Catilinarische Vershwörung." *Athenaeum* 40 (1962), 103–25.

_____. *Res Publica Amissa.* Wiesbaden, 1966.

_____. "Das Kompromiss—Angebot an Caesar i. J. 59 Chr., ein Biespiel senatorischer, Verfassungspolitik." *MH* 32 (1975), 197–208.

Meyer, E. *Caesars Monarchie und das Principat des Pompeius.* Stuttgart, 1922.

Michel, A. *Rhétorique et philosophie chez Cicéron.* Paris, 1960.

Michels, A. *The Calendar of the Roman Republic.* Princeton, 1967.

Mitchell, T. N. "Cicero before Luca (September 57–April 56)." *TAPA* 100 (1969), 295–320.

_____. *Cicero: The Ascending Years.* New Haven, 1979.

_____. "Cicero on the Moral Crisis of the late Republic." *Hermethena* 86 (1984), 21–24.

_____. "*The Leges Clodiae and Obnuntiatio.*" *CQ* 36 (1986), 172–76.

M. C. Mittelstadt. "Cicero's Political velificatio mutata, 54–51 B.C.: Compromise or Capitulation?" *PP 40 (1985), 13–28.*

Mommsen, Th. *Die Rechtsfrage zwischen Caesar und den Senat.* Breslau, 1857.

_____. "Die Gardetruppen der römischen Republik und der Kaiserzeit." *Hermes* 14 (1879), 25–40.

_____. *Römisches Staatsrecht.* 3d ed. Vols. 1–3. Leipzig, 1887–88.

_____. *Römisches Strafrecht.* Leipzig, 1899.

Morgan, M. G. "*Imperium sine finibus:* Romans and World Conquest in the First Century B.C." *Panhellenica: Essays in Ancient History and Historiography in Honor of T. S. Brown.* Lawrence, Kan., 1980, 143–54.

Mueller, R. "Die Wertung der Bildungsdisziplinen bei Cicero." *Klio* 43 (1965), 77–173.

Nisbet, R. G., ed. Cicero, *De Domo Sua.* Oxford, 1939.

Norr, D. "Zur sozialen und rechtlichen Bewertung der freien Arbeit in Rom." *ZRG* 82 (1965), 67–105.

North, H. *Sophrosyne: Self-Knowledge and Self-Restraint in Greek Literature.* Ithaca, 1966.

North, J. A. "The Development of Roman Imperialism." *JRS* 71 (1981), 1–9.

Nybakken, O. E. "Humanitas Romana." *TAPA* 70 (1939), 396–45.

Ogle, M. B. "Horace, Epistle 1.19.28–29." *AJP* 43 (1922), 55–61.

Oost, S. I. "Cato Uticensis and the Annexation of Cyprus." *CP* 50 (1955), 98–112.

Ooteghem, J. van. *Pompée le grand.* Brussels, 1954.

Orban, M. "Réhabilitation de la parole dans le *De Oratore* de Cicéron." *AC* 19 (1950), 27–44.

Ortmann, U. *Cicero, Brutus und Octavian–Republikaner und Caesarianer: Ihr gegenseitiges Verhältnis im Krisenjahre 44/43 v. Chr.* Bonn, 1988.

Palmer, R. E. A. "C. Verres' Legacy of Charm and Love to the City of Rome: A New Document." *Rendiconti della Pontificia Accademia Romana di Archeologia* 51–52 (1978–79, 1979–80), 111–36.

Parrish, E. "The Senate on January 1, 62 B.C." *CW* (1972), 160–68.

———. "Crassus' New Friends and Pompey's Return." *Phoenix* 27 (1973), 357–80.

Payne, A. N., Jr. "*Cicero's Proconsulate.*" Ph.D. diss. Cornell University, 1969.

Petrochilis, N. *Roman Attitudes to the Greeks.* Athens, 1974.

Philippe, M. "La Lex Clodia sur le banissement de Cicéron." *Athenaeum* 65 (1987), 465–92.

Philippson, R. "Das Sittlichschone bei Panaitios." *Philologus* 85 (1930), 357–413.

Pocock, L. G. "Publius Clodius and the Acts of Caesar." *CQ* 18 (1924), 59–64.

———. *A Commentary on Cicero In Vatinium.* London, 1926.

Pohlenz, M. *Antikes Führertum: Cicero de Officiis und das Lebensideal des Panaitios.* Leipzig, 1934.

Pöschl, V. *Römisches Staat und griechisches Staatsdenken bei Cicero.* Berlin, 1936.

Rawson, B. "Pompey and Hercules." *Antichthon* 4 (1970), 30–37.

Rawson, E. "Cicero the Historian and Cicero the Antiquarian." *JRS* 62 (1972), 33–45.

———. "The Interpretation of Cicero's De Legibus." *ANRW* 1.4 (1973), 335–55.

———. "The Eastern Clientelae of Clodius and the Claudii." *Historia* 22 (1973), 219–39.

———. "Caesar's Heritage: Hellenistic Kings and Their Roman Equals." *JRS* 65 (1975), 148–59.

———. "More on the *Clientelae* of the Patrician Claudii." *Historia* 26 (1977), 340–57.

Reitzenstein, R. *Werden und Wesen der Humanität im Altertum.* Strasbourg, 1907.

———. "Cicero's 'Staat' als politische Tendenzschrift." *Hermes* 59 (1924), 73–94.

Rhodes, P. J. "Silvae Callesque." *Historia* 27 (1978), 617–20.

Rich, J. W. *Declaring War in the Roman Republic in the Period of Transmarine Expansion.* Brussels, 1976.

———. "Silvae Callesque." *Latomus* 45 (1986), 505–21.

Rickman, G. *The Corn Supply of Ancient Rome*. Oxford, 1980.

Rist, J. M. *Stoic Philosophy*. Cambridge, 1969.

Robertis, F. M. de. *Il diritto associativo romano dai collegi della reppublica alle corporazioni del basso impero*. Bari, 1938.

Rundell, W. M. F. "Cicero and Clodius: The Question of Credibility." *Historia* 28 (1979), 301–28.

Sabine, G. H., and Smith, S. B. *Cicero: On the Commonwealth*. Columbus, Ohio, 1929.

Sanders, H. A. "The So-Called First Triumvirate." *MAAR* 10 (1932), 110–13.

Sarsila, J. "Some Notes on *Virtus* in Sallust and Cicero." *Arctos* 12 (1978), 135–43.

Schadewaldt, W. "Humanitas Romana." *ANRW* 1.4 (1973), 43–62.

Schmidt, O. E. *Der Briefwechsel des M. Tullius Cicero von seinem Proconsulat in Cicilen bis zu Caesars Ermordung*. Leipzig, 1983.

Schmidt, P. L. *Die Abfassungszeit von Cicero Schrift über die Gesetze*. Rome, 1969.

———. "Cicero De Republica." *ANRW* 1.4 (1973), 262–333.

Schulte, W. K. *Orator Untersuchungen über das Ciceronische Bildungsideal*. Frankfurt, 1935.

Seager, R. "Clodius, Pompeius and the Exile of Cicero." *Latomus* 24 (1965), 519–31.

———. *Pompey: A Political Biography*. Oxford, 1979.

Sealey, R. "*Habe rationem meam*." *CM* 18 (1957), 75–101.

Seel, O. *Cicero*. Stuttgart, 1961.

Shackleton Bailey, D. R. "Expectatio Corfiniensis." *JRS* 46 (1956), 57–64.

———. "The Credentials of L. Caesar and L. Roscius." *JRS* 50 (1960), 80–83.

———. "The Roman Nobility in the Second Civil War." *CQ* 10 (1960), 253–67.

———. *Cicero*. New York, 1971.

———. "Brothers or Cousins?" *AJAH* 8 (1983), 191.

Shackleton Bailey, D. R., ed. *Cicero's Letters to Atticus*. Vols. 1–6. Cambridge, 1965–68.

———. *Cicero: Epistulae ad Familiares*. 2 vols. Cambridge, 1977.

———. *Cicero: Epistulae ad Quintum Fratrem et M. Brutum*. Cambridge, 1980.

Shatzman, I. "The Egyptian Question in Roman Politics (59–54 B.C.)." *Latomus* 30 (1971), 363–69.

———. "The Roman General's Authority over Booty." *Historia* 21 (1972), 177–205.

———. *Senatorial Wealth and Roman Politics*. Brussels, 1975.

Sherwin-White, A. N. *Roman Foreign Policy in the East*. London, 1984.

Shimron, B. "Ciceronian Historiography." *Latomus* 33 (1974), 232–44.

Skinner, M. B. "Clodia Metelli." *TAPA* 113 (1983), 273–87.

Smethurst, S. E. "Cicero and Isocrates." *TAPA* 84 (1953), 262–320.

Smith, R. E. *Cicero the Statesman.* Cambridge, 1966.

Solsmen, F. "Die Theorie des Staatsformen bei Cicero de republica I." *Philologus* 81 (1933), 326–41.

———. "The Aristotelian Tradition in Ancient Rhetoric." *AJP* 62 (1941), 35–50, 169–90.

Sprey, K. *De M. Tullii Ciceronis politica doctrina.* Zutphen, 1928.

Stanton, G. R., and Marshall, B. A. "The Coalition between Pompeius and Crassus 60–59 B.C." *Historia* 24 (1975), 205–19.

Steidle, W. "Einflüsse römischen Lebens und Denkens auf Ciceros Schrift De Oratore." *MH* 9 (1952), 10–41.

Stevens, C. E. "The Terminal Date of Caesar's Command." *AJP* 59 (1938), 169–208.

Stockton, D. "Cicero and the *Ager Companus*." *TAPA* 93 (1962), 471–89.

———. *"Cicero: A Political Biography.* Oxford, 1971.

———. *"Quis iustius induit arma."* *Historia* 24 (1975), 222–59.

Straaten, M. van. *Panétius: Sa vie, ses écrits, et sa doctrine.* Amsterdam, 1946.

Strachan-Davidson, J. L. *Cicero and the Fall of the Roman Republic.* London, 1896.

Strasburger, H. *Caesars Eintritt in die Geschichte.* Munich, 1938.

———. *Caesar im Urteil seiner Zeitgenossen.* Darmstadt, 1969.

Summer, G. V. "The Last Journey of L. Sergius Catalina." *CP* 58 (1963), 215–19.

———. *"Lex Aelia, Lex Fufia."* *AJP* 84 (1963), 337–58.

———. *The Orators in Cicero's Brutus: Prosopography and Chronology.* Toronto, 1973.

———. "The Coitio of 54 B.C., or Waiting for Caesar." *HSPh* 86 (1982), 134–39.

Süss, W. *Cicero: Eine Einführung in seine philosophischen Schriften.* Wiesbaden, 1966.

Syme, R. "The Allegiance of Labienus." *JRS* 28 (1938), 113–25.

———. "Observations on the Province of Cicilia." *Anatolian Studies Presented to W. A. Buckler.* Manchester, 1939, 299–332.

———. *The Roman Revolution.* Oxford, 1939.

———. *Sallust.* Berkeley, Calif., 1964.

Taylor, L. R. *The Divinity of the Roman Emperor.* Middletown, Conn., 1931.

———. "The Election of the Pontifex Maximus in the Late Republic." *CP* 37 (1942), 421–24.

———. "The Date and Meaning of the Vettius Affair." *Historia* 1 (1950), 45–51.

———. "On the Chronology of Caesar's First Consulship." *AJP* 72 (1951), 254–68.

———. "Political Motives in Cicero's Defense of Archias." *AJP* 73 (1952), 62–70.

———. *Party Politics in the Age of Caesar*. Berkeley, Calif., 1964.

———. "The Dating of Major Legislation and Elections in Caesar's First Consulship." *Historia* 17 (1968), 173–93.

Taylor, L. R., and T. R. S. Broughton. "The Order of the Two Consuls' Names in the Yearly Lists." *MAAR* 19 (1949), 3–14.

———. "The Order of the Consuls' Names in Official Republican Lists." *Historia* 17 (1968), 166–72.

Thompson, L. A. "Cicero's Succession-Problem in Cicilia." *AJP* 86 (1965), 375–86.

Treggiari, S. *Roman Freedmen during the Late Republic*. Oxford, 1969.

Twyman, B. "The Metelli, Pompeius and Prosopography." *ANRW* 1.1 (1972), 817–74.

Valeton, I. M. J. "*De Iure obnuntiandi comitiis et consiliis.*" *MN* n.s. 19 (1891), 75–113, 229–70.

Vogt, J. *Ciceros Glaube an Rom*. Stuttgart, 1935.

Ward, A. M. *Marcus Crassus and the Late Roman Republic*. Columbia, Mo., 1977.

———. "The Conference at Luca: Did It Happen?" *AJAH* 5 (1980), 48–63.

Weigel, R. D. "Lepidus Reconsidered." *AC* 17 (1974), 67–73.

Weinstock, S. "Clodius and the *Lex Aelia Fufia*." *JRS* 27 (1937), 215–22.

———. *Divus Julius*. Oxford, 1971.

Wiedermann, T. "*Fetiales.*" *CQ* 36 (1986), 478–90.

Willems, P. *Le sénat de la république romaine*. 2 vols. Louvain, 1878–83.

Wiseman, T. P. "The Ambitions of Quintus Cicero." *JRS* 56 (1966), 108–15.

———. *New Men in the Roman Senate*. Oxford, 1971.

———. *Catullus: A Reappraisal*. Cambridge, 1985.

Wistrand, E. *The Policy of Brutus the Tyrannicide*. Göteborg, 1981.

Wistrand, M. *Cicero Imperator: Studies in Cicero's Correspondence, 51–47 B.C.* Göteborg, 1979.

Wirszubski, C. *Libertas as a Political Idea at Rome*. Cambridge, 1960.

———. "Audaces: A Study in Political Phraseology." *JRS* 51 (1961), 12–22.

Wood, N. *Cicero's Social and Political Thought*. Berkeley, Calif., 1988.

Yavetz, Z. *Julius Caesar and His Public Image*. London, 1983.

INDEX OF NAMES

339

INDEX OF SUBJECTS

344